Beverley Tucker

The Johns Hopkins University Studies
in Historical and Political Science

Ninety-Sixth Series (1978)

1. Neighbors in Conflict: The Irish, Germans, Jews, and
   Italians of New York City, 1929–1941
   By Ronald H. Bayor
2. Beverley Tucker: Heart over Head in the Old South
   By Robert J. Brugger

NATHANIEL BEVERLEY TUCKER
c. 1843

Beverley Tucker

HEART OVER HEAD IN THE OLD SOUTH

ROBERT J. BRUGGER

THE JOHNS HOPKINS UNIVERSITY PRESS
BALTIMORE AND LONDON

This book has been brought to publication with the generous assistance of the Andrew W. Mellon Foundation.

Manufactured in the United States of America

The Johns Hopkins University Press, Baltimore, Maryland 21218
The Johns Hopkins Press Ltd., London

Library of Congress Catalog Card Number 77-16294
ISBN 0-8018-1982-2

Library of Congress Cataloging in Publication data will be found on the last printed page of this book.

To my father
John R. Brugger
and the memory of my mother
Angeline M. Brugger
(1917–1976)

Contents

	Illustrations	xi
	Preface	xiii
ONE	The Cradle of True Patriots	1
TWO	The Virtuous Loser, A Man of Heart	20
THREE	To Build the Ideal Society	45
FOUR	The Prophet Delivered	66
FIVE	In His Father's Chair	91
SIX	"Checking the Car of Destiny"	114
SEVEN	Community and Therapy: The Hero as Healer	136
EIGHT	"Thro' the Lips of Madmen"	162
	Afterword	196
	Guide to Abbreviations Used	211
	Notes	213
	Essay on Sources	259
	Note on Psychological References	277
	Index	285

Illustrations

NATHANIEL BEVERLEY TUCKER, c. 1843 (A charcoal drawing from an early photograph by George S. Cook [?]) Courtesy of The College of William and Mary *Frontispiece*

ST. GEORGE TUCKER (From a copper engraving by Charles B. J. F. de St. Mémin) Courtesy of The College of William and Mary   *3*

FRANCES BLAND RANDOLPH TUCKER (A copy by Asher Durand [?] of a portrait done c. 1785 [artist unknown]) Courtesy of Dr. Janet C. Kimbrough, Williamsburg, Virginia   *3*

HENRY ST. GEORGE TUCKER (A copy by Rudolph V. Smutney of William James Hubard's original portrait [date unknown]) Courtesy of the Virginia Historical Society   *27*

BEVERLEY TUCKER, c. 1810 (Portrait from a miniature by Joseph Wood) Courtesy of The College of William and Mary   *27*

JOHN RANDOLPH OF ROANOKE, c. 1810 (Engraving by W. G. Jackman) (From Hugh A. Garland, *The Life of John Randolph of Roanoke*, 2 vols. [New York: D. Appleton and Company, 1850])   *27*

THE SITE OF TUCKER'S EARLY LAW PRACTICE (From adjoining sections of Bishop James Madison's *A Map of Virginia Formed upon Actual Surveys, and the Latest and Most Accurate Observations* [Richmond: n.p., 1807 (revised 1818)])   *30*

CENTRAL MISSOURI DURING TUCKER'S YEARS IN THE WEST (From Henry S. Tanner, *A New American Atlas. Containing Maps of the Several States of the North American Union* [Philadelphia: Henry S. Tanner, 1823])   *48*

ELIZABETH TUCKER COALTER BRYAN (From a miniature [artist unknown]) Courtesy of Mrs. Keith Kane, Charlottesville, Virginia   *73*

LUCY SMITH TUCKER (From a miniature [artist unknown] c. 1850) Courtesy of Dr. Janet C. Kimbrough, Williamsburg, Virginia   *73*

THE TUCKER HOUSE, WILLIAMSBURG (From a late-nineteenth-century photograph) Courtesy of the Colonial Williamsburg Foundation   *92*

VIRGINIA IN 1834 (From Joseph Martin, *A New and Comprehensive Gazetteer of Virginia and the District of Columbia* [Charlottesville: J. Martin, 1835])   *94*

WREN BUILDING, The College of William and Mary (From an early wet-plate photograph) Courtesy of the Colonial Williamsburg Foundation   *97*

THE DUKE OF GLOUCESTER STREET, WILLIAMSBURG (From a watercolor by Thomas Millington, 1836) Courtesy of the Colonial Williamsburg Foundation   *102*

THOMAS R. DEW (Portrait attributed to George P. A. Healy [date unknown] probably done in the early 1840s) Courtesy of The College of William and Mary   *107*

JAMES HENRY HAMMOND, c. 1840 Courtesy of South Caroliniana Library, University of South Carolina   *117*

DUFF GREEN (A watercolor engraving [artist unknown] apparently dating from the
    antebellum period) Courtesy of The Library of Congress   *120*
ABEL P. UPSHUR (Stone engraving published and probably cut by Charles Fenderich,
    Washington, D.C., 1844) Courtesy of the Virginia Historical Society   *137*
BEVERLEY TUCKER, c. 1846 Courtesy of Dr. Janet C. Kimbrough, Williamsburg,
    Virginia   *167*
WILLIAM GILMORE SIMMS (From William Gilmore Simms, *Poems, Descriptive,
    Dramatic, Legendary and Contemplative*, 2 vols. [Charleston, South Carolina: John
    Russell, 1853])   *170*

Preface

THIS BOOK sets out to sharpen our understanding of the Old South, especially its intellectual life, by examining carefully one man's experience in that society. Several issues fixed my attention on Beverley Tucker, but he might easily have escaped notice. Born in 1784, dying in 1851, he is best known for being professor of law and a secessionist at the College of William and Mary in the antebellum period; in that role he followed his more famous father, St. George Tucker, who had taught there in the 1790s. Beverley is also known for a few pieces of romantic writing. *George Balcombe* and *The Partisan Leader,* both published in 1836, remain prominent examples of antebellum Southern fiction, painting slavery in flattering tones and encouraging the impression that Southerners had developed a superior society. *The Partisan Leader* was notorious in its day. Subtitled "A Tale Of The Future," it predicted that this civilization south of the Potomac would soon find it necessary to revolt against federal tyranny. Indeed, Tucker took less pride in his literary skills than in his power of prophecy. Appearing in June 1850 at the Nashville Convention, where he hoped to lay the groundwork for a new republic based on old principles, he made an urgent call for secession as the first step toward building a glorious Southern empire.

Such pleas went for nothing. In 1850 compromise measures in Congress promised to quiet the furor over slavery in the territories, and all but a few Southerners wanted to be about their usual business. Their leaders trimmed accordingly. Henry S. Foote, the Mississippi politician whose defense of Southern rights in the summer of that year had no place for disunion, denounced Tucker or the floor of the Senate as a petty pamphleteer, "a newspaper scribbler, a novelist, a sort of political harlequin. . . ." Tucker was a secessionist before the South was willing to secede, and his failure appeared so complete at the time of his death that those historians who stumble across his path usually see him as one more exhibit of Southern eccentricity—rather like his half brother, John Randolph of Roanoke. In the words of Vernon Louis Parrington, Tucker was a misanthrope who "tucked [Parrington enjoyed a pun] the horizons of Virginia about him like a Hudson's Bay blanket and defied the cold winds of the North."[1]

Tucker is of more serious interest, however, and first caught my eye for the part he played in passing on political values and states' rights beliefs in antebellum Virginia. He taught constitutional law at a time when training in such theory, as in public ethics, had noteworthy influence on political attitudes and behavior. Certainly many contemporary Virginians noticed a direct and dangerous connection between Tucker and states' rights fervor. *The Petersburg Intelligencer,* for example, complained in 1850 that Tucker sent his students *"into the world with dogmas and crotchets which may stick to them for a lifetime."* They, in turn, were aware of receiving special instructions from him. "You have molded my heart when it was plastic," a former pupil—a Richmond judge and states' rights Democrat—wrote Tucker in 1849; "it has hardened, it is true, but the impression you have given it is only the more enduring." Several of his students carried the lessons they learned to the Virginia secession convention in the spring of 1861. The question of secession or union remained open when one of them, Robert L. Montague, counseled Virginians to draw courage from the "departed and venerated" Judge Tucker, who had told his students that, before any other colony had declared independence in 1776, old Virginia's "'voice of defiance was always ringing in the tyrant's ears; hers was the cry that summoned him to the strife; hers was the shout that invited his vengeance.'"[2] Tucker's young men figured prominently in the secession of Virginia, no doubt partly because of the impact he had on them.

In truth Tucker belonged to a disunionist underground, and thus in the matrix of the friends he kept he provides a glimpse into the way Southern radicals prepared for the sectional crisis they foresaw and tried to hasten. Tucker belonged to a committee of correspondence that included, from time to time, such implacable Southerners as Thomas R. Dew, Abel P. Upshur, Edmund Ruffin, Duff Green, William Harper, James Henry Hammond, and William Gilmore Simms. Tucker and these men planted and nourished the seed of separatism in the antebellum South; they made up a coterie of nation builders. Writing one another, mounting essays in newspapers, writing fiction, calling for agricultural reform, teaching law, history, and morals, lecturing lyceum audiences, agitating at conventions, and trying to form a Southern rights party, these "Southrons" were among the patriots who in the end got their revolution but lost their war for independence. Tucker sheds light on their part in fomenting rebellion and on their reasons for doing so. He is important to any understanding of the secessionist movement in the Old South.

Yet more than anything else, Tucker permits us to see in detail the changes that occurred in patterns of Southern thought and society in the first half of the nineteenth century. His life story is useful as microcosmic history, suggesting how certain young Southerners matured and gained a moral sense in this period, became acquainted with ideas, and developed habits of thinking. Tucker offers a case study in the growth of the states' rights, proslavery persuasion, his later extremism providing a refracted view of the ideology he shared with many other men who were less visible. Thus this book is fundamentally about process, about how changes in thought and moral sensibility took place. Besides dealing with Tucker as a personality, I have broached here—and I hope have begun to answer—questions about the Southern manner of acculturating and training young men in these years, about the connection between men of ideas and political action, and about changing disciplines of mind in the South between the Revolution and the Civil War.

Conceptual and personal issues help to explain why, over the past five or six years, this book has held my interest as it has. A biography dealing with intellect in a slave regime, it seemed for one thing to work against the grain: historians usually consider ideas to have been of little concern in the Old South and as a result have not paid them much attention. Louis Hartz, for example, in his classic study of American liberalism, wrote that social thought in the slave South was a "simple fraud."[3] From the beginning, Tucker suggested to me that it was neither quite so fraudulent nor so simple. Second, my interests really do take me beyond biography, and I have grown well aware of the weaknesses of this traditional form of historical scholarship. Balancing limits of breadth, however, are the possibilities of depth, and I have found a challenge in making the most of them. Lastly, perhaps most revealing, issues in the imbibing and holding of beliefs have fascinated me. Researching and writing the Tucker story, I gradually realized that this problem of process was a personal concern, something left hanging from the Vietnam War years, when I and many other young persons had to question how we had come by the beliefs that suddenly were so salient, to decide which of those conflicting principles we finally felt were compelling, and to ask whether we had unraveled ourselves honestly.

For such private reasons, this book grows out of the current historical interest in *mentalité*: in past values and views of the world, in the quality and meaning of the ties people establish among themselves. Treating Beverley Tucker as a serious subject, though not taking him at face value, I have tried to explore a man in his culture. To make that effort, as Winthrop Jordan put it in a passage on Thomas Jefferson and slavery, "is to savor complexity."[4]

My thanks go to the many persons who have shared the challenges of writing this study and to those whose resources have made it possible. My deepest debt is to David Herbert Donald, in whose seminar at Johns Hopkins this work began. His stern criticism and warm support are familiar to all his students; he has broadened and deepened my vision. Kenneth S. Lynn was helpful at several stages of the project; Louis P. Galambos, dropping criticisms from his own historiographical vantage point, seductively served them with cold beer and fresh oysters. Patricia Denison Brugger, along with Kathy Dalton, James Hoopes, Richard J. Kent, Linda A. Burcher, and Daun Van Ee,

offer proof that young scholars learn most from one another. Several of
my colleagues at Virginia, Paul Gaston, Joseph Kett, Dan Flanigan, and
Chuck McCurdy, have offered useful suggestions; Michael Holt and William
W. Abbot read the entire manuscript and helped both to clarify thoughts
and to round rough edges.

But I also have incurred debts to Willie Lee Rose, William W. Freehling,
Ronald G. Walters, and John Higham, all of whom, in Baltimore, leveled
questions in seminar and over lunch; to Robert T. Hogan, Professor of
Psychology at Hopkins, who made my year as a fellow in that department
stimulating and enjoyable; to Bertram Wyatt-Brown for his aid in moving
the manuscript from dissertation to book; to Robert S. Brown, Charlottesville psychiatrist and friend of history; and to Charles T. Cullen, editor of
the John Marshall Papers. Special thanks to Lenard R. Berlanstein, Jack
Censer, Rick Cottom, Drew Gilpin Faust, Frederick H. Graefe, Bill Harris,
Charles F. Hobson, and Steven Hochman; to Ms. Gene McKinney of
Charlotte Court House, Virginia; to Patrick S. Mulligan of Notre Dame,
the Navy, and elsewhere; and to Carl Oblinger, Nolan Yelich, Mary Yeager,
and—small tribute to the stimulus good students provide—to members of
my classes here at Virginia. Michael A. Aronson and Mary Lou Kenney
have been especially kind editors. The failings of the book remain mine;
these friends have done their best to minimize them.

At every stage of this project I have enjoyed the fullest cooperation from
research librarians and other interested persons. Mr. David Tennant Bryan,
Richmond, has generously permitted me to quote from the Bryan Family
Papers in the Alderman Library; Dr. Janet Kimbrough, a Tucker descendant
now living in the family home in Williamsburg, graciously showed Pat and me
about the house in the spring of 1972, talked with us of family lore, and now
consents to my using here likenesses of several family portraits in her possession. For permission to quote from unpublished manuscript materials and
for assistance during my research visits, I owe thanks to Mattie V. Russell
and Patricia Hummer of the William R. Perkins Library, Duke University;
Richard Shrader of the Southern Historical Collection, University of North
Carolina, Chapel Hill; Howson W. Cole of the Virginia Historical Society,
Richmond; to the staffs of the Manuscripts Division, Library of Congress,
and the Virginia State Library, Richmond. For help in answering inquiries
about this research project, thanks to staff members of the Boston Public
Library and the New-York Historical Society. Also to Frances H. Stadler of
the Missouri Historical Society, St. Louis; Nancy Lankford, P. B. Weiner,
and Debbie B. Miller of the State Historical Society of Missouri and the
Western Historical Manuscripts Collection, both at the University of Missouri
Library, Columbia; Allen Stokes of the South Caroliniana Library, University
of South Carolina; Mrs. B. D. Aycock of the Union Theological Seminary,
Richmond; Mrs. Mary Lane, Historical Foundation of the Presbyterian and
Reformed Churches, Montreat, North Carolina. Adelaide Eisenhart, Florence

Felter, and Elinor Baden of the Eisenhower Library at Hopkins worked cheerfully on my behalf. Michael F. Plunkett and William H. Runge of the Alderman Library, University of Virginia, exemplify the helpfulness that every scholar relies upon. But among all these fine people I reserve deepest appreciation for Margaret Cook, Curator of Manuscripts, Swem Library, William and Mary, for her devoted help and constant good will. She and her coworkers—in particular Linda Schon, Pam Boll, Louise Kale, and Hank Grunder—made research in Williamsburg so pleasant that the place feels like home.

I am grateful to the Ford Foundation, the Woodrow Wilson National Fellowship Foundation, the Wilson Gee Institute and the Summer Grants Committee, University of Virginia, for the financial support so necessary to the research, writing, and revision of this book. The aid of the University of Virginia Small Grants Committee helped to pay for typing the final draft of the manuscript—a chore that Donna Perfater, Ella Wood, Lottie McCauley, and Kathleen Casey cheerfully saw to completion.

Both Pat's family and mine, living nearby in Washington, were wonderful in helping to see us through the past few years. To mention the boundless generosity of my aunt, Ms. Helen Wellenstein, is only to begin a list too long to include here. Our love to everyone on it. And my warmest thanks to Laura and Rebecca, whose affectionate patience has been mature beyond their years.

CHAPTER ONE

The Cradle of True Patriots

IN BEVERLEY TUCKER'S later life the "old Virginia" of his lectures and essays became, as often as not, "poor old Virginia." In his speech at the Nashville Convention he went further. He made Virginia a goddess, the waxy muse of purity, truth, and strength. Having originally given life to the country, and always selfless, Virginia would make great sacrifices for the Union, he declared; she would divide her bread with the hungry, even shed to her undergarments to clothe the needy. But there was a point at which her political scruples drew rein, and "Woe to him," cried this gray-haired man, fierce in his frustration, "who with profane hand ventures to touch that last safeguard of her stainless honor."[1] Tucker thought it was his duty to maintain the purity of this goddess, to seclude her and the rest of the South from the social malaise, moral ills, and political danger threatening in the nineteenth century.

Especially when he was an old man, Tucker's depth of feeling often led to overstatement, and Virginians in the antebellum period did take pride in their state. Yet pride has a way of revealing weaknesses and worries. A commentary on his notion of mission, Tucker's patriotic devotion to an apotheosized Virginia more clearly reflected his sense of self. Counting himself a true son of Virginia, he considered her the mother of men larger than life. What higher honor was there, asked the hero of a romance Tucker had published in 1836, "than to be sprung from a race of men without fear and without reproach—the ancient cavaliers of Virginia?"[2]

I

It may help us to understand the author of these warm sentiments to know that half his ancestry was not Virginian at all. His father, St. George Tucker, was born in 1752 into the family of Henry Tucker, a member of the Bermuda gentry. It was a large household—the lad grew up under the ministry of four older brothers and two older sisters—and a proud family, fully aware that Tuckers had been on the island since sometime in the early seventeenth century, provided high-ranking officials to the local government, and performed service to the Crown abroad. The family also had a pride of place; the Bermuda of St. George Tucker's boyhood was so beautiful that one member of the family later put his affection for it in verse form. Those children of the next generation who never knew the charms of the isle read and reread his description of this "darling spot" of Nature and conjured up thoughts of tall palmetto trees, rich banana plants with broad branches to the salty breeze, lemon and orange groves, and "foaming surges" that lashed at white beaches. Opportunities in this otherwise paradisiacal setting were limited, however, and when it came time for St. George Tucker to embark on a suitable career, his father's need for economy ruled out a London legal education. The young man bundled up some letters of introduction, bade his family farewell, and in 1771 sailed instead for New York and the College of William and Mary in Virginia.[3]

It was a time when legal schooling carried practical lessons. After only a year at William and Mary, Tucker began professional training with George Wythe, a rising lawyer and a clerk of the Virginia colonial legislature in Williamsburg, who during the Stamp Act furor in 1765 had forcefully argued the constitutional case against Parliament. St. George Tucker found Wythe persuasive. The nature of the Empire limited parliamentary authority in America; colonial legislatures, not Parliament, were responsible for "internal Government" and taxation. The question was whether Englishmen could prevent Parliament from assuming the unchecked power which, in the preceding century, Parliament itself had rebuked in the Crown. Tucker believed that principles of English liberty were at stake. While on a visit home, he decided to join the continental rebels.[4]

Returning to Virginia late in December 1776, Tucker arrived in Williamsburg just in time for a holiday reunion with friends and a victory ball to celebrate Washington's success at the battle of Trenton. No doubt he then broke the news, making his welcome all the warmer, that with him from Bermuda he had brought a ship loaded with salt. Tucker was always a man of Benjamin Franklin's public spirit and shrewdness; while the Virginia assembly accepted this valuable wartime commodity "most Cheerfully," it paid what Tucker called "a very generous price" for it. During the following year he made similar voyages, outfitting ships at Charleston with indigo for the West Indian arms, ammunition, and salt trade. He was instrumental in the American capture of war supplies on Bermuda and even promoted a scheme for the rebel capture of his home island.[5]

Besides these supply expeditions, St. George Tucker saw some military action. After 1779 he served close to Williamsburg as a staff officer; he took the field early in 1781 to help repel the invasion Lord Cornwallis mounted from the south, and as a major in a brigade of Virginia militia took part in the battle of Guilford Court House, North Carolina. It was not an altogether flattering affair for the Americans, who lost both the field and their artillery. Nor was it entirely glorious for Tucker, who suffered a minor bayonet wound while trying, with his friend and immediate superior Colonel Beverley

ST. GEORGE TUCKER

FRANCES BLAND RANDOLPH TUCKER

Randolph, to halt the flight of their militia unit. Tucker remained with the army during the more memorable entrapment of Cornwallis at Yorktown; he came to know General George Washington and the Marquis de Layfayette and witnessed the surrender of British forces in October 1781.[6]

Yet Colonel Tucker's most pleasant wartime campaign was surely the one he waged for Frances Bland Randolph, a widow whom he first met during a rare attendance at church in the autumn of 1777. The eager young newcomer could hardly have focused his charms on a worthier object. Once called "the most beautiful woman of her age," Frances appeared in a painting done in 1785 as a woman of striking dark eyes, classically proportioned features, and compelling presence. The lovely widow was also landed. Her husband had been John Randolph, who belonged to the substantial family of Richard and Jane Bolling Randolph of Curles, and when John died in 1775, he left his wife several sizable estates. Marrying Frances in September 1778, St. George Tucker joined her at Matoax, the family plantation in south-central Virginia, which comprised over thirteen hundred acres of Chesterfield County and employed dozens of slaves. The new couple also supervised affairs at the Bizarre and Roanoke estates farther west. Taken together, these properties seemed to afford the new family ample comfort. It was true, looking at the ledger more closely, that the plantations came to Tucker heavily burdened with debt. But treaty complications after the war prevented British creditors from forcing payments. Things looked tolerably well.[7]

Besides the widow's plantations, St. George Tucker shouldered additional responsibilities as the father of three stepsons. The oldest, Richard Randolph, was eight years old when his mother remarried; Theodorick was seven. By all reports these boys were spirited enough, but there was another who was even more so. John Randolph, who later added "of Roanoke" to his name, was at the age of five especially restive, peevish, and precocious. He was a beautiful child, with his mother's large dark eyes and delicate features, a lad of intelligence and sensitivity.

The Randolph boys soon had younger half brothers and a half sister. First born to St. George and Frances was a child whom they named Ann Frances Bland and called Fanny. In 1780 Frances had her first Tucker son, who bore the illustrious name Henry St. George; another son, Theodore Thomas Tudor, was born in September 1782 and was named in honor of St. George's older brother who had settled in South Carolina. Two years later, on September 6, 1784, Frances gave birth to a third son. He was her first child born after independence had been won, the first one whose birth had not coincided with some war-caused dislocation. He was christened Nathaniel Beverley—Nathaniel after St. George's brother, who was with Thomas Tudor in Charleston, supposedly studying medicine but really writing poetry; and Beverley apparently to honor the Randolph who had fought with Tucker at

Guilford and who was soon to be governor of Virginia. The father of this newest addition received congratulations on the birth "of another Beauty, for such no doubt it must be."[8] The family called the child Beverley.

II

Because "Matoaks" was the original name of Pocohantas, the native American princess who adorned the early Randolph genealogy, Beverley's birthplace itself recalled the pristine past. The spot haunted his later imagination. Only a few miles west of Petersburg—a village on the falls of the Appomattox River—Matoax may not have been as impressive as most eighteenth-century estates on the lower James. All the same the white frame home, nestled among pine trees on a bluff overlooking the Appomattox, surrounded with shrubbery and abundant orchards,[9] surely made for much boyish merriment. There were fields and fences, horses and wagons, and dogs to scamper with; there was the Appomattox with its steep banks, tributary streams, and opportunities for adventure. Richard, Theodorick, and John, when not occupied at their studies, were the sort to lead the eager Henry and Tudor—with Beverley relentlessly trying to tag along—through gardens and across log bridges, up into tree houses, over stone forts and perhaps onto rafts of their own making.

By the few accounts available, these earliest years of Beverley's life were warm, orderly, and secure. Competently, lovingly, Frances Tucker set the tone of family life at Matoax. Though a firm mother, she was nonetheless gentle in her demands, especially interested in her sons' preparation for schooling and—if we can take John Randolph's word for it—attentive to their religious instruction. She read to the children tales of the kind common in the day, including the moralisms of "Frank Goodchild and Tom Idle." Gifted enough, as one Virginian remembered, to "charm a bird out of the tree by the music of her tongue," Frances encouraged her sons to practice oratory and often listened to her sons' readings and recitations. Too young for such training, Beverley nonetheless learned to mimic his brothers' speechmaking attempts; to the amusement of everyone in the family, the older boys taught him to recite lines he pretended to understand. The children's governess, an orphan girl, was an additional figure in these playful affairs, as was a young black woman, whose unwritten mandate gave her wide authority in the house and whose benevolence made a deep impression on her youngest charge.[10]

The duties of Richmond law practice and public service forced St. George Tucker to spend long periods away from this domestic scene at Matoax. In the fall of 1786 he attended a meeting at Annapolis to consider problems of interstate trade under the Articles of Confederation. When a larger gathering met at Philadelphia in May of the next year, Tucker was not among the delegates—Virginia luminaries abounded—but in October 1787, when the legislature in Richmond ordered a state convention to consider ratifying the proposed federal Constitution, Tucker opposed the new charter. Though he favored strengthening the domestic trade authority of the Congress, St. George Tucker agreed with his old friend Beverley Randolph that the Articles of Confederation provided for healthy state autonomy and were "the less of two Evils."[11]

While Tucker cautioned his friends against the proposed Constitution and worked at his law practice in the state capital, his wife's health suddenly deteriorated. However anxious he was for her, practical matters delayed his return home. Day after day, as October turned to November and November wore on, Tucker complained that the debate over the new Constitution and proceedings in court seemed to inflict ruthless claims upon him. On December 1 he was still in Richmond, "engaged in much business," and days later he reported that he had missed the stagecoach to Petersburg, but that on the morrow nothing would keep him from Matoax. When Tucker did return to his wife's bedside, he was powerless to halt her decline. Frances endured an agonizing illness with what a neighbor called "much patience and resignation" until on January 18, 1788, she died. For her epitaph St. George Tucker shortened a line from Horace's *Odes* which, in a contemporary translation, asked "Wherefore restrain the tender Tear?" He buried Beverley's mother next to her first husband, beneath a clump of pine trees near the mansion.[12]

Grief at the loss of his wife did not permit Tucker to postpone for long certain hard decisions. He decided to leave Matoax. By the terms of the will of 1775, the Randolph lands would soon begin to devolve upon Tucker's stepsons—the last of whom, John, would reach his majority in six years. Furthermore, the Randolph debts remained unsettled, and by early February, seven states had already ratified a frame of government that would measurably aid British creditors in recovering their prerevolutionary claims. Tucker may have anticipated hard times. In any case, his career was the law, not farming. The offer of a seat in the newly reorganized state judiciary greatly appealed to him. He accepted a general-court circuit the month following the loss of his wife, conducted a search for a more economical and convenient home, and in January of the next year wrote John Page, an old associate and master of Rosewell plantation, north of the York River, that he was once again a resident of Williamsburg.[13]

At the age of four Beverley thus suffered the shock of his mother's illness and death only to feel shortly thereafter the effect of a deeply significant family move. An entire world ended in the course of a single year. In the child's mind Matoax belonged to his mother and she to it. It was a place, however dimly remembered in later life, of motherly warmth, feminine care, and the security of family wholeness. In a poem referring to those days, Tucker later wrote that as a boy he had lived "where love was sincere & artless"; at Matoax he had known a motherly love "more sweet than the violet's breath," and had deeply missed that love once it was gone. While in his retrospective lines Tucker described Williamsburg as a place of blooming roses, mockingbirds' songs, and gardens with fragrant violets, his heart had remained elsewhere. Beverley after his mother's death was a "wild and wayward boy" who wandered among the cottages and yards of the village feeling little joy.[14] While Matoax was a kind of Eden that gripped his consciousness, Williamsburg represented the Fall.

The town might have depressed him in any circumstances. Although still in many ways a charming place of old homes, backyard gardens, and tree-shaded streets, Williamsburg suffered both in prominence and upkeep after the removal of the Virginia capital to Richmond in 1780. One visitor in the early nineties, the New England geographer and clergyman Jedidiah Morse, pronounced everything in the town "dull, forsaken, and melancholy—no trade—no amusements—but the infamous one of gambling—no industry, and very little appearance of religion." On the eastern end of the broad main thoroughfare, the Duke of Gloucester Street, the old colonial capitol was nearly in ruins; farther west the former governor's mansion was in decay. Bruton Parish Church, an Anglican landmark, was in disrepair. The marble statue of colonial governor Norborne Berkeley, which admiring Virginians had placed near the capitol in 1771, was now "exposed to the rudeness of negroes and boys. . . ."[15]

Of course things were not all bad, and in 1792 when Morse published these observations in his *American Geography* St. George Tucker nominated himself to refute them. Morse badly exaggerated the tawdriness of the village, thought Tucker, who insisted there were enough "genteel families" left in Williamsburg to form "a very agreeable society." He singled out for aesthetic notice the courthouse square, about ten acres of "delightful verdure" in the very heart of the town.[16] On the northwest corner of this extensive green was the weatherboarded home that St. George Tucker had purchased late in the year Beverley's mother died.

III

It was a two-story house, but not really large enough for the family and the servants Tucker brought with him to Williamsburg. So he added wings to the structure, extended the first floor rearward, and drew the roof over the first floor extension to provide a roomy second story.

Doubtless Tucker did much designing of this work himself. Like Thomas Jefferson, whom he visited occasionally, he was a man of wide accomplishments and a student of nearly universal interests. Tucker was capable of composing robust doggerel on a notebook page facing a plan for a steam-powered water pump; he kept records of astronomical observations, designed signaling devices and an air furnace, and collected materials on natural history and animal husbandry. St. George Tucker was an eighteenth-century rationalist, a deist who confided in Reason, believed in human progress, and clung to the certitude that man could find happiness on earth. When in 1795 he visited the famed Natural Bridge of western Virginia—a massive stone arch spanning a Shenandoah Valley canyon—rather than succumbing to its striking natural beauty, rather than writing a poem about it, he measured it.[17]

The verse that Tucker did write—and he became in Williamsburg the head of a small literary circle—was extensively footnoted and avowedly didactic. This instructive purpose shaped the treatment Tucker gave his favorite poetic subject, the American republic, and was especially evident in *Liberty, A Poem on the Independence of America,* which he wrote during the revolutionary war and published in Richmond, when he thought it timely, late in the Confederation period. *Liberty* traced the migration of the muse of human freedom, hounded always by abject failure, from ancient Greece to medieval England and then, in search of a haven, to America. On the fertile and promising shores of Columbia, under the revolutionary leadership of the godlike Washington, Adams the superb, the wise Franklin, and other men of large dimension, Liberty's happiness and safety seemed finally within grasp.[18]

Tucker glorified revolutionary experiences and spoke glowingly of patriotic leaders as a way of preserving gains secured. Historically the benefits of liberty were fleeting ones, lost to oppression, ignorance, corruption, and to "internal broils" that had sapped republican strength in ancient Greek city-states. Ambition, the thirst for conquest and wealth, cast the "'baleful spell' of luxury"—the "deadliest foe to liberty and health." Tucker constantly returned to the theme that Americans themselves posed the worst threat to their liberties. He begged Columbia to be ambitious only for freedom and to profit from the muse Liberty's earlier misfortunes. From the English experience with despotic government under the Stuart kings, Americans could learn the lesson of "corruption's deadly poison"; opposition leaders Algernon Sidney and John Hampden of the House of Commons were no more suspicious of powerful government than Americans needed to be. Tucker found in "poverty, and toil" a prime ingredient of sound national character, for Liberty and peace adorned a "humble cot." With virtue and wisdom, good will and moderation, lectured Beverley's father, the victors of the Revolution might somehow avoid the pitfalls of bygone freemen.[19]

Since these beliefs were grounded in rural simplicity and virtue, in public vigilance and local responsibility, political events in the 1790s deeply stirred Tucker. His brother Thomas, a congressman from South Carolina, and his friend John Page, a Virginia representative, kept the concerned judge abreast of all developments in the federal capital. Home from grammar school in the evening, Beverley must often have heard in his father's study indignant talk of the growing differences between Jefferson and Hamilton in Washington's cabinet, of John Adams's proposal to create regal titles for federal officials, and of Hamiltonian fiscal measures and plans to encourage manufacturers. As Washington's administration divided bitterly over the question of the French Revolution, St. George Tucker, like other Jeffersonians, sympathized with the Republicans.[20] But as that revolution failed of its loftiest purposes, he grew even more sharply conscious of the fragility of free government.

Tucker took to his pen, and one result was a series of satirical rhymes ridiculing the Federalists and their policies. "The Probationary Odes of Jonathan Pindar, Esq." appeared principally between June and September 1793 in the *National Gazette,* a pro-Jefferson newspaper in Philadelphia, and then in booklet form three years later. In the growing pretension of the federal government, in the apparent conspiracy of commercial and manufacturing interests against the general welfare, St. George Tucker saw a betrayal of revolutionary idealism. Fears of a decline in republican zeal, voiced in *Liberty,* seemed to stand confirmed. Hamilton may only have seated himself on a "paper throne" made of speculators' bonds the secretary of the treasury would pay in full, of national bank stock he would issue. It was resplendent all the same. Moreover, Tucker doubted that the national debt was the boon Hamilton argued it was; "to encrease this blessing and entail/To future times its influence benign," he suggested dryly, *"New loans* from *foreign nations* cannot fail,/Whilst *standing armies* clinch the *grand design."* The goddess Liberty had been "hoodwink'd" under the Federalist regime, thought Jonathan Pindar, and for the disastrous turn of events since 1789 he blamed *"young Ambition."* Like the weights that moved inside the clock high above the town square, intrigue played quietly, surely, and invisibly behind the face of distant authority.[21]

In another role, St. George Tucker made the difficult descent from the principles of Jonathan's "Odes" to the real problems of the new government. The poet was also a law professor, having assumed Wythe's chair of Law and Police at William and Mary when in 1790 the older man left Williamsburg to become chancellor of the state equity court in Richmond. While Tucker's students noted the need for public virtue in a system of self-rule, they also learned the absurdity of titled republican leaders, the inexpediency of governmental grants of vast tracts of land to individuals, and the threat a large national debt posed for the government. With special vehemence Tucker talked about the danger the 1798 Alien and Sedition Acts represented to personal liberties.[22]

While teaching the concepts of equality under law and the Law of Nature, St. George Tucker asked Virginians to fulfill the promises of revolutionary rhetoric in yet another way. He proposed the abolition of slavery. In May 1796 he published his lecture on emancipation and later addressed it to the General Assembly for its consideration. The pamphlet had brevity, clarity, and force. On the title page was a quotation from Montesquieu too direct to be misinterpreted. "Slavery," the French student of government had said, "not only violates the Laws of Nature, and of civil Society, it also wounds the best Forms of Government." In a system acknowledging that all men are equal, Tucker added, slavery was "contrary to the Spirit of the Constitution," and he thought this cancer could be eliminated through the enactment of a bill that would free—after a term of indentured servitude—all female slaves born after its passage and all their descendants. In elaborate calculations he estimated that the plan would take more than a century to complete; the number of slaves in Virginia would not begin to diminish for forty years after adoption of the bill, and the number of blacks under the age of manumission would continue at a steady level for many years. The restrictions Tucker's bill placed on free blacks—they were to enjoy only limited civil and political rights—gave evidence both of his frank recognition that racial equality was impossible in Virginia for generations to come and of his hope that stringent controls might encourage the freedmen to seek a better life in the vast lands of the west.[23]

Tucker's plan to end slavery was perhaps the best testimony he offered of his cast of mind. He was an immigrant of lofty patriotism, a republican committed to this experiment in free government, an Enlightenment figure whose approach to problems was practical and empirical. He was optimistic, moderate, pragmatic, and yet firm in his demand that Americans act on the principles they professed. The manumission plan, which received polite notice but produced no action in Richmond, Tucker considered a matter of first importance not only to the "moral character and domestic peace" of Virginians but even to their "political salvation." Eliminate the evil, he pleaded; rescue posterity from the calamity and reproach, which are otherwise unavoidable." As he demonstrated in his law lectures no less than in his poetry, St. George Tucker's object was to promote "the Happiness, Union, & Harmony of the United States."[24]

For the Tucker boys, their father's suspicion of government, ideals of public virtue, and concern with the problem of slavery were matters of table talk and neighborhood, just as acceptable as the humidity of the tidewater and the ordered politeness of Williamsburg society. Critical evaluation of these ideas could only come with greater maturity. How Henry, Tudor, and Beverley evaluated them had much to do with the way they fared in the small world they knew.

IV

While St. George Tucker labored in poetics, pamphlets, and the classroom, his son Beverley spent boyhood years in Williamsburg that he later remembered as miserable and dissatisfying. For everyone in the Tucker house during the 1790s there were adjustments to family change. Some of it was happy. In October 1791 the Tucker children gained a stepmother in Lelia Skipwith Carter, widow of the landed George Carter of Corotoman on the Rappahannock and daughter of an English baronet who then lived in Mecklenburg County. Lelia's children joined the family: Charles, a few years younger than Beverley, and a little girl, Polly. In 1792 the Tuckers announced the birth of a son, named after his father, who as "Tutee" quickly became a family delight.[25]

The theme of tragic death—certainly a common one in this age—recurred in the Tucker family with a frequency that badly scarred Beverley's memory. Gloom punctuated years that might have been the most carefree and pleasant in his life. In 1792, the year after the Tucker-Carter marriage, death claimed Theodorick Randolph, until that time a student at Columbia College in New York City. In April 1795 Beverley's brother Thomas Tudor, whom St. George Tucker thought the most promising of his boys, succumbed to illness, and in September of that year the family received another blow when the baby, "Tutee," suddenly died. The following year Beverley's eight-year-old sister Betsy fell mortally ill, and as the bereaved family recovered from that loss, Richard Randolph, now the father of three, abruptly died at Bizarre Plantation in June 1796. In December of the same year, as Beverley reached the age of twelve, the Tuckers suffered once more when a child who might have cheered the distressed family was born lifeless. Of the Randolph boys, only John was left; of the Tucker children only Fanny—whose health was never good—and the brothers Henry and Beverley remained.[26]

Conceivably these family deaths, particularly among the children, promoted in Beverley an unconscious sense of specialness, of being "chosen," and perhaps of guilt over being spared himself. Surely his encounter with the enforced rigors of school furthered any such feeling and did nothing to make these death-ravaged years happier. After some early training with John Coalter, a young law student who boarded at the Tucker house, Beverley set off for the Reverend John Bracken's grammar school at William and Mary in 1791. Worse than ill-prepared, the lad was precocious. As the youngest boy in an indulgent family he had developed, together with a memory for numbers and verse, a smug assurance of superiority. The result was that he soon lost interest in school and grew impatient with his teachers. Lessons that Beverley could not master in short order he dismissed outright. When Bracken tried to stimulate the indifferent pupil by placing him at "the foot of the class," Beverley was stunned. "Beaten and disgraced" as the class dunce, his reaction was defiance, which made for more punishments; at home his obstinacy caused the children's governess to hope that "with whiping [*sic*] and mortifying" the boy's conduct might improve. Beverley "was punished in school, and discountenanced at home" until, he recounted in a passage that revealed his bitterness and suggested his shame, "I almost learned to hate every one with whom I had to do."[27]

As Beverley's embarrassments increased, he began to see himself as a person of uncommon talent, held down in fetters, requiring only release to feel his own full force. He was restless, and proud of his occasional demonstrations of quick insight or sudden, decisive action. In his scholarly humiliation he drew comfort from the thought that he was too busy for the topics covered in class, too preoccupied contemplating matters his master was yet unready to treat. He was like a "high mettled colt," he told himself, with an instinct to run at full speed. Hitched to the loaded wagon of classroom forms—tedious steps in geometric logic, rote method—the colt lurched and foamed in frustration. Friendless, Beverley stalked a private realm, a protective enclave in which he indulged his fancy, thought lofty thoughts of what he would become in later life, and sought to escape his persecution and sorrow.[28]

St. George Tucker had little patience with the boy, frowning on what he referred to as Beverley's "freaks & eccentricities." Here were correctable character defects. Faced with the problem of raising children capable of republican citizenship, and no doubt reflecting the demand that men of St. George Tucker's rank in Virginia society produce boys who were also "young masters," the elder Tucker strove to develop self-discipline in his boys and encouraged a Spartan air of direction and determination. He once designated his household "Fort St. George," with tongue only partly in cheek, and posted "Garrison Articles" accordingly. Tucker's discipline led John Randolph to remember his stepfather's rule as "austere," and a descendant to recall him as a "rigid parent." For Henry's and Beverley's father, discipline was necessary for the improvement of a young man's virtue and understanding. Both qualities were necessary before he deserved public patronage, and both were indispensable to preserve republican government; neither had anything to do with daydreaming or self-indulgence.[29]

It helped to point to examples, and in bringing up his sons, Colonel Tucker (as did so many other fathers in these years) relied heavily on revolutionary models of character. Yet there was in the Tucker clan an undertone of competition that emphasized the service and duty ethic even further. Bermuda letters carried to Virginia regular accounts of global sufferings the younger generation endured in His Majesty's service. Cousins of Henry and Beverley appeared heroically at seizures of Indian strongholds, rose to high colonial office, received special citations, went on secret expeditions, served on flagships. God preserved them through horrible campaigns and incredible adventures. Duty was paramount, and as long as they were "all exceedingly well spoken of" and "received promotions equal to their expectations," the boys were a blessing to their proud parents. Probably the highest statement of the service ideal in the family was a Bermuda Tucker's apology when his son escaped drowning along with his shipmates in a South African harbor. The young officer was ashore on leave when a storm arose off the Cape of Good Hope; the weather changed so suddenly that the lad was unable to return aboard before calamity struck. Surely the Virginians would understand.[30]

Faced with this subtle rivalry, Henry and Beverley tried hard to perform up to standard. Occasionally they felt inadequate. After one report from Bermuda, Henry could only confess that his undertaking of law seemed fainthearted and his accomplishments provincial in comparison to his cousins' adventures in the Empire. While their "exalted positions" and the "high and unimpeachable integrity of their characters" gave Henry pleasure and evoked admiration, there was also the uncomfortable reflection that he was "as yet unworthy of them, and their greatness."[31]

This admission was especially telling because of Henry's distinction in the Tucker family of Williamsburg. Henry's mark was Beverley's target. Henry was cheerful when Beverley was glum, successful when Beverley strained not to fail, and in authority while Beverley was accountable to him. As the eldest son, Henry assumed the special role of subaltern to his parents; he became the repository of special confidence and, predictably, began to fulfill prophecies of leadership and success. While someone had to "whip and mortify" the younger brother during the painful period after his mother's death and the move to Williamsburg, Henry was able to pass news to Judge Tucker on his circuit and to receive instructions as a responsible intermediary. While Beverley in early schooling had "his freaks & eccentricities," St. George Tucker reported Henry "just about the same as usual." From relatives came expressions of confidence in the firstborn, with the hope that St. George Tucker's younger son would do as well.[32]

Henry's duties included tutoring Beverley. During the summers of the 1790s, while Judge Tucker tended to business in Richmond or while the boys visited the Randolphs' Bizarre estate, Beverley and his stepbrother Charles regularly worked at lessons they then submitted to Henry, who, they found, was a conscientious master. Henry often spent two or three hours a day hearing his younger brothers recite, and once wrote his father that, although he was especially busy reading his own books "all day from six to six," he intended to have Beverley and Charles read Roman history and some geography in addition to their regular summer studies at the grammar school. He was sure the boys would "have plenty of time to do *both*." He proposed, with his father's approval, to see to it that they did.[33]

Henry for his part did well at William and Mary. He read diligently, agreed with his father that perseverance led to "true knowledge," and when in 1799 he read his baccalaureate address, it was something of a sensation.

His composition, "On the Nature of Civil Liberty and the Form of Government Best Adopted to Its Preservation," assured his listeners that representative democracy—with frequent elections—was the best system for upholding civil liberty. Newspapers, Henry learned, praised what they called a "noble exhibition"; friends hoped that his oration and the others made on that graduation day would help revive the sagging scholarly reputation of the college.[34]

V

The College of William and Mary at the end of the eighteenth century was indeed a monument to unrealized dreams. For many years before the Revolution, William and Mary had been an Anglican institution beset with faculty divisions and stifled by its provinciality. Then in 1779 the college seemed about to show the way of academic reform in republican America. In that year the college Board of Visitors, including the energetic Thomas Jefferson, updated and secularized the curriculum, increased nonfaculty power in governance, and altered the financial base of the college—which the disestablished church no longer subsidized.[35]

But the reforms proved more formal than real, the issue of reform only demonstrated divisions of interest in Virginia making the future of the institution less certain than ever, and new problems arose to plague the college. At the beginning of the nineteenth century a mere twenty or thirty students were enrolled. From their appearance, wrote the Irish traveler Isaac Weld, "one would imagine that the seminary ought rather to be termed a grammar school than a college"; the main campus building, which Christopher Wren had designed but which Jefferson dismissed as a "rude misshapen pile," struck visitors as being kept in an "extremely indifferent" condition. In this bleak picture one bright spot was the local attention the school received when students of natural philosophy, after several spectacular and embarrassing failures, successfully launched a hot-air balloon in the spring of 1801. Enormous, ornamented with sixteen blue stars, inflated by burning spirits of wine, the bag rose from the courthouse green that May evening to the cheers of proud townspeople and vindicated students alike. It flew off in the twilight until, reported aeronaut Joseph Watson, it strikingly resembled a moon in partial eclipse. Considering the mixed successes and local triumphs of William and Mary, he might have been speaking of the college itself.[36]

Although the move Beverley made in 1801 from the grammar school to the college course was not as marked as one to Princeton or Columbia—where his Randolph half brothers had gone at his age—the step was nonetheless important. First of all, his academic work was more demanding, and apparently more interesting, and he had more occasion to make use of the respectable college library. His father enrolled him in the moral philosophy course, distinguished from natural philosophy much as the liberal arts are from science today, and Tucker soon found himself engaged with logic and the philosophy of the mind, rhetoric and belles lettres, ethics, natural law, the law of nations, politics, and political economy.[37] Second, he developed broader friendships among those students from western and northern counties who joined him as advanced students. When Henry began legal training in 1800, the circle of Beverley's friends also included young men in the law course. Some of them—Benjamin Watkins Leigh, Chapman Johnson, Joseph C. Cabell, and members of the Watson family—were especially promising. Each year several students boarded in the spacious Tucker house, so that there was a continued bantering among the young men during meals, and frequent exchanges of ideas with Professor Tucker in his well-stocked study just off the wide foyer.[38] Beverley had reached a point of intellectual embarkation.

He was soon immersed in politics. In fact an 1803 survey of American higher education found no institution in the country where political subjects were studied "with so much ardour" as at William and Mary. These studies helped give intellectual underpinning to lessons that Tucker and no doubt many other students there already had learned. Adam Smith's *Wealth of Nations,* for example, contained rigorous criticisms of industrial economies based on the exploitation of wage labor, observations that Virginians in their simple society could find comforting;[39] another work making a deep impression on young Tucker was Montesquieu's *Spirit of the Laws.* Montesquieu, whose ideas were plainly evident in St. George Tucker's writings, advanced the proposition that a single word could capture the spirit of different forms of government. In a despotism, that word was fear; in a monarchy, honor; in a republic, virtue. Montesquieu's republican virtue, like St. George Tucker's, was Spartan: a set of rules built on selflessness, public spirit, and moral will.[40]

But political interest at the college was not purely academic. Besides busily reading what someone called the "sacred trinity" of John Locke, Jean-Jacques Rousseau, and Thomas Paine, many students wore the red cockade of the French revolutionary patriots; the academy rang with denunciation of Federalist Party intrigues; a faculty member who came down on the wrong side of the Alien and Sedition questions in 1798 found himself an object of campus ridicule. The president of William and Mary, Episcopal bishop James Madison, earned some notoriety in Virginia by preaching that the Kingdom of Heaven was in truth a republic of equal souls.[41]

Thus experience challenged theory in Tucker's intellectual development. For one thing he could not help noticing that the "equality" in Rousseau's writings had a counterpart in a real issue at William and Mary, the matter of numbers against quality. After 1779 student matriculation fees were a major source of college revenue, so that fiscal interests worked against selectivity of admission. For a coterie of students—some studying law or living at the Tucker house—the result was an influx of the unworthy, who came to the school less for improvement than for diversion. Chapman Johnson found students in 1799 "less assiduous" than he had expected, and another student described three out of four of his colleagues that year as devoid of ambition, sluggish of mind, and wasteful of time. It appeared to Henry and Beverley and their friends that the reputation of the college had to rest on talents, on a "love of Science" that bad habits among unsuited students clearly offended. A certain community had to remain, a commitment to mutual improvement and to a sense of generosity among gentlemen that selfishness, vanity, and violence among men of lesser quality subverted.[42]

Furthermore, antireligious militance among wearers of the red cockade left Tucker with lingering misgivings. Probably never strong, piety at the college was one of the first casualties of the Jacobin enthusiasm, reaching what was perhaps an all-time low in the wake of a visit "Citizen Genet," the French revolutionary ambassador to the American people, made to Williamsburg in 1793. When one student arrived at the college, he was frankly surprised to find that Bishop Madison believed in Christianity at all. The bishop but infrequently mentioned faith in his moral philosophy course, and he raised hoots and jeers from impious students when he did. Skepticism, college extremists demonstrated for Tucker, had a way of growing into contempt, scorn into depredation. Not long before Tucker began college courses, "Jacobin" students broke into a Williamsburg church, smashed the communion table, scattered prayer books and Bibles about the courtyard, destroyed one stained glass window, and then smeared dung over the pulpit from top to bottom.[43] This attack, though unusually offensive, still had an undeniable connection with the antiauthoritarian climate of opinion among students. Tucker found the effrontery of this infidelity bothersome, the brutishness of its anti-institutionalism repelling.

Finally, in William Godwin, the English rationalist and defender of the French Revolution, Tucker found an exemplar of the uncomfortable thrust and radical excesses of Jacobinism. Godwin argued in his 1793 *Enquiry Concerning Political Justice* and later in his novels that society forced persons to hide from themselves through conventions and taboos; he hoped to place political, social, and even personal relations on a solely rational footing. Godwinism became the subject of raging interest among William and Mary students. At about the time Tucker began higher studies, a debate at the college—which was famous for its disputations—considered the question whether gratitude was a virtue.[44] The presumption was that Godwin would dismiss that feeling as sentimental nonsense. In this animated discussion Tucker was able to see the potential conflict between polite culture and intellectual commitment, between "heart" and "head," between the norms of conformity and objectivity. Though in misunderstanding Godwin Tucker made him a cruel parody of the Enlightenment and free enquiry, the more important point was that he saw in Godwin's "reason" and optimism an emotion-stripped abstraction that bothered him and greatly influenced his view of the intellectual life. While scoffing at the attachment one felt, say, for a mother, "rationalism" for Tucker challenged the order, regularity, and security of social form.

Contrasting with the shocks of radicalism and dryness of abstraction were Tucker's readings in ethics at William and Mary. They had an appealingly conservative tone. William Paley's *Principles of Moral and Political Philosophy,* first published in 1785, was an attempt to combine elements of the Anglican faith, English utilitarianism, parts of Locke, and the ethical objective of earthly happiness. Paley skirted deism, some thought, and spoke of natural rights. But his synthesis finally brought the reader to caution and even pious resignation. For Paley, a Yorkshire clergyman, the sacred scriptures were the ultimate source of ethical principles. "The will of God is our rule," Paley told his audience, and God meant for mankind only what would "promote the communication of human happiness." Prudence in one's dealings with superiors, politeness to equals, and charity to inferiors and dependents, Paley believed, would sustain "those conditions of life, in which men generally appear most cheerful and contented." While Paley's contemporary Jeremy Bentham denounced oppressive custom and the cant of tradition, Paley spoke more guardedly of "habit and fashion" among people, "the exercise of social affections" in society, and the "duties and obligations of civil life."[45]

When Beverley turned his attention to logic and the nature of the mind, he encountered the work of William Duncan, Thomas Reid, and Dugald Stewart; in rhetoric, examining the proper uses and form of oratory and literature, his source was the widely used handbook of the Reverend Hugh Blair of Edinburgh. These writers of what became known as the Scottish Common Sense School deliberately avoided the abstruseness of earlier eighteenth-century thought and urged a return to "natural realism." In this common-sense view it was fundamental that the mind perceived not simply ideas or images but objects themselves. There was a direct and necessary connection between objects and perceptions. Scottish realists thus discounted the "delusive" idealism of George Berkeley, the "scepticism" of David Hume, the mystical "phenomena" of Immanuel Kant and the intermediary "ideas" of John Locke. Realists appealed to the trustworthiness of man's senses, placed credence in "facts" as opposed to the recondite, and assumed that "first principles" found in all men made their good sense and intuition philosophically reliable. Scottish realism came as a rejoinder to overly ambitious thinkers, as a reminder of man's limitations and his dependency.[46] Beverley found this lesson instructive.

Critical as Tucker's readings and experiences at William and Mary were in his development, more important was the meaning he attached to them. For one who took refuge in brooding daydreams and who nursed memories of lost affection, the arrogance and "coldness" of eighteenth-century reason was understandably suspect and unsatisfying; similarly, the boldness of red-cockaded extremists violated the custom and predictability of Williamsburg society, which Tucker's motherless world had made particularly attractive to him. Certainly the forces working on the young scholar reached depths he was unaware of. Proudly impulsive as a child, having chafed under fatherly discipline, Tucker now might very well have doubted that Montesquieu's republican virtue was possible in all men; while Beverley resented paternal authority and resisted the private discipline that "self-rule" called for in St. George Tucker's household, the young man clung to the principle of public morality all the more tightly.

Giving shape to Tucker's intellect and personality were elements peculiar to him, and yet his reaction to them outlined larger contours of his culture. Beverley's raging anger as a "discountenanced" schoolboy suggested the importance of one's "face" when certain kinds of persons filled traditionally defined roles in society and when other persons therefore ascribed certain attributes to them. Thus Beverley's difficulties at school were no different than those any Southern lad suffered when, having learned that honor was central to his self-esteem in a role-conscious society, he felt shamed, and had to react in a fitting way. Forced at school to submit to a man who seemed of lesser station than his father, Beverley's problems with self-discipline only mirrored a broader issue in Southern society, the tension between the need slaveholders had to exercise nearly absolute power within their realms and the contrary need, which St. George Tucker knew to be so important in free government, for men suspicious of power. Before the Revolution, the domestic authority of the Virginia gentry had helped produce impatience with external restrictions;[47] independence brought the source of authority home and called for men capable of exercising power with self-control. For Southerners of Beverley's generation the republican's role could be an uncomfortable one indeed.

The idiosyncracies of Tucker's story also tell something of the intellectual setting in which young men trained for leadership in nineteenth-century Virginia. Tucker was drawn to the works of Paley and to common sense for reasons that joined together external events and the undercurrents of his mind. Yet the point was that all students at William and Mary in his day studied in a trough between systems of perceiving reality. One way of examining the world, the Enlightenment and its rationalist approach, appeared to Tucker—and he was not alone—to have run its course in human affairs, to have been carried to extremes that discredited it; a coherent alternative had not yet appeared to him. Judge Tucker hoped that his son would continue, as he had, to consider ideas testable, pragmatism a virtue, and skepticism a rule. It remained to be seen whether the second generation of Virginia patriots would find St. George Tucker's frame of mind acceptable.

CHAPTER TWO

The Virtuous Loser, A Man of Heart

BEVERLEY APPARENTLY PLANNED to present as his baccalaureate address an essay in praise of American literature: it purified the morals, cultivated the intellect, and refined the taste of republicans. He never finished the oration. In February 1802 William and Mary shook with student rowdiness and then more unrest when the faculty meted out punishment. The state of affairs so mortified Professor Tucker's good friend in Norfolk, Phillip Barraud, that he recommended closing the college doors forever lest the institution become a "Harbor for wild Beasts" and "mad-headed boys." Beverley himself had to admit to John Randolph, whose brief stay at the college in 1793 had ended with an unhappy dueling incident, that the prevailing dissipation surpassed even the frolics of Randolph's day. Students, said Tucker, enjoyed mint juleps in the morning, gin twists at noon, wine at dinner, and cards afterward.[1]

So that Beverley might no longer consider himself a member of what he wryly called "this *respectable* body," the boy's father withdrew him from school that February and gave him law books to read.[2] The study of the law, thought St. George Tucker, would impose the discipline of rigorous reasoning on the mind of his son. Instead the young man developed other ideas about reason, found diversions, and suffered disappointments. Results were not entirely pleasing.

I

The elder Tucker took responsibility for the intellectual upbringing of his boys seriously, and his purposes were largely hardheaded. A sound education made for a gentleman, inculcating good morals and practical habits; professional training was of great help in establishing a gentleman's financial security. A man had to be able "to place his reliance on *Himself*," he wrote. He saw to it that each of his sons, as well as an orphan who became his ward in 1801, set about their education with eyes fixed on both their "Improvement, & future advancement in Life." Yet St. George Tucker's very practicality bespoke the political theory he had in mind and the social ends he held as the longer goal of schooling. Besides realistic assessments, principles of republican government dictated the need for self-reliance; eminence and service went together as the primary objects of improvement. Every man, he had written the Randolph boys in 1787, "is respectable in society in proportion to the Talents he possesses to serve it."[3]

From Beverley's earliest memory, the law was the preferred mode of serving the new republic. John Coalter, tutor for the Tucker boys during their first years of schooling, had spoken to them of the lawyer's role in preserving the "Liberties of the People"; St. George Tucker taught his students that the science of law was the "inseparable companion" of liberty. Moreover, law was a family hallmark, a pursuit that aroused Tucker's expectations. He promised himself and his father to proceed in his legal studies with renewed scholarly attention, vowing "to proceed in it with a degree of alacrity" that he had previously avoided in his studies. He was anxious to make a beginning on his own. "I feel myself," he confidently wrote John Randolph, "fairly entered on the road to *independence,* and with the aid of my father hope to surmount every obstacle in the way."[4]

St. George Tucker began his son's legal training with the text most American law students used in that day, Sir William Blackstone's *Commentaries on the Laws of England.* First delivered as the Vinerian lectures at Oxford in 1733, published in the late 1760s, and soon afterward transported to the American colonies, the four-volume *Commentaries* had explained and justified the common law of England—and the rights of Englishmen—at an especially opportune time for colonial lawyers. On the floor of the House of Commons in 1775 Edmund Burke credited colonial rebellion to the vigilance of lawyers and to Blackstone's description of common-law rights.[5]

Even so, there were American objections to Blackstone, and after independence these criticisms came to a head. Blackstone had limited his text to English law and had ignored colonial statutes; independence and then the ratifying of the Constitution—introducing peculiarly American principles of government—also brought a minor revolution in laws relating to property and to other affairs. Republicans declared that the Englishman's tract was that of a conservative monarchist. His volumes were simply inappropriate for use in free America.[6]

Tucker supplemented his reading of Blackstone that spring of 1802 with lecture notes his father was preparing for a critical edition of the *Commentaries* (to be published the following year) in which he intended to meet these objections. The appendices were extensive. Besides explaining and modifying the text, Judge Tucker discussed the constitution of Virginia, Virginia courts, and state statute law. He included an essay denying that the federal courts could appropriate and apply English common law throughout the states; to do so would create an unwritten federal criminal code and

would slight the state judiciaries. Further reminding readers of his continuing hope, he attached to the first volume his plan to end slavery in Virginia.
St. George Tucker's aim was to prevent the abandonment of the *Commentaries* by making them palatable to the American taste, a purpose he achieved.
In the years following the appearance of his edition, it enjoyed considerable
success among men studying for the bar as apprentices to practicing lawyers.[7]

Tucker's tract also became notable for the lessons it provided on the nature
of the federal system. Beverley read in his father's volume ideas that Americans in the antebellum period later knew—and often denounced—as the states'
rights school of constitutional theory. It was a view of the Constitution based
on the letter of the document, the intentions of the men who framed it, and
the history of its drafting and adoption. St. George Tucker worked mostly
from American state documents rather than from what he discounted as the
musings of Europeans unfamiliar with republican government. He drew on
The Federalist essays of Alexander Hamilton, James Madison, and John Jay;
the Virginia General Assembly resolutions of 1798 condemning the Alien
and Sedition Acts; and the report that Madison, heading a committee in the
Assembly, wrote in 1799 enlarging on the theory of that protest.[8]

Tucker's case was forceful and persuasive: the Constitution, a written and
therefore limited charter of government, created a federal agency of "carefully prescribed" powers. Tucker held that, to maintain the republic, it was
crucial to keep the powers of both federal and state governments to manageable proportions, but the central government had the largest potential for
evil. It had in federal public lands a source of treasure that it might misap-
propriate; it attracted persons unscrupulous about the defined boundaries of
its powers. The necessary and proper clause of Article I, Section 8, for example, had become a pretext for assuming unspecified powers. The clause was
supposed to hold the federal Congress to its responsibilities and to those
alone; it made the linkage between grants of authority to Congress and the
laws it passed a test of their constitutionality, a means by which the federal
judiciary could act as a bulwark against "undue extensions" of congressional
power. "It is the due restraint, and not the moderation of rulers that consti-
tutes a state of liberty," St. George Tucker warned, "as the power to oppress,
though never exercised, does a state of slavery." The duties of the federal
government were "the exact measure of its powers."[9]

Judicial review by independent courts was an important restraint on government. But in the American federal system, wrote Tucker, the ultimate
watchmen over the central government were the states who had sent delegates to write the compact and whose people had ratified it. The federal
framework was one of states voluntarily joined together "without ceasing
to be perfect states," entrusting certain powers to the federal government,
their servant, while *"retaining an entire liberty"* to exercise as they thought
proper "all those parts" of their sovereignty unmentioned in the act of union.

The tenth amendment to the Constitution recognized this relationship. It was what Tucker called a "just inference and conclusion" from the nature of the federal structure that, although states had no explicit veto authority over acts of Congress, in serious cases they might interpose themselves—as had Virginia in 1798—to protect their citizens from the exercise of ungranted and injurious congressional power.[10]

St. George Tucker left his son, and the great many other law students who used his volumes, with a mixed message. On one hand it contained open-ended possibilities. He maintained that the states were the authors of a system designed to curb, not to grant, power to the federal government, and there was room for growth in this theory. Tucker failed to spell out precisely how or to what extent the states could "interpose" on behalf of their citizens when in legislature or convention—he did not say which was proper—one of them believed it necessary to protect individual liberties, or when—he did not elaborate—the federal government took to "intermeddling with the domestic concerns of any state." Nor did Tucker quibble over the exact quality or divisibility of the "sovereignty" he said belonged to the people and to the states as their means of expressing their sovereign will. Furthermore, Tucker's love for the Union was not blind devotion. The Constitution needed amendment, he thought, to limit further the power and influence of the President, to preserve the liberties of the people, and to ensure the independence of the states within the federal structure. He faced without fear the chance that the confederacy might break up. The Constitution must, he said, "be received, respected, and obeyed" as the supreme law of the land—until, he began that injunction by saying, the people, "whether the present, or any future generation, shall think it necessary to alter, or revoke [it] . . . ."[11]

On the other hand, Tucker's edition of the *Commentaries* carried a burden of enduring precepts and issued a call for responsible caretakers. If ever a "fair experiment" could be made of democratic government, wrote St. George Tucker in a brighter vein, it was in "United America"; and then, tying a knot between republican fear of tyranny and the ground rules of politics which helped make the Constitution a focal point of antebellum controversy, he insisted that the republic would endure only as long as its citizens obeyed laws and venerated the principles of the Constitution. In the body of the *Commentaries* Blackstone for his part presented the common law as at once a matter of marvelous logic and inscrutable wisdom. Unfolding through experience, said the English jurist, the common law was an extension of divine law and therefore deserving of man's reverence. Rights and liberties under the law were, or should be, beyond man's tampering. Property rights, the touchstone of liberty, were inviolable. The *Commentaries* were a brief for tradition, trust in experience, and the providential movement of history. The common law, as Beverley came to agree, was "a

venerated edifice of antiquity," which no one but the "rash and inexperienced" would try to tear down.[12]

Besides, it was possible for young Tucker to find in the *Commentaries* a
good argument for genteel political leadership. His father, though he spoke
of the people as sovereign, emphasized that citizens needed to pay the
"strictest attention" to the "morals and principles" of the men they chose
to represent them. Though the elder Tucker described the American system
as a democracy, it was one in which every man could only expect elevation
to public offices "to which his talents and integrity may qualify him."
Blackstone addressed a home audience. But when he wrote of the role of
the English gentleman, Virginians like Beverley had little trouble imagining
ways to apply these maxims to themselves. As jurors or justices of the peace,
gentlemen determined right and dispensed justice; as lawmakers, English—or
Virginia—gentlemen were guardians of the constitution, who would watch
for and avert "every dangerous innovation" while promoting solid and well-
considered improvements. Gentlemen, according to Blackstone, were bound
by nature, honor, and faith to transmit the constitution and laws of their
country to posterity "without any derogation."[13] Susceptible to this appeal
as the younger Tucker was, he lay charged with awesome responsibilities.

II

But legal study was tedious, and it did not take long for the first flush of
Tucker's eagerness to fade. Only a week after picking up Lord Coke's
Institutes, he longed for the more pleasurable fare and instructive pages
of Hume and of Rousseau. Though his professional reading enabled him to
talk of arcane common-law terms and of mysterious medieval relationships,
though he joked of learning "so many hard words in so short a time," he
still found it hard to rouse himself for the musty folios of Littleton. Nor
was he alone, for St. George Tucker's pupils regularly complained of the
labor and dryness of law study. Both Chapman Johnson and Joseph Cabell,
who later became distinguished Virginia lawyers, complained that the rigors
of the elder Tucker's course confined attention "almost solely to investigations entirely uninteresting, perhaps unimproving, and entirely loathsome";
law students could agree that the subject deserved every censure "the lazy,
the idle, or industrious" had bestowed upon it.[14]

Perhaps, thought the struggling scholar, it would help to escape the hard-
ship of his father's regimen. In the summer of 1802 St. George Tucker
agreed to let Beverley continue his legal studies with his old grammar
school tutor, John Coalter, in Staunton. Coalter had established a successful law practice there and, after his wife's death, had married Beverley's
older sister Fanny. By late July Beverley and Coalter had arranged a regular
reading program, and Tucker proudly had sent his father word that he had

grown to be "something of a student." Still, the study arrangement was less than ideal. Coalter's library was often inadequate for the student's purposes, so that texts either had to be borrowed nearby or, with the usual delays, mailed from Williamsburg. Anyway, Coalter was often busy with his own work. Beverley studied with him in the mornings then worked by himself in the afternoon, poring over the newly published edition of Blackstone when he had finished Coke on Littleton, and asking his father's occasional help by letter. Without much supervision, Beverley found considerable difficulty in "connecting the ideas" of some commentaries and "fastening upon the opinions and arguments" of others.[15]

Before long the deadening effect of legal studies again made Tucker unhappy and impatient. He complained at the end of the first half-year in Staunton that he had read very little else than the law since arriving there. His mind seemed "palsied" with it; his ideas seemed limited to the conduct of a suit. Though he labored to win his father's approval, he could demonstrate more effort than accomplishment when St. George Tucker administered an informal examination in the summer of 1804. It seemed as if he would never finish Blackstone's four volumes; he wondered if he would ever be able to prove himself as successful as his brother Henry who, just establishing law practice in Winchester, was meeting every expectation.[16]

Much as Beverley wanted to please his father, he had difficulty confining his reading to the law. Doubtless he followed Coalter's prescription of Shakespeare after a day at the bar. But history offered the most enjoyable escape. While trying to read Coke, Tucker found time to wade through an abridgement of Gibbon's *Decline and Fall of the Roman Empire.* At one point, after he had completed Blackstone's third volume, Tucker so exerted himself reading a section of William Belsham's *Memoirs of the Reign of George III,* celebrating the Whigs' victory over despotic power, that he suffered an eye affliction. It "utterly disabled" him, he said, and made it temporarily impossible to read his law texts.[17]

For a tidewater gentleman in his early twenties, the isolation of life beyond the Blue Ridge Mountains was itself painful. Tucker eagerly sought ways to escape it. Christmas visits to the cheerful fire in Williamsburg were often extended over a month or more, and on one such stay at home, Fanny—who had returned home with Beverley—reported that she had never seen him as "uniformly happy." In the fall of 1804, following St. George Tucker's election to the Virginia Court of Appeals—the highest court in the commonwealth—Beverley happily met his parents in Richmond to see his father sworn in and to attend the usual round of dinners and parties. The experience of social life in the capital was exhilarating. He was flattered when his father introduced him to the leading families of the city; he delighted in talking to Carringtons, Pages, and to the eminent George Hay— United States District Attorney in Richmond, whose home opposite

Capitol Square was a kind of headquarters for city society. "I have readily been surprised," Beverley confidently wrote his sister in provincial Staunton, "to find how many acquaintances I have in this town, & how fast I should increase the number were I to continue here."[18] There were parts a man of his upbringing should play, and he was eager to fill them.

III

In these anxious years Tucker's chief diversion from legal training was his half brother, John Randolph. The roots of their attraction lay in long summer vacations that Henry and Beverley had spent with Randolph in the 1790s at his plantation home, appropriately named Bizarre. Excursions to the country were boyhood escapes from school, fatherly discipline, and the restrictions of town life. For Beverley, whom Randolph described affectionately as a "saucy" child, anticipating a visit with Randolph gave him "the fidgets to be off." Tucker felt that the plantation beckoned him. A "country life in the society of the friends of our youth," Randolph once wrote him—and Beverley heartily agreed—provided "as much happiness as is compatible with our imperfect condition."[19]

Apparently such happiness was indeed meager and fleeting, for the closeness the two men developed was one based on persistent melancholy. Randolph stood in frank need of a confiding friend. His much-beloved Maria Ward had suddenly broken off their marriage plans in 1801, leaving him dejected. His depression also grew out of the loneliness of Bizarre; the estate in south-central Virginia seemed in fact to work havoc on all who lived on it. Judith Randolph, widow of John's older brother Richard, complained of its "uniformity & dullness," and while there, her more sensitive and imaginative sister Nancy found herself given to "wild, delusive speculations." Even during these politically successful years, Randolph could find periods between congressional sessions at Bizarre just as dreary. He required "the society of a rational friend," he wrote, and he welcomed Tucker to fill that need, to help him cope with his morose impulses. Fearing that Judith nourished melancholia that would destroy her, Randolph spoke for himself too when he begged Tucker to visit and divide with him "the task of soothing her wounded spirits."[20] Tucker came to exercise a certain charm over Randolph.

Such closeness carried a subtle challenge to Tucker's father. While Beverley studied with Coalter, his temptation to visit Bizarre was one that he knew St. George Tucker would have him resist; although once at the Randolph plantation Tucker hoped for the rains that would close the roads and delay him there, he knew doing so would be against his father's wishes. When in 1804 there was a plan afoot to move Tucker to Bizarre permanently in the belief that he could, in Judith's phrase, "pursue his studies with as

HENRY ST. GEORGE TUCKER

BEVERLEY TUCKER
c. 1810

JOHN RANDOLPH
OF ROANOKE
as a young congressman

much advantage *here* as anywhere in the World," the elder Tucker vetoed
the proposal, doubting Beverley's claim that he could pass time with Randolph undistracted. Then in 1805 Randolph and St. George Tucker split
painfully, and for Randolph bitterly, over financial details of the bequest
that Randolph's father had left him and that Tucker had administered.
Afterwards Bizarre became a kind of enemy camp in Judge Tucker's eyes.
There was an edge in Beverley's comment a year later that visiting Randolph
was a case of improvement and pleasure going hand in hand.[21]

At first Randolph's lure was his brilliance and political success. Although
depressed and lonesome at Bizarre, Randolph in Washington was already
a legend in his late twenties. Widely read, often a spellbinding speaker, the
Virginia congressman made up for his squeaky voice—perhaps the result of
a hormone deficiency—by wearing a hunting coat and brandishing a riding
crop on the floor of the House. He was originally a Jefferson Republican, a
formidable member of the Congress, chairman of the Ways and Means Committee, and a trusted Jefferson lieutenant.[22]

Randolph overreached himself. As manager of the prosecution in the im-
peachment trial of Judge Samuel Chase, he failed to win conviction of this
Republican party enemy and disappointed the President. Embarrassed,
losing influence, Randolph was principled, critics now said, to the point of
being brittle and peevish. He differed with the administration in 1805 over
the question of whether to compensate victims of the Yazoo land-fraud
swindle, referring to such favoritism as a "monstrous sacrifice of the best
interests of the nation on the altars of corruption." A year later he broke
further with Jefferson when the President made a frankly devious attempt
to acquire West Florida. Alienation from Jefferson over these questions of
political morality, setbacks in grubby legislative workings, and a pervading
sense of disgust led Randolph to the role of spiteful moralizer. He soon was
chief of a congressional faction, the Quids, whose stated purpose was to
remain true to Jeffersonian principles even as the President abandoned
them.[23]

In Tucker's restless state, Randolph's political disenchantment easily
became his own, and as his half brother's disillusionment made for intellectual changes, Tucker shared them. Both men loved history; both of them
read extensively in the classics. More important, it was during these years
of the second Jefferson administration, Tucker later recalled, that Randolph
became a convert to Edmund Burke. Earlier a wearer of the red cockade, a
user of the French revolutionary calendar, and an admirer of Thomas Paine,
Randolph after 1805 began to suspect, as Tucker put it, that there might be
"something in the enjoyment of Liberty which soon disqualifies a people
for that self-government." Burke was sober on the subject of liberty.
Human nature, he wrote, was a matter less of reason than of intuition, of
natural instincts that men could not ignore. Like Blackstone, Burke called

attention to institutions as protectors of individual rights. When Randolph
took up Burke, so did his brother. Tucker now spoke pointedly of questioning the "infallible wisdom" of Jeffersonian councils, a reference that was
not wholly political, for Burke even more than Paley or common-sense
philosophy represented in Tucker's mind a revolt against the Reason Jefferson symbolized.[24] The intellectual affinity that Tucker and Randolph
developed had an important influence on the younger man's growth of
mind.

   This harmony of thought had its counterpart in aesthetics. Through
Randolph, Tucker acquired, first of all, a taste for the aristocratic mode—
the noble manner. Though in fact Burke was as pragmatic in practical
political affairs as Randolph was dogmatic, Tucker saw in his brother the
image of Burke and the fulfillment of the English tradition of Whiggish
opposition. Randolph was a country gentleman—Blackstone's English
squire—at home with his hounds, horses, and servants; duty to his people
and locale carried him off to the seat of power to remind forgetful men,
with exquisite aloofness, of their obligation to preserve proven good and
to stand by old morality. Furthermore, Randolph embodied for Tucker the
romantic man. Heroic, morose, proud, doomed, contemplative, Randolph
was a figure, said Tucker later, whom Byron alone could paint.[25]

   Finally, Tucker's "Brother Jack" provided with the game of politics a
retreat from the rigors of study. As soon as political warfare broke out
between Jeffersonian moderates and Randolph's doctrinally righteous
Quids, Tucker became intensely, even though vicariously, involved as an
anti-Jefferson partisan. He wrote excitedly that he had never before realized
"what a damnable Sin was heresy, whether in politics or religion." Learning
quickly the Quid lexicon, reciting it devoutly to Randolph, Tucker discovered in being one of these "sinners" a welcome relief from Coke and
Littleton. If, admitted the young man, he had "lost a great deal of time
(speaking, take notice, as a student of law)" during one summer with
Randolph at Bizarre, it was an "evil" that he was willing to bear. Perhaps
it was unfortunate that he had neglected the law, Beverley told Randolph
with a wink. But worse, he said, "in acquiring from you some of the knowledge of more general subjects, I acquired also a taste for them, which made
me return to my more serious studies with disgust."[26]

IV

In the summer of 1806, when Tucker was at last prepared to take his law
licensing examination—what he called hopefully his "degrees as a man"—
St. George Tucker advised his son to open an office in Fredericksburg.
There, on the falls of the Rappahannock River, commerical growth promised
legal opportunities. A clever young man would take advantage of them.

THE SITE OF TUCKER'S EARLY LAW PRACTICE
Marysville, middle left, was also known as Charlotte Court House; Richmond appears
at the upper right.

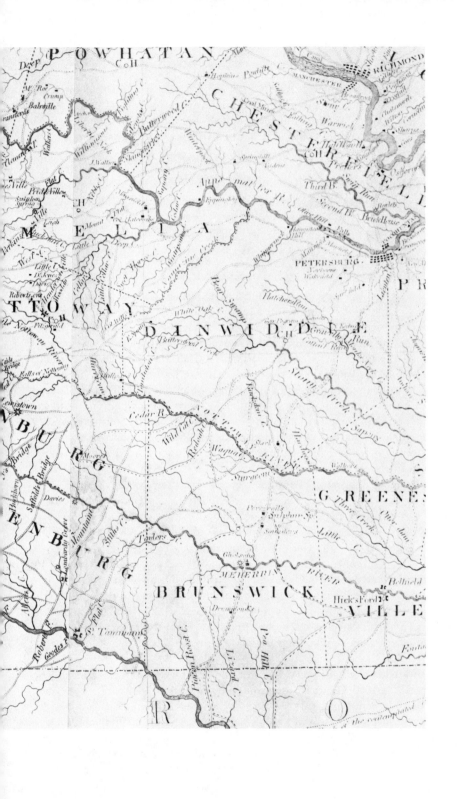

Tucker resisted the Judge's advice, supposedly on the grounds that the river town with its bad company might lead him into temptation. Tucker's real complaint against Fredericksburg, though he did not tell his father of it, was his wish to be close to Randolph; at Charlotte Court House, south of the James near Bizarre, he could see his brother every day he was home from Washington. In this cause against head of family, Beverley enlisted the help of Henry St. George, who in Winchester had already become a prominent member of the bar. St. George Tucker finally gave in. While Henry, too, regretted the arrangement, he tried to be consoling: better that the younger Tucker's test of maturity take place in a theatre of his own choice.[27]

In deciding on Charlotte Court House over Fredericksburg Beverley chose feeling over shrewdness, but the choice had its merits. There were three levels of Virginia courts in 1806 and he hoped to make his mark on two of them locally.[28] Besides the Charlotte County Court business, Tucker counted on recognition at the Prince Edward bar, where one of the Virginia district courts met twice a year and where a prominent lawyer's recent advancement to the bench created a vacancy; in Halifax, where accomplished lawyers appeared wanting, he saw even greater opportunity. At Charlotte— barely more than a rural crossroads for most of any month—Tucker planned to have a small house in which, he said expectantly, "I shall enjoy, in the fullest extent, all the pleasures of my own company, & that of my books."[29]

Nonetheless, Charlotte Court House was the scene of embarrassing failure. The summer of 1806 had been dry, and with bad crops there was a slow-down in litigation the following fall and winter. "As to business," Beverley wrote home in February, "I am just where I was. I have never received a cent, nor am I by any means sure of receiving any. . : ." Competition at court turned out to be stiffer than anticipated. Although there were occasionally encouraging signs—one client who paid Tucker a ten-dollar fee told him that he had "got the full value of his money"—for the most part the young lawyer's reports made dismal reading. He was especially distraught to find that his early career compared badly to the novice lawyers who had gone before him in the district. The cottage he had hoped to occupy never materialized. It was late January before he found a suitable boarding house, and when he did he was surprised to find that rental terms excluded bed, bedding, furniture, candles, and firewood—leaving him further in need of fatherly aid.[30]

With Tucker's worst fears confirmed and his considerable pride offended, gloom at Charlotte Court House took on morbid dimensions. "I see no one," his father learned, "hear from no one, and witness nothing that can excite an interest in you, or even in myself." He spent sleepless nights haunted by "cares and doubts" about his future in the profession; self-doubts, he wrote, were "perpetually hanging round" him. Writing letters that exhaustively listed his black feelings, he grumbled when his family did not write frequently enough. He was "cut adrift by all the world," surrounded by strangers, deprived of those persons who knew and cared for him. Not until March 1807 did he hear from either Henry or Fanny, and then he found that their news had staled and sentiments cooled over the distance traveled; he would have preferred their affectionate messages, like Newton's comet, not only hot but "solid and substantial also." Disappointment and mortification, he admitted, had "broken and humbled" his spirit.[31]

The failure of Tucker's attempt to make good on his first decision against paternal advice increased that tension he felt in his relationship with St. George Tucker. To Randolph, Tucker confided that he had a right to expect more from his father, who had seemed to show "*comparative* liberality" to Henry when the older brother was a fledgling lawyer in Winchester. Beverley's belief that Henry had received preferential treatment served only to increase his "restive indignation." Uncomfortable in his unmanly reliance on fatherly care, Tucker at the same time cried loudly that St. George Tucker wished to cast him off; he had been rebuffed where he was "best entitled to look for assistance and support. . . ."[32]

Yet the wedge driven most deeply between the unhappy attorney and his father was the love Tucker professed for Polly Coalter. A younger sister of his law tutor, Polly was a befreckled and sprightly Scotch-Irish girl who had been an agent of cheer during the years Beverley studied law in Staunton. While ill success during the first year at Charlotte Court House damaged Tucker's pride and set back his campaign for an independent livelihood, failure was worse because it put off marriage to Polly. Fatherly exhortations to brace and cheer up under the professional strain seemed to ignore the "anxious solitude" that Beverley endured without Polly.[33]

In the summer of 1807 Tucker decided at least to confront St. George Tucker with his intention to marry. He wrote of his "inviolable attachment" to Polly and of hers for him. Although he was still receiving support from his father, he expected soon to require that help no longer because Randolph—perhaps because himself a disappointed suitor—had offered to furnish Beverley with a house for his bride. Besides, he said, professional prospects looked brighter. Surely Judge Tucker would bestow his blessing on a union promising, as Beverley believed, more happiness than he could ever deserve.[34]

The elder Tucker's reply, issuing from deep parental love, was nonetheless a judge's verdict of guilty, carrying a sentence of several years of hard labor without Polly's wifely companionship. Bad crops, a resigned professorship, and threats of war made it clear that Beverley could look for nothing from his father. Nor should he become a burden on Randolph, thereby adding to his financial difficulties.

The conclusion to St. George Tucker's brusque message was a crushing disappointment. That Beverley, knowing his father's predicament, with neither a shilling of property, nor any income from his profession, nor with "any certain hopes or prospects of future success," should have endeavored to "gain the affections of an amiable young Lady," was utterly incredible. "That you," Beverley read, "should . . . have persisted [in doing so] in defiance of my well known sentiments, and of your own better Judgment, if you had ever exercised it," was something St. George Tucker would with anyone else have thought impossible. There were stinging references to Beverley's "uniform disregard" of his father's opinions, such impertinences having marked his conduct "on various occasions." Had Beverley postponed his designs until able to support a family it might have appeared as some mark of respect to his father's advice. "Abandon every Idea of marrying," demanded St. George Tucker, "until by Industry and Assiduity you have laid an actual foundation for your mutual support, & that of your family, without the aid of your Brother. . . ."[35]

Tucker set out that fall more determined than ever to prove himself, and for a time he felt as if he were gaining ground. But once again misfortune dropped him back. With the December 1807 embargo on American shipping, Tucker's business fell until he had to describe it as "snail slow in profit." Receipts were next to nothing in proportion to his work. Time, it seemed, was "wasting away, and days which might be devoted to happiness" were lost in painful reflection. He felt he had aged six years since writing the hopeful proclamation of his love for Polly, and when Beverley looked at his circumstances at the beginning of 1808, it seemed futile to go on. The spring district court at Prince Edward Court House provided no business; he went there, he told Randolph, "only to see every body else flourishing—while neglect awaits and poverty scowls upon me." He could as easily see his way to the grave as to the end of his present difficulties.[36]

For Tucker failure at Charlotte Court House had about it a cruelly mocking quality. His family was known as that of Judge Tucker of the supreme bench, and of the respected Henry St. George, who had married happily in 1806 and the next year won election to the Virginia legislature at age twenty-six. Inability to match them greatly added to the younger son's chagrin. Moreover, his father made the fulfillment of his love for Polly depend upon success in a profession that was becoming in the early nineteenth century a field of posturing, fluid oratory, and impromptu persuasion—a way of demonstrating gentlemanly virility. But here Beverley stood exposed, for he discovered when beginning practice that he had none of Randolph's talent for public speaking. A stammerer who never fully overcame his uneasiness, he derided what he called a "flippant readiness of speech."[37]

Tucker reserved feelings of deepest self-pity for the pain his father caused him in these several years of elusive success. It seemed that only belatedly or begrudgingly did St. George Tucker provide the financial help the young man so desperately needed. During the early months of 1808, when Judge Tucker neglected writing, Beverley decided that the elder Tucker "did not care to think about" his son's plight. Although a message from Williamsburg finally arrived, Tucker wondered aloud whether a register of deaths with apologies for not writing constituted a letter at all. Other mail, filled with "honied words" from his father and professions of affection, he rejected as insincere.[38]

V

St. George Tucker had expected Beverley's study of the law to discipline his intellect and prepare him for leadership in Virginia life. But instead of submitting to the logic of the law, Tucker tried to escape it; rather than learning to participate in the shaping of events, he condemned them. A frustrated young lawyer sensing social and professional change in Virginia, he began to believe himself a victim of wayward forces that were responsible for his troubles.

By no means were these changes the result of revolutionary experimentation. The Virginia constitution, which the Assembly had adopted with uncertain authority in 1776, protected important features of the colonial charter and remained a conservative influence during the early years of the nineteenth century. It left untouched, for example, a system of county rule through justices of the peace by which these magistrates, who virtually filled their own vacancies, had wide legal and administrative authority. Nor had the traditional rule by men of birth and breeding changed much. Parties and issues continued to be of lesser importance in most elections—voting remained by voice—than private connections and the quiet marshaling of influence. The "Richmond Junto," an informal group of Democrats related by blood and friendship, met in occasional caucuses to name candidates for state and federal offices, at other times kept in contact by letter, and gave every appearance of flourishing on the same principles of deference so characteristic of earlier Virginia politics.[39]

Nonetheless, as Tucker knew, things were not the same. Travelers invariably remarked on the best evidence of change, the "poverty and wretchedness," "briars and weeds" laying bare the disappointments of Virginia agriculture. Virginians themselves, in the agricultural societies and farming tracts that appeared in these years, painfully noted the damage done "the land of our ancestors." This economic decline undermined an entire social order built on simple, one-crop planting. Especially in eastern Virginia, continuous tobacco growing had destroyed land values, called into question the worth of slave labor, led to a sharp decrease in farm income, and furnished what St. George Tucker summarized as "the most awful and instructive lessons." Landholding ceased to be the sole source or best measure of wealth.[40] The moral here was one men and women who considered themselves an elite of ease and leisure commented on: land-holders of substance may have been respectable in the eyes of lower folk because financially successful, not because landed; other men, successful in other areas like the law or trade, might just as easily claim social recognition.

Moreover, putting republican principles into practice in Virginia had led to subtle changes in its political culture. The very role of government in the commonwealth was far different than in the colony. There were in the late eighteenth and early nineteenth century local and state offices to fill, state functions to perform, internal improvements to be made, contracts to be let. As the General Assembly convened in December 1806, a writer for the Richmond *Enquirer* apologized to his readers for having nothing to report for three days except the readings of petitions about "Roads, Bridges, Ferries and Inspections." In the myriad activities of state government were interests and opportunities tempting the most virtuous legislators. In addi-tion, demographic shifts pointed out the main chance in Virginia and promised political tensions; settlers filling the western reaches of the state sympathized little with eastern matters of slavery, called for more internal improvements and branch banks, and questioned inequities in legislative representation. Even the Richmond Democratic caucus, the "junto" that maintained control over the politics of the capital, hinted at differences in the political climate, for this network resulted in part from the felt need of older leaders to link together and to exert themselves prudently in the face of change, just as criticism of the junto provided proof of that challenge.[41]

Early-nineteenth-century developments in the political economy and the political life of Virginia also had their effect on the bench and bar, topics of special concern to young Tucker and his family. By the time Beverley began his law practice, complaints about the state judiciary had prompted reforms aimed at decentralizing common-law and chancery courts on the appellate level and speeding the judicial process. With population growth in the west and an increased volume of litigation, justice had become badly mired down. In 1802, the Richmond monopoly on chancery appeals gave way to a system of three intermediate or superior courts of chancery in several regions of the state. An 1808 measure altered the earlier system of district courts of common law at a central spot for several adjacent coun-ties in favor of a plan of superior courts that met twice a year in each county. The law received support for making justice accessible to more Virginians, but also criticism for the inconvenience it caused bench and bar. Finally, legislative attempts to clear the docket of the Supreme Court of Appeals created continuous controversy in these years. Reminded of the backlog of cases, legislators in January 1807 actually reduced the size of the court from five to three members, increased its number of terms each

year, and limited appeals; then in 1811 the Assembly decided to provide
five judges for the court and to require it to sit permanently until its annual
business was completed.[42]

As happened in other states during the Jeffersonian period, debates in
Virginia over the court system focused a great many prejudices. In the
House of Delegates and in the pages of the *Enquirer,* irreverent advocates
of judicial change went beyond comments on crowded dockets and the difficulty of traveling to distant courts. Critics of the Virginia judiciary attacked the "pomp" of the judges the commonwealth had in a "multitude,"
complained of their "exorbitant" salaries, and called them "pampered
individuals." Lawyers received their drubbings as well. "Professional
quibbling," read one piece, so mangled most lawsuits that an ordinary jury
was often helpless to make a fair judgment; Richmond lawyers reportedly
obstructed structural reform of the judiciary because of their selfish interest
in the appellate business there; William Wirt—an ambitious lawyer himself—
twitted Virginia lawyers in his *Letters of the British Spy* for their "arts &
frauds." Suspicion of the bench and bar in fact contained hostility toward
the traditional ruling gentry of Virginia, and here was ill feeling that was
subversive of old order. Nathaniel H. Claiborne, a delegate from Franklin
County in the west, declared during a speech he made in 1810 and published in pamphlet form that "every powerful family in the State" seemed
bent on placing one of its members in judicial office. A contributor to the
Enquirer saw in the abuses of county magistrates and their clerks the same
kind of antidemocratic jobbery: "the present vicious tho' constitutional
mode of electing these officers . . . is worse than *Aristocratical—,* it is
Oligarchical. . . ."[43]

To be sure, not all proponents of judicial improvement made democratic
attacks on bench and bar; bar members themselves favored many procedural
and organizational adjustments, and in any case disputes over the judiciary
in Virginia were far less rancorous than in more highly differentiated societies like Pennsylvania or in frontier regions like Kentucky. But the undercur-
rent of animosity toward the gentleman was there, and besides the threat to
the independence of the judiciary that the Tuckers recognized in legislative
tampering with the courts, it also invited reflection on the quality of public
life in Virginia. In the Tucker and Randolph families such thought led to
pessimism. Like Wirt in his *British Spy,* first published in 1803 and circulated widely thereafter, and like Sir John Foster, the British minister who
traveled in Virginia in 1806 and 1807, the Tuckers noted a decline in civic
spirit in the new commonwealth. In their view, a passion for the spoils of
office was developing; legislators were not of the same cloth, had little
respect for a balanced constitution, and were unwilling to avoid the party
haggling that endangered free government. According to Tuckers and
Randolphs there were "flatterers & adherents" in Washington; in Richmond

what "public virtue—public honour[,] public honesty and independence of
character" there had ever been had vanished.[44]

It surprised no one that Beverley's criticisms of the changing order were
especially harsh, and deepening his disappointment at failure was a sense of
betrayal. In Blackstone's *Commentaries* he had read that the judiciary was
the high priesthood of the constitutional order, independent of either interest or influence, exercising judgment with a "delicacy of sentiment" that
was "peculiar to noble birth." Yet after several years of law practice in
Southside Virginia (the south-central counties of the state), it seemed clear
to Tucker that Virginia judges were often not what they were supposed to
be. Since law practice, especially in the Richmond appellate courts, could
pay considerably more than the sum the legislators provided judges of even
the highest courts, there was some substance to Tucker's charge that the
best men did not always sit on the bench. There was also evidence that, as he
suspected, judges did intrigue in Richmond for and against legislation and
candidates of interest to them, violating the rule of judicial neutrality.
"Learning and genius, moderation and sobriety and dignity" were not as
likely to bring a man to the bench, Tucker concluded, "as acrimony and
intemperance of political zeal, and a general turbulence of Character. . . ."[45]

At the Virginia bar the young Charlotte County lawyer saw erosion of
quality that was cause for even greater outrage. Hoping to be able to play
the part of a "barrister" rather than that of a mere "bailiff," Tucker expected to find an informal ranking in the profession, by which the men of
superior schooling undertook the most intellectually challenging assignments,
practiced before the higher courts, and were rendered appropriate deference.
But if the law, as Wirt observed, was "the road to honour" in Virginia, the
way was growing crowded. The bar examination procedure in Virginia had
never been quite as difficult or tightly administered as in some other states,
so that by the early nineteenth century there were in truth a great many
pliers of the trade arguing before county and superior courts, refusing to
defer to men like Tucker, and absorbing much of the "plain business"
which, in lean times, better-trained lawyers were glad to accept. While
Tucker scorned having to "go beg for employment at the hands of a mean
and sneering herd," men whom he called "pettifoggers" and described as a
cross between a lawyer and a constable appeared in every corner of the
country, brought to court the lesser disputes of neighborhood and family,
and worked for supper and horsefeed. What was worse, these unprofessional
upstarts, with what Tucker called a "ready knack of saying a great deal they
really do not understand," often had a driving ambition to win election to
the legislature.[46]

Tucker's case illustrated the effects that organizational changes in the
Virginia judiciary brought members of the rural bar. Since in practice
judges of the superior courts drew lots each term to determine which of

the circuits they would travel, it was that much more difficult for a young lawyer to establish rapport with any one of them, to learn their foibles, and to gain their respect. More seriously, the judicial reform efforts of the General Assembly made the practice of law physically more difficult and loosened the structure of the country bar. The 1808 superior court statute increased markedly the number of places Tucker and his peers had to be in order to keep up their practices; in Tucker's attempt to appear at nearby county courts and superior sessions at Staunton, Prince Edward, Brunswick, and elsewhere, he attended by his count fifty-six sessions a year. Changes in the location of chancery courts and, in some instances, calendar conflicts between chancery courts and common-law courts had their effect on established equity practices. As the importance of the county courts diminished and the practice of law for most men became a traveling road show, the discipline and character of the bar became more difficult as well. It was no longer a closed fraternity of local gentlemen who set standards of competence and behavior. Circles of friendship became looser and less effective professional barriers, and men whom Tucker considered interlopers grew more common. His verdict was severe. Country practice, he said, was utterly disgusting, "producing neither honor nor profit and justifying the hope of neither."[47]

Thus at Charlotte Court House Tucker found himself unable to play the role he felt assigned. Angry, nursing his disillusionment, he had trouble even with his peers—who included such competent Southside lawyers as William Leigh, James Wood Bouldin, and William Bruce. Although Tucker from time to time spoke proudly of the friendly sentiments colleagues directed his way on court days, he admitted that only with difficulty could he maintain the gentlemanly ethic, "the scrupulous rule of forbearance," which his father had known at the bar and wanted to pass on to his son. Occasionally Tucker found it necessary to use the "bitterness [of] sarcasm" in exchanges with courtroom adversaries, a tactic that was, he explained, more successful and less likely to offend permanently than straightforward insult. In any case, he used invective only in self-defense. While St. George Tucker, a practical man, advised "diligence, punctuality, and a conciliatory manner" in his son's professional demeanor, Beverley bewailed the refusal of the public to recognize young and struggling legal talent.[48] Did birth and breeding matter nothing?

VI

Frustration at Charlotte Court House heightened Tucker's romantic sensibility as it deepened his feeling of dignity. For one thing, the young lawyer endured halting success and explained money shortages by seeing his condition as one of a gentleman of "fallen fortunes," a phrase he used in describing a local physician whose ancestors "chose rather to leave him an unblemished name than a splendid fortune." In short, Tucker was a virtuous loser. Assisting in the prosecution of a certain murder case would have "stained [his] fingers," he told his father—despite a fee of two hundred dollars; the pleasure this show of gentlemanly taste gave Tucker was, he said, worth twice the money. He rejected other fees because they were so small as to seem trifling. In one letter home reporting few courtroom successes, Tucker declared a hope that he would never in his "pursuit of fortune be tempted into conduct which would make wealth worse than poverty."[49]

Discrimination was one rule, largess another. Good causes abounded, and Tucker was generous in his support of charity subscriptions, even if forced to borrow to cover his pledges. Genteel indulgence offered an alibi for embarrassment, provided some relief of mind, and sustained his polite manner in others' view. Tucker tried to conform to his father's rule of being "frugal but not *parsimonious.*" Besides, if he avoided liberality on grounds of poverty, no one, he explained, would have believed him; his "character for veracity" would have disappeared along with his "reputation for generosity."[50] True gentlemen needed both.

Tucker's outrage at democratic dilution at the bar grew into a high sense of worthiness. Scorning the people at large and disdaining to deal with them, he began to lord his "family Pride" in Bermudian origins, to speak freely of the need for rule by the select gentlemen of wealth, education, and substance, and to delight in Randolph's studied aristocracy of taste and manner. Virginia, Tucker decided, was traveling down the road to "self-abasement" in her neglect of quality. It seemed that "learning and truth and honor and everything venerable in society" was being "thrown into the mire and trodden under the hoofs of a swinish multitude."[51]

It was but a short step from virtuous loser to persecuted minority. Politics for Tucker, earlier simply a diversion, now became a morality play and a way of bolstering his self-esteem: the struggling young lawyer fancied himself one of Randolph's Quids, that "Spartan band" of "honest and independent" men whom Beverley extolled for their courage and consistency. When in 1808 Randolph faced reelection to Congress, Tucker's failures made vindicating his brother that much more important. The campaign, he believed, was a contest of "power and villany against liberty & truth," an attempt to uphold a spotless integrity that seldom survived in the public theater. Tucker did his duty for Randolph on court days. He was, he thought, a chief among the outnumbered antiadministration men in his baliwick, even as his brother led the Quids in Congress. Opening bundles of papers that Randolph sent him from Washington, Tucker was pleased that gentlemen pressed around his table; when he ventured to speak in this "great drama," he received some of the "estimation" which, he admitted, meant everything to him. "[W]ere it not for the political fever of the day, which produces an excitement not too strong to find its vent in words," Beverley wrote his father in 1808, "I do not know how I could support myself."[52]

Few beginning lawyers in Jeffersonian Virginia may have suffered quite this anguish. Tucker's antagonism toward his father, familiarity with revolutionary examples of duty fulfilled, rivalry with Bermudian servants of the public weal, and interpretation of Blackstone on the gentleman's responsibilities were all his own. Yet Beverley's troubles on entering the profession were really illustrative commonplace. Setting up law practice in these years was generally discouraging. Moreover, his responses to changes in Virginia portrayed vividly the surprise and anger so many young men of his period voiced when they believed their social route detoured in early-nineteenth-century America or clogged with newcomers to the climb. The presumption that traditional kinds of service would continue necessary, and would be demanded of the men who had provided it, was critical to the social expectations of that generation of Virginians whose fathers had exercised such authority. Prepared for service, they, like Tucker, could be keenly sensitive to any tremors that gave promise of quakes to come.[53]

In the tone and substance of Tucker's response he showed how far he had moved from the "head" of St. George Tucker's generation to the "heart" of nineteenth-century romanticism. Randolph was an immediate cause of this shift; with him Tucker associated autonomy in a form he may not have set out to achieve, but was willing to applaud. Randolph—now fully an enemy of Jefferson—was a dashing figure, who proclaimed that his ideas were "attached to no theory" and were formed "without any regard to the doctrines of any sect, or individual." Randolph—and his snub of authority had special appeal to Beverley—confided in his intuition "careless of consequences." Here was feeling that permitted distance from one's discomfort. Awareness of the simple beauty of feeling perhaps more than anything else grew out of Beverley's refused permission to marry Polly and his suspicion of fatherly neglect. Tucker spoke of a sharpened knowledge of "those feelings which were designed by nature for our greatest blessings"; he now saw the nonrational qualities of emotion and impulse as genuine, as naturally good. "Philosophers may preach up the empire of reason as they will, and deny the absurd influence of brutal instinct," wrote Tucker warmly. "I believe it impossible for the mind to be divested of it until it has first laid aside every generous and honorable principle." His older brother Henry, now a delegate to the General Assembly, worried that such warmth might bring Beverley to "acts of imprudence."[54]

Other sources of Tucker's romantic sensibility carried more general themes. Young men wary of changes would, one might expect, find little to recommend ways of thinking that were so much a part of bygone order and that settled for tentative truths. Tucker brought into relief the change in attitude these altered circumstances tended to produce. His inability to overcome his failures helped him to reject what seemed in retrospect an eighteenth-century—and fatherly—pretension to rationality, an obsession with practicality, and a mistaken confidence in the power of man to improve his condition. Too, although Beverley's early loss of mother encouraged a fascination with the edenic past, and though his peculiar isolation and anguish at failure brought special apprehensions about the future, his nostalgia only carried to extremities feelings he shared. Given the faded glory of William and Mary and of Williamsburg and the despoiled state of Virginia, many young men of his generation were not far behind him in their submission to feeling and haunting memory. "I never walk the streets without experiencing the most gloomy sensations," wrote one William and Mary student of his stay in Williamsburg; "but it is a kind of pleasing melancholy, that the mind rather courts than despises. It is a dignified pleasure that is always excited in the mind when viewing the vestiges of departed grandeur."[55]

Tucker was vaguely aware of the repudiation implicit in these quiet intellectual changes. A young man struggling to succeed and at the same time to prove himself independent of his father, he was not, he reported home, a "very faithful disciple" of all St. George Tucker's doctrines. But Tucker's renunciation of his father had its ambiguities. Whether the elder Tucker had justly or unjustly "thrown away" his affection for the unhappy young lawyer, nothing could bring Beverley to an open spurning of his father's love. Nothing was so essential to his happiness as that paternal approval. "I never think of him," Beverley insisted of St. George Tucker, "that my heart does not swell with grief and indignation at the indifference with which he sees me suffer all the wounds his neglect and adverse fortune together can inflict—but my attachment," he protested, "is not for a moment diminished by it."[56]

The uncertainty of this paternal repudiation revealed itself in Tucker's grappling with revolutionary truths as handed down to his generation. First of all he divided that legacy in his mind and convinced himself of his apostlehood. While for example Tucker damned Jefferson's embargo, and his father implicitly, the young lawyer was still able to venerate St. George Tucker as revolutionary figure—as his "rebellious" father; with Randolph and the Quids holding fast to the ideals that the government seemed to be discarding, Beverley could align with them and at once sustain his own best vision of his father while challenging paternal judgment. Second, Tucker's concern with proving himself capable of carrying on with the republican experiment was reflective of the larger anxiety members of his generation so often expressed on this score and of the suspicions such feeling could engender even after the party quarrels of the 1790s appeared settled. Tucker doubted himself and his peers—was suspicious, even contemptuous of them.

Never before as in the first decade of the nineteenth century were "men of integrity and firmness" more needed, he wrote. Nor were they more scarce, for great men were being replaced with lesser sorts. Youth, believed Tucker, had been taught to "look upon grey hairs with contempt," and he spoke apprehensive, even fearful, words when a friend's father died. "The prating youngsters," the twenty-three-year-old lawyer wrote Randolph, "who disgrace the hall of our Assembly, and sometimes that of congress, raise my gall."[57] Here perhaps was an explanation for the desuetude of earlier ideals: sires were giving way to unworthy sons.

VII

For a time marriage put Tucker more at ease. After receiving from John Randolph (against St. George Tucker's advice) a 300-acre tract of land, fifteen slaves, and animals to stock the new farm, and receiving from his father the family's 500 acres in Lunenberg County, two male slaves, and $500 in cash, Tucker finally wed his amiable Polly in February 1809. Polly adjusted quickly to the isolation of the small cottage that Tucker had built near Randolph's Roanoke estate the preceding year. She spun, sewed, and managed the simple household while Tucker, when not away at court, read law and looked to his affairs on the farm. The couple adhered to St. George Tucker's recommended regimen of rising early and keeping busy. The new husband found that directing his few slaves in the tobacco and wheat fields or going on rides to tend to legal business in the fresh reviving air of the early morning was the surest antidote to the glum feelings that had plagued him. Two years later Polly gave birth to a son, a "fine fellow" who, Tucker believed, more resembled his mother than him, and who was named after the child's uncle, "Jack" Randolph.[58]

Tucker's relationship with Randolph continued warm, and quickened during a pilgrimage they made together in the summer of 1810 to visit the old Quid, Nathaniel Macon, at his North Carolina home. About this time Randolph insisted on having a portrait of his younger brother to carry to Washington and to keep on view at the Roanoke home he now occupied. Tucker sat for the painting, a miniature on an oval piece of wood about four by five inches, in Richmond. It was a handsome bit of work, but the artist had a handsome subject. Randolph's memento captured Tucker's dark hair and well-proportioned head, his proud, straight nose, the eyes that were so much like Randolph's and apparently like the fixing, lovely eyes of their mother. The young barrister, persevering in his effort to win the recognition he deserved, offered the artist an intent gaze that he succeeded in capturing.[59]

Then suddenly, in the fall of 1810, an estrangement from Randolph caused Tucker anguish and distraction. It began with a mysterious dispute between John and Judith, and by March 1811 Tucker was deeply embroiled. First caught in the middle of the affair, then inadvertently on the side of John against his sister-in-law, Tucker soon became the object of a bitter campaign by which Judith tried to persuade Randolph that Beverley's brotherly affection was "hollow and insincere," a "design on his purse and property." Tucker was outraged. A face-saving adjustment of business assets between the two men soon turned into a sort of lovers' quarrel that defied solution. An exchange of revealing notes produced biting remarks and complaints of hurt feelings. Tucker prepared to move off his half brother's land. "Stay here," Randolph begged him, "if you have any remaining regard for me." But for the present at least, things were not the same; by October 1811, Tucker had established a new household—though only about four miles from Roanoke.[60]

He thought of going much farther. Tucker's criticisms of the Virginia bench and bar, after a moratorium following his marriage, grew severe in the year of his departure from Roanoke, continued so afterward, and spurred his talk of removing from the state altogether. He was willing, he said, to compete with "a moderate number of men of character and ability," but he had seen enough of law practice in Virginia to realize that "every disgusting circumstance" attending it when his father stood at the bar had "multiplied tenfold." Leaving Randolph's estate and dissolving in part the material obligations owed him gave release to Tucker's fancy. He tried to persuade his father that his fortune lay in South Carolina, where the Coalters had relatives. In Carolina the law was the profession of gentlemen and, in great measure, state regulations kept it free from "the intrusion of black-guards." In any case time was drawing short. John Coalter listened quietly in May 1812 to another of his brother-in-law's plans to migrate and then, he reported to St. George Tucker, advised this errant young man to *"Fix* himself, for *Life,"* establish his reputation, and get on with his career. Tucker's next move, Coalter emphasized, "must be his last."[61]

CHAPTER THREE

To Build the Ideal Society

BOTH TUCKER BROTHERS did their part in the conflict that broke out with Britain in 1812, but the war left Beverley no particular distinction. Henry St. George Tucker enrolled under him a gallant volunteer corps of cavalry, comprising the most respectable young men of Winchester, and participated colorfully in the battles for Washington in 1814. Beverley meanwhile served with an infantry company in the county militia, his single chance for excitement coming in the summer of 1813, when the governor called the Charlotte troops to Norfolk and into defenses against coastal marauders. The British disappeared. Instead of action, Tucker saw much garrison life during the war.[1]

Afterward, while Henry rode a crest of popularity to Congress, Beverley went home to continuing embarrassments. He had proudly noted in letters home that his service in the state adjutant-general's office had gained him the attention of his commander and offered an access to power; in brother officers he had experienced fine company and mutual respect, both sensations greatly pleasing Tucker. Yet his hope for a regular commission went unrealized. Beverley's law practice—which wartime militia duty had done nothing to improve—failed to lighten his pessimism, and he began once again to talk of pulling up stakes. So efficiently did multiple court sessions keep him from tidewater family and friends, he wrote early in 1815, that he and Polly might as well live in the wilds of Siberia as Charlotte County. Had his relationship with Randolph improved in the war years he might feel better about staying there, but it had not. While Tucker clung to the soil and name of Virginia, her society, he said, afforded no field for the rising generation.[2]

I

As did many other Americans in these postwar years, Tucker looked to the west. In June 1815, after placing Polly, Jack, and an infant daughter, Frances, with the Coalters in Staunton, he set off down the Ohio River for Kentucky and where else he did not know. The exploratory adventure finally carried him all the way to the Missouri Territory, and when he returned to Virginia in November, with his head "almost turned with hurry, hustle

and perplexity," he had made a tentative land purchase in the Saint Louis
area. Excitedly, he prepared his family and belongings for the trek west-
ward, hoping to be in Saint Louis on the first of January to close the trans-
action. Polly's brother John, now Judge Coalter of the supreme court of
appeals, subscribed to the Saint Louis land venture. In need of cash, Tucker
sold his interest in some Randolph land he had received through his mother.
He bought a carriage with brass fixtures and completed arrangements for
moving his few field slaves west after he was established there. He had no
time for a last visit to Williamsburg.[3]

In late November 1815 the Tucker party said its last farewells and pushed
off for the Cumberland Gap before heavy snows closed the pass to Kentucky.
Polly and the children rode in the carriage with "old granny Phillis," a black
woman who had been in the family for many years and whom Tucker described as one who had won the heart of everyone she had met. Other slaves
followed, driving the one or two wagons loaded with furniture and necessary household items. Tucker was everywhere, supervising the caravan from
horseback, knowing that any lapse in his attention could prove fatal. Such a
trip was difficult under the best winter conditions, but the company met
weather "bad enough to break the heart of any man in his own house." Of
the eleven days the Tuckers marched before reaching a real resting point at
Abingdon, Virginia, Beverley reported seeing the sun only three. The pace
was about twenty miles a day. There was snow overhead, mud underfoot,
and the clouds seemed to have piled up between the Alleghenies and the
Cumberlands. Everyone, he maintained, was cheery anyway.[4]

Having arrived safely on the Kentucky side of the mountains, Tucker
caught a fever that forced him to give up his efforts to be in Missouri by the
first of the year. Instead he spent the rest of the winter with Polly's sister
and brother-in-law, John Naylor, at their home near the Ohio River. During
the layover Tucker tried to convince Naylor of the riches beckoning at Saint
Louis. By spring, when at last the river was suitable for travel, Naylor had
agreed to join the Tuckers there and to send his pretty daughter Eliza ahead
with them. He helped Tucker lash together two flatboats for the trip down
the Ohio. Placed alongside one another, the boats formed a barge twenty-
five feet square, which Tucker and two "stout hands" hoped to control
using two oars in the bow and one in the stern of the craft.[5]

The next leg of the journey west was largely uneventful, at times even
pleasant. Unfamiliar with the Ohio and hardly an experienced boathandler,
Tucker was lucky after only a day on the river to tie up with a larger vessel
loaded with timber. He rested a bit easier. The Virginians also made good
time because they could now float on during the night, less worried about
collision with a heavier craft. Kentucky on the left bank and Ohio and
Indiana on the right slipped quickly past. Rain squalls and rapids provided
only a few anxious moments. The Tucker party covered a distance of six

hundred miles in eight days, a remarkable rate, and on June 7, 1816, debarked at Shawnee Town, Illinois Territory. "It is not possible," Beverley wrote happily, "to perform a journey of equal length in more comfort." In July, after a hot and dusty ride across the Illinois prairie, Tucker and the family installed themselves on a rented farm a few miles north of Saint Louis. Despite a dry season, he boasted a promising stand of corn and oats.[6]

Jack Tucker, by this time five years old, and his sister Fanny, about two, were of course not old enough to make their views of the new state of things very deeply felt; letters their parents wrote to Virginia usually mentioned larger business matters or simply the general state of health. Still, the children were very much a part of this affair. Riding in the carriage, unheated in the mountains and poorly ventilated during the ride through southern Illinois, must have been as miserable for the youngsters—who surely were no less impatient than children ever are—as the flatboat ride was thrilling. When the family reached the Missouri farm there were additional amusements; Jack no doubt considered Indian raids imminent and bravely prepared for them.

Frances was delightful, but Jack by 1816 had become a subject of special pride for Tucker. Randolph's namesake was, in Tucker's eyes, the luckiest imaginable cross of Bermudian and Scotch-Irish—"ballast to sail & Sail to ballast." It relieved Beverley when Jack seemed obedient enough to be above crying and beyond whipping; it made the father proud that, when his son set himself against something, it was "wonderful" what the boy would endure "sooner than yield his point—and that without being sad or sullen or resentful about it. . . ." Though "sometimes *fractious*," the lad was a constant cheer, and—in a reference that may have carried a plea as well as a description—if Jack had what his father told St. George Tucker was a "violent temper," the son was in "affection, generosity, courage, health, strength and beauty as fine a fellow as heaven could have sent me."[7]

Near the farmhouse Tucker rented outside Saint Louis was an orchard he blamed for carrying the fever that in September 1816 claimed the lives of "dear little Fan" and then Jack as well. Though Polly was not stricken with the same disease, she too was dangerously ill that sad month, and the severe shock she suffered at the children's deaths matched Beverley's own "complicated toil and affliction." They endured sorrow without the consolation of friendship. Nor did they have the comfort of shared suffering, for the blow struck at the end of a season notably free of disease and at a time when Saint Louis was universally healthy.[8]

Tucker thought he recognized in the uniqueness of the lot that befell his children the hand of an all-loving Providence: what was most noteworthy of his bereavement was the new sustenance of faith he was able to draw on. If the Almighty willed to take Jack and Fan from them, Tucker concluded in one of his earliest declarations of piety, then it was only a reflection of

CENTRAL MISSOURI DURING TUCKER'S YEARS IN THE WEST
Saint Louis and St. Charles are at the middle right. Arrow Rock, where Tucker later moved—about 150 miles west of Saint Louis—appears at middle left.

his own unworthiness as a parent. "That they are happy," he continued, "I have no doubt, and thus consoled I find it possible to bear my loss with a fortitude which twelve months ago I could not have comprehended." Polly's spiritual strength was even greater, and with the strength her faith provided, the couple decided to remain in Missouri—despite the mournful impulse to turn back to Virginia.[9]

II

The splendid abundance of Missouri provided Tucker renewed strength and vision. The depth of the soil was almost beyond comparison. Missouri farms afforded such a golden harvest, as Tucker reported them, that "it is not necessary to turn to the right or the left to put in the sickle to the best advantage." He told of an old soldier who had come to Missouri with nothing and a year later lived as well as most Virginia planters who worked three or four hands. In the spring of 1817 Polly claimed some 400 chickens under her care, enjoying for the first time in her life milk and butter in plentiful measure. The muddy Mississippi carried produce downstream; steamboats, new to the river, brought convenience and luxury from below. The soil, climate, population, and commercial prospects, said Tucker, improved in his estimate daily. He brushed aside the warnings of his father and urged John Coalter to join him in a land enterprise that he promised would certainly bring profits of from 1,000 to 10,000 percent. "Do not laugh and look wise, and say 'just like Beverley,'" he pleaded. "Do as I advise, and you can not have any reason to repent, and may have cause to rejoice."[10]

More important for Tucker than the bounties Missouri promised was the chance he had there to begin again. Missouri was a clean slate on which he could write as fresh a definition of himself as he wished. In the free air of Missouri he could almost laugh at his troubled past in Charlotte, Mecklenburg, and Halifax counties. "Halifax!!" he mused in July 1817. "That any man who has once turned his attention to this magnificent country should think of Halifax." How, he wondered, could anyone turn his eyes from the mighty Mississippi to the Staunton in Southside Virginia, marking "the windings of a scanty rill?" Not he; and the metaphor had to do with more than rivers. Tucker in Missouri escaped the confines of earlier distress. He was a new man, seeking a running lane in the race for position in this rapidly developing and socially unestablished region.[11]

Since Missouri was a frontier country, a dash of color often helped a man in this contest. Hardly anyone knew much of anyone else, so the frontier permitted, even required, a brash assertiveness, an occasional boast of hardiness, or an overstatement of trait. It helped one to stand out and be recognized. Such a swagger was the law office Tucker took for himself in the winter of 1816–17—the base of a hollow sycamore tree that he found near his home. It was no ordinary stump. Tucker's sycamore library was more than ten feet in diameter and high enough to stand in; it had a planked floor, a glass window, shingled roof, a stove and chimney. In it he placed shelves for law books and for the historical, political, and other books worth hundreds of dollars which, indulging himself in his new prosperity, he had ordered in 1816. In the spring thaw of 1817 Tucker moved his sycamore out of the timber and placed it in his house yard. He then waited for the world to learn of his eccentricity, hoping to see word of it "bruited from one end of the continent to the other." To Ritchie of the Richmond *Enquirer* he offered the sycamore story and the chance to launch the Tucker legend in Virginia.[12]

The game continued in the late months of 1817, when Tucker—admitted to the Saint Louis bar but apprehensive about his "knack of speaking"— bought a farm of his own, achieving at last the independence that had eluded him at Charlotte Court House. The ordinary structure that he built and moved into—two cabins joined with a covered walkway—might as well have been a castle, the several hundred acres he now owned, a fiefdom. In a christening service neighboring farmers must have talked about, Tucker named his home "St. George," in order, he said, "to record the lineage" of the plantation owner. Here certainly was an overture to his father, a public exclamation of filial loyalty despite "independence." But what Tucker also wanted to do was to bring Missourians to heel. Treating his land claim as if it were a tidewater principality was a way of calling attention to all the reasons why the Virginia gentleman in Missouri deserved recognition. Tucker admitted a certain self-consciousness—"I believe," he wrote his father, "you have always thought me a little inclined to be an aristocrat"— but made no apologies for speaking of "the stainless purity" of his name and race. Even if such pride were "a mere ladder of ambition," Tucker refused to kick it from underneath himself.[13] Like the sycamore study, it was a badge of distinction, a necessary and useful exaggeration.

The stratagem succeeded. While failures in September and October of 1817 made Tucker sorry that he had been drawn back to the bar, the tables had turned by mid-November. His pride in pedigree, and the attitude that impressed at least one who noticed him as belonging to a "very respectable gentleman of high political standing, from Virginia,"[14] gave leverage to Tucker's demonstrable legal knowledge and superior professional training. As the year drew to a close he was so busy that, for the first time since army days, letter writing was nearly impossible. Tucker's professional ambition was at last fulfilled. No mere country lawyer with little more status than a court clerk, Tucker established an office in Saint Louis; he was now employed in the only fashion he ever wanted to be, as a "counsellor & barrister" arguing contested cases of intellectual substance against respectable opposition. He felt redeemed, satisfied even if his payment partook "more of the nature of honor than of profit." He was one to be reckoned with and was living up to all that the title "St. George" suggested in the way of grace and prestige. To crown this new distinction, acting territorial governor Frederick Bates, a Virginia native, appointed Tucker to the Northern Circuit Court of Missouri in December 1817. Judge Tucker took care to see that John Coalter passed the news around in Virginia, so as to avoid, he said, crowding the eastbound mails.[15]

Assuming the bench in February of the next year, Tucker especially gloried in his judicial role because he was now able to shape professional character. Missouri courts, particularly those outside Saint Louis, were "new and crude," and lawyers lacked polish. Tucker believed that his own attention to professional conduct—for which he drew on the lessons and example of his father—had helped to earn him a seat on the bench. The profession, he wanted to teach his Missouri associates, was a noble fraternity, a system of brotherhood in which he, as judge, acted as the "older brother of the family." Tucker's role was to preserve courtroom harmony and good order without pomposity; where necessary, he intended to interpose judicial authority in the same temper he wished other members of the bar to cultivate themselves. If gentlemanly competition was distinctive of the legal profession and a credit to it, there was a particular need on the frontier to formalize relationships between contending attorneys and to establish gentlemanly subordination to "older brothers." Tucker strove to encourage a camaraderie that would unite and elevate the bar while, incidentally, closing it to the unfit. It weighed heavily upon Tucker that he was a leader. Plaudits he received from some bar members following his first court term gave him enough confidence that he spoke of being a kind of professional whip.[16]

In Judge Tucker's mind, professional uplift could only follow the building of a judiciary that would serve the needs and merit the confidence of the people. As matters stood, the Missouri territorial courts had notable limitations. They were, first of all, inadequate to the business at hand. For a region burgeoning in population and constantly forming new counties there were only two circuits. So oppressive was the case load at one session in the summer of 1818 that Tucker sat in court more than nine hours a day for nineteen consecutive days. Further, the court structure itself was deficient. A congressional act of 1816, authorizing the territorial assembly to create circuit court judges, led the legislature to abolish county courts and justices of the peace. The result was that, in addition to all criminal cases and civil suits of $100 or more value, Tucker also handled the tedious and routine matters of county administration. There was, moreover, a defect in the appeals system. Two of the three men on the superior court could decide cases, and of the three members two were the circuit judges themselves. The superior court, as Missourians duly noted, was "constructed on principles unheard of in any other system of jurisprudence, having primary cognizance of almost every controversy, civil and criminal, and subject to correction by no other tribunal!!!"[17]

These complaints against the territorial judiciary reflected a growing demand among Missourians for statehood. As was the case elsewhere with frontier people, Missourians were conscious of governmental arrangements and were anxious to receive the recognition of political maturity statehood conferred. Citizens observed that a federal government in which they were without voting representation had the power to tax them. They noted jealously the limits congressional authority set on their own legislative prerogative, and chafed under a territorial executive with absolute veto power. Statehood appealed to different people for different reasons, but for Tucker the prospect was most attractive because it promised constitutional and statutory reform. Judge Tucker did his part to further interest in this cause during his first year on the bench, moving about his circuit, talking to local political leaders, working silently, he said, to prepare for the change of government everyone considered imminent. Petitions to Congress had their effect. The hold of the federal government on Missouri seemed about to be loosened when in February 1819 the House of Representatives considered an enabling bill that would allow the territory to call a constitutional convention, organize itself, and apply formally for admission to the Union.[18]

III

It was quickly apparent in Washington that the Missouri bill created some difficulties. The admission of the territory, which everyone expected to adopt a constitution protecting slavery, threatened a delicate balance in the Union between free and slave states. Sectional suspicions surfaced on February 13, 1819, when Congressman John Tallmadge of New York tried to attach to the enabling bill an amendment prohibiting the further introduction of slaves in Missouri and calling for the emancipation at age twenty-five of all slaves born there after statehood. The House debated this amendment in the waning moments of the Fifteenth Congress, then again from December 1819 through March of the next year.

Probably Tucker no more than anyone else anticipated the outburst of sectional acrimony the Missouri bill caused. It centered on the question of slavery: slavery as a humanitarian problem, slavery as consistent or not with "republicanism," slavery and the natural rights ideal contained in the Declaration of Independence. Helping to raise the pitch of debate higher was the coupling of slavery with the West. Because of the immense opportunities there, the question whether the first state entirely beyond the Mississippi River was to be free or slave was an especially hard one.[19]

Immediately the Tallmadge amendment posed constitutional questions, and Judge Tucker therefore had an intellectual edge in Missouri. He opposed the Tallmadge restriction with all the energy he could discreetly display. Closest at hand were the county grand juries on his circuit. These bodies of citizens had a wide scope of investigative interest in frontier Missouri; while all forms of lawbreaking came under their purview, so did threats to the commonweal that later might be deemed more political than criminal. In the spring of 1819 the grand juries on Tucker's northern circuit were resounding in their indignation at the attempt in Congress to usurp the rights of Missouri citizens. These pronouncements, either composed by Tucker or at least made under his approving eye, often appeared in the local papers. One jury even called a rally to celebrate the anti-Tallmadge position, a gathering so successful that slavery restrictionists described it as a "mutiny." With Tucker's endorsement added, another grand jury manifesto made its way to President Monroe's desk in Washington. Even in remote Missouri, said Tucker in the introduction, men knew their rights; even frontiersmen were familiar with the Constitution, and with the "higher source" which was above all human devices.[20]

But Tucker's objection to the Tallmadge amendment revealed itself chiefly in a series of newspaper articles suggesting he did not take his fellow citizens' wisdom for granted. The five essays carried in the Saint Louis *Missouri Gazette* from April to mid-June appeared under the pseudonym "Hampden," a mask that Tucker drew from his reading in English political history. Pressed with court duties, Tucker for two of the articles relied on the help of another Virginian, a promising young Saint Louis attorney, Edward Bates, brother of the territorial secretary. With the aid of the younger Bates and the support of another friend who signed himself "Sydney," Tucker hoped to alert Missourians to their constitutional rights and to make the case conclusively enough that newspapers in Richmond and elsewhere would republish the arguments.[21]

With the Tallmadge amendment, Tucker explained in the "Hampden" article of April 21, Congress exceeded its authority. As preconditions to statehood, the federal government could require Missourians neither to emancipate their slaves, free future black progeny, nor exclude other slaves from Missouri. The formidable case he and Bates mustered in support of that position began with the states' rights theories both men knew from St. George Tucker's edition of Blackstone. The Union was a compact among sovereign states; entry to the federation therefore presupposed the sovereignty of the applicant. Any attempt on the part of the federal government to make admission to the Union conditional violated that original sovereignty. Furthermore, as Bates tried to show, the Tallmadge provisions struck at property rights, the preservation of which was the very object of society and the Constitution.[22]

Tucker himself was more specific. There was no authority in the Consti-

tution for the kind of action Tallmadge contemplated, and the Tenth
Amendment withheld from the central government undelegated powers.
While Congress was authorized in the document to make "rules and regulations respecting the territory and other property" of the United States,
Tucker maintained that the clause had only to do with the territories as
federal property. Congress, in this view, had no special power over things
local circumstances made peculiar to a given territory—the institution of
slavery in Missouri being an example; the authority Congress could exercise
rightfully over citizens of a territory and their property did not exceed
congressional powers over citizens and their properties in other parts of the
Union. Finally, Judge Tucker pointed out that forbidding the further introduction of a certain kind of property into Missouri, and disallowing future
dividends from presently held slave property, amounted to punishment for
an unprescribed crime. The Constitution forbade such bills of attainder.
Congress thus threatened the rights of all citizens, whether slaveholders or
not.[23]

To the arguments that statehood followed the pleasure of Congress and
that Congress therefore could impose any restrictions it wished on slavery
in an applying territory, Tucker answered by invoking the treaty agreement the federal government had made in 1803 when it acquired Missouri
as part of Louisiana. The Constitution made treaties with foreign powers
the law of the land, he wrote, and such agreements were on a par with the
charter itself. The Louisiana treaty was clear on several points. Congress,
first of all, was to form the territory obtained from France into states on
an equal footing with the others and, by implication, to admit them to the
Union. Citizens of what was then Louisiana Territory were to enjoy all the
rights and privileges of United States citizens. This treaty, argued "Hampden," not only obligated Congress to form states equal to any already in
the Union, but further guaranteed to Missourians the protection of all the
rights the Constitution recognized in other states of the compact.[24] Some
states were slave states; the option of slavery was therefore clearly open to
Missourians.

Antislavery advocates all the while made every effort to demonstrate the
embarrassing moral position in which enemies of the Tallmadge amendment
placed themselves. To oppose the restriction provisions, they said, not only
was to flout the beloved Jefferson and the intrepid Washington—not only
to share with Virginia an acknowledged curse and with Kentucky a proverbial
liability. No one who valued consistency, "A Farmer of St. Charles County"
declared in the *Gazette,* could talk of freedom while holding his fellow man
in slavery. No rational man could dare speak of usurpation when he himself
had usurped the liberty of other men. Pro-Tallmadge essays made sharply
sarcastic references to the crack of the slave driver's whip and the shrieks of
abused Africans as music melodious to "certain *republican* ears."[25] But

surely the most effective of all these attacks was the barb Tucker's own father provided. St. George Tucker's *Dissertation on Slavery,* as one *Gazette* contributor observed, contained a stinging indictment of those shortsighted, selfish, and morally obtuse slave owners who refused to consider gradual emancipation. So pointed were these published praises of Judge St. George Tucker, so touted his wisdom, that few readers of the *Gazette* could have doubted who the object of this lesson was.[26] Tucker's face must have reddened deeply when he saw his father's words used against him.

For certain he insisted in the "Hampden" essays that slavery itself was beside the point, and there was evidence that he did so with conscious sincerity. Of course he depended on his own slaves to do the hard work of frontier farming; intending to stay in Missouri, he had a real stake in the defeat of Tallmadge's amendment. Yet in 1819 he felt neither need nor wish to mount a defense of slavery. When he told readers of his essays that he thought it unnecessary to discuss "the propriety of slavery in general" his reasons may not have been tactical alone, for only a few years earlier he had spoken of inheriting his father's "prejudice against land and negroes," and of believing it conducive to neither his "interest [n]or comfort to possess such property." During these newspaper debates, Tucker wrote in a private letter that he cared as little about slavery as any man. He was willing to prove that he argued his constitutional case in good faith, not simply out of material concerns. If a pledge were demanded, he declared, he would emancipate all the blacks he had.[27]

Whether Missouri was to be a slave or a free state was a good question, he repeated in the final "Hampden" number; nonetheless, it was one that Congress rightfully had to leave to Missourians to decide for themselves in constitutional convention. Tucker insisted that the Tallmadge amendment represented an alarming movement toward the strengthening of central power at the expense of local authority. There were grounds for his concern. The Tallmadge question arose only a few days before the Supreme Court, in *McCulloch* v. *Maryland,* struck down state attempts to tax the federally chartered Bank of the United States and spoke firmly for the implied powers of the federal government. News of the decision had reached Missouri by the time Tucker wrote the "Hampden" articles. The scope of the federal government seemed also to be growing in the area of internal improvements, a subject of special interest to Tucker because his brother Henry chaired the House internal improvements committee in the years just before the Missouri controversy and was an able defender of federal power to undertake such projects. Too, the first protective tariff passed the Congress only three years before Tucker composed his essays, and such governmental favoritism deeply troubled him.[28]

In addition, the choice of "Hampden" and "Sydney" as by-lines suggests the meaning Tucker and the men close to him found in the Missouri struggle:

John Hampden and Algernon Sidney were seventeenth-century English Whigs whose tireless efforts to protect common liberties and the integrity of the Constitution against the power of Crown and Cabinet made them legendary republican figures. Although Tucker and Bates doubtless chose these names for their propaganda value, the larger point is that the same ideas of local discretion as opposed to outside dictation, of constitutional balance, of ingrained suspicion of government—it tended to grow and tyrannize—marked the "Hampden" of the *Missouri Gazette* as well. Tucker warned Missourians of the "increasing latitude" of Congress. He worried about the "indenture of posterity that a surrender to the lawless domination of Congress" would represent. If Congress could dictate one provision of the new Missouri constitution, it could prescribe more than one: it could dictate the whole charter. The balance of powers of the federal system could only continue and the ascendency of any "reigning faction"—whether northern or southern—could only be averted if people closely and jealously watched the government. Belonging to his father's tradition of suspicious regard for distant, central government, Tucker was a guardian of hard-won liberties, an "injured freeman" (in a phrase he used) seeking redress.[29]

Another theme in the "Hampden" series suggested the bind in which Tucker found himself during the controversy over the character of this new state. Even as he denied the relevance of slavery to the matter at hand, "slavery" crept into his writing as a metaphor for the servile condition he feared and loathed. Missourians, declared "Hampden," must resist becoming the "veriest political slaves"; "when freemen are to be made slaves in order that slaves may be freed," he wrote in a private letter, "I am ready to go all lengths."[30] The "liberty or slavery" device had appeared in earlier American rhetoric, and Tucker's use of it underscored his grounding in the republican tradition of political thought and moral watchfulness. But for Tucker and for any other Southerner who "saw" no evil in slavery, a turning point was reached. Pointing out the dichotomy between slavery and freedom only played into the hands of pro-Tallmadge essayists, who noted Tucker's reliance on it and ridiculed him for it. As the moral perception of some republicans changed, so that this either/or distinction implied a contradiction in American life and the need to rid the republic of slavery, so too did Tucker's conception either of morality or of republicanism have to change. Tucker faced the question whether republicanism and slavery could be made to fit together any longer, whether the good society could continue as he had known it, half slave and half free.

Tucker's first impulse was to seek preservative ends with radical means. When critics abused "Hampden" as a false republican, found him unsound on the Declaration of Independence, and denounced him as a shame to the example of antislavery Virginians or the revolutionary generation, Tucker seemed to strive that much harder to be like the champions of American

independence: if he could not write essays condemning slavery, he would
be patriotic and good in louder ways. Thus there was a clear revolutionary
ring in his "Hampden" essays. Missouri, he exclaimed, was simply at the
point of becoming an independent state, at the threshold of nationhood. Although as citizens of the territory Missourians had consented to rely on the
federal government, Tucker argued, they remained dependent only as long
as they wished. When Missourians withdrew that consent, elected delegates
to a constitutional convention, and solemnly formed their own charter,
they became *"lawfully* independent." Congress could hardly dictate to
such a free people the manner in which they were to form their sovereign
and independent state. Tucker invoked those fathers of the Revolution of
1776, "from whom we receive all our ideas of political rights." Doubtless
he startled some Missourians by talking freely of an uprising which, with
the aid of the Southern states, would resist with force of arms any attempt
on the rights of the new state. Just as an arrogant British duty on tea had
incited rebellion in 1773, Tucker declared, congressional meddling in the
affairs of Missouri would produce revolt in 1819.[31]

In the tempest of the Tallmadge question Tucker exchanged the posturing of the sycamore study and the homestead "St. George" for the more
serious stance of a revolutionary statesman. "We are not cast down," he
wrote President Monroe in August, when the Senate had defeated the
slavery restriction amendment and Tucker considered the matter at rest.
"We feel as if we had been appointed to a high destiny—to stand in the
breach between our native states and their assailants—and to call back our
countrymen to the forgotten principles of their forefathers."[32]

IV

There was something about Missouri, wrote Timothy Flint, the New England missionary-journalist who lived there in 1820, which cast a spell over
the settler. In the remoteness of the frontier there was a "charm of romance"
that spurred the imagination, gave rise to extravagant popular reports, and
drew even more hopeful people to what the Reverend Flint called the "hills
of the land of promise." Tucker was especially susceptible to this sorcery.
He came west with an imagination already enkindled. Neither the occasional
hard times he and Polly experienced on the frontier nor even the tragedy of
losing Jack and Fanny could dispel Tucker's enthusiasm. He was determined
that Missouri would be different. He saw there more Virginians than Yankees;
he found a "comfortable proportion" of men who did not, he told Randolph
alluringly, hold the "doctrine of presidential infallibility."[33] If few Missourians, thought Tucker, boasted superior genius, they were on the whole
men of long views and great enterprise. The climate was favorable, the
materials malleable.

Tucker's dream was to create in the uncorrupted land across the Mississippi what he called a "true Virginia settlement." From the beginning of the Missouri experience he had tried to surround himself with friends and relatives. Not long after he came to Saint Louis the families of Polly's two Kentucky sisters, the Naylors and McPheeters, joined him on small sites near St. George. But when in 1818 Polly's oldest brother David Coalter consented to come to Missouri from South Carolina, Tucker's settlement design took on new dimensions. More land was needed, and since real estate around Saint Louis had grown prohibitively high, Tucker and several of his friends took off in January 1819 to locate a more suitable site. A half-day's ride northwest of Saint Louis was Saint Charles, a trading post overlooking the Missouri and a likely prospect for the new state capital, and not far north of the town the party found a splendid 6000-acre tract of bottomland between the Dardenne and Peruque creeks. Tucker and his associates spent the year drawing final plans for the community. If the prejudiced notions of our Northern friends do not prevail, Tucker wrote home, "we shall have in this quarter a neighborhood hardly to be surpassed on the Continent."[34]

This neighborhood was to be a slaveholders' Camelot. Tucker and his friends were to live with their families and slaves on huge contiguous plots of land. The men would spend their lives there in dignified repose, reading good books, writing memorable letters, and, when their country called, drafting papers on public affairs. There would be good conversation during frequent visits to one another's estates and after services at the settlement church. They would provide a fund of intelligence fully adequate to the work of shaping Missouri. Tucker and the men he drew around him, Flint noticed—though he did not then fully understand their purposes—felt on the subject of Missouri "all the ardour and freshness of youthful poets."[35] They themselves expected to form the ideal society in this new state.

At first it seemed likely that they would realize their dream. Many of the men who joined in the Dardenne undertaking were truly notable, their families attractive, their work important to the establishment of the new state. Their vision was attuned to Tucker's. Charles S. Robinson, together with William Lacy—a wartime friend of Tucker's who had entered the ministry—served as chaplains to the clan. Most of the newcomers were South Carolinians. There were two professors of South Carolina College who planned to join the faculty of the Missouri state college; a son of the distinguished Columbia judge Abraham Nott also came to the Dardenne. Other men enlisted by marrying one of the five daughters Polly's brother David and his wife brought with them to Missouri. Two of the girls came married: Frances to Dr. David H. Means, a planter destined to become a leading champion of Southern rights; Catherine to a widely known legal prodigy, who in 1820 became chancellor of the Missouri equity courts,

William Harper. William Campbell Preston, another Carolinian of later renown as a states' rights stalwart, bought vast acreage on the Peruque Creek and in 1822 came out to the Dardenne to marry Maria Coalter. Edward Bates, Tucker's collaborator on the "Hampden" articles, established close ties with the group in 1823 when he wed Julia Coalter. The Dardenne community was as proud and as intertwined as any in Virginia or Carolina.[36]

Tucker's part in bringing together these Southerners gave him inexpressible pleasure. "I came here like the patriarch of old, leaning on my staff," he wrote his father, "& behold I am become a great nation."[37] This exclamation and others like it suggested how meaningful for Tucker the Dardenne undertaking was. It transposed to Missouri a society he had failed in, giving him another, and now better, chance to succeed in it. The Dardenne plan also reflected the nostalgic strain in his personality and served notice of the lengths to which he was willing to go to give it substance. Tucker's idea of the colony was in part based on his wistful view of Matoax and the surrounding plantations in the numbered days of his boyhood when his mother was alive and well and the family happily together. His utopia, instead of forward-looking or experimental, sought to restore that proud "Virginia" of extensive land tracts supporting gentlemen who, in his father's youth, rebelled when the Crown threatened their liberties. The hopes of fulfilling this dream, as well as his acting it out, explained the ferocity of the attack Tucker made on Northern "prejudices" during the Tallmadge controversy. In Tucker's own case the plan for the community was especially exciting because it partook of the imagination; it answered deep-seated needs.

More broadly, Tucker's Dardenne scheme was interesting because it was so out of place, standing in stark contrast to prevailing Jeffersonian ideas of what the West would become. For most Fourth of July orators in these years, the promise of the West was of the small farmers it would sustain on frontier freeholds—of the simple and virtuous "yeoman" whose homestead would bring subsistence with the prospect of commercial gain.[38] The Dardenne plan was a harbinger of contrary expectations. It illustrated in fine detail a developing Southern belief that the West could provide the setting for slave as well as free society. Tucker and his colleagues hoped to superimpose a structured social system that included slavery on a fluid situation that rewarded individual enterprise.

Why the Dardenne colonists chose this alternative to the Jeffersonian vision was in large measure a matter of simple familiarity: like any other pioneers, Tucker and his friends were inclined to duplicate in the West what they had known in the East. Yet the meaning Tucker himself attached to the community, and the appeal the plan carried for other slaveholders who were involved in it, suggest that habit did not tell the whole story and that these Southerners, rather than casting off earlier ideals, had chosen to emphasize certain themes in them. Tucker's restorative impulse highlighted the timeless quality, central to the Dardenne plan, of the society these men believed necessary to stable, free government. The Dardenne community also spoke to Tucker's accommodation with the problem of slavery and republicanism. He was, he said, establishing a "choice society" from the "finest materials" and most sincerely pious men he knew.[39] These moral men were trying to demonstrate the fitness of hierarchy.

Letters Tucker sent east, testifying to the superiority of the Dardenne society, sought to gain adherents to this cause. More South Carolinian slave-holders were reportedly on their way west to join him, and they surely were to become men of power and influence. His party was on good land and in Missouri to stay. When in 1820 the new Congress resumed debate on Missouri statehood, Tucker became impatient with the threat the government in Washington posed to his design. For the Dardenne experiment he was willing to "put everything to the hazard"; confident of final victory, he urged his Virginia friends to join the enterprise.[40]

Such notices served their function well until in early 1820 the message borne in one of these beckoning private letters appeared in the Richmond *Enquirer,* a newspaper to which, it happened, the editor of the Saint Louis *Missouri Gazette* subscribed for Virginia news.[41] The description Tucker gave of the Dardenne community and the implications of its purpose—a slaveholder's Valhalla—were dangerously frank, hardly intended for the eyes of simple Virginians and positively not for domestic Missouri consumption. Nonslaveholders, simple men of modest means, men proud of their independence, read that Tucker had successfully "spread a spirit of resistance" against the slavery restriction amendment in Missouri. Tucker seemed to believe that he was a manipulator of public opinion. It was as if commoners were blessed with his presence. He spoke bullyingly in the letter about throwing nonslaveholders who opposed him across the river into Illinois; he applauded too loudly the arrival in Missouri of large numbers of men of property and slaves, and the consequent growing "homogeneity" of the region. If ordinary Missourians had earlier known little of the ideal the Dardenne settlement represented, they now knew more than enough. Joseph Charless, the *Gazette* editor who in the preceding year had printed the "Hampden" articles, now republished the anonymous "Letter of a Missourian to Virginia" in full with sarcastic notations.[42]

The appearance of the reprinted *Enquirer* letter generated hostilities that merely emphasized already existing ill feelings toward Tucker and men like him. Pro-Tallmadge replies to the "Hampden" letters clearly had contained an undertone of resentment against privilege and status.[43] The "Hampden" articles, as detractors noted, had a certain pompous quality that Tucker may have thought befitted his station; men calling themselves "clodhoppers" had

poked fun at the "polite and dignified" members of the "lawyer junto."
Publication of the "Letter from Missouri" permitted open season on Dardenne colonists, slaveholders, lawyers, men of property, and all pretension.
Charless gave no quarter, stopping only short of naming Judge Tucker as
the author of the letter. Particularly nasty references suggested that, already in a sinecured position, the writer was especially venal for wanting
his propertied friends in similar places. A later letter to the editor proposed
caustically that a grateful people, saved from Congress, ought certainly to
name the author of the "Letter" a senator, a general, or governor. "Hampden Jun[ior]" asked *Gazette* readers to imagine him traveling through the
Dardenne in his gilded coach with a footman shouting for peasants to
clear the way.[44]

The abuse "Hampden" suffered during the 1819 debates over the Tallmadge amendment and the ridicule the Dardenne association prompted in
1820 suggested how precarious the plantation ideal was in the West. While
Tucker and his friends of proud breeding had intended the Dardenne settlement to be a model community that other Missourians might adopt, after
1820 he began to see it as a cantonment, built on high ground against a
flood of immigration that brought with it problems of crowding and quality. Irish by the thousands arrived in Saint Louis after 1818, and many of
them debarked the steamboat without means of livelihood; while Tucker
thought the Catholic bishop of Saint Louis a man of talent and urbanity,
the Virginian could scarcely conceive a "viler flock" than these listless Irish
newcomers. Tucker complained too of "straggling vagabonds" who floated
up and down the river during the summer, then wintered boisterously in
Saint Louis. Footloose land speculators undermined stability and security.
The "sounder part of the population" might have kept these unsavory elements under control, reflected Tucker, but in the years after the Panic of
1819, the flow of families from Virginia and the Carolinas subsided. Earlier
he had described the Dardenne colony jokingly as a "city of refuge." More
seriously, it became in the 1820s a place for the "sober men from *old*
States" to band together midst the whirling uncertainty of the frontier.[45]

V

Partly on the grounds of what Judge Tucker called the "indecent attack"
mounted against him in the *Gazette* in early 1820, he resigned from the territorial bench on the last day of February.[46] For most of that year he remained withdrawn from public life. Perhaps because his friends knew that
the cinders of the *Gazette* episode were still warm two months later, they
decided not to nominate him as a delegate to the constitutional convention
Missouri was at last able to call in June of that year. The *Enquirer-Gazette*
letter and its aftermath hurt Tucker, and the irony of his omission from the

convention, after he had been so feverish a constitutional theorist in the Tallmadge debate, hardly struck him as amusing.

But Tucker had known disappointment before, considered attacks from some quarters compliments, and furthermore was determined to stay in the fight. The excitement of state building was simply too much for him to resist. Believing that the good republic and a sound society could be made in Missouri, he saw himself as a teacher of the virtues necessary for self-government and of the discipline required for social stability. On the eve of the constitutional convention he knew he would not attend, he wrote a public letter warning of inferior leadership, of the abuse men of ability and integrity suffered, and of jealous factions. When the new state governor Alexander McNair later named Tucker judge of the state third circuit, it seemed to the Virginian only fitting. Tucker's message to the first Saint Louis grand jury after the adoption of the state constitution was but a variation on his usual reminders to Missourians of the responsibilities they faced as republic makers.[47]

Economic depression in Missouri following the Panic of 1819 made Tucker's talk of republican austerity timely. Just at the time the new government was forming, one Saint Louis bank folded, and the second was of no use in providing Missourians badly needed currency. Throughout 1820 immigration dropped off. Hard currency flowed east or simply stopped circulating. Credit disappeared, land values plummeted, foreclosures rose in number, and then crops failed to meet expectations. By early 1820 increasing pressure on the General Assembly brought several relief measures. One was a "stay" law that suspended for two and one-half years the payment of debts owed on land; another act established a state loan office that resembled colonial land banks in being a makeshift institution using land as capital. It had authority to print interest-bearing certificates that the legislature intended to pass as money, and to provide ready loans to needy farmers. The government declared it would pay salaries in loan-office certificates and accept them in payment of taxes. While in the fall of 1821 it appeared as if the act might prove successful, a few months later the bills depreciated greatly in value, and the state government faced bankruptcy.[48]

For Tucker this relief legislation raised serious problems, since the federal Constitution specifically forbade states from impairing the obligation of contract and prohibited them from issuing bills of credit. The Missouri loan-office act was admittedly ingenious. The legislature avoided making the loan-office certificates explicitly legal tender—an act of palpable unconstitutionality—but clearly pronounced the paper acceptable for taxes and payable for salaries in lieu of gold or silver. The question was whether such notes were bills of credit—notes issued solely on the faith of the state and redeemable at a future day. Relief legislators argued that state resources backed the loan-office certificates. Private persons, however, could not sue a state; they seemed to have no recourse but to accept the promise of the state to back the paper with something of intrinsic worth. The expected collision between legislature and judiciary came in February 1822. Sitting at the Saint Louis circuit court, Tucker struck down the loan-office law in the case of *Missouri* v. *Lane* and then in April declared the stay law unconstitutional in *Glasscock* v. *Steen*.[49]

These decisions were courageous—the first in the state against the relief plan of the legislature—and they placed Tucker in an exposed position at a time when desperate debtors were little given to patience with what appeared legal niceties. The popularity of the legal profession reached new depths. Tucker's decisions, declared outraged Missourians in newspapers and in meeting places, were an affront to the dignity of the people and their elected representatives. Judges were supposed to expound the law, not repeal it. Politicians on the stump during the summer election campaign denounced Tucker; the Saint Charles *Missourian* spoke heatedly of falling under "the crush of judicial oppression," and men talked openly of the tricks of lawyers, the relationship between the courts and creditor interests, and of the "pomp and learning" of judges.[50] Most threatening were the moves to amend the constitution so as to make judges elective at the hands of the legislature, to open a way for a reduction of judicial salaries, to abolish the chancery court system altogether, and to place chancery cases in the common-law courts.[51]

But instead of dismissing antijudiciary elements, Tucker lectured them; instead of striking down laws and leaving legislators to their own devices, he offered them alternative ideas. During the spring of 1822, he published in the Saint Louis *Missouri Republican* a series of five laborious articles on political economy over the signature "Necker," an allusion to Louis XIV's financial oracle. Relief to the insolvent, argued Missouri's "Necker," would most effectively follow upon the repeal of the stay law and the loan-office laws, and the reestablishment of the state credit. He proposed the funding of the state debt—including loan-office certificates at current market value—and the establishment of a long-term sinking fund to retire that debt. "Necker" in the *Republican* goaded lawmakers to place the state on a firm fiscal footing.[52]

On the bench Tucker prodded Missourians to prepare themselves for high responsibilities. His judicial opinions groaned under the weight of his moral and political homilies, but no matter how condescending they seem now, and may have appeared then, they were meant to be anything except self-serving cant. Loan-office money cultivated contempt for the rights of others and a disregard for what men were accustomed to hold respectable, said Tucker in *Missouri* v. *Lane*. Valueless currency led to "total depravation of the moral sense, and dissolution of moral obligation. . . ." The founders of the republic feared as much and provided accordingly in the Constitution.

But only discipline and virtue would make that republic work. Men needed to be reined in; there was no hope for a society of Tucker's design unless men developed not merely a proper opinion of their duties, but a right *"habit* of thinking."[53]

Tucker drummed into his readers the need for an independent judiciary. It was a necessary check on the misrule of other branches of government, and constitutional restraints on the power of the legislature were guarantees to the whole community that the assembly would exercise its "necessary power" only for purposes the people provided for in the charter of government. To assailants of the judiciary, Tucker patiently explained that judges could never enforce laws they saw as unconstitutional: judges swore to uphold the fundamental law according to their own lights, and this conscientious duty included preventing the rampages of an "unfettered majority." Rather than a public enemy, the judiciary was thus a benign safeguard, Tucker insisted, placing between the people and tyranny "the shield of the constitution." If judges were as older brothers to members of the legal profession, they were fathers to society at large; they were above petty interests, men on whose judgment of "great questions of common right" personal considerations weighed not "even as a feather."[54]

The more often Tucker repeated his lessons, the more fiercely he clung to them. The legal profession was a social watchdog with the teeth of the common law. The dignity and authority of the bench represented the last hope of property against the ignorance and willfulness of the legislature. The supremacy of the law was the mainstay of minority rights in the face of numbers. Experiences in Missouri during the relief controversy gave Tucker a firsthand example of the catastrophe resulting when his doctrines were forsaken. If in this crisis he did not lose his faith in republican institutions, he reported to his father, he had seen the people of a republic exposed to the cant of demagogues, a society careening out of control. He looked the "demon of misrule" in the eye. More than ever he could savor Virginia's example of old forms, her respect for the "wisdom of former days."[55] Depression-crazed, poorly led Missouri confirmed his worst fears of universal suffrage.

In 1822 fall elections brought victory to the antirelief forces and spelled the defeat of the amendments designed to bring the judiciary to heel. Tucker was delighted. He had warned of bad leadership prior to the 1820 constitutional convention; he had outlined republican duties before the Saint Louis grand jury after his appointment to the state bench later the same year. He spoke in the *Lane* and *Glasscock* decisions in early 1822 of sound leadership, stability, virtue, and discipline. Election results suggested that, with Tucker's guidance, Missourians had passed their test and had escaped the misfortune that befell Kentucky following a similar legislative-judicial clash in the spring of 1822. The opportunity he had to pass on the

loan-office and stay laws was, he admitted, "the most fortunate circumstance of my public life."[56] By the fall, Tucker believed himself a statesman
proven right.

But more than that, Tucker was battle scarred, valiant. It was given to
him to be the first judge into the breach in early 1822, and he did not
shrink from this calling. Nor was he unconscious of his courage. It was
sweet to reflect how far he had come in ten years—from a dejected veteran
without a law practice to a champion of judicial independence and the
supremacy of law in a state that he had much to do with forming. Thrilled
to throw himself into the battle to be "sacrificed," as he said after *Missouri*
v. *Lane,* he hoped to gain immortality as he was. Where, he asked, was the
Virginia newspaper coverage? Where was Ritchie in these moments of trial?
He sometimes felt, he wrote home, "like a man who has received his death
wound in the dark, in attempting to rescue innocence from the hand of a
ruffian, and is bleeding away his life in obscurity." He sent off his decisions
to his father, soliciting his support, hoping that they would appear in Virginia papers.[57] If he were to "die" gloriously, he hardly wanted it to be
anonymously, in the dark alley of the Missouri frontier.

Tucker was already longing to return to Virginia even in his moment of
triumph—but Missouri nonetheless had offered it to him, and it was the
first real triumph in his life. The debate over the Tallmadge amendment
and the debtor-relief controversy did not finish the fight, but matches were
won, and Tucker's earlier ill fortune helped him savor these successes. "I
have a pride," he had a way of saying afterwards, "in thinking that Missouri is not just like the other western States, and that the difference has
been in part produced by me."[58]

CHAPTER FOUR

The Prophet Delivered

BUT THESE SUCCESSES were not long-lasting, and as Tucker grew contemplative and restive in the late 1820s, he became more than ever a man awaiting a crisis call. Earlier, during the doleful period spent as a lawyer at Charlotte Court House, he had drawn some comfort in speaking vaguely of just such an impending storm. What sort of calamity it was to be, how it would come, and what form it would take, Tucker never made clear. But the storm may have been a metaphor his readings in aesthetics suggested to him: if order was beautiful, chaos was sublime. The beautiful, wrote Edmund Burke in 1759, was of limited dimension, unobscure, serene. Sublimity on the other hand invoked the vast, the rugged and negligent—the dark, awe-inspiring, and tempestuous. Hugh Blair, an Edinburgh scholar whose text on rhetoric William and Mary students used in the 1790s, warned that sublimity was too intense, "too violent . . . to be lasting." Tucker was nonetheless willing to risk it. He dreamed of a cataclysm that would be more than a metaphor, of a social-political cloudburst that would wash away evil as it cleansed and reinvigorated. When such a crisis occurred, Tucker believed, men "who can neither see nor hear would be made to feel."[1]

I

Following Tucker's success in the struggle for debtor relief and judicial independence was an illness, apparently the complication of several abscessed teeth, which struck him in the summer of 1825 and brought him very near death. Bedridden, his jaws nearly locked, weakened by his inability to eat solid foods, and at the mercy of physicians who applied painful scalp blisters and laid open his cheek to ease feeding, Tucker endured considerable discomfort. He suffered from loose teeth and inflamed gums, complained that his tongue was swollen and sore, and that his mouth felt continually "as if scalded with hot water." For many weeks he could communicate only with slate and chalk, and even in May of the next year he spoke with great difficulty.[2]

He tried to remain cheerful. He enjoyed the respite from court work. Wholly dependent on his wife, he and Polly became closer than they perhaps ever had been. Yet Tucker's greatest delight was the "life of literary leisure" he discovered during the compelled silence of his illness. He read as he had not for years, often for twelve hours a day, digging into the variety of books he had on hand and even forgetting his usual urge to visit Saint Louis. Frightened lest he lose his faculty of speech altogether, keenly sensitive that he had "thoughts worth uttering," he also began to write. His mind seemed to be in a state of constant fermentation, demanding release, and when he sensed the pressure mounting he took up his pen and let it lead him where it would. Besides meditative letters, he composed long, reflective essays. "[T]ho' no human eye may ever read a word that I am writing," he explained in December 1826, "I often succeed in pouring out my thoughts upon paper with as much fervor as if I were speaking, and had the world for my audience."[3]

Thus giving himself to contemplation and writing, Tucker began an autobiographical essay, a recounting of observations that "crowded on" him when he was "worn down by disease." His narrow brush with death made this introspective glance not only possible, he thought, but necessary. Hoping to give an account of what had made him what he was, Tucker's aim was to make his deliberations a way of teaching morals. He was his own best pupil; the autobiography was an "offensive . . . distressing . . . searching . . . healthful" exercise, a matter of recording testimony the memory bore against itself, of "holding up the mind" to one's eyes and sketching the image it presented.[4]

After a short while Tucker put aside these painful reminiscences in favor of a more ambitious plan. He set about writing a theological treatise, based on his explication of scriptural passages, which he hoped to publish in Virginia. Though the effort did reflect a kind of Pauline experience—struck dumb, Tucker suddenly felt helpless and afraid, spiritually kindled—the collection of twenty or more sermons was also the fruition of a spiritual concern that had been growing quietly for years. His move to Southside Virginia to open a law practice had placed him among rural people whom revivals stirred at that time, and while Tucker deprecated these frenzied and faddish displays of conversion, he nonetheless admired Polly's Scotch-Irish piety. About the time of the move to Missouri, Tucker discovered a need for Christianity himself. Throughout the 1820s he was a prominent member of the Dardenne Presbyterian Church.[5]

The touchstone of Tucker's theology, as he expressed it in his draft sermons, was the postulate that God was neither an impersonal Watchmaker nor an Angry Punisher of Sinners. Tucker's Deity was a warmly personal God who ached with the wish that men love Him, a being who as Christ on the cross stretched out His arms "in the attitude of imploring Love." God wanted to make men happy. If they were weak, imperfect, incomplete in God's image, prone to sin by setting their wills against His, God wished His creatures to control that propensity for sin. To such an end He established through the Scriptures a "means of our government in this life." Ensuring obedience to this moral discipline by fear alone could only have brought men misery and torment and would have defeated God's purpose of benevolent supervision. Tucker believed that the Almighty preferred to engage obedience by means of a "principle of Love." If men obeyed God's plan for their happiness, obeisance would infuse "pleasure into the performance of every duty discharged under its influence."[6] Tucker thought he saw a movement in Protestantism, which in his isolation he believed himself leading, away from groundings in fear, toward the feeling and loving honesty of a child. He advised his clerical friends to return to simple, touching exhortations.

Tucker's message inescapably reflected his own deepest concerns. Like his autobiographical sketch, containing an indictment of a household in which boys were brought up to "hate kings, despise priests, and deride religion," his religious essays were in part a commentary on his father and an attack on the "perverse ingenuity styling itself Reason" that had marked St. George Tucker's generation. Enough, said Tucker, with preaching about the punishment of God; enough of the "cold, hard, severe, technical pulpit disquisitions" he had so often heard when a boy. Tucker's evangelical God was not to be God the Father—the godly father—of that earlier day. God was not a hard and cruel authority figure; there was nothing in the figure of Power to excite love. Nothing, moreover, could "so point the sting of Conscience to an infidel father's heart," claimed Tucker, in a remark aimed to sting one man at least, "as to see his own child bowing to the cross that he had spurned thro' life." Yet nothing could so satisfy a son's heart, it seemed, as to win his father to that same conviction of the cross. St. George Tucker in Williamsburg heard beseeching requests from his son to forsake sin, to join the fold of Christ, to heed Beverley's message. "I would rather," he wrote his aging father, that the religious essays made "the desired impression on your mind than on all the other minds of the world."[7]

Interesting as was Tucker's newfound faith for what it said about his own emotional needs, it also placed him in the mainstream of moderate evangelism. His religious reflections, he learned after probing talks with friends among the Presbyterian clergy, greatly resembled theological doctrines prevailing at eastern seminaries like Andover and the recently established Yale Divinity School. Part of the movement within American Calvinism that had begun with Jonathan Edwards in the early eighteenth century and had then continued with Samuel Hopkins, liberal Congregationalism and New-School Presbyterianism voiced confidence in common sense and the dictates of the heart. Like Tucker's homespun theology, this evangelical impulse led to the position—far from the innate depravity and the inert helplessness of sinners—that God wanted men to be saved and that men, instead of passively waiting for the gift of the Holy Spirit, could by act of moral will play a part in bringing themselves this infusion of grace. Tucker found Hiram Chamberlin, an Andover graduate and missionary who met the judge soon after arriving in Missouri, one link with this evolving liberal theology; probably it was Chamberlin who introduced Tucker to the *Quarterly Christian Spectator,* a magazine that Chauncy Allen Goodrich published at Yale and that contained the essays of the foremost "New Haven" evangelical, Nathaniel William Taylor. Taylor's views on common sense in theology and on heart in the process of conversion codified Tucker's own. So excited was Tucker about the *Spectator* that he wrote Goodrich warmly of it, agreed to become local agent for its distribution, and had it sent to his friends and family in Virginia.[8]

The evangelism that became so important to Tucker in the late 1820s was especially noteworthy because it merged with his republican belief in civic responsibility and heightened his moral sensitivity. According to Hopkins and later evangelicals like Goodrich and Taylor, one telling effect of regeneration in the Holy Spirit was the capacity for truly selfless love. Such "disinterested benevolence" encouraged one to believe that the good he was doing was absolutely so and gave spur to that moral activity because of the sharp contrast between the regenerate and the unregenerate condition. Since man could play an active part in saving himself, much good could, in fact, be done.

This urge to do good before it was too late brought evangelicals like Tucker to speculate on the consequences of national evils and missed moral opportunities. A Richmond evangelical magazine edited by the Reverend John Holt Rice, whom Tucker had met before leaving Virginia and whose work he immensely respected, declared in 1826 that time was short for God's work; the "predominating influence in the country" was one, as to feeling, of "pain and sorrow which language cannot express; as to *conviction,* that SOMETHING MUST BE DONE, *and that quickly.*" Tucker sounded the same theme when he heard that former-presidents Adams and Jefferson had died on the Fourth of July of that year. He interpreted their nearly simultaneous deaths as a sign of God's displeasure with His people. Though Americans enjoyed numberless blessings, here was cause for more vigilance than self-congratulation. Hearken to the word of the Lord, Tucker pleaded with listeners to this sermon on the moral state of the Union. He reminded them that God had given fair warning. "'If ye will not hear, and if ye will not lay it to heart to give glory unto my name,' saith the Lord of Hosts, 'I will send a curse upon you, *and I will curse your blessings*: Yea I have cursed them already because ye do not lay it to heart.'"[9]

Instead of worrying about the attacks Chamberlin and others told him his book of essays might draw from Old-School Presbyterians, Tucker took delight in the prominent place where his feeling had led him. Finding it comfortable to believe that God took an active part in men's affairs, he occasionally even betrayed his impatience with the work of regeneration. In one of his manuscript sermons he tried to explain why a benevolent deity permitted evil in the world. Pain and deprivation, Tucker argued, made for savory moments of pleasure; if the world was not a "place of unmitigated bliss," he wrote, better that it was not. The "acid of pain and sorrow" made the cup of life—rather than a "cloying sweet"— a "racy and refreshing draught." Here Tucker's view of pain as the necessary instrument of God's benevolence and his romantic view of crisis neatly merged; suffering made for strength and resolve in the individual just as crisis did for society. "A little taste of danger," said Tucker in May 1826, "is necessary to make security valuable."[10]

II

An intellectual release during Tucker's confinement and compelled silence, writing was also an emotional escape that betrayed a longing for home. Though he made brief visits east several times in the mid and late 1820s, Tucker wanted to return to Virginia for good. Working alone in his study late at night he fancied that there were at that hour spirits abroad on the earth—witches and warlocks astride their broomsticks—whom he could join in freedom, spreading his wings to "stretch away over hill and plain" toward "scenes of former joys and friends of other days." Writing allowed him to forget the "what is here," he told Bet Coalter, his twenty-year-old niece in Virginia, with whom he now developed an intimate correspondence. His feelings were "entirely Virginian."[11]

The inability of westerners to understand this affection for a spot of earth convinced Tucker how out of place he was in Missouri. When John Coalter, Bet's father, decided to sell the family estate near Fredericksburg in January 1826, Tucker told Bet he lamented its loss "more than I can well explain to myself," and he advised her to welcome the phantoms of the past that old places conjured. His sorrow at the Coalter sale probably led him to begin thinking of a romance he wanted to write. He would tell of a Virginia native on the Missouri frontier, heir to the family's tidewater Virginia plantation that conspirators try to deny him. With the help of the hero of the tale—another Virginian—the young man in Tucker's imagination would return home to Virginia, defeat his adversaries, and take his rightful seat. Certainly the Coalter sale reawakened memories of leaving Matoax estate and then losing it to foreign creditors, but in Tucker's mind there was also a connection between the sentimental and the political. Without roots in the soil, he asked, how could frontiersmen appreciate state sovereignty? Tucker was, he admitted, "emphatically and truly an exile."[12]

Contributing to his disaffection was the failure of the Dardenne community. While reasons for the breakup were mixed, Tucker attached considerable blame to the state legislature. In 1823 the general assembly abolished the office of chancellor in an economy move that had anti-aristocratic overtones; his close friend William Harper thus lost his position and shortly thereafter returned to South Carolina. To Harper's departure Tucker attributed great changes in the character of the Dardenne neighborhood. There were other losses as well. William Campbell Preston and his wife left Missouri not long after their marriage in 1822. David Harper Means and family left in the spring of 1826, just as Tucker struggled to recover from his illness. With Means gone, Tucker was left downcast. In five years, he wrote sadly, the community had lost enough "talent and public virtue" to furnish a whole state.[13]

As the Dardenne community dwindled, Tucker's sense of isolation increased. Distant from Virginia—where there was pressure for a constitutional convention to reform legislative apportionment and redistribute the tax burden between east and west—Tucker was also removed from Washington, where Randolph, named a senator in 1825 to fill an unexpired term, was embellishing his reputation as a political maverick. First, Randolph made it a point to embarrass his old political enemies John Quincy Adams and Henry Clay by dwelling on the "corrupt" arrangement that had sealed Adams's election in the House. Then in 1826 Clay and Randolph put together a comic opera in which a secretary of state and a senator fought a duel over these charges. Out in Missouri Tucker watched nervously, surveying newspapers for Randolph's speeches and writing him encouraging letters. Old differences were forgotten as the two men blasted Adams's proposals for an active, powerful central government. "The aspect of political affairs . . . makes it not impossible," Tucker reported east, "that every Son of Virginia may ere long find himself called home by a sense of duty to her."[14]

By late 1826 Tucker was alone in a way that left him free to meet any such duty as he wished. Word reached him in November of his father's death in Staunton, the Shenandoah Valley town where for many years St. George Tucker had vacationed during the late summer and early fall. Occurring only a few months after the deaths of Adams and Jefferson, the passing of the elder Tucker—the family's own revolutionary—could have given this restive son cause for reflections; he might have expressed remorse at the loss of a father with whom he had quarreled so bitterly and whose spiritual life had been the object of so much filial concern. But Tucker's letters contained scant mention of the event.[15]

The following year, personal tragedy on tragedy provided him evidence that God did indeed take part in men's lives. In the fall of 1827 Polly died suddenly in the course of a pregnancy that Tucker had hoped would bring them renewed joy. Grief-stricken, he made a trip to Virginia between the fall and spring circuit courts. Returning reluctantly west, he tried unsuccessfully to lose himself in his work. Still shaken by Polly's loss, cherishing the "careless chat of old friends," Tucker in October 1828 married Polly's niece Eliza Naylor, who had come with the Tuckers from Kentucky in 1816. He wed her despite the objections of the Naylor family, who distrusted doctors' advice that marriage might miraculously cure her consumption. Optimists were proven wrong. Tucker sat by Eliza's bedside the following March and helplessly watched her die.[16]

"I can add no more," Tucker wrote Randolph in the black despondency that followed Eliza's burial, "I am alone, without plan or purpose." His gloom in the next year reached depths he had never before plumbed, even as a failure in Charlotte County twenty years earlier. He relied the more heavily on Bet Coalter for understanding and solace; "few in this world," she heard, were "qualified to minister to the distempers of a mind like mine." Aware of the "destructive ravages" of melancholy, and on guard for his sanity, he walked, read, rode until he could no longer stand, and composed verses he hoped would purge him of his sorrow.[17] Nothing, it seemed, could dispel his morbid daydreams.

Tucker's only recourse was to place his trust in God. Perhaps he had been punished; perhaps further suffering would be necessary to prepare him for the world to come. Tucker grew closer to the Reverend Chamberlin, confessed his sins, thanked the Divine Master for the strength to bear the burden laid upon him. Since Tucker wanted to believe that God was loving, he sought to assure himself that his misery belonged to a Providential plan. God, he had written in 1826, used evil as an instrument for good; "all [H]e does, however inscrutable to us, is for the good of [H]is creatures. . . . Surely," Tucker had then decided, "we cannot believe that it is for the sake of any trifling or fleeting benefit that he afflicts us. . . ." Now it was Tucker's part to discover what God would have him to next. "My task of life is done," Bet's uncle wrote in his bereavement. "No doubt if [God] chooses to keep me here, he will appoint me other duties." If Tucker had a wish, he said, it would be that the scene of those earthly duties be laid elsewhere than in Missouri. He swore he would return to Virginia.[18]

III

Retired army general Thomas Smith, a Virginia native who was now a farmer and government official in west-central Missouri, had known Beverley Tucker from the days when the judge toured the Boone's Lick country on the territorial circuit. In early 1830 they became better friends. In February of that year Tucker sold his land near Saint Charles and moved west to join Smith in Saline County, a region of great promise about a hundred miles distant from the scenes of Tucker's sad memories. There he hoped the evening of his life "would be as bright as the morning and noon have been dark and tempestuous."[19]

ELIZABETH TUCKER COALTER BRYAN

LUCY SMITH TUCKER

Part of the attraction Saline County offered Tucker was General Smith's daughter Lucy Ann. Intelligent, exceptionally beautiful, Lucy was the delight of many suitors. Once in the neighborhood, Tucker quickly joined their ranks, and it may have surprised him that the young woman gradually directed her attentions his way. His face was more than a little worn; his illness of 1825–26 had left his lower jaw slightly deformed. He no longer was quite the slim and straight figure an old War of 1812 veteran remembered seeing on one of Tucker's visits to Virginia. Yet Lucy's favorite was a man of still-handsome features whose eyes remained "keen as a nighthawk's." He was, moreover, a mature man, considerate, imaginative, gallant to a fault, and God-fearing; he could write flattering poetry and tell wonderful stories about people and places in the east. Tucker and Lucy were married on April 13, 1830 at the Smith house near Jonesborough in a private ceremony attended by a few friends of the couple and the Smith family. Always a lover of old-fashioned fun, and able to enjoy himself for the first time in years, Tucker—to the dismay of his Presbyterian brethren—was soon seen at social gatherings dancing and frolicking with Lucy.[20]

Surely it was a sign of Tucker's change in fortune that he found for the site of his new home a lovely expanse of land that became available just when he needed it. It was not far from the Smith estate, between the Salt Fork and Arrow Rock, in rolling country among "beautiful and romantic" hills covered with prairie grass and dotted with clusters of trees and brush. "Ardmore" the place had been called, and Tucker took it up as "the family seat" of a "powerful and noble family" along Scottish lines. He looked for an artist who might do justice to the view from the dominating hill on which he planned to build a brick house with a wide veranda. Were Ardmore in Virginia, he said, he could have called the spot the "sweetest on earth."[21]

Though Tucker's marriage to Lucy seemed to restore and ensure happiness, it also required of him new demonstrations of energy. Lucy was a vibrant seventeen, he a twice-married forty-six. Understandably Lucy's parents had seen her younger male callers as more likely marriage partners, and they seem to have assented to the Tucker proposal with some reluctance. Just as understandably, Tucker felt an unstated obligation to warrant Lucy's love, to be as young and active as he could be to belittle their age difference. Lucy's pregnancy the summer of 1831, rather than proving Tucker's vigor, further taxed his strength. Aware that he was older than the fathers of most infants, and certainly acquainted with the ravages of death, Tucker's impulse was to establish himself, to capture a reputation that would stand firm even if he were taken away. Tucker could now speak heartily of his bloodline continuing, with God's blessing, to the millennium,[22] but "Tucker of Ardmore" had to give his heraldry substance.

Tucker took a hard glance at his life's work. He had struggled with only mixed success as a lawyer in Virginia, had done better practicing in Missouri, had even risen to the territorial and state circuit court bench. But his judicial career had never flowered. He might have sought his father's vacated United States district court position in 1825, when St. George Tucker retired, but the son was unsure of his competence in federal, international, and admiralty law and worried about the opposition to "hereditary succession" that might have formed at the Virginia bar. Tucker missed possible elevation to the Missouri supreme bench when a vacancy occurred while he was incapacitated in 1825–26. Although he continually denied any desire for the plaudits of society, it bothered him that "faction and accident" had prevented his rising to a "proper station" in the Missouri courts. In the autobiographical sketch he began when ill and voiceless, Tucker approached this matter of ambition with noteworthy frankness. As a lad in Williamsburg, he had had, in this retrospective view, an "instinct for genius" that turned his eyes to the "highest pinnacles of fame and excellence," but, too impatient to trudge the usual winding path to those summits, the boy was— in Tucker's portrayal—like a young eagle fallen out of its nest. Awkward, ignored for the time being, the eagle would grow strong wings, develop fully, and then mount the heights of acknowledged genius, where eagles belonged.[23]

The author of this self-examination was that young eagle grown mature, still fluttering about ignobly. What had Tucker done that would endure after his death, he asked himself; how would his young wife and yet unborn child remember him? What was the duty God had preserved him to perform?

IV

For a time it looked as if the wings that were to carry the eagle aloft were political, that Tucker's duty was to play as a representative from Missouri the part Randolph had on the crag of Washington. No longer a judge bound to the ideal of nonpartisanship, Tucker entered the fray of Missouri politics, which, in its exuberance, offered much opportunity. During the campaign for legislative seats in the summer of 1830, lines in Missouri were drawn roughly between friends of Thomas Hart Benton, senator and supporter of President Jackson, and those of Henry Clay, the Kentucky senator who favored federal measures to encourage economic growth. Standing for reelection in the new legislature, and often voting with Clay, was the other Missourian in the upper chamber, David Barton. Though candidates for the assembly exchanged views on the tariff and on Jackson's May 27 veto of the Maysville Road bill, a project the President said would unconstitutionally allocate federal money for a local improvement, it was not always easy to tell who stood where in the campaign. Candidates of unknown pedigree called themselves Jacksonians; Jackson men, together in their affection for the President, included squatters and rising businessmen, Virginia nabobs and plain men no less proud of their plainness.[24]

Because Tucker was willing to count himself in the Jackson camp—betting that the President's Southern background would keep him to a states' rights course—the instability of that coalition greatly concerned him. Factions rallied behind local leaders like his friend and collaborator in the states' rights cause, John Miller, now governor, and Spencer Pettis, a friend of Benton's and a hellion who since 1828 had been the Missouri representative in Congress. And there was Benton himself, a man Tucker knew and liked, who had studied law under his father and who in Washington had developed a fond appreciation for John Randolph. Leaders aside, issues like a proposed constitutional amendment limiting state judges to four years on the bench divided the Democrats in the summer of 1830; Jacksonian enemies of pretension pilloried Jacksonian defenders of judicial independence, Tucker among them, for siding with entrenched privilege and with those Clay newspapers supporting lifetime tenure. Winning the August election, the Democracy next disagreed over a successor to Barton: while the choice of Benton and his friends was John Miller, the governor's patronage decisions had displeased other Jackson men. Besides, Miller's states' rights position raised doubts among many legislators. Less than two years earlier, South Carolina, denouncing the 1828 tariff act, had invoked states' rights while threatening the Union. For many Missourians, to speak of that theory was to endorse what the *Missouri Intelligencer* obliquely referred to as the "wonderful blustering in South Carolina."[25]

In response to this party confusion, Tucker published a series of newspaper essays that he hoped would promote the election of a states' rights senator, like Miller, and secure support for South Carolina. Writing between the August election and the December convening of the legislature, Tucker as "A Friend of State Rights" began with the premise that states' rights was sound doctrine because the states were sound. With no need for a large revenue, armies or navies, foreign ambassadors, or any of the "pompous and costly machinery" that plundered and oppressed citizens as it distracted them, state governments were simple, responsive, and benign. The establishment of the federal government in no way altered the integrity of these institutions. On the contrary, since the central authority was subject to all the temptations Tucker cited, the system required the balance strong states provided. States' rights men need not, therefore, apologize for their errors, as Daniel Webster demanded in the Senate; the guardian of states' rights was a true friend of the Union, and furthermore a wise observer of the operations of government.[26]

Readers of the *Western Monitor* in and around Fayette learned that Americans were forgetting old ideas of community rule. In the separate states, wrote Tucker, homogeneity, ties of blood and marriage—a familylike regard of men for one another—worked as a moral brake on the wheels of authority. At the federal capital, on the other hand, men had now acquired power to legislate over the interests of people whom they did not "care for," and the result was injustice and oppression. If, as intended in 1787, communities were to rule themselves, men had to look to their states to do most of the work of government. In order to revive the vitality of those state governments, Tucker suggested that the federal public lands be returned to them. Though this scheme would have an unequal effect, and though it depended on the willingness of the federal government to give up this rich source of revenue, Tucker stood by his belief that once the states secured control of their own soil, Americans could again appreciate the meaning of state sovereignty. Indeed he defended the pluck of South Carolina in these same terms of community self-rule. Men cared more naturally for their neighbors than for distant peoples and, in office, governed them more justly; preserving that rule justified defiance.[27]

Such ideas had much to commend them. Yet on balance, Tucker's mood was quarrelsome, his rhetoric inflated. Later that year a fight with Presbyterian elders over his active social life cast this testiness into bold relief, and as the messy, drawn-out affair grew worse, Tucker's friends tried in vain to edge him toward humility, reconciliation, penitence. The *Western Monitor* articles, too, contained more than his usual truculence. Disappearing from his admonitions to Missourians was the pedagogic, patient tone of his open letters during the debtor-relief controversy. He wrote in 1830 as a republican moralist independent of elders, occasionally resorting to the bombast he criticized revivalist preachers for using when trying to shock sinners. The "Northern grandees" who insisted on making the federal government "complicated[,] splendid & expensive" were "bloated vampyres sucking at the heart's blood" of the country while lulling its people to sleep and, "by a sort of accursed magic," inspiring them with bright visions of national glory. "Awake!" Tucker shouted at his Missouri readership. "Awake! or that sleep is your last."[28]

In particular, Tucker's references to self-seeking Northerners in these newspaper essays suggested that his thought, unconscious needs, and circumstances surrounding him were forming a volatile emotional substance. Sharpening his republican vigilance was an evangelical urge to spiritual will, to saving activism. The absence of his father, the sense of having been chosen for God's work, and the wish to stake himself in the new game he played for Lucy's benefit freed him at the same time that these changes placed him under new pressures. Having gone west to make his fortune, Tucker—though he was by no means a poor man—had to admit that his search for wealth and substance was a continuing one. I live in the hope, Polly had written only a few years before, "of one day seeing my Husband free from embarrassment & able to wear a good coat & even boots if [he] should fancy them."[29]

"Yankeys" served a symbolic purpose in Tucker's mind. As members of a "universal race," they lacked ties to soil and tradition that made them "belong" and that made for community in the way Tucker defined it. Tucker, though no longer literally speechless, was in Missouri effectively silenced—at least unable to be heard where he thought it counted—and he resented Northerners for their figurative power of speech, for what he said was their "intellectual arrogance," their numbers of publishing houses compared to the South; Yankees "wrote all the books." Tucker's Christian benevolence might have restrained him in these attacks on his brethren, but he denounced Yankees as "like the Pharisees of old" and therefore as spurious Christians, puritanical but hypocritical, laughing superciliously at the poverty of the South while they milked its wealth, blaming the misfortunes of the section on its inferior habits, on laziness and slavery. Finally, Yankees, according to Tucker, were a "huckstering, chaffering," people, coldly cynical in their dealings with other people. They were outsiders who were ruthless and therefore vulnerably "successful." Tucker's hatred of "yankeys" was a kind of antisemitism without Jewry, a hobbyhorse that observers noted he was riding, and a response to perceived wrongs and "foreign" values growing uglier.[30]

Tucker's essays failed of their immediate purpose: in December the assembly passed no resolutions supporting South Carolina, and his friend John Miller lost his bid for the Senate. The former judge nonetheless succeeded in a larger way. As his identity as the author of the *Western Monitor* articles became known, Tucker was established as a states' rights champion in Democratic circles. Further, his attempt to provide a focal point for the party appeared the more in order as it failed. Missouri legislators sent to the Senate Alexander Buckner, a state senator who had encouraged men to think of him as a Jacksonian and who, once elected, favored a protective tariff and extensive internal improvements at federal expense. Clay forces in Missouri and Washington laughed, and their talk of "Bucknerizing" the Jackson party again highlighted the organizational and ideological weakness of the Missouri Democrats, while giving Tucker some claim to leadership among them.[31]

In 1831 the open break between Jackson and Calhoun also made Tucker conspicuous in Missouri. Earlier he had applauded the challenge South Carolina offered central authority. With the ante now raised, with the vice-president's July letter publicly acknowledging his leadership of rebellious Carolinians and elaborating the state-veto theory he had posed anonymously in 1828, the Missouri states' rights leader wrote South Carolina governor James Hamilton, Jr. Tucker expressed sympathy for the suffering state and warned of the measures an aroused Jackson might take against her; he spoke darkly of a decay in the republic, which he hoped Hamilton and his cohorts would help halt.[32]

At a convention of Democrats in October 1831 Tucker acted on his belief that "the politics of the day turn on State Rights and their defense." It was a special session—called to nominate a successor to congressman Pettis, whose duel with his challenger in the race just ended had eliminated them both—and Tucker himself aimed to fill that vacancy. Democrats were in a quandry.[33] On one hand the organizational flabbiness of the party pointed to the nomination of a man of ideological ambiguity, whose personality could unite the uneasy coalition; on the other hand, recent developments in Washington, South Carolina, and at home divided and befuddled Missouri Jacksonians and seemed to call for a clarification of party doctrine, a healthful purge.

Tucker chose the second alternative without hesitation, and the principles he wanted to guide every "Constitutional Democrat" were the resolutions the Virginia legislature had passed during the controversy over the Alien and Sedition Acts in 1798. Defining the powers of the central government, clarifying the terms of the federal compact, the Virginia resolves condemned all "latitudinarian constructions" of that charter. And since the Virginia resolutions, for all their talk of strictly defined powers and undiminished state sovereignty, said nothing about state veto over federal laws, Tucker sidestepped for the moment charges of extremism. When he obtained the floor at the Columbia gathering he berated assembled party leaders for the disregard of principle that had led to indirection and deception. With the guide of the Virginia resolves in hand, Democrats would have little trouble forming uniform opinions on issues of Bank, tariff, internal improvements. Principle, he said, would provide a real bond of unity and allow concert of action; it would cull out spies, inspire the weak, and detect heretics. Here he took his stand. Tucker could hold to no other principles himself and challenged other party members to put themselves to the same test. Having thrown down this gauntlet, he was understandably disappointed when, instead of taking it up, the convention called for unity and fashioned an equivocating platform. On the fifth ballot the Democrats nominated Robert William Wells, whose strongest recommendation seemed to be his availability.[34]

Yet the blessings of the October convention would evaporate by the time the regular congressional canvass got underway the following spring. Galled at the "spellbound lethargy" of the party, Tucker decided to take his case to the people. His stand on principle in the convention address received immediate notice. Governor Miller praised it. Tucker heard encouraging estimates of the number of transplanted Virginians who were prepared to rally around him as the disciple of the "true faith once delivered us, by our political Saints." Alphonso Wetmore, a publicist and active Democrat, believed that the party would unite on Tucker in the 1832 election. "Keep to the same independent, dignified, consistent course," another of his backers promised, "and you will not labour in vain, nor spend your strength for nought."[35]

The campaign Tucker mounted was informal, solitary, and sometimes intoxicating. He took the field in March 1832, traveling first to the southern counties where he was less known—the single Missouri representative was to be elected from the state at large—and where Miller advised him to spend most of his time. Supporters printed and distributed copies of his address to the Columbia convention while Tucker made his way alone from courthouse to courthouse in his search for true Democratic votes. The Columbia *Missouri Intelligencer,* never sympathetic to Jacksonians of any stripe, reported April 7 that the candidate's recent remarks there were "more exceptionable, if possible, than those contained in his handbill," but when he arrived in the area of his old Dardenne home, Tucker found such "a perfect jubilee" that he remained there for several unplanned days. "Men of all parties forget differences of opinion in my favor," he wrote Lucy joyfully, "and men of my own party renounce old grudges against me with perfect frankness, and join heart and hand in my support." Tucker's reception in Saint Louis, a stronghold of Clay sentiment, was less affectionate. Still, when he arrived there in late April he launched a bold attack on the "Protean" Federalists who had so conveniently and completely forgotten the "true character" of the Constitution. He wrote the speech for publication, and after he left Saint Louis a supporter there told him confidently that the harsh treatment the Clay papers gave it was solid assurance of his growing popularity.[36]

Though Tucker's protracted absence from Lucy and Ardmore while campaigning made him sick with loneliness, there were compensations. His sacrifices gave Lucy the nobility of a Shakespearean heroine, he thought, waiting for him at Ardmore as "the wife of an honorable and brave man." If, to his regret, Tucker's public stance did not help endear him to General Smith, he nonetheless wrote Lucy that it was as "the husband of *your father's daughter*" that he waged his war. He could be defeated but not disgraced in the congressional race. "No dearest," he declared after a weary day; "*Your* husband shall never give you cause to blush except with pride & pleasure." A belief in duty alone could thus take him away from home; his heart was not made for "the bustle of this sort of life." When he was dead and gone he only wanted his newly born daughter to remember him as meeting that duty.[37]

As it turned out, Tucker was neither defeated nor disgraced; he was sidestepped. By late May, with other self-appointed candidates besides Tucker entered in the race, party leaders began to worry that division of the Democratic vote would give the pro-Bank, protariff "Jacksonian" William H. Ashley the election. For reasons of party discipline, Senator Benton overlooked the need for "principle" for the time being and lent his support to the Wells campaign; local party committees tried as best they could to mobilize support behind the convention nominee. Tucker made an attempt to see Wells about who should withdraw, even hoped that Governor Miller might set up an impartial panel to make the decision, but Wells refused and the governor deferred to regular party machinery. There were weeks of indecision. In Saint Louis someone started the canard that Tucker had dropped out of the contest, suggesting to a Tucker man that the Clay party thought Wells an easier Democrat to defeat. Most of the summer Tucker spent weighing his chances and listening to the advice of supporters. Then in late July the state central committee of the Democrats decreed in favor of Wells. Disgruntled, the states' rights candidate withdrew from the race.[38]

It was oddly fitting that Tucker's disappointment proceeded from the development of party. He had learned from his father to mistrust parties, those engines of interest and instruments of faction that could only work against the loftier good of the republic. Neglecting this lesson, Tucker had tried for two years to organize the Democratic party in Missouri around principles that would serve what he saw as that higher end. But in Jacksonian politics, structure more than principle was shaping the character of political parties. Organization was an end in itself, not a result of fusion on principle. With sound enough organization, principle might be inessential or secondary to the acquisition and exercise of power. Further, the personality that inspired this organization itself undermined principle: Jackson's "spirit of command" had an alluring quality about it, Tucker observed, a promise of security and purpose seducing even the "purest and most devoted Lovers of Liberty." The nature of Jacksonian organization seemed to reduce the function of principle in politics; presidential popularity could dangerously distract attention from it. If God was helpless to redeem a man unwilling to be saved, Tucker asked Lucy during the last days of his campaign, "what can *man* do for a people bent on self-destruction—bent on sacrificing all permanent and general good, for occasional individual advantage?"[39]

The movement to rally the Jackson party in Missouri around the cardinal doctrines of '98 thus whimpered to a conclusion. Tucker's partisans consoled him with talk of foul play, with words of campaigns to come, and tried to buoy him with uncomplimentary asides on the sagacity of Missouri voters. "You could not represent them," one of Tucker's campaigners told him after Ashley's election in August; "*no* man of good taste could possibly do it."[40]

Comforting though these words may have been, Tucker by the fall of 1832 had reached a dead end, and it was more than political. Forced after his debilitating illness in 1825–26 to hold communion with himself, to turn to theological speculation, Tucker saw in his personal tragedies of the years following a sentence of divine punishment, and in his bereavement believed that God would endow the remainder of his life with special meaning. Removed from Randolph and from what seemed more than ever the scene of action, Tucker pined for Virginia while refusing to leave the West abject and defeated. His public appeal in the spring of 1832 produced neither the congressman who could return east to awaken sleepy republicans nor quite the man of distinction Tucker wanted to be for the sake of his young bride and child. Tucker's life had reached an impasse.

Then it seemed as if events came to his rescue. In November 1832 South Carolina antitariff men succeeded in calling a state convention to condemn the most recent tariff and the 1828 law it was supposed to reform. Moderates were unable to cool tempers. On November 19, South Carolina pronounced both tariff laws null and void, declared them unenforceable in the state by federal officers, and dared the newly reelected Jackson to collect the duties. The convention invited other states to similar resistance. Men all over the country immediately took sides. Hotheads spoke of arming for civil war; constitutional theorists emerged in every courthouse square and in the columns of every newspaper.

In Tucker's address to the Columbia convention he had spoken of the need for men of principle in the Democratic party, men who could answer the "crisis call" when it came. It may have sounded at last. And as the news of the defiance of South Carolina reached the West, Tucker opened a letter from John Randolph, ill in Virginia, apprehensive about public events. Randolph had written the letter, disjointed though brilliant, over the course of a week. On Saturday, November 9, he simply took his pen and wrote Tucker,

I have been unable to prosecute this letter until now, & have just strength enough left to say in three words

Come to me.[41]

V

On the day after Christmas, 1832, Tucker finished a long essay on the South Carolina crisis by declaring that he was a disinterested man. "I am not and probably shall not again be a candidate for anything in your gift," Missourians soon read in the Saint Louis *Free Press*. He made a moving call on westerners to support Carolina in her exposed position and served notice that he was leaving them for Virginia hoping, he said, to render service to his native state. "She is my mother," Tucker said solemnly, "and to be with her in her hour of trial is a duty of which by no act of mine can I divest myself."[42] Nor, he might have added, would he if he could. Nullification gave Tucker his excuse to return home with a mission.

Obviously his purpose in that journey was to oppose, with all his energies, the theory of power President Jackson took to his strong stand against

South Carolina. Besides alerting the federal army and navy for action, Jackson published through his secretary of state, Edward Livingston, a message on nullification denouncing state veto as treason. In this proclamation of December 10, which reached Tucker before his departure for Virginia, Jackson flatly denied the doctrine of state sovereignty. Such a notion appealed to "State vanity" and found advocates in the "honest prejudices of those who have not studied the nature of our Government sufficiently to see the radical error in which it rests." The proclamation spoke of the "unity of a nation" and made no effort to conceal the implications of such a concept. The Constitution formed a government, Jackson and Livingston made clear, not a league.[43]

Yet Tucker's mission to Virginia was not in support of John C. Calhoun. For one thing, Tucker mistrusted the nullification leader, now entering on his Senate career. As secretary of war under President Monroe, Calhoun had advocated several projects of disputed constitutionality; as Jackson's vice-president, he had frankly sought to succeed the old general to the White House. Only in the summer of 1831 had Calhoun openly espoused the cause of constitutionalism that Tucker had known from his own boyhood. Tucker admitted in newspaper articles that he had "no love" for this complex man, whom he had bitterly attacked in the former vice-president's "high and palmy days," and he expressed none now.[44]

There was the gleam of ambition in Calhoun's eye, and furthermore there were problems with the theory of resistance he now used. It seemed, at first glance, stock Virginia doctrine. Calhoun began with the conception of the Union that St. George Tucker had discussed in his edition of Blackstone: the general government was a creation of the people of the states acting in their sovereign capacity; the Constitution was the expression of the compact thus formed, and it granted certain specific authority to the central government as the agent of the states. The final arbiter of disputes was therefore the states, and Calhoun here cited the 1798 Virginia Resolves that Tucker had tried to make the test of Democratic orthodoxy in Missouri. But Calhoun went beyond these resolutions in contending firmly that a state in solemn convention could, in fact, nullify and void federal law. State nullification in this manner, said Calhoun, would force the general government to set in motion the amending machinery provided for in the Fifth Article of the Constitution; only if three-fourths of the states in convention sustained the federal authority in the dispute would the questioned statute become the law of the land.[45]

Tucker thought Calhoun's theory was preposterous. South Carolina, while asserting her sovereignty, had made herself a recalcitrant vassal, a rebellious province. Sovereignty was hopelessly confused—in one sense lying with the convention of the nullifying state and in another sense with the collective act of the other states. Further, wrote Tucker, there was the practical problem of individual persons, all of whom, while the challenging state remained in the Union as a troublesome member, continued to be citizens both of the state and of the United States; perhaps, like collectors of tariff revenues at Charleston, their duties would conflict. Seeking constitutional shelter from attack as a public enemy and at the same time trying to prevent her citizens from carrying out official tasks, South Carolina fell between two stools. The Virginia resolutions of 1798 scarcely set this awkward course. James Madison, the elderly author of the resolutions, lent support to this much of Tucker's view by pointing out in an article he published in 1830 that the Virginia resolves had made a case for state remonstrance in the Union, but not for nullification. Tucker in fact did not simply deny nullification, he denounced it as smacking of the abstraction he detested in metaphysicians. It was paradox and sophistry, "mystery mystified, and confusion worse confounded."[46]

The key to the question of state and federal power was sovereignty, Tucker wrote, and his conception of sovereignty—instead of ethereal like Calhoun's—was "real and substantial." He defined it as the ultimate lawful power to protect right and to redress wrong. By this definition, the existence and character of sovereignty had less to do with speculation about whether it could be divided or not than with its effects. Turning on who carried the keys of life and death in common matters of human affairs, Tucker's view of sovereignty paralleled the argument his father had made earlier in the debate over courts and common law. Advocates of extensive federal powers in the early republic had claimed that, because the common law was known to all American courts, there was reason to include under the purview of federal courts disputes at common law throughout the country. St. George Tucker, along with others interested in maintaining the integrity of the state courts, had countered that each colony, and then state, had built its own unique set of court decisions on the foundation of the English common law. States had distinct "common laws," and as a result there was no "United States Common Law."[47] Similarly, Beverley Tucker reasoned in 1832–33 that the authority governing the dealings of everyday life on the basis of the common and statute law was the true sovereign, and accordingly there was no "United States Sovereignty." He trenchantly noted that in matters of personal injury, debt, or common crime no one in the country looked to the federal government. "A strange sort of sovereignty" was that of Jackson and Livingston, Tucker exclaimed, exercising "no control over these acts" that were "destructive to the peace and well being of society!"[48]

Calhoun's nullification tactic also troubled Tucker because it was fundamentally conciliatory. Nullification was a way to preserve the Union by allowing a state, while remaining in it, a means of protecting its own minority interests by voiding oppressive laws and appealing to its sister states for constitutional amendment. Calhoun reluctantly admitted that a state might secede if the necessary number failed to uphold the nullifying act, but, if nullification could in theory lead to secession, it was clearly not supposed to. However ensnarled this plan was logically and practically, and despite apprehensive interpretations moderates gave it, Tucker saw Calhoun's device as the truly temporizing measure it was. It was at bottom a way to avoid disunion, not to precipitate it.[49]

Secession, Tucker said in his newspaper address to the people of Missouri, was the only defensible and effective recourse of an aggrieved state. If the laws of the United States had to be executed, and if the President of the United States had sworn to enforce federal laws throughout the states, then a wronged state simply had to cease membership in the Union. While a nullifying state placed its people in an ungainly position, helpless and open to ridicule, a seceding state, Tucker believed, put itself and its citizens in a constitutional sanctuary, safe in independence. Of course no state would resort to this remedy except in desperate circumstances. But once outside the Union, the need for a congressional declaration of war would restrain the chief executive from pressing matters, and politically the state could render itself impregnable. Secession in Tucker's mind was the natural channel the federal form of government provided dissident states; in a system of divided operations it would not even impair the normal business of the central agency.[50]

It could not have surprised Tucker, and it probably pleased him, that his brother Henry counseled prudence in the nullification crisis. Serving then as president of the Supreme Court of Appeals in Richmond, Henry had made investments and earned rewards strengthening the sense of responsibility his younger brother had noticed in their childhood years. Henry, too, was opposed to an oppressive tariff. It was unfair and unnecessary. But he regretted both the divisiveness of South Carolina and his younger brother's excitement. "We are standing here upon a Volcano," he wrote Beverley from Richmond. "Materials are collected which are ready to Explode, and I am sure you cannot be willing to furnish the Spark. . . ." The charter of federal government, he continued, might be clarified in convention so as to avoid clashes of the sort South Carolina seemed intent to bring on; meantime tempers must cool. "No, my dear Beverley," wrote Henry in a tone that must have rankled, "the fault is not in the Execution of the law; the fault is in the rash and ill advised course of South Carolina, on the one hand, & of that constitution on the other, which *we* have been taught to consider as 'the most stupendous monument of human wisdom.'"[51]

The younger brother marched ahead despite that monument and these rejoinders. Indeed, given the view of the Union he had learned from what Henry called the brothers' "pure and common source," secession was hardly a breakthrough in political theory. Nor was Tucker the first critic of federal policy to bandy about talk of seceding from the Union. But the

hopes and then failures of the Missouri experience had raised the consciousness of a man already sensitive and troubled; the nullification controversy
brought him the chance to speak—though he did not yet shout—of misgivings about change he had until then only muttered. Tucker was apparently
the first Southerner to dedicate himself to the cause of secession as a means
of establishing a separate people. If the ideal society could not be formed
in the Union, it would have to be found out of it. There was nothing to fear
in secession, Tucker tried to convince his Missouri audience. By any definition, sovereignty was incapable of rebellion. There was nothing higher for
it to rebel against. Secession would be peaceful, even joyous from the long
view, for "a new nation would have sprung up among the nations of the
earth."[52]

VI

Such assurances were for the fainthearted. The Virginian who answered the
crisis call in the dying days of 1832 returned there with every hope of a
storm that would be sublime in its effect. In the *Free Press* Tucker called
on men to steel themselves for the choice they would have to make. Letters
home to Lucy, once he was underway, betrayed the thrill of anticipated
conflict. Docked at Louisville on New Year's morning 1833, he excitedly
wrote Lucy of his vindication as a prophet. He had predicted that the old
soldier in the White House would react to the South Carolina nullifying
ordinances as belligerently and wrongheadedly as he had. "I am now equally
clear in the opinion," he told her, "that it will go on to the extreme of disunion, accompanied by a bloody struggle." A week later he was in western
Virginia, his spirits still high, buoyed by some local newspaper articles that
supported his prediction of "awful consequences" and led him to talk of
spending the rest of his life in the tented field. While his husbandly attachments and patriotic duties painfully divided him, it was a bracing pain. He
conceived of Virginia as another Scotland, with the gallantry the poet
Robert Burns ascribed to that proud, outmanned region. Tucker was on an
imaginative crusade, reveling in romantic allusions, yearning for the sublimity
of pitched battle, banners, confusion, valor, and victory.[53]

His reunion with Randolph in mid-January heightened the euphoria of
the journey. As Tucker expected, Jackson's proclamation defying the nullifiers had invigorated the sickly Randolph and given spur to his emotions as
well. Joined occasionally by close friends, nearly a hundred miles from Richmond—where a sober General Assembly voted to send Benjamin Watkins
Leigh to Charleston as a peacemaker—Tucker and his host spent days talking
in the desolation of Roanoke plantation. It was a communion of minds that
Tucker never forgot, the realization of a dream he had expressed for years
during the Missouri exile. In caring for Randolph, Tucker seldom for a mo-

ment left his brother's side. Each night the two men dined together by candlelight and then, in their beds, talked until the early hours of the morning. It was a time to mull over the political battles of the past fifteen years, to celebrate the harmony of their beliefs, and the opium Randolph took to ease his misery no doubt helped raise these discussions to a rightly inspirational plane. Tucker warmed at the pleasure Randolph showed at his "steadfast and solitary adherence to principles," his "spirit and ability" in maintaining them. Together they mustered their energies to alert the public and to expose Jackson's heresy.[54]

Their vantage point in events was not a prominent one. In Washington friends of the administration introduced in the Senate on January 16 a bill, which, after reiterating the constitutional theories of Jackson's December proclamation, requested extraordinary powers to use against South Carolina. The Force Bill was a device showing Jackson's determination to uphold federal power in the face of Calhoun's folly, even as the President supported the efforts of Clay and others in Congress to disarm the nullifiers by lowering tariff duties. To Jackson the Force Bill and tariff reform would bring moral victory and sectional detente. To the nullifiers in South Carolina, the Force Bill and its explicit threat of war brought serious soul-searching. To Calhoun, just arrived in Washington and seated in the Senate, it was an immediate test of resolve and skill.

For Randolph and Tucker in the wilds of Charlotte County, Virginia, the Force Bill was a boldly contrived engine of executive oppression. Here surely, thought Tucker, was an affront to the dignity of the states that would unite Virginians in indignation and force a showdown with the imperious chief magistrate. Isolation fed these expectations. Tucker penned fiery letters for the enfeebled Randolph, helped plan a large meeting of anti–Force Bill Democrats at Charlotte Court House on February 4, and sent Thomas Ritchie's Richmond *Enquirer* a caustic, though germane, fable based on Aesop. It was about a pond of frogs who organized a republic, then underwent a change of heart and prayed to God to send them a king, and finally were devoured by the crane the Almighty sent to rule them. Though Tucker thought in terms of building a movement, he more nearly headed a conspiracy. He naturally sent his incendiary letters to men of known sentiments who needed no persuasion; the encouraging reports Tucker received from Richmond told him only of the delight his rhetoric brought "good men and true."[55] Ritchie refused to print the frog-pond parable.

The Charlotte Court House rally was a more credible success. True, voters who gathered that Monday in February had a long history of following John Randolph's lead—they were hardly newly won converts to states' rights—but the rousing meeting provided Tucker and other stalwarts in Virginia a needed lift. After listening hushed as Randolph spoke from his seat on the platform, the assemblage adopted a series of resolutions that

Tucker had written beforehand. They contained little that was new. Condemning nullification as "weak and mischievous," the resolutions nonetheless voiced a right of secession. Through the resolves Tucker asked Virginians to swear their first allegiance to their state and asked President Jackson to rid himself of misleading, designing, and ambitious counselors. Ritchie agreed to publish this communication, and Tucker ensured the widest possible distribution of the resolves by sending copies to federal and state officials, to Leigh—the Virginia delegate in South Carolina—and to friends Tucker and Randolph had among the nullifiers there.[56]

In mid-February, after the Charlotte resolves had "roused" the people of that and nearby counties and debate on the Force Bill in the Senate approached a climax, Tucker and Randolph carried the fight to Washington. Randolph's remarks against the Force Bill at Charlotte Court House had already arrived in the capital. "[C]ravens take heart," believed Tucker, "just knowing that the shattered remains of his carcass are here." While Randolph took a seat in the Senate gallery near the South Carolina Senator and glowered at Daniel Webster—a Force Bill proponent—Tucker began writing a series of public letters over the signature "a friend of state rights" and "a true friend of Andrew Jackson." Most of the essays appeared in the *United States Telegraph,* with the assistance of its editor, former Missouri resident Duff Green; all of them, intended for Southern legislators and the Chief Executive, urged steadfast enmity for the Force Bill and a return to sound states' rights principles. The first letter appeared on the nineteenth and advised the planting and slaveholding country to adopt a policy of *"prudent boldness."*[57]

In the event Jackson was not following the series, Tucker after a few days in Washington took it upon himself to pay a call at the White House. At first the doorman politely informed the visitor, who as other Americans in 1833 rode up to the presidential mansion as one would stop by the home of any gentleman, that the President was too busy to see him. Tucker insisted on leaving his card and made it clear that he would not leave until he had seen someone competent to take it, an aura of importance that next brought forth a porter who explained again that the President was engaged with heads of departments, that a great number of visitors had been turned away for that reason. "So I understand; and I anticipate such an answer," replied the Virginian coolly. "Nevertheless I will wait for it." Faced with this persistence, Jackson's household staff now asked Tucker to step into a parlor where, he recalled for Lucy, "the old man soon came to me." Though the two men each took pride in quickly gutting an adversary, they found it easiest to explore their grounds for agreement in the "long and free" discussion that followed. "I soon found I had nothing to do but to let him talk," was Tucker's report, "and when I had got the length of his foot, I took him up and made him say all I wanted him to say." As the afternoon wore on,

Jackson seemed to have decided no more to issue a proclamation of force against South Carolina than to burn his shirt. The encounter left Tucker lightheaded with excitement and satisfied that he had succeeded in driving a wedge between the old soldier and the consolidationist secretary of state who had written the Force Bill. "Now mind!" Tucker cautioned his wife in Missouri. "This is all a state secret. Nobody knows that I have been there, & no one dreams of my reception."[58]

Perhaps he knew his man and was correct that Jackson had doubts about his heavy-handed enforcement bill. But the hated measure did pass, the President did sign it, and with the later passage of Clay's compromise tariff bill the nullification crisis subsided. In Tucker's view of things there simply were not enough "good men and true" that winter, in Virginia or anywhere else.[59]

All the same, this aborted revolution, a rehearsal and hint of the sublime, gave Tucker exhilaration even as it marked a defeat. On the very day that the Senate passed the Force Bill over Calhoun's protest, on the same day that might have found Tucker writing letters of despair in his Washington hotel, he had been in the East Room of the White House enjoying a debate with the President himself. For a few moments Tucker splashed in the font of power; while arguing with this old general—whom he found amusingly inept at theorizing—he could believe for an instant that he was making history. Everything he did in this crisis assumed a new importance. The whirl of events seemed to lift his articles for the *Telegraph* to the level of state papers. During the frenzied weeks Tucker spent in Washington he was often in the Capitol and in and out of senatorial offices, accompanying Randolph on visits the stooped Quid paid his many old friends. Tucker had long talks with Benton, who had praised Tucker's December address in the Saint Louis *Free Press,* and who now, it seemed, regretted his failure to join Tucker in early defiance. Alabama radical Dixon H. Lewis met Tucker, as did Tennessee Senator Hugh Lawson White, who had married a sister of Lucy's mother. "I am on the best terms with the great folks," he happily wrote Lucy; "*no man* stands on higher ground at this moment than I."[60]

The experience changed Tucker's imagination of his possibilities. Close to power, feeling the effects of his association with it, even his influence upon it, Tucker was content not to wield it as he had as a Missouri judge ten years before. His unpleasant and unsuccessful congressional campaign no doubt helped him reach the conclusion that public prominence was "a very small affair," that the things "greatness toils for" were simply "contemptible." Though readers of the *Telegraph* letters mistook them for Randolph's, it was a sign of Tucker's new pose that he was content to bask in reflected glory. With an independent income, he wrote Lucy, he could remain in Washington and do more as a private man than anyone in office —and without the inconvenience of a popular mandate. He believed that his being there gave him more influence in government than "any office but the presidency" could give him. *"I will never again hold any public employ-ment,"* he vowed to his wife: he could be more effective relying on his ideas and his pen.[61]

As most Americans cheered the end of the nullification imbroglio, Tucker warned that the day of reckoning was merely delayed. The compromise tariff was but the appearance of reconciliation, only postponing the crisis. Nullification confounded the public on the subject of constitutional govern-ment; secession was simple, clear, and sound. The "ball of Revolution" would roll on, he predicted, and he notified his father-in-law, who had not found Tucker's position during the controversy edifying, that he must not hang up his sword. The prophet's vision was apocalyptic. *"It cometh,"* he proclaimed of disunion, *"and will come."* To hasten the day it was necessary to place Randolph's banner of states' rights firmly on the ground of seces-sion. But who, Tucker asked Senator Benton, would plant it there?[62]

The answer was not long in coming. In June, while en route with his family from Missouri to Virginia where he was again to take up residence near Randolph, Tucker heard of his half brother's death. Detained in Vir-ginia awaiting settlement of the tangled Randolph estate, Tucker then received word of his election to the chair of law at William and Mary. He accepted; the mantle had passed to him.

CHAPTER FIVE

In His Father's Chair

IN A LETTER to Kentucky Senator John J. Crittenden, the law professor hinted that life "in the midst of the dead" had a certain pungency. Williamsburg had continued to decline during Tucker's years in Missouri. In 1832 the colonial capitol burned entirely to the ground. According to the William and Mary faculty (and the comment was registered in the official record of the college), the tawdry condition of the Wren Building chapel shocked not only visitors but also the religious sense of the community at large.[1]

Tucker was happy to be where he was. He was home, soon even living in the same sprawling white frame house he had known as a boy. Inviting Crittenden down from Washington for a commemorative ceremony to be staged on the very ruins of the capitol, Tucker suggested that he lived with the past as never before. He assured Crittenden that the appearance of the old place was unchanged; the senator might even mistake his host for the spirit of St. George Tucker. "I am literally sitting in my father's seat," proclaimed the incumbent with satisfaction, "exercising the same functions that he made the business of his life." Appearances, however, were misleading.[2]

I

No doubt for many Virginians in 1834 life contained assurances of continuity and gave promise of reasonable progress. Edmund Ruffin, a Prince George County planter with an active Petersburg printing office, carried on the earlier agricultural reforms of John Taylor of Caroline by publishing in 1832 a booklet on soil enrichment that soon became a standard reference throughout the country. There were advances in transportation. Farmers in the Shenandoah Valley stood to gain by the construction of the Chesapeake and Ohio Canal along the Potomac; they anticipated even speedier access to eastern markets when the Baltimore and Ohio Railroad completed its track to Harpers Ferry. The Virginia assembly, fostering public improvements through private enterprise, thereby encouraged attempts to dredge rivers, to subsidize turnpikes, and to cut a canal connecting the West to the James River. Richmond and Petersburg were growing, filling with people who engaged in iron making, flour milling, ship loading, cotton and tobacco manufacturing.[3]

Yet in other ways, and to other people, time in the early decades of the nineteenth century had badly treated Virginia. Leader in population over the first three federal censuses, the state in 1820 dropped to second, and in 1830 to third place in the Union—losing representation in Congress with each new apportionment. Income levels in Virginia lagged behind the rest of the United States, and the commonwealth neither kept abreast of commercial and industrial developments in the North nor equalled advances

THE TUCKER HOUSE, WILLIAMSBURG

there in public education. Only by selling surplus slaves to planters in newer areas, Virginia landholders complained, could they meet western competition in agricultural commodities. In what was known as "lower Virginia"—the eastern counties along the inlets of the tidewater region, and the old tobacco-growing areas southwest of Richmond where Tucker had practiced law as a young man—the sense of declension that he had noticed earlier had worsened in his absence. While in the 1830s Virginia as a whole grew in population at just one-sixth the national rate, many lower-Virginia counties sustained losses. Despite efforts to restore soil productivity in this older part of the state, farmers often found it easier to resettle in Alabama or Mississippi than to stay and try to reverse their fortunes.[4] Residents of lower Virginia looked out on a world that was in many respects leaving them behind.

Though Tucker may not have used every such index of change, once in Virginia he could not help breathing the piquant air of decline, tension, and defensiveness. He knew all too well that efforts to change the political structure of the commonwealth placed eastern Virginians in real danger of losing control of state government. Beginning in October 1829, after many years of western prompting, the Virginia constitution had received close scrutiny at a convention held in Richmond—a distinguished assemblage that included as senior delegates former-presidents Madison and Monroe and the aged Chief Justice Marshall. Since the revisions the convention made to the 1776 frame of government were minor, it did not win great favor among unenfranchised city dwellers and its work received sharp criticism in the underrepresented west. Discontent over sectional inequities intensified there. The growing number of western Virginians—most of whom were nonslaveholding small farmers—supported every expectation eastern landowners had of renewed struggle and the eventual end of their hegemony. Not surprisingly, given this apprehension, they discovered in the convention a sentimental message that made for rhetorical flourish at the time and later provided the stuff of magazine sketches and historical addresses.[5] It was the last appearance of a generation whose political universe was manageable; it was the very exhibit of past greatness.

The problem of diminishing control would have been serious in any regional society. In a biracial society ordered by the labor system of slavery, control was everything. The Nat Turner slave revolt of August 1831, involving the brutal deaths of about sixty whites in the country below Richmond, brought home this point to Virginians perhaps as never before. Tucker cared scrupulously for his own slaves. He ensured that families remained together, took pains to see that they were "well and comfortable, and as happy . . . as belongs to human nature to be in their condition." All the same, he could readily understand the fears—the "constant dread," as one Virginian had written him in Missouri—that Turner and his band awakened in all whites, and especially in slaveholders. The rebellion provoked a dramatic discussion of slavery in the following session of the General Assembly, where conservatives withstood attempts to alter the status quo only by a rather narrow margin; heated exchanges laid bare slaveholder-nonslaveholder strains and demonstrated how truly precarious eastern containment of this sensitive issue could be. Later in 1832, when Thomas Dew of William and Mary summarized and extended arguments supporting slavery in his booklet on the debates, he gave form to the uneasy public mood in lower Virginia.[6]

Yet another reason for this uneasiness was the vulnerability of slavery should the federal government become its antagonist. Although Tucker's powers of persuasion had failed to align his state with South Carolina in the recent crisis, slaveholding Virginians, like nullifiers in Carolina and other Southerners, were aware that questions of federal power were critical at a time when their own strength in the Union was apparently shrinking and when abolitionists were stepping up their efforts, however obliquely, to move Congress in their direction. The possibility of federal intervention

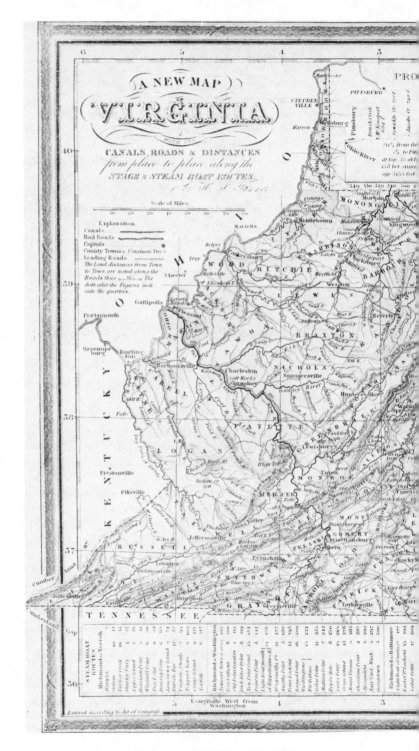

VIRGINIA IN 1834

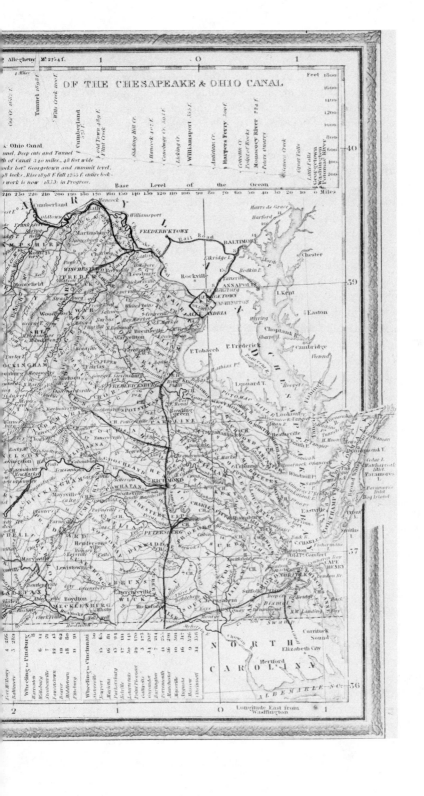

in slavery affairs explained in part the intensity of the response so many residents of lower Virginia made to Jackson's stand during the nullification affair. Democratic leaders like John Tyler and former-senator Littleton Waller Tazewell left the party because of the President's aggressive nationalism. Popular meetings in Amelia and James City counties decried Jackson's move toward consolidated government, his subversion of states' rights. On the Eastern Shore, Abel P. Upshur—a leading conservative and a state superior court judge—organized a rally in February 1833 that denounced Jackson for violating the restraints of the federal system and creating a military despotism.[7]

All this talk about constitutional revision, slavery, and the parameters of federal power made clear Tucker's way as this man who called himself a prophet returned home. Lower-Virginia society was overlaid with reasons for apprehension; men on both sides of salient issues conducted a search for first principles, necessarily facing political realities in terms of established channels of thought and expression. What was the law of nature? Virginians asked themselves again; How did one define the rights of property and the limits the state could place on it? To what end were governments formed? Critics of malapportionment, narrow suffrage, and unequal taxation rested their appeals on the revolutionary truths that power derived from the people, men were equal, and that every citizen was entitled to an equal voice in government. Opponents of slavery declared it an "act of injustice, tyranny, and oppression, to hold any part of the human race in bondage." Supporters and enemies of nullification, besides arguing over the expediency of state veto, differed on the character of the Union. In this state of affairs Tucker could talk freely about what had been bothering him for a long time. He was attuned to the fears of lower Virginians.[8]

In short, Tucker's wares were marketable. Friends jumped to define his role as a spokesman, apologist, and teacher. Thomas G. Peachy, rector of the college, accompanied word of Tucker's election with the news that "proper" states rights men already had begun to congratulate themselves on now having in Dew and Tucker able instructors in the "true orthodox political faith." Ruffin's *Farmer's Register* cheered the Tucker appointment no less heartily. In South Carolina William Campbell Preston, a former member of the Dardenne clan, urged the new law professor to "shake the mildew from the public mind" in Virginia. Edward Bates in Saint Louis hoped Tucker would combat the "manworship" of Jackson partisans. Duff Green, the erstwhile Jackson man now in Washington using his *United States Telegraph* to support conservative Southern leaders, had anticipated Tucker's challenge by telling him that the people had to be "convinced and *alarmed* to do right." "We congratulate the friends of William and Mary, lower Virginia generally, and the Constitutionalists of the South upon this appointment," proclaimed the *Richmond Whig* in July 1834. "It is important that the law classes particularly, should be instructed by Professors of sound politics as well as good legal attainments."[9] Next to readings in history, the editor of the *Whig,* John Hampden Pleasants, explained, training in law was most influential in forming political opinion. Tucker's teaching post was a political portfolio.

II

In the early afternoon of October 27, 1834, a faculty meeting in the old Wren Building formally opened Tucker's first year of teaching. Making his way to the college along the Duke of Gloucester Street, with its colorful matting of fallen maple leaves, Tucker may well have reflected on the irony of his William and Mary appointment. Though he was now to serve in the law professorship that well-known predecessors like George Wythe and his father had made famous in Virginia, he himself had not been a particularly successful Virginia lawyer. In the very chamber where the faculty would convene, he, as an indifferent pupil, had often received the rebukes and even thrashings of his earnest schoolmasters. Tucker's early

WREN BUILDING, THE COLLEGE OF WILLIAM AND MARY

feelings about his new role had in truth been guarded; at first he described the professorship as "better than nothing" while awaiting disentanglement of the Randolph will.[10]

But Tucker warmed to the task, welcoming, he said, the return to law books after several years of farming and writing. The job provided a fairly steady income, and he felt needed. The Reverend Adam Empie, President of the college and instructor in belles lettres, logic, and ethics, greeted the new professor at the faculty gathering that October afternoon. Tucker extended a firm hand to Thomas Dew, the proslavery pamphleteer, who was professor of political economy. Other colleagues included Robert Saunders, mathematics; William Barton Rogers, and after 1835, John Millington, chemistry and natural philosophy; and Dabney Browne, classical languages. Before the end of this perfunctory meeting, Professor Tucker managed to request some repairs to the law classroom and succeeded in having *The American Jurist,* a Boston quarterly seeking to raise professional standards and promote fellowship at the bar, added to the library subscription list.[11] He looked forward to being a busy and important figure at the college.

Tucker may further have considered himself at the forefront of an academic movement. It was true that in 1834 most men studying for the legal profession did so in the same way he himself had thirty years before, either by reading texts in the office of a practicing attorney or in a private law school. Because Virginia standards of admission to the bar remained loosely administered, and because of the wide availability of St. George Tucker's edition of Blackstone's *Commentaries,* the apprenticeship method was well grounded in Virginia. In other parts of the United States this clerkship arrangement was just as prevalent; some northern states in the first decade of the century even required law-office study for a prescribed period before a candidate's licensing examination. Private law courses, by which prominent judges or lawyers took on a group of apprentices and systematized their reading, though occasionally influential, continued few in number and were mostly short-lived. The most famous of these schools was the one that Judge Tapping Reeve founded in Litchfield, Connecticut, in 1784 and that John C. Calhoun attended. In Virginia, Henry St. George Tucker had conducted a private school in Winchester—one of several in the state—while a judge of the chancery court between 1824 and 1830.[12]

There were, however, a growing number of academic law schools in the country in 1834, and their importance was growing. By the time Tucker assumed his professorship, the colleges and universities offering programs in law included important nineteenth-century additions. In 1817 Harvard began schooling legal practitioners; in 1823 Chancellor James Kent introduced law lectures at Columbia University; in 1824 Yale incorporated as an adjunct to the college a law course already being taught in New Haven. For most of the 1820s David Hoffman, a jurist whose broadly conceived *Course*

of Legal Study gained wide attention, labored to institute his reformed
curriculum at the University of Maryland. When the University of Virginia
opened its doors in 1825, law was one of the six subjects of instruction.
Unlike almost all apprenticeships, law studies at colleges were regular and
rigorous; while private courses of the Litchfield and Winchester type were
an improvement over clerkship training, academic law schools had an
institutional link that helped to ensure their longevity.[13]

Moreover, academic law schools laid claim to professional leadership.
Many of the great minds at the bar—Joseph Story at Harvard, Kent at
Columbia, Hoffman at Maryland—were in the forefront of the effort to
justify the prerogatives and prestige of the profession to American society.
The law, they pointed out, was a science that required devoted study and
long preparation. The truly sound lawyer was a scholar, and men trained
in academic law schools were best suited to take the lead in the profession.[14]

While Story believed the lawyer should be more a classical scholar than a
professional antiquarian, academic law schools nonetheless reflected a
movement in the profession to draw in the boundaries of the lawyer's interests, to redress popular hostility toward the profession as elitist by assuming a narrow, workmanlike stance. At the Harvard and Yale law schools,
students were expected to be interested solely in technical training. Some
students had already finished baccalaureate work, true; but for those who
had not—and such degrees were by no means required for admission—liberal
studies at the college were not made easy. Both institutions were in the highly
competitive business of teaching occupational skills.[15]

The Jurist, which Tucker ordered for the William and Mary library,
reflected these new professional attitudes. While earlier attempts at professional journals in the century had directed themselves to the widely read,
broadly educated audience for whom Blackstone had written his *Commentaries* in the eighteenth century, readers of *The Jurist* found reviews of noteworthy court decisions, useful tips on pleading, and forms for making wills.
Short articles on the great lawyers of the past and present carried the lesson
that the legal craft, though it called for extensive knowledge, was nonetheless open to anyone of good will and abundant energy. The lawyer was an
honest, contributing member of society; and above all he was nonpolitical.
To the editors of *The Jurist,* who included in the 1830s several students of
Story at Harvard, the working definition of the profession had grown
restricted. Politics, itself growing professional, was outside the parameters
of the study of the law.[16]

Further, at Harvard law school in this period and perhaps at Yale as well,
the avowed object was to teach national law, to search out principles in the
statutory law of the states that were common to all or most jurisdictions of
the country. Perhaps Nathan Dane, the Massachusetts jurist who founded
Story's law chair and favored teaching the "most national" law, and Story

himself, whose performance on the Supreme Court left little doubt of his own theoretical leanings, believed between them that such a nationalist scheme was academically preferable. Perhaps this interest at Harvard grew out of a Northern concern with legal-commercial matters that were by their nature interstate in scope. In any case, this line of inquiry led students to conceive of the law as something evolving toward uniformity, as tending toward consistency throughout its parts. In this view, peculiarities of state law were aberrations, unimportant dropped stitches in the fabric of national law.[17]

On the afternoon of the October 27 faculty meeting, reading from a text that Tucker had taken great pains to prepare, the new law professor gave an inaugural lecture that demonstrated how out of step with these professional trends he was. Much of what Tucker told his incoming law students was no doubt standard fare. He made clear the seriousness of their undertaking. Law study was the *toga virilis,* the business of adulthood; it would be arduous, laborious. To choose it was to separate oneself from that common herd of young men who, as one who had resisted legal study was bound to know, "shrink from everything that demands exertion and perseverance." There was perhaps no discipline, warned Tucker, that taxed the powers of the mind more severely than the law.[18]

Yet in contrast to legal schooling at Harvard and Yale, Tucker's William and Mary course was to concentrate on Virginia statutes, almost entirely on Virginia court decisions, and on the common law as a foundation of both. He paid little attention to comparative state law and avoided any "national" frame of reference. He expected his students to view law, not as something evolving toward unity, resolving differences among constituent parts, but as something building logically on past experience. The locus of study was to be neither the future nor the whole. It was to be the past and the particular. Tucker's lawyers were above all to be Virginia lawyers.

Furthermore, they were to be statesmen. William and Mary after Jefferson's 1779 reforms had made as little distinction as possible between disciplines: study in law offered the kind of education that befitted not only the lawyer but the lawmaker as well. Standing on tradition, Tucker this October afternoon told his students that they were enrolled in anything but a limited professional course. It was his duty at the college, he said, "to present views more important to the statesman than the mere practitioner." He was to be an educator of leaders, not simply a herdsman of specialists.[19]

The social function of the legal profession, as Tucker defined it in his introductory lecture, was enough by itself to draw him away from narrow specialization. Because the bar, statesmanship, and the gentlemanly mode all joined in Tucker's mind, he saw the profession as being ideally built on the eighteenth-century English model he had clung to so stubbornly as a struggling young lawyer at Charlotte Court House. If barristers were well educated and prestigious, and if solicitors resembled tradesmen, Tucker's aim was to prepare barristers. Barristers were statesmen and jurists in the making, men who could expect "to hold a place among the great ones of the earth." Conceived not as a collection of practitioners but as a closed fraternity of gentlemen with large obligations, the bar, Tucker told his students, was like a "talisman" in which they could put their trust, knowing that whatever they sought they would receive. They should look upon their profession, he said, "as the source from whence are to flow all the comforts, the honors, and the happiness of life."[20] The bar was part of a predictable system of social relations.

Given the cadence of academic legal training elsewhere, Tucker was out of step, but his obsolescence insured the saliency of his role at William and Mary. On the evening of October 27 his fireside gave off an especially warm glow. The college had opened, Lucy Tucker wrote her family in Missouri, with more students than ever in recent memory. Not only had her husband's students acclaimed his inaugural lecture, but a committee of them wanted to print it in a pamphlet and even to have it published in the new magazine, *The Southern Literary Messenger,* which Thomas W. White edited in Richmond. Later in the fall and into the winter, as the lecture circulated, Tucker's satisfaction mounted. A young Missourian studying at the University of Virginia saw the introductory lesson and pledged his reliance on Tucker's constitutional teachings; White of the *Messenger* wrote the new professor that in the state capital the lecture was a topic "of much and deserved eulogy." The old Quid Nathaniel Macon, to whom Tucker had sent a copy, warmly hailed his effort.[21]

III

Slowly the excitement of his introductory lecture died down, and by the late fall Tucker had settled into the agreeable routine of teaching. Meeting his class three times a week, Tucker enlarged on assigned readings that included the texts of Stephen and Mitford on pleading—he found these older works and this difficult craft of the law in need of closer attention—and employed Starkie's standard guide to the rules of evidence. He fulfilled his promise to make students lawyers of the commonwealth above all, by requiring them to know Lomax's digest of Virginia realty law and to study Benjamin Watkins Leigh's compilation of state statutes; Tucker also relied heavily on the two volumes of Virginia law that Henry Tucker had written for use in his Winchester Law School. In lectures Beverley gave examples of legal principles in daily practice and listened with the ear of a former judge to the answers students gave his gentle but insistent probings. His moot court was no innovation in legal training, but as one who earlier had described judges as "elder brothers" of the bar, Tucker apparently enjoyed using this teaching device and had students keep a record of its proceedings. Tucker the professor made none of the complaints about the dullness of the law which, as a student, had claimed almost as much time as his reading. Young men at William and Mary benefited from his own sour experience.[22]

They knew that Tucker's course truly had reached high pitch when he began talking about the Constitution and principles of government. He did in fact arrange his syllabus with a crescendo in mind. Blackstone and his father, Tucker explained in his introductory lecture, had dealt first with the origins of political rights, then moved on to matters of individual rights and civil relations between persons—the stuff of everyday law practice.

THE DUKE OF GLOUCESTER STREET
looking toward the college, in Tucker's day

Tucker used his father's edition of the *Commentaries* as a point of departure, but he reversed this sequence. Beginning with material like pleading, wills, contracts, Tucker expected to bring the minds of his own students to governmental theory "sobered and subdued" by the rigors of elementary work.[23] He further sobered his students, and played on the sentiment of everyone connected with the college, by stressing the tradition they shared. A narrow view of federal powers and a hearty defense of the states' reserved powers were synonymous with William and Mary and, by implication, with the Tucker family. "The Virginia School of Political Science and Constitutional Law," the second professor of that name reminded an alumni gathering, "is the School of William and Mary"; Wythe had established law school and political faith during the Revolution, and sons of the college, said Tucker, have made those beliefs "the faith of Virginia." Such enthusiasm was catching. The "days of glory" one sensed in the Wren Building and "sound *state rights Republican* doctrines" simply belonged together, decided a student of Tucker's law course; "why should not the Ancient university of William & Mary be the repository of the orthodox political faith?"[24]

No one expected Tucker to treat constitutional law as so much logic-chopping, and he did not. He framed his lectures in early promises and later crises. Besides poring over the explanatory appendices of St. George Tucker's Blackstone, students read *The Federalist* essays that Tucker believed critical to an understanding of the Constitution. The papers of Madison, Hamilton, and Jay shed light on the "true intent & meaning" of the document when it was ratified; adhering to the rule of evidence that *contemporania exposito est fortissima,* they represented what the parties to the contract thought they were entering into at the time. Tucker prescribed as examples of later glosses that kept to the true path the 1798 Virginia Resolutions, so important to him during his brief involvement in Democratic party politics several years earlier, and Madison's 1799–1800 Report on the replies that other state legislatures made to Virginia. Scarcely willing to omit the lessons of more recent controversies, or to neglect his own contributions to this literature, he included on his list of readings copies of the newspaper essays he himself had written in the midst of the nullification conflict.[25]

With good reason Tucker took a sense of urgency to these discussions. New York Chancellor James Kent's text on the Constitution and American law, which Tucker had students read as a case study in centralist reasoning, was in the early 1830s perhaps the most influential American treatise on such matters. Moreover, Joseph Story, who taught law at Harvard and like Tucker was influenced by the nullification controversy, published in 1833 three volumes of *Commentaries on the Constitution,* which soon appeared in abridged form for use in Northern colleges and academies. Tucker rightly recognized a threat in the work of Kent and Story. Like George Bancroft, the Boston Democrat whose recent *History of the United States* Tucker was reading for review in the *Messenger,* Story made the argument for an American nationhood with roots deep in the past. This approach, if widely enough accepted and followed to its logical conclusion, easily permitted the belief that the federal government was national, and therefore superior to the states, instead of an agent government with defined and limited powers. The ideas of Story and Bancroft invited the central government, with all its destructive potential, to enhance its powers.[26]

Blackstone's *Commentaries* provided all the elements Tucker needed for his lectures: Blackstone spoke of the genius of custom, the limits of reason,

the sanctity of the right of property, and implied that the law was properly
the domain of the better sort of men. The appendices of St. George Tucker's
1803 edition helped republican students to handle the common law in
American terms and enabled his son later in the century to hammer at
changeless constitutional principles.

Nonetheless, the key to Beverley Tucker's training of statesmen was the
felt need to go considerably beyond this textbook, even beyond his father's
edition of it, which (he told his students) he treated "with filial reverence."
Tucker leavened his father's teaching with his own instructive experience.
Blackstone, for example—fascinated with savages and expecting to find
important truths in antiquity—discovered in primitive society a suggestion
of man's natural, and therefore real, capacities. But Blackstone had never
traveled to the wilds of America; he had never known an aborigine. Tucker
not only trusted the real over the theoretical, he had observed "reality"
firsthand—having gained as a circuit-riding frontier judge a knowledge of
Shawnee and other Indian tribes that was more than passable in Williamsburg. In the lectures on government he began to develop in the first year
of teaching, in his lessons on the original state of society and the real nature
of man, Tucker made the most of this resource. He focused the "eye of
science" on those rude forms of society, examining "the first germs of
civil authority" through "a sort of moral microscope."[27]

Peeping through the lens Tucker had polished for them, his students
could see that man and society had always existed together. Man was
"emphatically a social animal," he taught; "The very laws of his nature impose society upon him." It was abstractionist folly to talk of a time when
men consciously bound themselves together and created society. The utter
helplessness of newborn children and the insecurities of man's primitive
existence had made social organization crucial to his survival from the
"dawn of time." Like Blackstone, Burke, and other adversaries of rapid
change and social instability, Tucker saw men as humble participants in a
divinely ordained order that sometimes eluded complete understanding.
Yet in this case at least, God's plan made itself intelligible. Of necessity
seeking security with others, man from the moment his Maker created him
felt the implanted urge to establish supremacy over "brute creation." Man's
weakness was his strength in another sense too, because the long dependency
of a young person had the effect of building affections that offset the brutishness of his nature. "It is by this fostering process," said Tucker in a passage
interesting in light of his own extended dependence, "that the heart is
warmed to a sense of inextinguishable obligation. . . ."[28]

For Tucker, government—and in these passages he was also talking about
sovereignty—insured the protection of society just as society provided for
the security of the individual. Again he spent much time searching for
origins. In one lecture he spoke of government as growing out of external

conflict. Primitive tribes, homogeneous in their ties of blood, marriage, and friendship, tended to repel one another, he had noticed; differences between persons of different tribes could easily produce strife. The earliest forms of government, Tucker surmised, lay in parleys between hostile groups, councils leading to agreements that were binding on all tribal members. In a later class he stressed internal "dissension" in society as a second source of government: To prevent wrongs to persons and property inside the group, he said, men eventually had recognized an authority enforcing retribution and inflicting punishment.[29]

Both these observations returned the attention of Tucker's students to his constitutional theory. Government, distilled to its essence, held each citizen accountable for injuries committed. In describing governments in their role as domestic arbiters, Tucker demonstrated the plausibility of his working definition of sovereignty. Essentially, "government" was that authority redressing wrongs and preserving peace and security in society; political bodies without this function were not truly "governments" at all, but jurisdictions or agents of the sovereign. Secondly, government was responsible to other sovereignties for the actions of its members. Tucker deduced that men were therefore duty-bound only to the group that was answerable for them. Had Tucker transposed this principle from primitive to current circumstances, he would have denied the inference that United States reciprocity treaties with other countries made the federal government sovereign; it was manifestly an agent of sovereign states. In fact Tucker's implication that a Virginian committing a crime in Maryland, say, was in some sense ultimately responsible to his home state revealed the meaning he attached to communities like Virginia, supposedly tied together by ties of blood, marriage, and friendship. "The inseparable connexion between allegiance and protection," he said of an issue nullification had raised, made it impossible to owe allegiance to more than one government.[30]

Tucker's students may very likely have asked him during these discussions whether safety from danger within and without told the whole story, whether any natural rights transcended the accidents of political organization. Of course Tucker had trouble with natural rights. By definition they existed independently of time and place and hence antedated the society Tucker said man always had lived in. Still, he did not deny man's claim to personal security—or to liberty, the preservation of which was so fundamental a concern of republican government. To talk meaningfully of rights to life and liberty, Tucker embedded them in what he felt was concrete social reality. While personal freedom and security were precious rights, taught Tucker, they were only valuable insofar as they permitted the pursuit and enjoyment of property.[31]

Property was the cornerstone of Tucker's conception of rights. It was "concrete" because natural and universal. Everyone shared the sense of ownership; respect for property, said Tucker, could be found in the codes of simple and complex societies alike. Unlike Blackstone, who spoke of property as an absolute right sanctified by English common law, Tucker stressed that property was a creation of society, growing out of the formation of society and giving it order and structure. There was no society without property, and the security of persons within that order was best guaranteed when connected to the safety of property. The maxim that no man's belongings could be taken without his consent was not merely a protection for the sake of property alone. Experience and history, said Tucker, drawing on both Blackstone's glorification of the common law and Burke's praise for the English Constitution, taught that "property thus becomes the measure of the value of liberty." Linked to property, liberty was no longer a speculative matter, no "imaginary divinity," and Tucker contended that liberty was to be enjoyed, not worshiped. To enjoy liberty was to hold and revere property; to worship liberty was to spin metaphysical webs around it—as indeed enemies of lower Virginia and the South seemed to be doing.[32]

But the enjoyment of liberty was bound to cause problems. The liberties of some men infringed on those of others, and as men competed for the bounty of God's earth, inequalities were assured. In contrast to St. George Tucker, who in his edition of the *Commentaries* spoke approvingly, if vaguely, of the revolutionary "spirit of equality," his son focused the attention of his students on the self-evident fact of inequality. While he did not deny that men in a moral sense were born and remained equal, Tucker argued that the very working of the principle of equality made them materially unequal. All primitive men had the same right to stalk deer that roamed their region. If some of them fared better than others, built up a store of provisions, and became substantial members of the tribe, it was simply a result of their original parity. Surely, thought Tucker, unlucky or unskilled hunters could not complain of the way the rule worked in practice. Equality naturally begot inequality, a principle he was scarcely the first to pronounce.[33]

Tucker did, however, shift the burden of the argument. Speaking first of savages sharing the chances of feasting on the same deer, he then suggested that the results of bygone hunts rightfully had their effect down through generations. He also changed the terms of the theorem from possessions to social status and implied that one could move the level of the Indian-chasing-deer metaphor from individuals to the scale of families, nations, or races. Necessity, Tucker told his students, imposed the only limit on what one might lose in this natural process. Only when a man was "bound to all that he can perform" could his "liabilities be carried no further."[34]

IV

The departure Tucker made from his father's assumptions was most evident in a lecture he delivered in December 1834 on slavery—a subject, he said, "too interesting to be passed in silence." In 1800, there had been about 300,000 slaves in Virginia, and St. George Tucker had then warned his municipal law class that any postponement of an emancipation plan would make the task of freeing them quite difficult. The mythological Milo had only grown strong enough to carry an ox by beginning when the beast was still a calf; if Virginia complained at the beginning of the century that the calf was too heavy for their shoulders, what would they do with the ox of a black population doubled in thirty years?[35]

St. George Tucker's son told his own law class that it was now time to look into the subject of slavery "more narrowly." Milo's calf had indeed grown into an unshoulderable ox. For St. George Tucker the section of Blackstone that dealt with the legal grounds of slavery had prompted discussion of a manumission scheme; Beverley Tucker protested that Blackstone's "preemptory judgment" unfairly placed Southern slaveholders "in the condition of convicted delinquents." "The time is rife with proofs," he warned in this lecture, his second published in the *Southern Literary Messenger,* "that unless we mean tamely to surrender a most important interest, we must hold ourselves always on the alert to defend it with tongue and pen."[36]

THOMAS R. DEW
as a William and Mary faculty member

This candor merged nicely with intellectual currents already working at William and Mary in the person of Thomas Dew. Dew, whose tall, slender

frame and large nose lent themselves to silhouette drawings in students'
notebooks, had received his professorship in 1824 after a fine record as a
student at the college. Unlike Tucker, Dew had been abroad; like Tucker,
he had private reasons why the part of apologist or spokesman pleased him.
A frail, ascetic man, Dew's health and demeanor severely restricted the
rewarding things he could do in a relatively simple society. He gained a wide
reputation in Virginia for his history lectures, which, besides emphasizing
the rise and fall of ancient republics, gave ample attention to the development of chivalry and the extremism of the French Revolution. Dew was
also popular with members of the Board of Visitors and students for his
espousal of free trade. He attended the free-trade convention in Philadelphia
in 1831; in his political economy lectures, antitariff doctrine was fundamental.[37]

As Tucker began teaching at William and Mary, Dew was probably best
known for the pamphlet he wrote in 1832 discussing the recent legislative
debates on slavery. Much of the essay affirmed Tucker's own ideas. Dew
made it clear—as had Tucker in his 1826 theology manuscripts—that God's
benevolence was the key to an understanding of His ways. In Burkean
terms familiar to Tucker, Dew wrote that circumstances formed institutions,
that wisdom grew out of experience rather than speculation. In other
respects Dew led where Tucker had not yet gone, at least in writing; more
than a summary or critical recounting of the debates, the *Review* defended
slavery not merely as excusable but as a positive good and a measure of
cultural advancement. History, according to Dew, showed that slavery was
"inevitable in the progress of society," a necessary consequence of the
"principles of human nature and the state of property." Slavery was neither
unjust, for masters were like parents to slaves, nor was it evil, for Holy
Scripture sanctioned bondage and prescribed standards of behavior both for
masters and servants. Jefferson's criticisms of slavery in his *Notes on the
State of Virginia,* wrote Dew, simply were not borne out by the facts.[38]

Tucker had never denounced slavery, but neither had he publicly defended
it before 1834. At first his argument was low-keyed. Tucker complemented
Dew's apology by challenging Blackstone's view that slavery was unjustified
either in law or logic. Slavery hardly made sense as the result of a bargain or
contract, read the *Commentaries,* because in bartering there had to be an
exchange of things of comparable value, and nothing was equal to one's
liberty. Tucker replied that, since Southern slavery was peaceful, benevolent,
and mutually beneficial, accepting it for the rewards of security and happiness might be a fair exchange after all. Blackstone also raised the question
of slavery and the laws of war. Hugo Grotius, in a seventeenth-century text
that was still in use in Tucker's college days, had defended the enslaving of
war prisoners as better than killing them. Blackstone in the eighteenth century argued that the wartime right to kill rested only on the necessity of

self-defense, and that once a victor took a man captive he no longer needed to slay him—so that neither could he justifiably enslave him. Tucker upbraided Blackstone for what he thought was a practical absurdity and looked for truth in the real necessities of man's primitive state. It would be foolhardy, answered Tucker, for tribal leaders to turn loose "savage and treacherous" captives; it was better to annihilate completely their "power of arrogance."[39]

Tucker also continued telling his students what he had said in his inaugural lecture: slavery preserved the character of republican leadership. Following Aristotle, Burke, and Dew, Tucker held that man was too weak both to labor and to find time and energy necessary to the role of sovereign citizen. Repeatedly he reminded his students of Burke's remark in Commons in 1775. Where slavery existed, free men were exceedingly jealous of their liberty; in a slave society said Tucker, using Burke's words, freedom was not only a boon "but a kind of rank and privilege," a certain "haughtiness of domination" fortifying the spirit of independence and rendering it "invincible." Tucker argued that slave labor had this crucial and notably practical advantage. By filling the demeaning stations of society, slavery permitted free men to command high wages, to feel the utmost confidence and self-respect, and to undertake public service.[40]

The South seemed to Tucker increasingly unique in being a bastion of republican strength. As many Northern states liberalized suffrage requirements in this period, laboring men with relatively little property were able to vote and to hold office. Even some Southern states joined in this movement. South Carolina and Virginia, for the present moment anyway, resisted change, and Tucker challenged his students at the end of 1834 to keep Virginia strong. Though *"publicly"* Northerners chided Virginians for what they called "aristocratic features" of government, *"privately"* observers looking south admonished Old Dominion statesmen to profit by Northern error and to hold fast to their more tried and tested institutions. Thus Tucker met head-on the continuing charge that slavery and republican liberty were paradoxical and incompatible. Not only did liberty coexist with slavery, free government depended on it. "When power has marched unchecked and unchallenged over the prostrate democracy of free labor and universal suffrage," he declared in his lectures, it has always found in Virginia "the most formidable barriers to its progress."[41]

Such references were on the whole scholarly and emotionally contained. By the fall of Tucker's second year of teaching, his expressions in favor of slavery had grown more moving. No doubt he felt himself prodded into taking this more exposed stance. In reviewing two books on slavery—one by the writer James Kirke Paulding, an unusually friendly Northerner, and the other a polemic "vindicating" the South from the "treason and fanaticism" of abolitionists—Tucker took note of the rising pitch of antislavery and anti-Southern agitation. He thought it was based more than anything on the dreams Northern reformers like the Reverend Charles Grandison Finney had of perfecting human nature. How could anyone look attentively and understandingly at this perfectionist-inspired abolitionism, asked Tucker in the essay readers of the *Messenger* saw in the spring of 1836, "without deep and anxious interest?" He spoke of the calumnies put forth and the wrongs meditated by reformers who sought to destroy the South "under the mask of Christian Charity and Brotherly Love."[42]

Attacking such hypocrisy, Tucker pointed out that slavery, not abolitionism, was the result of true charity and mutual love. In the Southern arrangement between black slave and white master, he saw the hand of God. Differences between whites and blacks, for example, neatly complemented one another. Reciprocating the loyal devotion of the slave—a loyalty peculiar to blacks—the slaveholder took care to treat the slave in a Christian manner, and to Christianize the black man in the process. The emotions this situation engaged were like those between nurse and child or, ambiguously, between brothers. Far more than simply "patriarchal," Tucker explained, these sentiments belonged "to a class of feelings 'by which the heart is made better.'"[43]

V

Returned to the tidewater region that he had known as a boy and installed at the old college, Tucker believed himself a symbol of continuity, a link with the past. In truth he was a reflection of change, the exponent of a tidewater society, especially of its elite, which many years earlier had been fruitful and confident and now was crouched in defense. At one level Tucker represented this change because he played a part in voicing the proslavery position a great many other Virginians now shared with him. Earlier, his appeal on behalf of Southern rights had attacked the protective tariff and the expense of a remote, growing government—the inequities of a federal system becoming oppressive. In the environment of Williamsburg his indignation rang in proslavery tones—doubtless in part because of Dew's influence on the new law professor, but also because Virginia had special meaning for Tucker. Once back there, it was easy to view abolitionism as a threat to her safety. Tucker was also moved by what he perceived as a tactical switch of an old cultural enemy. "Yankeys," who represented the antithesis of Southern values and who for self-gain repeatedly had tried to smudge constitutional limits on federal power, now openly threatened to abolish what Tucker had concluded was "the basis of all our institutions."[44]

One might have supposed that Tucker was simply parroting provincial and class defenses, but certainly there was substance and lineage to his thought. For one thing, his republican upbringing had put him on guard against distant attempts to meddle in local affairs and had ingrained a belief that men should bend self-will and selfish interest to the higher good of the commonweal. He was, furthermore, a Burkean of sound credentials. Long before lower Virginia required the manning of academic battlements, Tucker had taken from Burke the lesson that legislators should try only what was practicable, avoiding the use of abstract theory in facing actual problems, and above all respecting tradition—the "temper" and habits of a community. As a student of Burke's own sources, including Montesquieu and Coke, Tucker since a young man had held firmly to the belief that antiquity brought legitimacy, that truth lay with the "immemorial" and that wisdom and prudence rested on past experience. Perhaps more than anything, Tucker's faith formed his thinking. As a godly man, he believed that the hand of Providence was at work in earthly affairs and therefore that bondage had its place in a divine plan that would ultimately provide everyone caught up in slavery the means to salvation.

Sincere as Tucker's adherence was to these ideas, they did present logical difficulties. His thinking and lectures drew on common-sense realism and romantic feeling. Though both intuition and sentiment supported his reliance on nonrational urges to truth, together they created problems. The society Tucker wanted Virginia to resemble was a fantasy, a wish based on the idealized past. Yet common sense, a prosaic empiricism, taught him that what was sensible, especially what was concrete, was firmer ground for action and belief. Thus a split opened in Tucker's thinking between the imperatives of nostalgia and present actuality. In different form it became a more serious problem involving principle and time—elements of which were contained in his sources. Colliding with Burke's pristine past was the progress Burke said was ordained by God; Blackstone's common law was supposed to be both immutable yet adaptable. Tucker's thinking built on this uncertain ground. He wanted to preserve principles that apparently recognized providential change in the face of changes he found disconcerting. When he said Southern responsibility for the black men extended through "God's appointed time," he gave away the game. How much time passed before changes were discernible as divinely sanctioned was the point in question. If government grew organically out of society and if laws reflected the character of society, laws should embody social change, and the majority of Virginians in 1835 might have decided the fate of slavery in the state.[45]

The ambiguities of Tucker's thinking were those other Virginians shared. Past and actuality, principle and progress pulled in opposite directions. Wary of rejecting revolutionary ideals, tidewater and Southside Virginians all the same contradicted them or selected from them carefully. At the 1829–30 convention, western delegates, calling for reapportionment of the Assembly, spoke eloquently of the rights of men; easterners, as if to deny change, expected their neighbors in the developing west to recognize instead of the principle of equality that of property—to the extent that slave holdings counted toward heavier eastern representation. The stablest self-government, said supporters of the leasehold franchise, resulted from the rule of men who owned the land. Yet this view denied propertyless workers, new to the city, a hand in what everyone proclaimed was a government of the people. Abstractions in the Virginia Bill of Rights were acceptable as far as they went, defenders of slavery admitted in the 1832 legislative debates, but history had demonstrated their practical limits.[46]

These twists and turns were by no means peculiar to the ideas Virginia slaveholders employed in the 1830s. Nor was Tucker unusual in holding together in his mind beliefs that could work at cross purposes. But such contradictions tend to resolve themselves by giving direction to new thoughts, and Tucker's own dilemma as the son of a prominent revolutionary helped make his case illuminating of his generation of Virginians. Like them, only more obviously than they, he wrestled with himself in the presence of an unrealized goal. In the mind of his father, blacks were fully men, and men—despite their acquired differences—were equal in a secular sense that made slavery a patent evil; the removal of slavery from all the United States, "the restoration of the blessings of liberty to those oppressed in bondage,"[47] was the fondest hope St. George Tucker had for the new republic. His younger son demonstrated that ideals have a way of souring. Never quite reachable, set aside because of racial fears and practical problems, this vision of the revolutionary generation haunted the next. Tucker had to contend with the tyranny of a decaying dream.

The republic St. George Tucker had hoped to create called for changes his son could not admit; changes Beverley Tucker could not control imperiled what remained of his father's world. At Charlotte Court House, during the years when he might have blamed the egalitarian shifts that thwarted him on the principles of self-government that the elder Tucker professed, the young lawyer had begun fashioning a solution to this problem. Rather than turning his anger on his father, he had declared that revolutionary concepts of patriotism and republicanism had become perverted by "the hacks of the votaries of passion," as he said, "& the hunters after office and power."[48] In Beverley's mind leveling tendencies were therefore the abandonment of old faith, apostasy.

Now caught between the oppression of unattainable virtue and the pressing need for cultural survival, Tucker in similar fashion placed the onus of fatherly repudiation on the intellectual and social currents that hastened change and that, like perfectionism, seemed to upset tolerance, proportion, and order. Tucker's denunciation of perfectionism had the honed edge of frustration. The belief that men were capable of moral progress bringing them to holiness, "even as God is holy," Tucker saw as blasphemy, the height of spiritual arrogance. Perfectionism was pretension;

it was also delusion. Borrowing the words of the French anti-Jacobin poet Alphonse de Lamartine, Tucker declared the cruel truth that man was not so capable of education as philosophers imagined. "Let research discover, let science teach, let art practice what it may," he observed ruefully; man was feeble, humble, bound to earthly unhappiness, and subject to forces he could not understand. Yet the worst of it was that perfectionism was impudent. Since the days of the revolutionary fathers "great light has risen on the world," he sarcastically told students in his first year of teaching; the sons of those statesmen—Northern antislavery reformers and even some Virginians—now seemed to find fault with them for tolerating slavery. These younger people mocked the accommodation of their fathers, renouncing the "sins" of those forebears to whom by God's command men owed honor in life and reverence in death.[49]

Loath to follow this example, Tucker instead proclaimed filiopiety all the more insistently. Let the sacrilegious "desecrate and demolish the tombs of their fathers," he said; let them build monuments to their own praise.[50] He would pass along to his students teachings in law and government that it was especially important to portray as the faith of their fathers. Having laid the mantle of paternal orthodoxy on the institutions of Virginia, having condemned their critics as defilers of graves, Tucker could view himself— and he stood a chance of being accepted—as a custodian of the past and defender of the reasonable.

CHAPTER SIX

"Checking the Car of Destiny"

ALL THE NATIONS that ever had enjoyed liberty, Tucker taught his law students, passed through an appointed cycle. Though in the first flush of self-rule men guarded their freedom with jealous devotion, before long the prosperity of liberty "debauched the mind" and the pursuit of gain became the ruling passion of society. Demagogues then won popular favor by spreading about the spoils of the public treasury. Panderers seduced citizens into wearing "badges of party and trappings of distinction." Tucker described this period of decay with all the color and detail of an eyewitness. It was the time of tumultous elections, mob rule, of leaders drunk with ambition and rabble drunk with flattery and alcohol. The decline of virtue had proceeded dangerously far. Just the same it might be possible, he told his classes, to devise a means of "checking the car of destiny in its fatal career," to postpone the day when the liberty and happiness of Virginia would "but furnish school-boys' themes in distant lands."[1] Perhaps individual men could, by sheer moral resolve and force of will, divert the course of history. Tucker thought he might be one of these men.

I

"If the esteem of the wise and the good, and the confidence of the public is honor," Tucker wrote his wife Lucy in the fall of 1835, "I never gained so much of it in any one year of my life as the last." To lower Virginians he and Dew were pillars of the old college, where enrollment after 1834 began a steady and prosperous rise. Tucker rejoiced that he was no longer the unknown figure he had been when he returned to Virginia two years before. He had noticed the embarrassment this anonymity had caused his wife; at last, he said, he seemed to have earned the "deference and respect" that Lucy expected her husband to command.[2]

Tucker was especially pleased with his apparent drawing power. As he began his second year of teaching, the number of students in the law class grew to more than a dozen. They were, like William and Mary students generally in the second quarter of the nineteenth century, virtually all Southerners, almost exclusively Virginians, and overwhelmingly men from the tidewater area.[3] Tucker's pupils were products of rural Virginia and came from families that in many cases had suffered all the trials of economic stagnation and political unease so irksome to Tucker. Fathers of these law students shared the professor's alarm at "the progress of dissolution" in political affairs and the loss of "youghful vigor" in the body politic; they agreed with Tucker that Virginia society was the victim either of moral, physical, or political decay "or a combination of them all."[4]

By asking sons of these Virginians to join evangelical piety with classical ideas about republican morality, Tucker made American virtue, public and private alike, matters of deep concern. During a half century of liberty, the country had known every conceivable earthly reward—Tucker had noted in 1826 and now repeated—but Americans hardly seemed happier as a result. He saw signs betraying "the distempered anguish of the mind" as surely as pale cheek and sunken eye announced disorders of the body. There were wide discrepancies between human laws and the law of God as revealed in Scripture. Tucker thought the lower classes wanting in temperance and industry, the higher classes lacking in sobriety and chastity. He further abhorred a prevalent "atheism of the heart" that resisted the reign of God not in theoretical but in practical, unintentional ways: while many Americans could point to a Bible on their shelves, few, he conjectured, opened it or read it.[5]

To deal with this decline in virtue Tucker made an appeal for Christian education. In a piece he wrote during his first year at William and Mary, he exhorted readers of the *Southern Literary Messenger* to make religious instruction of Virginia youth the "ratchet" that would secure any gains the preceding generation had made in "the business of evangelizing the world." Tucker went beyond a discussion of the need for such religious training to talk about the best approach to it. He condemned the "heavy lumber of theological learning" with the "nice and shadowy distinctions" that puzzled the understanding and afflicted the spirit; he admonished parents to let the "heads" of their children alone. The aim of moral education was not the "scholarly pretension" known as knowledge but the "*sense* of good and evil" growing out of sound moral surroundings. Salvation lay in a faith "by which the *heart* believeth with righteousness." Enlarging on the religious reflections he began in Missouri, and publishing some of them at last, Tucker argued in the *Messenger* that the reasons for faith were less important than its intensity.[6]

Tucker made his instruction in law a form of Christian education. His lectures warned that temptations to political evil, as with sin, were everywhere, traps that would drop unwatchful free men from their precarious grace. The work of the teacher, he had remarked several years before his William and Mary appointment, "whether political or religious," was not so much with immediate as ultimate concerns, with the larger questions that struck at purposes for existence or dealt with the survival of society. "When it is 'war or peace,' 'Heaven or Hell,'" he declared, the teacher had to do more than simply expound doctrine. He had to bear a message that would be visited on the very souls of his listeners.[7]

Tucker now told his law students that they composed the "body guard" of the goddess Liberty. They were, as he made clear in his first lecture and on countless occasions thereafter, to wield the "weapons" of the law in her defense, to be the men who would arrest the decay of republican principle as the manifest wages of sin. While Henry St. George Tucker spoke to his own law students about the need for enlightened leaders to exert "an ameliorating influence" in public affairs, to abide by orderly change and compromise, to learn "some moderation and forbearance," his younger brother at William and Mary girded warriors for apocalyptic battle.[8]

II

The surest way to hasten the day of deliverance was to build a separate nation; but how did one convince the nation that it was ready for building? Many Southerners in the summer of 1835 may have cheered the Charleston mob that burned abolitionist leaflets sent unsolicited through the mails. Politically the region still was far from united. Probably the majority of voters continued to count themselves Jackson Democrats. The opposition, organizing as Whigs, was strong in important places in the South. Centered in South Carolina was a Calhoun faction that had followed the senator out of the Democratic party during the tariff and nullification controversy. There were states' rights Whigs in Virginia who, like Tucker, were unsure of Calhoun. In Richmond the proadministration *Enquirer* tried to lull readers into accepting as Jackson's successor the crafty New Yorker, Martin Van Buren. Here was a possible opportunity. Tucker, so eager to bring the South together, and aware of Van Buren's shaky popularity there, believed Southerners might unite against the heir apparent. Reminding a Petersburg Whig that one could not fight Van Buren with an abstraction, he was one of the first to enlist in the movement to make Hugh Lawson White President.[9]

White, who was senator from Tennessee in the mid-1830s, appealed to the law professor both because of his reputation for unimpeachable integrity and because, as Lucy's uncle, he was Tucker's own relative as well. White had been cool toward the nullifiers but in Tucker's eyes was sound all the same; a member of the original Jackson coalition, White had parted ways with his old Tennessee friend over the President's partiality for Van Buren. Tucker had doubts that his uncle could carry the South, the only section warm to him, or even Virginia, where Whigs of the Clay stamp leaned toward the more malleable William Henry Harrison. But the Tennessean was a good excuse to proclaim principle and to call for concerted action. In the second half of 1835 Tucker spent much time writing letters extolling White's gentlemanly character, attending White meetings, and making an occasional speech in his behalf.[10]

For a short while White's fortunes seemed promising. Governor Tazewell wrote Tucker that he supported the labors of the Tennesseean's friends. There were encouraging words from John Taliaferro, the Whig congressman, and Tucker's Richmond friends were active in supporting White. South Carolina senator William C. Preston in Washington and James Hamilton in Charleston agreed with Tucker that Jackson was a despot and Van Buren a political magician. Duff Green labored in Washington to build an organization of principled men to halt Van Buren. Exchanging allusions to republican decay, members of this informal caucus harbored a hope that "far sighted" men of will could come together in support of the Tennessee gentleman. Still, White's antinullification votes in 1833 left his support in Charleston uneven. In Virginia, Harrison and White men divided in the 1835 elections, and voters gave the Jackson party a majority in the legislature. Tucker no doubt shared John Coalter's disgust at the prospect of Van Buren's election the following fall. When acting as Tucker's boyhood tutor, Coalter had described the lawyer's part in maintaining republican zeal in nearly lyrical terms. "As to politics," he now wrote, "*I give* them up, as I do the wheat crop—a total failure in both is the fate of Virginia."[11]

JAMES HENRY HAMMOND, c. 1840

Just as White's presidential hopes began to fade, James Henry Hammond, a first-term South Carolina congressman, cheered Tucker with the noise he needed to rouse would-be listeners in the South. The newcomer's background had not obviously prepared him for lasting fame. Of mixed New England and Carolina middle-class stock, Hammond had compiled a creditable record at South Carolina College and tried school teaching before his admission to the Columbia bar in 1828. Soon afterward he embarked in political life as an opponent of high tariffs and within several years had published a militant newspaper, placed himself at the cutting edge of nullification leadership, married into wealth, and opened a cotton plantation he called "Silver Bluff." In December 1835, newly arrived in Washington, Hammond entangled himself in a series of petitions demanding an end to slavery in the District of Columbia. While such petitions had become rather routine, usually submitted with disclaimers and tabled without comment, Hammond on December 18 called on the House to reject them altogether as unconstitutional and therefore impossible requests, the work of "ignorant fanatics." The young representative relished the part he played in this preelection maneuvering, taking the principled high ground that more seasoned politicians, including Calhoun, normally avoided. In February of the new year Hammond made a rousing argument for slavery as "the greatest of all the blessings which a kind Providence has bestowed upon our glorious region." Especially astonishing to Hammond's audience was his willingness to face squarely the subject of disunion. The instant Congress legislated on slavery, declared the twenty-eight-year-old legislator, he would abandon his seat, go home to preach disunion, and if necessary fight a civil war that would "sink the republic in blood." His was a "voice of thunder," he shouted, and it clapped loudly enough to be heard in Williamsburg.[12]

In the Southern fight against abolitionist mailings, antislavery petitions in Congress, and designs on slavery in the District, Tucker sensed the makings of a political din that might not only awaken the South to public events but also change their course. Hammond seemed to him the only man in Congress willing to raise such a racket, and inkling changed to certainty when Hammond obligingly sent Tucker a franked copy of his most blustering speech. Here at last was a politician of mettle. Unlike the ambitious, equivocating Calhoun—who had yet to answer a Tucker letter of the preceding summer—Hammond was bold, unyielding, and courteous. The law professor quickly fastened on this new friend, writing him the same day he received Hammond's address, then sending off a second letter the next day. Tucker, who had not met Hammond, explained that his openness was not rashness; he was addressing a brother in ideas, and what he wrote was for the eyes of "every true hearted Southern man." Were Tucker on the floor of Congress, he said, he would speak all that he had written and more.[13]

"If you people are prepared for your threatened crusade," Tucker advised Hammond and the South Carolina delegation, "now is the time and this is the topic." Abolitionism was providential; he hoped that antislavery agitators like Arthur and Lewis Tappan had finally, forcibly, opened the eyes of the South. The delegation should depart Washington for home, Tucker wrote, lead South Carolina out of the Union, seek the certain support of Britain and the probable help of France. South Carolina would form the nucleus of a new nation. If the federal government sent any military force to coerce the state, he was sure other Southerners would see that the objective was to destroy slavery and to "light the flames of servile war." If, on the other hand, the United States left South Carolina alone, the enviable prosperity of an independent Carolina would soon prompt the remaining Southern states to join the confederacy, wisened by their unhappy experiences in the old one, "homogeneous & united" in common conceptions and interests. Time was of the essence, urged Tucker. Before long men would cry once again that events had passed them by. Sound the alarm, he pleaded with Hammond: "There are many who think with me and decisive action anywhere would increase the number a hundred fold."[14]

But the South Carolina delegation did remain in Washington, and a crisis again passed. Instead of the birth of a new nation, certain ordinary things happened. First in the Senate, then in the House after much longer and more complicated wrangling, compromise and subterfuge quieted the issue of anti-slavery petitions. Because Van Buren was reluctant to commit himself on that awkward question, he and his strategists in February persuaded Henry L. Pickering, a Carolina congressman of hitherto solid reputation as a nullifier, to propose a settlement by which the House would refer all such memorials to a select committee with instructions to report that the federal government "ought not to interfere" with slavery in the District. Given a middle course, Southerners split. Hammond made splenetic attacks on Pickering for conceding the all-important point that, though it was inexpedient to do so, Congress might in fact interfere with slavery in the District.[15] Heartily approving Hammond's speech, Tucker recognized in this "inexpediency" reference a Trojan horse inside Southern defenses. Van Buren appeared stronger than ever.

III

Compromise in the Senate and concession in the House were all that remained of the gag-rule controversy in the spring of 1836. Isolation and loneliness colored Tucker's Williamsburg. To Lucy, who was visiting her parents in Missouri, he mailed letters that asked why her father remained a Jackson partisan. "We have given up our hearts to manworship," he concluded. "We shall sleep and wake in fetters." Not even the consoling missives of Hammond were available, for the young Carolinian had taken ill in mid-February, had left his seat, and was preparing to sail for Europe. Tucker tended to his gardening, a favorite pastime, and reworked his lecture notes. He also answered mail, much of it from Thomas W. White, the struggling, self-deprecating editor of the *Southern Literary Messenger*. Tucker had been supplying him with sketches of the frontier and a few book reviews, and White begged for more material.[16] Once again writing became a way to keep busy and to attract attention.

Partly through this willingness to write but mostly because of Tucker's extremist politics, he soon became part of a network of Southern separatists. Among them was Duff Green, whose *United States Telegraph* had carried the Virginian's attacks on the Force Bill and who, as an occasional visitor at the Tucker home, fascinated law students with his lively table conversation.

DUFF GREEN
in his antebellum years

Green had asked Tucker in 1835 to help prepare a collection of history, reading, rhetoric, and even arithmetic textbooks that would impress on young Southern minds the great blessings they enjoyed as freemen and their "high obligation to maintain [their] liberties." Together the two men hoped to persuade Judge Abel P. Upshur, the conservative from the Eastern Shore and another favorite at the Tucker household, to establish a review of Southern politics. Involved in this second plan was the Virginia publisher and agricultural reformer Edmund Ruffin, well known as an excitable hater of Northerners. Green and his Williamsburg friend also spoke of schemes that would place reliable states' rights men at editorial desks in Washington and Richmond.[17]

Tucker was convinced that the truth could make Southerners free; if Southerners realized that they were a peculiar people, they would separate from the North. His book reviews for the *Messenger,* so carping, so overdone, made arguments on behalf of an embattled minority. They also called for the preservation of a unique morality. In Europe and the North "grimace, obscenity and buffoonery" had triumphed over "taste and wit . . . sense and decency." Running through Tucker's disgressive essays, reaching a thousand or more readers, was the cry that "We in the South" could escape the corruption prevailing elsewhere. Southern literary men, having neither wish nor need for universal acclamation, had no intention of writing for the "perpetual motion" of changing manners and tastes. "We are absolutely sure," wrote Tucker after reading Edward Bulwer-Lytton's *Duchess de la Valliere,* "that in our unrefined, unenlightened, unpretending, uncanting community of white and black," such portrayals of depravity could scarcely draw together enough theatergoers to "pay the candle snuffer." Virginia had neither great cities, fashionable sinners, nor "mobs civil or literary." "We stand on our defense against imported innovations," Tucker declared, and if such prudery earned the ridicule of degenerate Europeans or Northerners," we are willing to stand condemned."[18]

Of Tucker's several attempts to define Southern manners and values, making that morality distinctive enough to justify nurturing it, the most ambitious were the two pieces of fiction that he published in 1836 and that gave him minor claim to a novelist's reputation. The first one to appear, a romance of Missouri and Virginia entitled *George Balcombe,*[19] surely was conceived in the West and was probably begun there. It wove itself around a flimsy structure of intrigue, pursuit, and capture. In opening the tale Tucker had his youthful narrator William Napier, a Virginian and a William and Mary graduate, meet George Balcombe while traveling on the Missouri frontier. The older man—also a Virginian schooled at the college—Tucker depicted as an established figure, an Indian fighter respected by friend and foe alike, a planter of exceptional wisdom and deep piety. In the course of enjoying Balcombe's hospitality, Napier discovered that he had been cheated out of his father's tidewater Virginia inheritance by a libertine named Montague, who happened to be in Missouri and who was one of Balcombe's rare enemies.

With the help of a crude but dependable corporal, a western Virginia native who resembled James Fenimore Cooper's Natty Bumppo, Napier and his new friend began a campaign to bring Montague to justice. During the chase Tucker took his reader to a revival meeting, furnished descriptions of the work and confusion of Missouri courts, and even included a realistic skirmish with Indians. When Montague escaped eastward to destroy evidence that could make Napier master of his family's estate, Tucker shifted the scene to Virginia, where a joyful reunion took place between the young man and his slaves and where Tucker set the scene for a dramatic conclusion. Struggle against injustice, the triumph of right, but above all acquaintance with Balcombe brought Napier education and maturity.

Like *Balcombe* in being sentimental and unpretentious, Tucker's second publication in the presidential election year was a highly controversial campaign tract. The title page of *The Partisan Leader* was wholly fictitious. Its author, "Edward William Sidney," was a by-line Tucker contrived for himself; the publication date, 1856, was part of the ruse announced in the subtitle, *A Tale of the Future.* It was a story Tucker and his secret publisher, Duff Green, hoped would produce consternation among Van Buren Democrats and bring about the awakening of Southerners.[20]

The future Tucker foretold in this unfinished account was one of sectional strife and Southern independence. The time, in his imagination, was 1848–49. The lower South had just left the Union, peacefully seceding in protest as President Martin Van Buren managed deviously to gain a fourth term in office. Having hesitated in that moment of decision, Virginia next found herself fighting a guerrilla war with the federal government in her attempt to join the happier, more prosperous, and sounder Southern league. Van Buren, loathsome and conniving, surrounded with all the frills of monarchy and supported by the worst conceivable sycophants, tried relentlessly to crush the Virginia insurgents.

Revolt against tyranny and war for independence caused a division within the noble Trevor family of Virginia, a split that furnished Tucker with his meager plot and provided a backdrop for his frequent digressions on states' rights constitutionalism, free-trade economics, and proslavery paternalism. Arthur Trevor began the story by leaving home in eastern Virginia and traveling to the southwestern mountains of the state to join the rebels. The reader learned in a flashback of several hundred pages that Arthur's father, Hugh Trevor, was a moderate Jacksonian whose love for the Union only recently had given way to an acknowledgment of Van Buren's chicanery. His oldest son had attended West Point as a Jackson appointee, had become an ardently loyal career officer, and now for political reasons led elements of the army sent to occupy and pacify Virginia in late 1848.

Tucker's leading figures provided carefully drawn, though not complex, character studies. Douglas Trevor, another of Hugh's sons, had—like his brother—served in the army but had resigned his commission over a question of honor that was instructive both of Trevor manners and Van Buren treachery. Disillusioned with his commander-in-chief, Douglas at this point came under the influence of two men. One was his uncle, Bernard Trevor, a punctilious gentleman of gruff militance but also of frankness and kindly warmth; the other, known only as B——, was a South Carolinian who acted as a kind of Southern seer and strategy advisor to the Virginians. Bernard and B— persuaded Douglas to head a guerrilla band in a war of liberation, and it was Douglas's base that Arthur Trevor joined in 1849. With the aid of a wily Virginia mountaineer who served as guide, Douglas routed the federal "bluecoats" at a series of sharp engagements before he was suddenly captured in his hour of triumph. The partisan leader was on his way to stand trial in a Star Chamber of Van Buren's creation when Tucker left readers awaiting the next installment.

In several respects Tucker's romances were period pieces. Homely, idealizing the past, the pleasantry of country life, and the ways of slave-holding society, Tucker's fiction resembled the work of John Pendleton Kennedy, the Baltimore lawyer whose *Swallow Barn* and *Horseshoe Robinson* were popular at this time; the Tucker stories were also like the writings of a Virginia country doctor, Alexander Caruthers, whose *Cavaliers of Virginia* appeared in 1834-35 and told of revolutionary heroism in the tidewater.[21] Tucker's books also gave evidence of Sir Walter Scott's influence on American fiction of the day. Tucker made no effort to conceal the likeness *Balcombe* and *The Partisan Leader* bore to Scott's *Waverley* romances, with their colorful bravado, self-consciously authentic manners, and stylized characters. Relying, as did Scott, on a proto-realism of setting and speech, Tucker created incredible people in laboriously detailed surroundings.[22]

Moreover, Tucker's romances conformed to the critical presuppositions of Scottish common-sense thought. For Tucker, as well as for most early-nineteenth-century American writers and critics, literature was less creative than serviceable, less expressive than judicial. Schooled in Hugh Blair's standard text in rhetoric and familiar with those organs of conservative Scottish criticism, *Blackwood's Magazine* and the *Edinburgh Review,* Tucker wrote reviews and fiction drawing on the belief that art ought to reflect prevailing standards of taste; good taste meant delicacy and refinement, the qualities that would become "Victorian" later in the century. The writer, as Tucker explained in an 1835-36 exchange of letters with Edgar Allan Poe, then one of the editorial assistants in the *Messenger* office,[23] was to be paternal, protective, corrective. Thus Tucker's criticism and fiction had a watchdog quality about it. His characterization was unambiguously instructive, his language was pure to a fault (he would not stain the paper with the profanity of one villain), and love affairs—except when he illustrated the ruin of lust—were rigorously innocent.[24]

Yet regenerative purpose, more than aesthetic standards, explained the tone of Tucker's writing, and here his work departed from the ordinary. There were plausible developments he wanted to forestall, deliberate social and political points he wanted to make. In the wake of Jackson's two administrations, a multiterm President—served by officials devotedly loyal, not to the country or the Constitution, but to him personally—was a distinct possibility that Tucker rightly feared. The use of federal courts to implement political policy was a maneuver any President could execute; the federal creation and use of special courts—"Star Chamber" or military tribunal—was also conceivable and just as sinister. No President in Tucker's lifetime succeeded in bending the judiciary to his will in the way Tucker described, but his insistence that one could do so revealed something of his frame of mind in 1836 and suggested the approach this law professor took to the federal courts. In Tucker's digressions on free trade he spoke bitterly of the effect the protective tariff had on Virginia and called for an end to this misgovernment. Furthermore, *Balcombe* and *The Partisan Leader* were sermons on true nobility that spoke to Virginians of the decline of public leadership.[25]

In both these narratives, and especially in *Balcombe,* Tucker gave readers a glimpse of the society he had hoped to establish in Missouri and now wanted to restore and to isolate in the South. Besides being struck by the harmony in the God-loving, self-sufficient plantation community Tucker lionized in *Balcombe,* readers could hardly miss noticing the moral strength of his leading figure. George Balcombe embodied all the qualities that justified and sustained Tucker's vision of the ideal society. Balcombe was a man of holiness, kindness, generosity; from him all the persons in his care derived spiritual and physical strength. Balcombe was at once a descendant of Plantagenet nobility and a republican saint, thereby combining potency and self-control. He was an archetype of the Virginia gentleman, a peculiar man "in whom the spirit of freedom was so blended with loyalty" to the original principles of self-government that the chief dangers to a republic, servility and selfishness, were unthinkable. Balcombe was a philosopher-prince whose intellectual power held Napier spellbound and whose "hardiness of thought and freedom of speech" quickly fatigued lesser minds. Balcombe could lead men into battle as easily as he could hold forth on the nature of honor, instinct, religion, gentility, and slavery. Although Balcombe scrupulously took "no part in the scramble for office" in Missouri, men recognized in him a natural leader.[26] There was little subtlety in these lessons.

Less deliberately, Tucker betrayed in *Balcombe* and *The Partisan Leader* his concern that men did not defer to their natural betters and his uncertainty therefore whether the harmony he described could be preserved, or even existed. Though in these novels he praised western Virginians as practical, hard-fighting, loyal to their slaveholding neighbors, he did not treat lower-class whites as equals. Both Balcombe's useful ruffian, John Keizer, and the partisan leader's scout, Jacob Schwartz, were physically inferior to lower Virginians. They were short men with small eyes, pinched features, and dark complexions. Unattractive though these mountaineers were, better-educated Virginians depended on them—their buckskin glazed with grease and mottled with blood—to interrogate and lead other ruffians, disembowel deer, and show the way through the wilderness.[27]

It was a problem for the aristocratic Balcombe and B—— to win the support of such brutish men, and to resign themselves to their reliance upon
them. In Tucker's earlier romance, Balcombe obtained Keizer's aid simply
by lending support to the frontiersman when everyone else in the locale
dismissed and distrusted him. The narrator smoothed over differences between the two men by emphasizing the similarities of their intuitive "operations of mind." By the time Tucker wrote *The Partisan Leader,* the western
Virginian was considerably more in debt to his tidewater benefactor. B——
had "picked up" Schwartz nearly forty years earlier, Douglas Trevor learned,
"a little, dirty, ragged boy, without money, without friends, without education, and without principles." B—— had supplied all these wants, he contended. Would the westerner recognize his debt? Of course he would, B——
assured himself; "he is bound to me by gratitude such as few men are capable
of." The stakes in the relationship were high for the aristocratic Virginians,
for whatever "large experience in knavery" Schwartz had, it was in the mountains where these westerners made their home that the Virginia rebels sought
sanctuary; only with the loyal support of the west could the cavalier expect
to meet outside threats.[28]

Tucker's claim on the loyalty and respect of the Virginia mountaineer was
too loudly proclaimed to be entirely convincing. He was flattering, but even
more hopeful. Although B—— told Trevor that as partisan chief he would
command Schwartz "body and soul," that the westerners would be devoted
to his service "without envy, jealousy, or grudging," Schwartz had independence of mind that left his "leaders" queasy. Schwartz's impertinent
questioning of Arthur Trevor, when the lad approached the partisans' hide-
away, made the young aristocrat's face blush, and the mountaineer's unwillingness to take Arthur's identity on his gentleman's word hinted at the
sectional antagonism and democratic lack of deference that made Tucker
increasingly anxious. It was uncertain that Schwartz did know what he was
"fit" for; it was unclear whether poor whites did know their place in
Tucker's social hierarchy.[29]

On another level Tucker's romances of 1836 contained the recurring
theme that individual men could, in fact, arrest the car of destiny. The
heroes of *Balcombe* and *The Partisan Leader* were heroic beyond the needs
of a literary device. They were, as Arthur Trevor said of his brother the
partisan commander, endowed "with almost superhuman powers." Because
Tucker hoped he might assume these heroic proportions, his principal characters were thin disguises that told his readers, as if he desperately wanted
them to know, what he thought of himself. George Balcombe, who resembled Randolph at his best, was also—as Poe suggested—Tucker as he wanted
to become. Further, in *The Partisan Leader* Tucker made clearer than he
ever had before the differences between "head" and "heart," and in so
doing said a great deal about himself and the way he expected to arrest

corruption in the history of the republic. Throughout his life he had viewed himself as somehow divided between mind and feeling, and B——, wise, deliberate, and learned, represented Tucker as a sharp-minded strategist. Like Tucker for the moment, B—— bided his time. Keeping himself "out of harm's way, and free from all suspicion," B—— told Douglas Trevor that when the time came he proposed "to act a part which shall make me a conspicuous mark for the malice or policy of our enemies." Furtively, while pretending to keep himself "on this side of the line" of propriety, B—— and Tucker labored for the insurgent cause.[30]

That portion of his divided self from which Tucker drew the greatest sustenance, however, was the side Bernard Trevor depicted for his readers. Instead of biding his time, instead of controlling his passions, Tucker really wanted to embody the pluck of Randolph, the hair-trigger jealousy of liberties that distinguished English gentry and true Virginia gentlemen. At bottom, he conceived of himself as a man of "heart" who, like Bernard, was quick and intuitive in his conceptions, strong in his convictions, and "habitually satisfied with his conclusions." Like Tucker obscure, Bernard had a hasty temper that gave him the appearance of being rash; his ill success in life "seemed to justify" his being unheeded, loved by few and "misunderstood by many."[31]

But Bernard became a surprise hero in the midst of crisis, and while his ebullience neared the comic in *The Partisan Leader,* Tucker was deadly serious. Bernard, deficient in the "cold prudence which takes advantage of circumstances," nonetheless "was eminently gifted with that more vigorous faculty *which makes them.*" Earlier neglected and ridiculed, now in 1849 old and ill, Bernard virtually by himself set off the Virginians' "war of right and liberty." Marching a small band of men on the polling place near his Southside home, he broke up the attempt of federal troops to fix a critical election for state legislators. It was a telling fantasy. Armed with pistols and a dirk, face flushed with anger, Tucker's Bernard forced the cowardly politico who had withdrawn under Van Buren's pressure to confess his sin and to stand aside. "AND I AM A CANDIDATE," cried the old hero with gusto. "I am a candidate," Trevor repeated as his friends hoisted him onto their shoulders, "on behalf of VIRGINIA, her RIGHTS, and her SOVEREIGNTY."[32]

Assurances of romantic heroism enabled the real-life Bernard to pass off the moderation of his older brother as wrongheaded meekness. *The Partisan Leader* commented sardonically on the relationship the Tucker brothers shared and the comparison many Virginians apparently drew between them. Tucker's sketch of the elder Trevor brother Hugh, so distinctly a likeness of the legislator and jurist Henry St. George, carried the message that there was hidden danger in responsible caution. Hugh was prosperous, handsome, talented, amiable, influential in society, and successful in all his undertakings.

"Wealth had flowed into his coffers, and honors had been showered on his head." Still, Hugh was a man of faint heart and uncertain mind. He "had sometimes deemed it wise to compromise when men of less cautious temper would have found safety in prudent boldness," and the plight of Virginia in 1849 stemmed from the heed citizens mistakenly paid to such hesitating leadership. In this "tale of the future" Beverley surmounted Henry at last. Hugh came to regret his "former overcaution," his service in the cause of peaceful union, and to change his mind about his younger brother. With the outbreak of hostilities, Bernard, in Hugh's eyes, was no longer "inconsiderate and imprudent." Tucker had Hugh tell Bernard's daughter that her father was a noble, generous, and wise man. "I would to God," added he, sighing heavily, "that I had half his wisdom."[33]

Except for Green's botching of its distribution, Tucker's book might have struck readers as the campaign excesses of an ardent Whig. Few of them, when *The Partisan Leader* reached bookstores in late 1836, could have realized the depth of its writer's bitterness or the extent of his efforts to make its prophecies self-fulfilling. Yet Tucker's letters to Hammond during the abolitionist petition debates in the spring of 1836 frankly laid the scenario for the crisis that would cheat fate, alter history, and return him to his rightful political influence. Men of "*will* . . . decision of character, boldness of zeal" would have to organize the provisional confederacy, Tucker had written the congressman. In the "day of danger" the men "whom God had qualified and placed in condition to lead, and have the courage to call on others to follow, are always followed."[34]

IV

Tucker was growing impatient. Men his own age, he wrote his favorite nephew, St. George Coalter, seemed intent on "dying out of the way before the crisis comes, & so leaving that job to the next generation." Failing to escape through death, the cautious seemed to reap reward for remaining alive and moderate: early in 1837 news spread that at the July commencement William and Mary would confer an honorary doctor of laws degree on Henry Tucker, whom his younger brother had recently portrayed as misguided and overrated. If the forecast of Southern revolt in the late 1840s was accurate, the maker of that prediction would then be nearing his sixty-fifth year. While Bernard Trevor was lame and ached from the gout, Tucker had evidence of his own advancing years in frequent aches and pains.[35]

Douglas Trevor, the partisan leader who gallantly led the Virginia guerrillas from their western stronghold to threaten enemy-held Richmond, demonstrated Tucker's belief that he could persuade the next generation of Virginians to turn about and face their destiny. The young gentlemen of the tidewater were to be Tucker's arm in his incapacity. To capture their interest he had to stage a kind of revival; "the South can do nothing without Virg[ini]a," one states' rights friend wrote him, and she appeared "irredeemably lost." By using history and creating myth, by employing both the shrewdness of B—— and the feeling of Douglas' lovable uncle Bernard, Tucker hoped to kindle interest in Virginia culture, to engage the enthusiasm of young Virginia, and thus to build an army of Douglas Trevors.[36]

History was Tucker's chief intellectual avocation, and it was partly an antiquarian interest. In early 1837 Tucker joined Edmund Ruffin in soliciting old Virginia letters and scattered papers that Ruffin hoped to publish before they deteriorated and were lost to later generations.[37] But history was also a fund of experience that gave grounding to Tucker's constitutional and legal ideas, a vein to be mined for principles. In the spring of 1837 he busily began assembling materials for a projected documentary history of Virginia in the late colonial and revolutionary period. The plan grew out of his disgust with the case Northerners Joseph Story and George Bancroft each had made for the national character of the colonial struggle against Britain. To set the record straight, and to dissuade Virginians of this nationalist view of the Constitution and the federal government, Tucker had to do a little original research. In March he wrote to Richmond for copies of the proceedings of revolutionary Virginia conventions and for other papers pertaining to the 1775–76 decision to rebel; he sent to Washington asking the help of Richard Crallé, a friendly newspaperman and longtime associate in the states' rights cause in obtaining copies of early Continental Congress documents. The sources he assembled and the use he made of the college library satisfied him that Virginia announced her independence on May 15, 1776, considerably before the Continental Congress adopted the Declaration of Independence. Virginia "by her own sole and separate act . . . took her stand among the nations of the earth."[38]

By commemorating each year the independence resolutions of the revolutionary Virginia assembly, Tucker hoped to replace July 4 and the nationalism it encouraged with May 15—to make reverence for the Virginia past and character a regular part of life in the state. Taking his case for a new holiday to the Petersburg Lyceum, Tucker wrote ahead directing Ruffin to hold the meeting on that very date. He then asked how many of his "large & respectable" group of listeners knew its significance. Tucker made it clear to Petersburg citizens that the independence of Virginia on May 15, 1776 set her off from the other colonies, who remained in "degrading thraldom," and with whom she had in the beginning positively no political union. The people of Virginia were sovereign then and remained so in the late 1830s. Their loyalties, preached Tucker, ought to reflect their primary allegiance to Virginia; the federal government was a creature of state citizenry, not its master.[39]

Tucker's concept of history allowed him some mythical license. Legend was not history, he admitted, but while reviewing a volume of Jared Sparks's *Writings of George Washington* Tucker argued that there were truths greater than historical accuracy. The value of Sparks's collection was not in its factual detail, but in its inspirational account of the way Washington disciplined himself as a young man and trained for greatness. Washington's early life and letters allowed later Virginians to "know him as he was," but more important "to mould [them]selves by his precepts and example." History was a source of moral lessons.[40]

Besides, the past had revitalizing power. By recalling the halycon days of William and Mary, Tucker thought he could bring his students' sense of historical responsibility to feverish intensity. In the halls of what he described in his first lecture as a "venerable but decayed seminary," students trod in the footsteps and sat in the very seats of men whom Virginians now pointed to as their most distinguished statesmen, jurists, and philosophers. Conscious of the backwater location of the college, and all too aware that the University of Virginia—with abundant state support—had replaced William and Mary as the leading academic institution in the commonwealth, Tucker bewailed the neglect Virginians paid this old "nurse of heroes." He vowed to restore the academy of his youth "to all its former prosperity and usefulness," and in its plight he admonished the young men in his law classes to relight the lamp of tradition and honor that once had made William and Mary great.[41]

Tucker tried, furthermore, to make love of Virginia a binding force among her citizens, the center of a kind of cult. He invited his earliest students to take up the cross of their homeland: to cleave to Virginia, to be alive as he was to all her interests, to be jealous of her honor and resentful of her wrongs, and to partake in all her struggles. He asked students to turn their hearts toward the Muse of Virginia in devotion as the Moslems turned their faces toward the tomb of the prophet in prayer. More than ever Tucker referred to his state as a "country." In *George Balcombe* he described a "sort of freemasonry" among Virginians who found themselves in other lands, a sense of origin that only the insensitive failed to prize; in *The Partisan Leader,* the "proud war cry" of Douglas Trevor's band of guerrillas was "OLD VIRGINIA FOR EVER."[42]

Tucker's *Partisan Leader* and public lectures were especially appealing to Virginians who had grown to manhood in the turbulent, frustrating 1830s. Testifying to Tucker's popularity among these would-be partisans, the secretary of the Lynchburg Young Men's Society referred to him early in 1838 as a "living oracle" of the opinions that were "coming to the rescue in these days of degeneracy." Invited to speak to the association that summer, Tucker was unable to deliver his address in person, but the essay he sent was read to hearty applause and demands that White print it in the *Messenger.*[43]

Tucker aimed to make the youth of Lynchburg a lighthouse of patriotic militance and local pride, and the address was important because it established a technique Tucker often used afterward. He told them first that freedom was fundamentally a matter of self-discipline, of placing moral chains on one's appetite (in Burke's phrase), so that justice could supersede rapacity, soundness and sobriety displace baser instincts of vanity and presumption. Since there was an "insoluble alliance between freedom and virtue," the preservation of republican government depended upon the strengthening of every incentive to selflessness. Love of community was foremost among such incentives.[44]

Tucker entreated the assembled young men to restore the lost grandeur of Virginia that he painstakingly pronounced dead. He beckoned them, shamed them. Patrick Henry's spirit was still; the cannon at Yorktown were rusty. In the eyes of her natives, Virginia was now nothing. Her glorious deeds were forgotten. Pride of sovereignty and independence men now derided as the "apery of children" and the business of cranks. But "O! gentlemen, can this be so?" Tucker suddenly demanded of his listeners; "Can you look thus coldly on the past?" They themselves could reverse the course of things, standing around Virginia as her hour of trial approached, guarding her "like a wall of fire." For these young persons of "incipient manhood"—whom Tucker said he would treat as grown men so as to bring them quickly to the "real graces" of maturity—adversity was to bring thrilling togetherness and the self-abnegation of combat. To us who remain, intoned Tucker, "it belongs to minister at the altar—to feed the flame—*and if need be, to supply the sacrifice.*"[45]

Certainly it helped Tucker's cause that there was an enemy against whom young Virginians needed to close ranks. In his paper for the Lynchburg youth group he gave his often-expressed hatred for the calculating and selfish Northerners a foundation in history. New Englanders originally had turned their backs on all the comforts of civilized life, all the "dear delights of home," for the sake of what Tucker considered a perfectionist conscience. Austere, brittle, restrictive, Puritans in no way resembled the liberty-loving, sensible Cavaliers of the Chesapeake, who had enjoyed living and understood the warm side of human nature. Without attachment to rich soil and missing the trust and cooperation rural life instilled, Northerners could understand neither the Southern white nor black, nor the "unsophisticated affection" that bound them together. The differences between Virginian and Yankee, as Tucker wrote in *The Partisan Leader,* were differences of light and darkness, heat and cold, life and death.[46] They were differences of heart and head. To be a Virginian was emphatically not to be a Yankee.

Tucker repeated the skillful bombast of the Lynchburg address—the call to dangerous mission, the warning of outside enmity, the confirmation of community rectitude—before other groups of Virginians. His principal audiences, however, were college men, and his entire reward was the few

honors they could bestow. Before the Franklin Literary Society of Randolph-
Macon College he made a grandiloquent plea for the study of political science
by all young Virginians, an address that appeared as a booklet in the summer
of 1840 and received condescending criticism in the leading national arbiter
of letters, the *North American Review*. Tucker's message to Randolph-Macon
students approached mystical fervency: "Ye are yourselves the temples both
of freedom and of Him who made you free," Tucker advised; "Beware lest
you profane them." When he appeared later at Hampden-Sidney College, by
request of the Philanthropic Society there, he alerted students that "the seeds
of death" were germinating in the republic and that the most important tasks
before the youth of Virginia was to "arrest their growth." No people could
be free who did not *"in the strongest sense of the word,* WILL *to be so,"* he
insisted in this presentation, also published in pamphlet form, "and Government *is* a matter of choice."[47]

Honorary membership in these and similar campus service and debating
societies and the regularity of Tucker's speaking schedule suggest that he did
stir the communal memory in a section of the state where consciousness of
power lost, of status surrendered, and of wealth declined was part of the
heritage parents passed on to their children. In the hard times that followed
the financial depression of 1837, this awareness was particularly keen, under-
lining comments Tucker made even before the Panic struck. "Look at the
ruins which strew the face of your lower country, the remains of churches
and the fragments of tombstones," B— told Douglas Trevor in *The Partisan
Leader*. "Ask for the descendants of the men whose names are sculptured on
those monuments and their present condition will tell you that [Virginia's]
prosperity has passed away." Furthermore, Tucker's call for devotion to
Virginia was in part an attempt to unite a state still divided by sectional ill
feeling, whose lieutenant-governor in 1836 warned of the need for "a closer
association, moral and political," between east and west and for "a greater
equalization of advantages (to the most neglected portion of the State). . . ."[48]

But Tucker's appeal to young men lay chiefly in their being young, in
their need, especially during troubled times, to find a way of explaining the
world to themselves. The ideology Tucker offered them was perfectly suited
to this need. It was easily understandable, widely applicable, and a formula
for bold action that allowed every joiner to participate in the heroics of
crisis. It was Tucker's office, he said, to produce men suited to the emer-
gencies that would later "summon them from obscurity, and marshal them
to their places as leaders of men, and *masters* of circumstances and destiny."
His students left Williamsburg convinced that they were part of a movement
that would enable them to overcome the forces that had humbled their
fathers. One former student, assuring Tucker that he had received all his
ideas of government from him, boasted that he and young men like him
could "wrest Virginia from her mire and degradation . . . and exhibit her

once more to the world cleansed and purified. . . ." Richard Cocke, beginning law practice in Powhatan County, spoke of Tucker's "higher destiny" than material or political gain; his was the "far nobler aim" of stimulating "Virginia's rising youth."[49]

The professor's appeal to emotion was effective in itself, for it was a technique that resonated with young men's heated impulses toward self-proving independence. He was a comrade in that effort. "You are 54 in years," said one loyal student, "but not more than 21 in feeling." To feel was to talk lustily of charging forward into action, and such talk was catching. Only the general adoption of Tucker's principles, wrote a spokesman for the Lynchburg Young Men's society, could dispel the clouds that obscured "the glory of our Ancient Commonwealth." Principle was required—but together with ideas, he continued, "all the power and energy that accompany them . . . from the feeling and patriotick heart."[50]

V

Tucker was trying to change the course of Southern history. He expected in the late 1830s to summon the moral energy necessary to bring men to grace, to revive civic virtue apparently only found among fervent patriots; this mission led him to call for a Southern consciousness and to celebrate the heroism required to form a new nation. Revitalizing Virginia, he hoped to make her once more the "mother of statesmen." He himself wanted to be like the Washington whom he extolled in reviews for the *Messenger,* and like St. George Tucker, whose instructions at the college he claimed to be duplicating. But by 1840 Tucker's calls for action appeared to many persons who knew him no less impotent than petulant. Despite his popularity on the young men's lecture circuit, his view of himself as a hero was more sanguine than accurate.

For one thing, *The Partisan Leader* was neither a political nor an artistic success, to judge from response to the book. Upshur, in a review that would cause him no little embarrassment, applauded his friend's work in the January 1837 *Messenger,* and there were appreciative notices in the *Richmond Whig.* Nonetheless, most reaction was uniformly unenthusiastic. A correspondent in the February 9 *Enquirer* denounced it—and the *Messenger* besides for Upshur's praise of it—as stripping literature of her ornaments "to gild the poison and garnish the Sepulchre of liberty." All conspirators, he continued, had "begun their work by deluding and corrupting the young." In the same paper on February 16 "A Voice From the South" called *A Tale of the Future* "the prophecies of a vizored and crack-brained Politician." Editorial comments and letters in other Virginia publications were no more receptive, and the *Georgetown* (D.C.) *Metropolitan* dismissed the tract as "silly and trashy."[51]

Moreover, Tucker's novel registered few gains among friends and family. Shortly after Upshur's review appeared in the *Messenger,* White reported that the magazine lost sixteen subscribers in Richmond alone and that the most emphatic cancellation had been Henry St. George Tucker's. Angered by the blatant extremism of *The Partisan Leader,* hurt by his brother's portrait of him as the "contemptible imbecile" Hugh Trevor, Henry begged Beverley to renounce the book that was "very generally" attributed to his pen. In a long letter to Henry the younger man tried in vain to absolve himself of fraternal ill feeling. "Neither character," he insisted of Hugh and Bernard Trevor, "was meant for you or for myself." Bet Coalter Bryan, the niece on whom Tucker could always rely for incisive criticism, wrote pointedly that his passions had overrun him while he composed his tale of the future. Tucker's penchant for sarcasm, she said, too obviously had embittered him; it was unbecoming for a professor. Upshur tried to remain cheerful; the book has to have a "salutary effect on public sentiment," another supporter assured its author, "when it throws the menials of power into such spasms." Still, Duff Green complained of low sales, and Tucker gave up plans to write a sequel to the story.[52]

At the same time Tucker's virulent secessionism embarrassed the college, for critics of the political temper of William and Mary could easily link his *Partisan Leader* with the inaugural address that Dew delivered when he assumed the presidency of William and Mary in the fall of 1836. Reflecting beliefs Tucker had expressed earlier, and perhaps a joint faculty effort, Dew's essay was a pious dedication of the college to the truths of "moral and political education"—an emphasis on religious training and grooming for statesmanship, which, the new president explained, involved a "generous exercise of the feelings of the heart." As slaveholders and sons of slaveholders, young Virginians would thus be readied to defend what Dew called "the justice of our cause" in the face of "demon fanaticism" and in spite of the debasing tendencies of democratic politics.[53]

In the February 1837 *Messenger* a contributor who signed himself "N" used Dew's address to attack William and Mary for its preoccupation with pride, patriotism, and ambition. Such sentiments, so "easily kindled in the youthful breast," made political studies a dominant interest at the college, even an obsession. After leaving Williamsburg, complained this nameless critic, excitable young Virginians felt compelled to enter politics—even if it meant departing the state to find room to do so. In their haste for political notice they often fell into the hands of party hacks. One of the worst afflictions of the commonwealth, the correspondent tersely observed, was "the morbid desire of her sons for political distinction." Even in 1837 it was difficult for readers of the *Messenger* to know how widespread were the sentiments "N" expressed, but at Fourth of July observances the following summer in Fredericksburg there was open talk that faculty members at the college were "Nullifiers." The inference was that morbid political desires could easily lead to political extremism.[54]

In response to such charges—and he was moved to publish a reply to "N" —Tucker pointed out that the college course of instruction remained essentially the same as thirty or forty years before and that Virginians lived "surrounded by the proofs of its excellence. . . ." Soon after, in a lecture closing the school year, Tucker went on to claim that he was not indoctrinating his students; he was honing their minds. He aimed at understanding, not empty recitation. He was uninterested in attuning young men to any party platform or leader, as Democrats apparently were convinced. He counseled students not to adopt his opinions with "too much confidence," reminded them that he had never promised to impart political truth. Tucker claimed no infallibility. His business, he said, was to teach men "to observe, to compare, to think." "How uncandid and unworthy of the relation I bear to you," he told these departing students, "to take advantage of my position for the purpose of infecting you with my partialities or dislikings."[55]

But Tucker protested too much, for finally his lessons were studies in received truths and lonely duties. While he denied implanting doctrine, he did admit instilling a "disposition" in his students to see political and constitutional questions in the bent light of high principles and low necessities. In matters of mere expediency, experience was the only teacher, and here Tucker invoked his historical lessons and called for observing, comparing, thinking. Elsewhere faith instead of intellectual detachment was the rule. If "where certainty is attainable it may be criminal to doubt," he said at the end of his 1839 course on political philosophy and constitutional law, "in matters of high moral or political duty it is always so." Tucker saw to it that his students knew what these certainties were and that they carried heavy responsibilities with little reward. Though he had trained them as "true political scientists," less-endowed theorists and party functionaries, he warned, would condemn his students and try to limit them to "inaction and obscurity."[56] Disdain for public opinion virtually became their test of loyalty to him.

These remarks offered evidence of Tucker's frustration and self-delusion in the late spring of 1839. His confidence in being among the moral and political regenerate led him to extremities where his following diminished. It was just as well to him. He who defied tyrants and resisted the "unbridled passions of the multitude" might indeed "have all the world against him." But such opposition only confirmed Tucker's belief in his own peculiar calling. His lectures and addresses became occasions for self-affirming imagery. "The man of virtuous wisdom cannot be hid," Tucker proclaimed for his students' benefit and his own; "his brightness shines through the cloud that would obscure him, and gilded with its beams, he wears it as his glory." Tucker compared himself to Aristides the Just, an ancient Greek of unswerving probity whose "crowning glory" was popular ostracism. Fantasizing that the cataclysm of secession would change things, Tucker used as another self-figure the Roman hero Camillus, celebrated in Plutarch and Livy, whose exile was a trial that prepared him to be "the savior of his country." In his address to Randolph-Macon students the following year, the author of *The Partisan Leader* revealed that Randolph had anointed his half brother "to embody and preserve" his work and suggested that, like Randolph, he would push ahead despite the "neglect and reproach" of the ill-informed.[57]

Thus Tucker's conception of himself and his powers began to strain and break away from reality. He was a prophet ignored in his own country, a man with a mission but only a small following. His frustration now led to dreaming aloud just as it had in his boyhood when the "high-mettled colt" chafed in harness hitched to a heavy wagon. Tucker's incredible metaphors of self suggested the kind of knots he felt himself tied in. They also placed him in a precarious psychic position, for they were self-images that scourged. How, Tucker may have wondered without fully realizing it, was one actually to be as sagacious and honorable as Balcombe, as statesmanlike as B——, and as bold and true as Bernard Trevor? Tucker's heroic figures carried another danger in that, since they subtly influenced his behavior, they limited his options, they worked against detachment, reflection, and choice. Whether employing the self-image of Randolph returned, of a classical martyr, or of romantic hero, Tucker left himself in jeopardy of truly becoming a mere caricature, a figure as uncomplex and reflexive as the characters in his romances. Finally, Tucker's delusive views of himself worked against him in more easily noticeable ways: many Virginians did dismiss this posturing zealot, and the circle closed.

As gravely as Tucker looked upon the course of public events, the 1840 presidential election campaign—with its log cabins, torchlight parades, and ridiculous slogans—was one of the most frivolous in American history. He referred to it as "this waste of time, this waste of substance, and, worst of all, this waste of excitement which, once spent, leaves the mind unfit for action."[58] Since the canvass in his view was one between disappointingly poor candidates, the results in no way could have pleased him. Still, he was surprised and angered when Virginia went for Martin Van Buren. To Tucker the incumbent President embodied the real challenge a growing North posed to the South politically and personified the moral decline, the chicanery, Tucker believed would loosen restraints in government and society. The car of destiny seemed to have overrun him.

CHAPTER SEVEN

Community and Therapy: The Hero as Healer

THE FIRST VOLUME of Alexis de Tocqueville's *Democracy in America* had been published several years before Tucker saw the book. When he did, probably late in 1838, he devoured it. Tocqueville had come to the United States in the early 1830s sympathetic to the liberal democracy he believed inevitable in Europe, but when he wrote his impressions they contained what Tucker considered an outsider's confirmation of his own earlier warnings. The young French nobleman, who spent most of his time in the North and West, noted an erosion of deference in Jacksonian America, unfortunate changes in political leadership, and a decline in public morality, all of which popular equality apparently invited. The dangers Tocqueville sensed while journeying about the country were the evils that Tucker, now seldom leaving his backwater village, knew were there.[1]

Tocqueville's larger point, and one that Tucker seized on, was the necessary relation between society and men's minds. Just as men could enjoy well-being and achieve fulfillment only in society, the character of a society set the direction of life and thought. Tocqueville's second volume, appearing in 1840, made the connection explicit. It tried to show how democracy suggested to Americans the perfectibility of man; it discussed why in democratic societies there was—as one of his chapter titles read—a "more ardent and enduring love for equality than liberty" and dealt with the way democracy influenced the relationship between masters and servants, the quality of family life, and the education of young women. The observations Tocqueville made in his first volume so excited Tucker that he began poring over them page by page, writing extensive commentaries, enlarging the work at one point, amending it at another. His notes soon grew lengthy enough to be published themselves. Judge Upshur, who read *Democracy in America* even later than Tucker did, encouraged him to make these annotations his own appraisal of American government and society. Give the commentary a form, Upshur wrote his friend, "which will enable it to stand alone, & be read for its own sake."[2]

Such a book would have been the masterwork that Tucker badly wanted to write. It also would have helped to mark his intellectual distance from more optimistic social observers or those more resigned to change. Tocqueville, preparing his countrymen for liberal democracy, predicted the lines along which America would develop; Tucker, finding good cause for his suspicion of events outside the South, typified the hope many Southerners placed in timeless social institutions. In the 1830s he had seen problems of change, sectional conflict, and Southern lassitude as challenges to individual will, as matters for heroism. That appeal had not won him the following he needed for his purposes. Tocqueville's book, demonstrating the ill effects of democratic society in the North, suggested another approach, perhaps more widely compelling. Tucker now stressed that Southerners had in peculiarly sound institutions both the means of moral improvement and bulwarks against the loss of social cohesion. Family, land, law, and slavery had a nuturing, shaping power that worked to sustain simplicity and goodness. "Our condition," he wrote in his notes on *Democracy in America,* permits "a hope of permanency." Had Tocqueville visited the South, he would have seen there a traditional way of life "which communicates stability and affords anchorage" in an unstable world.[3]

ABEL P. UPSHUR, 1844

I

In the journal Tucker kept while reading *Democracy in America* he made criticisms of Tocqueville's passages on the Constitution that might have made an instructive pamphlet. Instead of pressing them into publication, however, he deferred to plans his friend Upshur had for printing his own essay. Long in preparation, the *Brief Enquiry Into the True Nature and Character of Our Federal Government* appeared in the summer before the Harrison–Van Buren election. It brought to a head the bookish quarrel between Joseph Story and Southerners like Tucker and Upshur over the history and structure of the federal union.[4]

Tucker rightly claimed that the *Enquiry* was "laid in ideas derived from me." A passage from his Petersburg Lyceum address on the Virginia declaration of independence supported the attack on the "colonial nation" concept. Upshur's explanation of the fundamental role states played in the federated system was one closely paralleling Tucker's discussion of the test for sovereignty. The belief, reiterated in the *Enquiry,* that there was a "natural and necessary tendency" for the federal government to enlarge its power and patronage at the expense of the states was hardly original either with Upshur or Tucker. Still, Upshur's earlier praise for *The Partisan Leader* suggested that Tucker made these points the more immediate to him. Tucker obligingly reviewed the *Enquiry* for Edmund Ruffin's struggling *Southern Magazine* and obtained copies of the booklet for use in his law course.[5]

Tucker welcomed Upshur's project, yet he did not greet it with the enthusiasm he could have mustered ten years earlier. It was significant, for one thing, that he had not written the pamphlet. As law professor at William and Mary, where state sovereignty was a cardinal principle, it was Tucker who might logically have undertaken to rebut Story and amend Tocqueville in published form. During the recurring illnesses that forced Upshur, year after year, to postpone completion of the *Enquiry,* Tucker could well have shouldered the task of finishing the counteressay himself. Upshur's effort was of a kind that Tucker felt behind him. In *The Partisan Leader* he had referred to faith in the Constitution as a "delusion" that caused Virginians to sacrifice "the *substance* of liberty and prosperity to the *forms*" of an instrument "devised to secure, but perverted to destroy them." Upshur's *Enquiry* itself warned Southerners that it was too late to indulge in "undiscriminating eulogies of their Constitution"; the compact was "far from perfect." Bernard Trevor, Tucker's "heart" in *The Partisan Leader*—speaking of men who would surely trample the Constitution underfoot—counted himself among those who upheld it only "as long as there was hope."[6]

Tucker's hope had long since begun to fade, and it was small reason to sustain it that he and Harrison's vice-president, John Tyler, were old friends. For someone of Tucker's sensitivity, it was not an entirely comfortable friendship. While both men had been born on tidewater plantations, attended William and Mary, and in their early careers practiced law in lower

Virginia, Tyler—the younger by seven years—had been far more successful. When Tucker returned from Missouri, Tyler was an ex-governor serving in the Senate and one of the William and Mary Visitors to whom he was indebted for his professorship. Thereafter college affairs, social life, and common political interests frequently brought the two men together. In 1835 Tyler's oldest son began law studies with Tucker; he and Tyler talked at the meetings and parties surrounding every July commencement exercise. Tucker more than once may have visited Tyler's nearby Gloucester County estate. In 1836, when the pro-Jackson Assembly directed Virginia senators to vote in favor of expunging an earlier censure of the President from the Senate record, Tucker was one of those whose advice Tyler sought before deciding to resign rather than abide by the instructions. Next moving to Williamsburg to practice law, Tyler bought from Tucker the dwelling in which he had expected to retire from public life.[7]

Neither Tucker nor Upshur thought much of Tyler's superior. Tucker found in the President-elect nothing of the mettle of ideas; Upshur's comment on the Harrison inauguration was that in history nothing was so uniform as the "madness & follies of free government." But history was more nearly uniform in its caprice. In April—on Palm Sunday and a month to the day after Harrison's swearing in—the old Indian campaigner died, and as special steamer and train carried Tyler off to Washington, he left behind a circle of anxious friends who suddenly found themselves among the new President's "kitchen cabinet" of informal advisors. Here at last was a chance for Tucker, Upshur, and Dew to become the guiding lights of a virtuous chief executive.[8]

Among states' rights Southerners, Democrats and Whigs alike, Tyler raised understandable expectations. In the confusion of party alignments there seemed to lie great opportunity. If Calhoun and enough Democrats joined the President and his anti-Jackson Southern Whigs—whose Whiggery had never quite resembled Clay's—Tyler might, with scattered Northern support, forge a party strong enough to enact its own legislative program and to win his reelection in 1844. With such an organization, Southerners perhaps would find protection in the Union. Writing cheerfully to Tucker, Ruffin envisioned a new party of men acting on the constitutional principles to which they merely paid lip service as Whigs or Democrats. "What a change," William Campbell Preston, South Carolina senator, exclaimed to Tucker after learning of Harrison's death. "What a destiny for Tyler. I have confidence in him. I do not fear the result."[9]

All the same, Harrison bequeathed serious domestic and foreign problems. The country remained in the throes of a depression more severe than any to that time; there were ticklish foreign-policy questions that included an independent Texas and undefined boundaries in Maine and Oregon. Moreover, Tyler had an uncertain mandate and a divided administration.

Northerners could dismiss him, in the biting words of John Quincy Adams, who was now in the House, as having "all the interests and passions and vices of slavery rooted in his moral and political constitution. . . ." Kentucky senator Henry Clay, who had friends in the Cabinet, recognized in Tyler a longtime opponent of broad federal legislation and considered himself—not "His Accidency"—leader of the Whig party. At the special session of Congress to convene May 31, Clay planned to enact an ambitious program based on the 1840 Whig victory. Although Tyler's opposition to a federally chartered national bank had been axiomatic throughout his political career, Clay's proposals included just such a bank.[10]

Tucker believed the political evils of a United States Bank far outweighed its economic advantages. In a long letter to the President April 11 he offered to supply Tyler with appropriate arguments. Certainly the country needed sound currency and a source of credit, and a national bank would meet these requirements. But through such a bank the federal government gained a dangerous influence over the monetary system; as "head of the money power," the national bank became "either the instrument of the Government or a dangerous and troublesome antagonist [to it]," said Tucker, a "subject of contention & humbug, and a sharp weapon in the hands of a demagogue." He enclosed a plan that would provide, he thought, economic necessities without violating the constitutional limits on federal power. He acknowledged Upshur's help in drawing it up; he had mentioned it to Dew who, "tho' unprepared to adopt it," approved his colleague's "fiscal reasoning." Before writing the President, Tucker had taken the precaution of writing Clay, outlining the proposal and asking him to consider it.[11]

The plan called for a compact among the states, for a kind of fiscal constitution, and it might have produced a monetary institution highly protective of Southern interests. By Tucker's scheme the states would agree to form a federal banking association, each state subscribing an amount of money proportional to its strength in the electoral college and placing the funds in the United States Treasury. Governing the association would be a bicameral directorate with ten men in each "chamber." Senators and congressmen of nonslave states would elect six members of one chamber and four of the other; the slave states would choose the other ten members. Since drafts for funds would require the approval of both chambers, the machinery insured the North and South alike a concurrent vote in interstate financial policy. The association would issue bank notes acceptable as legal tender, act as the fiscal agent of the federal government, distribute profits to the states, and, if necessary, make up its deficits through the sale of public lands. Tucker's proposal would make a state-created institution, independent of Congress, a key element in the financial system of the country. Since states themselves would decide on charter renewals, the bank could

never become a "tool in the hands of the central power," and therefore,
Tucker explained in his letter to the President, "the atmosphere of Washington would be forever exempt from all storms arising" in the fiscal quarter
of the political horizon.[12]

Tucker accompanied this outline with political counsel. The state banking compact stood its best chance of enactment, he advised the President,
if Tyler disclaimed all aspirations to a second term. Should he fail to make
this renunciation, Clay Whigs and most Democrats were waiting to frustrate
and destroy him as a rival to established party leaders. Tucker argued that,
by replenishing the treasury, invigorating commerce, and placing circulating
money on a sound basis, Tyler could build himself "a monument more enduring than brass." At the same time he would demonstrate to the place-
seekers and professional power brokers in Washington the intellectual and
moral integrity of the Virginia statesman. Tucker challenged the President
to curb ambition in all subordinates and "most of all" in himself.[13]

Tyler found it impossible to separate the law professor's wisdom from
his idealism. The state-compact plan, which Tucker thought would give the
chief executive a rallying point above parties, was simply passed around the
cabinet, admired, and finally ignored as Tyler tried to temporize with Clay.
Henry A. Wise, a young Eastern Shore congressman acting as liaison between
Tyler and his informal counselors, was "taken with" the Tucker proposal
but had doubts about it, like Upshur, who feared "insuperable difficulties"
in working out the details of the plan. Clay rejected it outright because it
created an "authority apart from, and yet coordinate with the Constitution,
and independent of Congress." Not until April 25 did the pressure of Tyler's
business allow him to acknowledge the letter Tucker had sent to Washington
two weeks earlier. However interesting Tucker's proposal for a state-created
system, the President wrote his friend in Williamsburg, the subject of banking
required caution. Surely, he said, the country would not expect at the opening of the special session "any matured measure" from the new executive.[14]

While Tyler delayed, Clay acted, and when the Kentucky senator pushed
ahead with his plan to incorporate a new national bank, Tucker began a
series of open letters to Tyler showing how Clay's bill violated constitutional
provisions. Too sharply critical of Clay for the Washington *Madisonian* and
published instead in Ritchie's Richmond *Enquirer,* Tucker's articles upheld
Tyler, who on August 16 vetoed the act creating a "Fiscal Bank of the
United States" and whose action on another such measure the country
awaited. Tucker demonstrated the "impudence" of attacks on the President
for party irregularity. He recited the history of political parties to show the
tainted pedigree of Clay nationalism. The Constitution nowhere contained
the word "national"; the founding fathers had stricken it, and its frequent
use in 1841 was "but one of many proofs of the tendency of the Government to degenerate into the great consolidated mixed monarchy, which the

advocates of strong government at first desired, but dared not recommend to the people." The President's alleged collaboration on the second bank bill made his decision on the version the Senate sent him early in September especially difficult. Tucker shored him up. Insisting on a bank that only large and loose rules of construction could justify, Clay made it impossible ever again to rely on constitutional authority as a check to usurpation. Was the document to be understood as an instrument of power, asked Tucker wearily, or as a restraint on that power?[15]

The year was immensely disappointing for Tyler, and for his friends in the tidewater as well. The President's second rejection of the bank bill within three weeks left him lame and derided, his cabinet resigning, and Clay Whigs reading him out of the party with the dispatch of men who had planned an execution. Having tried to secure the support of both Whigs and Democrats by evenly distributing patronage favors, Tyler had won over neither. His Virginia advisors were little more pleased. In the summer of 1841 the President appointed Edward Everett, the Harvard scholar who edited the *North American Review* and was no friend of slavery, minister to the Court of St. James. Given slaveholder concern over English involvement with Texas, this choice left Tucker bewildered. Even the chief executive's second bank-veto message betrayed weakness, or ineptness, and perhaps a nationalist influence. Tyler had written that he viewed the Constitution as the "embodied and written will of the whole people of the United States." But by conceding that there was such a body politic, he granted the first premise of consolidationists and made his high-principled vetoes look somewhat ridiculous. "Ye Gods!" Upshur wrote Tucker on seeing the presidential message. "Why this is the very quintessence of Kent & Story." During Tyler's first half year in office, he had succeeded only in "mortifying his friends & strengthening his enemies."[16]

Of those friends, Tucker was perhaps left the most distressed by Tyler's early administration. The President named Upshur the new secretary of the navy. But the nomination brought embarrassment with it because John M. Botts—a Richmond lawyer and Whig congressman—took this opportunity to vilify Upshur, Tucker, and William and Mary for the rankest disunionism.[17] Moreover the rejection of Tucker's bank plan offered, as if he needed it, a further example of the baneful effects of party. Tucker in 1841 had planned to use Tyler as an agent in dissolving parties; he had hoped to place his friend above and beyond Democrats and Whigs, so that, free of the political organizations that kept divisive topics mostly submerged or discussed them in terms of intersectional alliances, the country could face the real issue of sectional rights. Once again no such "party of principle" had emerged. Tyler had turned out to be a mortal man, not much less ambitious than Van Buren, his administration just about as infected with intrigue and influence peddling as any other. The truth was that Tyler was no hero and Tucker none either.

While Tucker's banking compact might have resembled the political achievement of his father's generation, such leadership was now more difficult and less rewarding: the people were uninterested in high matters of state. So very few men, a young lawyer wrote Tucker after Tyler's second veto, "seem to understand any thing of Sovereignty philosophically viewed. . . ."[18]

II

The bypassed presidential advisor watched Richmond newspapers in the spring of 1842 for word from Rhode Island, where demands for constitutional reform nearly brought on civil war. The Dorr Rebellion was "democracy run-mad," exclaimed Upshur; it reminded Tucker that universal suffrage was but a "theoretical perfection." Democratic reform, he had written in his notes on Tocqueville, drew upon the presumption that a majority had a right to whatever seemed the greatest good. According to this maxim, he pointed out, minority rights were inconsequential, and the "aimless exercise of power" could lead nowhere except to "plunder and self-indulgence."[19]

Given Tucker's concern for tradition and common sense, one could see the wave of experimentation in the early 1840s as the best evidence yet that American society was coming apart. Utopian communities carried to disturbing extremes the American fetish for change, organization, and reorganization which Tocqueville had noticed as undermining traditional authority. Religious enclaves proclaimed the dawn of a millennial order and practiced celibacy. Robert Owen, establishing New Harmony, Indiana, denounced private property, organized religion, and the ties of marriage as impediments to social progress. Owen's friend Frances Wright, notorious to Tucker as an outspoken women's rights reformer, made her own attack on American domestic arrangements in the public support she gave slave emancipation and the abolition of marriage. At the Massachusetts settlement of Hopedale, begun in early 1841, men and women secluded themselves from the world in order to form a Fraternal Communion in which everyone would "stand on a footing of personal equality, irrespective of sex, color, occupation, wealth, rank, or any other natural or adventitious peculiarity."[20]

Such social movements went against all that Tucker knew from experience and felt to be true. They grew out of Rousseau's belief, which Tucker questioned, that man antedated society, that society was his convention, even his burden, and that by using his reason he might change society and perhaps even free himself from it. Tucker thought these conceptions neither self-evident nor supported in history; they were misleading abstractions. Before the college adjourned in the late spring of 1842, in an address to the student Temperance Society, he reminded its young members that men should keep moral goals within the bounds of human frailty and remember the integrative as well as individual purpose of moral striving. The passage from childhood to maturity brought change "from the belief that all is bright and beautiful and good, to the conviction that all is vanity," he said; the best one could do, and Tucker saw it as a first object of education, was to learn to exercise reason as a counterbalance to base instincts, "to play off the passions and appetites against each other," "to embue the heart with a lively scorn of everything . . . impure, brutal, or degrading." Thus for Tucker the absolutist piety of the millennial sects, besides the impetus it gave abolitionism, neglected the demonstrably seamier side of man's nature. The celibacy of the Shakers, the antimarriage rhetoric of Owen and Wright, and the polygamy of the Mormons all upset the relationship Tucker believed natural between men and women. Both socialism and communism denied divinely ordained principles of private property. In these experiments of Northern reformers Tucker saw the same heartless rationalism, the Godwinism, that he remembered from his days as a Williamsburg schoolboy.[21]

In battling the contagion of political change and social experimentation, Tucker discovered a comrade in the German-born liberal scholar, Francis Lieber. First known to Tucker as a contributor to the *Southern Literary Messenger* and as the author of an indifferent travelogue-essay collection that Tucker in 1835 refused to bother reviewing,[22] Lieber was a professor at South Carolina College in 1840 when he published the first volume of his *Manual of Political Ethics*. This book pleased Tucker. In the spring or early summer he wrote its author to congratulate him on the work and to praise it as an aid in "humbling the mind" of the beginning student of government. The *Political Ethics* in its cautious solemnity offered new testimony that the science of government was a labyrinth out of which the "thread of experience marked the only trustworthy path"; Tucker announced that he had adopted the text for use that fall in his junior year course in political law and government. With Lieber's friendly reply, boasting that his *Political Ethics* avoided the "easy preachings" of Rousseau and commending Tucker as a "true votary of knowledge," there was every sign that a friendship had been forged.[23]

A man of superior intellectual energy, who was also unhampered by Tucker's pessimism and parochialism, Lieber in many ways preempted the exercise the William and Mary professor had planned to perform in his commentaries on Tocqueville. Yet there were problems with the Lieber text, and when in the spring of 1842 Tucker read the second volume of *Political Ethics,* he doubtless began thinking once more about writing his own book. After all, *Ethics* could give as much satisfaction to nationalists like Joseph Story, to whom Lieber dedicated the work, as it did to readers who were jealous of national authority. Although Tucker agreed with Lieber that the primary role of government was simply to regulate men's relations with one another and to offer protection to citizens and their property, he could not accept without qualification Lieber's argument that the state might provide those services men were incapable of performing for themselves individually, including public schooling and internal improvements. Holding to the concept of a superior rule of law, Tucker rejected Lieber's view of public opinion as the "continual sovereign action of society" and his judgment that the state could interfere in private affairs when "demanded by the public interest."[24] Nor did Lieber once mention slavery in his *Ethics.*

Slavery was of particular concern to Tucker because this element in Southern society was a barrier against the atomistic individualism, the depersonalizing "progress" that he uneasily watched growing in the North and in England and—he apparently realized—that Northern reform movements themselves reflected. Early in 1844 he began an essay dealing with slavery as an alternative to the fracturing effects of modern industrial society.[25] While his acquaintance with that system was limited, he consoled himself that few abolitionists had ever been in the South. He cited the damning reports on British factory life Sir Robert Peel had compiled in the 1820s; he referred to Tocqueville's encounters with Northern businessmen and workingmen. On the basis of this secondhand evidence, Tucker pointed out that in Britain and the North powerful groups invariably sacrificed the interests of the weaker if by doing so they could advance their own, that the multitude begged for work and often labored for less than subsistence pay. "[M]odern discoveries in art and science," he maintained, only widened the gulf between classes and worsened strife between them.[26]

Free government and domestic peace, said Tucker, were doomed in such circumstances. However rigidly disciplined hungry factory workers were kept, their suppression could not insure order and tranquillity. In the "freedom" of impersonal competition, the goal of lifting oneself out of poverty became an obsession, Tucker believed, so that men and women, pursuing the grail of possible wealth, taught their children to love money above all things, and themselves learned "to look upon extortion and fraud and corruption and bribes but as means which may be sanctified by the good end to be accomplished." Money lust, he predicted, would become the "master passion" in competitive societies, and conflicting interests would always work to tear them apart. Downtrodden, jealous, the toiling citizenry eventually would turn on the few who were better-off and either by confiscatory legislation or by plain violence wreak vengeance on them.[27] Earlier Tucker had made his case for stability against the background of democracy, often using the excesses of the French Revolution to apply leverage in his discussion. In the early 1840s his apprehensions shifted to include an indictment of the selfishness, materialism, and dehumanized relationships of industrial life.

This change in Tucker's thinking paralleled a similar turn in Tocqueville's critique of American democracy.[28] It also resonated with the ideas of the British social and literary critic, Thomas Carlyle, whose work Tucker could have seen in any of several American and Scottish journals that the college library received. The two men were reaching similar conclusions at about the same time. Though the Virginian surely found this like-minded conservative reassuring, he did not necessarily ape Carlyle's ideas, as it may have appeared to unsympathetic Northerners. Carlyle's lectures *On Heroes, Hero Worship, and the Heroic in History* bore a striking resemblance to Tucker's own infatuation with the man of will, but they were published several years after *The Partisan Leader.* Carlyle's *Past and Present,* appearing in 1843 and summarizing his objections to competitive society, merged well with Tucker's own common-sense naturalism. Carlyle lamented the slow incursion of "the Gospel of Mammon," the free individualism that pushed men to succeed, drove them to mutual hostility, and made "cash payment" the only basis of their relationships. Was the serf so unhappy in his tie to land and lord? he asked; What did the worker's present freedom mean except the liberty to starve? Supply and demand displaced faithfulness, veracity, and real worth with puffery, falsity, and "Unnature." Society needed affiliation to hold it together, and men needed to venerate "Human Worth" in the security of social hierarchy.[29]

To complement these observations, Tucker brought evangelical lessons to his own commentary on the altered values of emerging society. Wealth was not true abundance, he cautioned; prosperity did not mean happiness. Completing his earlier case for slavery and settling finally on its place in a benevolent God's plan, Tucker argued that slavery enabled the South to enjoy a "constitution of society" built on a network of relationships "in obedience to the law of Love." It was clear to Tucker, and he was eager to share the good news, that God's purpose in creating the human race was the eternal happiness of all men through faith in their redeemer; in the end God equalized the happiness of all His creatures. Though the slave worked long and hard, he learned the Gospel from his master and was assured of his love; if slaveholders and the South had fallen behind in "the race of improvement and refinement," they had the satisfaction of doing God's labor, receiving the love of their blacks, and enjoying a moral sanctuary—evils elsewhere safely quarantined. Organizing society on the basis of love made the tasks of government comparatively simple, wrote Tucker, because it left no pretext to ambition, no motive for misrule. Southern society solved the problem of reconciling self-discipline with liberty by "restoring that beautiful harmony in which Power is gentle, and Obedience liberal, and the will of the superior prevails. . . ."[30] Slavery, even if it failed to pay high earthly dividends, was still a better system for all concerned than the competitive individualism and inhumane materialism of "modern" societies.

In the rapidly developing proslavery argument that Northern reformers considered diabolical and hysterically defensive, Tucker formed a link between William Harper's criticisms of free labor and the later, more famous,

"sociology" of George Fitzhugh. Harper's *Memoir on Slavery,* published in
Charleston in 1838, had described every stage of human society as having
"its own peculiar evils." Relying on the English writer Edward Gibbons
Wakefield's observations of his own country and America, Harper hit at the
"distress and pauperism," "the inequality and wretchedness," which, for
the British working classes, was the noteworthy evil of crowded, factory
towns. Fitzhugh, writing in the 1850s, carried the defense of hierarchical
society and the attack on industrial life to the point of suggesting the en-
slavement of free laborers. In Tucker's essay on the "moral and political
relationship" between slave and slaveholder, he elaborated on Harper's
surplus-of-labor observation and developed it further in discussing the
money-centered materialism that competitive society encouraged.[31]

Tucker may not have been entirely aware of making this advance in the
proslavery argument. Though he did keep in touch with a wide range of
Southern-rights advocates, his connections with other slavery apologists
were weaker than Northerners and moderate Southerners believed. Harper,
in the 1820s a member of the Dardenne clan in Missouri, gave Tucker credit
for ideas about the legality of slavery that the South Carolinian quoted
from the "Notes on Blackstone's Commentaries" but did not write Tucker
regularly. In the 1840s Tucker may have known of Fitzhugh, then a mar-
ginally successful planter near Port Royal, Virginia. But if Tucker ever met
Fitzhugh he made no mention of it in writing, and if Fitzhugh felt he owed
Tucker any intellectual debt he never acknowledged it. Tucker did once encounter the Reverend Thornton Stringfellow, a Baptist minister in Culpeper
County; his preaching while passing through Williamsburg in 1839 spurred
Tucker to stoke the spiritual fires he worried about letting cool. Because
he knew of Stringfellow, however, it was all the more remarkable that he
failed to keep in touch with this fellow Virginian, who made no secret of
his proslavery view of sacred Scripture.[32]

While Tucker joined most Southerners in rejecting the theory that blacks
were not humans at all, he was even a bit out of step with proslavery. He
defended the institution primarily as a familylike system of simple, inter-
dependent relationships. Yet this view placed everyone, white and black
alike, on a hierarchical scale. Many whites in the slaveholding region were
beginning to explain slavery as a way of controlling hopelessly inferior blacks
while allowing whites to live democratically. Here was one of the very ideas
that Tucker believed endangered Southern strength. He wrote that free men,
surrounded by slavery, were doubly jealous of their freedom, so that slavery
was the "only secure basis for a free government"; he made it clear that free
men in the South were white men, so that slavery provided a floor beneath
which no white man could fall. But he could not accept the corollary that
in black inferiority there was white equality.[33]

Tucker began writing his 1844 slavery essay as a scholarly discourse, hoping to read it at the spring meeting of the National Institute for the Promotion of Science in Washington. Upshur worked hard to place his Williamsburg friend on the speaking program, and at first the secretary of the society thought the topic—treated by someone of Tucker's reputation—interesting and timely. But the timeliness of Tucker's lecture was its undoing. Charles J. Ingersoll, a member of the program committee and a moderate Pennsylvania Democrat, vetoed Tucker's proposed topic. Upshur had some second thoughts as well, fearing that an address on the master–slave relationship would upset a delicate sectional balance among the directors of the institute —who included such unlikely colleagues as Senator Robert J. Walker of Mississippi and John Quincy Adams—while disrupting and perhaps destroying the fledgling scientific society at its carefully planned April gathering. "[A]n angel of light could not touch your topic at the time & place proposed," Tucker finally heard from a spokesman for the institute, "without producing a disastrous explosion."[34]

III

The powder Upshur wanted to avoid setting off was the issue of Texas annexation. Now secretary of state, following Webster's resignation, Tucker's longtime friend was deeply caught up in the mystery and mistrust that filled Washington in the early months of 1844. Tucker had heard from Upshur the year before that there was a "systematic Conspiracy against the South & its institutions" in the federal capital. The Northern vision of conspiracy, centering on the question of Texas annexation, was every bit as ominous. Although the early Tyler administration had maintained a policy of coolness toward Texas in her attempt to join the Union, this stance quietly changed in 1844 when increased British military, commercial, and antislavery influence became evident there.[35]

Tucker's own interests in Texas were considerable. In mid-March 1839 his friend Albert T. Burnley, a Virginia native, who was then a Kentucky lawyer and Texas adventurer, had taken fifty of Tucker's Missouri slaves downriver to New Orleans and next by packet to the newly independent republic. Burnley then put them to work near Galveston on "beautiful & valuable" land which, though Lucy Tucker opposed any move to the Texas frontier, he hoped Tucker eventually would settle himself. Later, when Burnley accompanied the Texas bond commissioner to Europe in an effort to establish the credit of the fledgling government, Tucker sent off the emissaries with encouragement and ideas for a system of paper currency based on public lands. Burnley held out the possibility that Tucker himself might make the next European voyage as a Texas diplomat. Delighted at the interest Tucker took in Texas, "& still more at the *evidences*" he was willing to give to it, Burnley thought that if the law professor only established residence there he would fill the "highest offices in the young Republic."[36]

As an independent country Texas held out considerable promise for Tucker. But he was in Virginia to stay, committed to the work of protecting Southern uniqueness. As a state Texas would strengthen the South; besides, as long as Texas was foreign ground, federal importation law forbade the return of his slaves either to Missouri or Virginia. Quite naturally Tucker became involved in Tyler's emerging Texas policy. Instrumental in the President's naming of Waddy Thompson, a South Carolina Whig friendly to Texas annexation, as minister to Mexico early in 1842,[37] Tucker was also a party to the subtle maneuvering of Upshur the following year. The secretary of state wrote Tucker excitedly in October 1843 reporting that possible Texas statehood—the only reason, he said, he remained in the cabinet— was "*the* question of the day." The destiny of the Union and the maintenance of international peace depended upon it, he declared. After making renewed attempts to discuss annexation with Texas officials, the secretary of state asked Tucker to draw up a preamble and transfer clauses of an annexation treaty. What form should the document take? Upshur wondered; Did governments transfer only territory? Was the consent of the people required?[38]

The legal status of Texas soil and the proper means of acquiring it were disputed subjects. Senator Walker, an archexpansionist whose published case for taking Texas covered its every benefit, and who sent Tucker an inscribed copy of his booklet, argued that Texas belonged to the United States as part of the Louisiana Purchase; the territory Spain had transferred to France in 1800 supposedly included land as far west as Texas. But the Spanish-French treaty was hardly accessible, and in any case the Adams-Onis agreement with Spain in 1819 established the southwest boundary of the United States as the Sabine River, the western edge of the state of Louisiana. The wider belief was that Texas, neither empty country nor a United States territory petitioning for statehood, was a foreign government. Formal, bilateral assent was therefore necessary before a congressional enabling act, and that assent meant a treaty. Tucker began a treaty draft. "It is not yet certain that I shall need it," wrote Upshur confidentially in December, "but the probabilities are that I shall, & that too within the present month."[39]

There was every reason then and in the following weeks to believe that such a treaty, which the President signed on April 12 and sent to the Senate for ratification, would win approval. Expecting the best, Tucker swallowed his anger at the rebuff the Institute for the Promotion of Science paid his address on slavery. Then misfortune befell pro-Texas southerners. On February 28 Upshur died in a naval gun accident. Calhoun, whom Tyler named to succeed the Virginian, was barely settled into office when an editorial in the *National Intelligencer* accused the administration of plotting to obtain additional slave territory by means of a secret arrangement with Texas. Though these negotiations were hardly secret, available evidence did nothing to put antislavery forces at ease. The New York *Post* published material disclosing the background of the Texas-American annexation treaty; in an ill-advised letter that newspapers soon printed, Calhoun wrote to the British minister combining a bellicose stand on Texas with a comprehensive defense of slavery. On June 8, before the Senate adjourned for the summer and the presidential campaign between James K. Polk and Henry Clay, it rejected the Texas treaty by a lopsided vote.[40]

For once Tucker neglected constitutional niceties. Defeat of the treaty, he was quick to point out, need not mean the end of annexation hopes. As early as May he commended to Senator Walker the alternative of acquiring the Texas republic by joint congressional resolution—a device that would pass with a simple majority instead of the two-thirds Senate vote the approval of treaties required. Tucker was convinced that the article empowering Congress to admit new states justified this course.[41] Later in the year he eased scruples further by recalling for Secretary of State Calhoun his own interpretation of the Louisiana treaty during the debate over Missouri statehood: taking Texas was only reannexing it.[42] After Tyler and Calhoun adopted the policy of annexation by joint resolution, Thomas H. Bayly— the Virginia congressman who often took counsel with Tucker and whom the law professor described as no leader but capable of "good service"— took the position in the House that the Constitution granted the federal government two classes of powers, foreign and domestic. In foreign affairs, where the interests of all the states were inseparable, federal power was to be broadly construed. Congressional power to admit new states included everything necessary and proper to its fulfillment.[43]

During the agitated Polk-Clay campaign that fall and in the congressional debates of the next winter, opponents of the joint-resolution method of Texas annexation caught the lame-duck Tyler administration in uncomfortable contradictions. Having originally introduced the issue as a treaty matter, Tyler and his counselors seemed thereby to have admitted the foreign status of Texas. The irregularity of the plan they now followed was embarrassingly evident. Moreover, in the Missouri statehood controversy, Southerners had argued that Congress could set no conditions on admission to the Union. Now, in the joint resolution that the House and Senate finally agreed to early in 1845, there were a number of stipulations involving boundaries and debts.[44]

On the Texas annexation question Tucker departed from constitutional principles he had defended throughout his intellectual life and broke rules to which he had always strictly held himself. While Texas was a free, sovereign, and independent state, according to Tucker, so were the other states of the Union, and, in considering whether to admit a preexisting, foreign government, only the Senate represented the states equally. Having been until now consistently jealous of the interpretation given central authority, Tucker now based his position on general, incidental, and implied powers. One former Tucker student, Robert Ould, chided another, who was pro-Calhoun and pro-Texas, for abandoning the faith learned in Williamsburg and wrote his old professor for assurances; "My dear Judge," asked Ould, "our bulwark is the Constitution, and not Texas, is it not?" To bystanders states' rights and strict interpretation seemed suddenly, cynically, inconvenient to the South. Here was a disregard of principle among usually moralistic men that Senator William S. Archer of Virginia, one of whose earlier speeches on Texas found its way into Tucker's library, noticed and warned Southerners against. Tucker must have smarted at charges that, in seeking to obtain Texas by whatever expedient was necessary, the South had sold its soul. What is to be thought, Henry Clay pointedly asked Tucker in January 1845, of those men who supported strict construction of the Constitution and yet contended for Texas by joint resolution? "They forfeit," he answered himself, "all consideration of respect to principle. . . ."[45]

IV

The point was that Tucker's principles were no longer constitutional. He "cheated" at a game he believed Northerners were no longer playing at all. In November 1841 the radical abolitionist William Lloyd Garrison had denounced union with slaveholders in the pages of his *Liberator*.[46] More seriously, several Northern states had passed laws which, by protecting the rights of free blacks, made the capture of fugitive slaves more difficult. Although in 1842 the Supreme Court in the *Prigg* v. *Pennsylvania* case struck down one such law as violating the constitutional provision that fugitives "be delivered up on claim," the decision was of little aid to the South. Justice Story's decision made it clear that the return of runaway slaves was the proper province of federal, not state, officials. Soon ingenious Northern statutes angered and frustrated Southerners more than ever.[47] So fragile was the legal position of slavery, John Quincy Adams had asserted during the 1842 House debates on the "gag" rule, that the commander of a federal army suppressing an insurrection of slaves had a perfect right to set them free. Here, Upshur had written acidly, was "quite a new discovery in constitutional law." Then in 1843 the Massachusetts legislature passed resolutions calling for the repeal of the constitutional clause allowing the South congressional representation for three-fifths of its slaves.[48]

One might have reacted to these apparent examples of bad faith with pleas of good sense. Henry St. George Tucker, since 1841 professor of law at the University of Virginia, issued just that call for moderation in the lectures he published during the Texas debates. He shared his younger brother's anger at the Massachusetts resolutions; they violated, he said, a sacred compromise between variant interests. But he strove to restore harmony. His message promised safety in the Constitution. Henry Tucker saw exemplified in the *Prigg* decision a judicial guarantee that the "trammels of the constitution" would ultimately prevail over any "lawless sectional majority." Persuaded that Northerners would respect the Constitution "even if they be desirous to change it," he saw additional security in the oath that members of Congress and government officials took to support that charter. Henry St. George did in truth occupy what he described in his *Lectures on Constitutional Law* as "an isthmus that divides two great contending parties in the nation." "I have endeavoured," the Hugh Trevor of *The Partisan Leader* told his classes in Charlottesville, "to maintain a course between dangerous extremes." Shunning both nullification and consolidation, he was sure he had followed "the track of the wisest and most virtuous of our statesmen."[49]

Beverley Tucker was no more convinced of his brother's wisdom in 1845 than when he wrote his romance of Southern insurrection. He doubted that true Southern statesmen clung to parchment protections; he now emphasized that the common law, not the Constitution, offered the South security and permanence. His lectures paid much attention to the eminent practicality of the English legal tradition. Reflecting the complexity of life itself, the common law resulted from long and varied experience, from repeated and patient trial. He found "scientific" support for his view in the first volume of *Political Ethics,* where Lieber described the common law, because neither compacted nor legislated, as closest to the solid bed of custom and nature.[50]

Tucker's love of the common law helped to explain his aversion to the codification movement of these years—the attempt to systematize and digest the written and unwritten laws of a state, transforming what reformers thought to be perplexity into what they expected to be coherence. Procedural reform, far less controversial than attempts to impose rationality on the substantive law, nonetheless aroused Tucker's interest. In Virginia, he knew, confused lawyers and irregular pleading had produced discomfort in the profession, prolonged lawsuits, and caused bitterness among clients who thought themselves bilked by a system of quibbles and deceits. Virginia law did not require county court or superiour court clerks to keep extensive records of the facts established in cases, so that inferences of law from them were hazardous; the writs lawyers did draw were too frequently "cumbrous and absurd." In the mid-1840s the Virginia Assembly considered solving the difficulty with a system of prescribed forms.[51]

Here, thought Tucker, was codification in minature scale. Expanding on lecture notes, he began in the winter of 1844–45 to compose an essay on the way common-law courts obtained facts in civil disputes. Tucker hoped that, by bringing the legislature and the profession to recognize the original simplicity of the art of special pleading, he could prevent the establishment of a fixed, artificial, and "premeditated" set of rules. The ancient exchanges of complaint, plea (the defendant's response, setting forth new facts as necessary), rejoinder, surrejoinder, demurrer, rebutter, surrebutter, and judgment, explained Tucker, were no more than the stages of fact-finding "to which every prudent and sagacious master or father of family resorts, whenever called upon to do justice between those who are subject to his authority." If lawyers and citizenry truly understood the grace and unerring reliability of pleading as it was meant to be practiced, the William and Mary professor was certain there would be no movement to replace it.[52]

In making his own plea on behalf of special pleading, Tucker presented a published brief on behalf of the common law at large. He criticized plans to codify the law—some of which would have introduced concepts from Roman law—as tainted with the smell of the Continent and contaminated by ideas unknown to the Anglo-American tradition. It bothered Tucker that codifiers were trying to outguess experience, to outdo reasonableness. "In the infinite variety of human transactions," he wrote in his manuscript on pleading, "all imaginable cases are brought under adjudication, and the law concerning each is ascertained and established with a degree of accuracy of detail to which no code could be expected to descend. . . ." He questioned whether "human ingenuity, reasoning *a priori,*" could ever match a system as wide, complete, and enduring as the common law.[53]

Tucker's confidence in the wisdom of the common law was a constant in his thought, and his effort to clarify special pleading in order to save it resulted from professional needs that other lawyers commented on as well. Even so, this work in defense of the common law reflected his view of sectional antagonism and eventual crisis. Possibly Tucker (like an anonymous writer in the *American Jurist*) saw in common-law safeguards of a master's claims in runaway-slave cases a "right of recaption" antedating the Constitution and federal statute. Yet the writ serving this purpose, *de homine replegiando,* in practice called for a jury trial to determine the facts of the case, and in Northern states law and sympathy sided with the black man. Too, Tucker realized that in any contest involving slavery reliance on the common law could cut both ways, since, among the rights it ensured, personal liberty was perhaps preeminent.[54]

Instead Tucker fastened on the common law because it was the stuff of nationhood: particular to each state, and therefore mirroring the sovereignty he said states retained in the federal system, the common law would outlast sectional clash and disunion. The common law—and Lieber's *Political Ethics* offered assurances of its durability—was most likely to survive the accidents of governmental change. Constitutional forms were as fleeting as the principles of the common law were firm; the South, Tucker hoped, would soon withdraw from the Union, and when it did the common law would remain. It would ensure order during crisis and continuity afterward. The "Law of Common Right," Tucker maintained, "can never perish while men retain a sense of value of rational liberty and the capacity to enjoy it."[55]

Too, replacing constitutional securities with those of the common law was one way Tucker could establish his own academic reputation, which, in Henry's shadow, had proved elusive. When Beverley first assumed his father's chair in law, he had written optimistically of editing a law journal for Duff Green and of soon making his lectures into a book that would bring both renown and profit. But Green's editorship fell through, and a decade later the volume of lectures was still forming. Tucker's notes on Tocqueville remained in manuscript, waiting to become the landmark commentaries on American society and politics he had planned. In the meantime Henry, at the University of Virginia—besides publishing his own lectures on government and the laws of Virginia—had in recent years turned out volumes on constitutional and natural law. The Tucker brothers exchanged copies of their work, and Henry, expressing thanks for some of Beverley's "beautiful productions," promised "to use them when the occasion will permit." Yet the younger man had spoken often of his jealousy of the university in Charlottesville and believed Henry's love for Union all but monomaniacal. Beverley's resentment at being the "other" Tucker continued to smolder.[56]

Not until late in 1844 did Tucker's book of lectures, a volume designed to meet what he said were the "earnest and oft'repeated" requests of his law students, finally near completion. It was a faltering finish. After mailing most of his bulky manuscript to a Philadelphia printer in November and waiting months for a reply, Tucker learned that the printer did not consider himself a publisher, that the principal publisher in that town "declined to meddle" with the Virginian's book, and that two of his lectures had disappeared along the way. Thus at the height of the Texas annexation discussion, while trying to keep Bayly in Washington supplied with arguments and rejoinders, Tucker was forced to take time to do annoying rewrite work. In the following spring, when Cary & Hart at last published the book, their blunders and carelessness had so botched the text that, as Tucker noted in a sharply worded errata sheet, "some of the allusions must be unintelligible."[57]

Less a climax than a summary of Tucker's thought, the *Lectures on the Science of Government* were repetitious and discursive, occasionally reflective, more often sentimental or indignant. What was to have been an intellectual triumph was merely a collector's convenience. Tucker included in this volume most of the discourses he had delivered to students and literary groups, his *Southern Magazine* review of Upshur on Story's *Commentaries,* and an address he had made to a Richmond mercantile association in 1841. He also reprinted the case he had made for states' rights federalism six years before at the Petersburg Lyceum. There were familiar references to repub-

lican government as a moral discipline that involved self-knowledge and the
will to conquer the "mystery of iniquity" in man's nature; there were
numberless asides on the heritage of Virginia and the need to resurrect
the pride and sustain the values of bygone, glorious days. In a dozen lectures until now unpublished, he reiterated the origins of society and government and repeated his view of natural rights, equality, and property. Tucker's
Lectures led to what he called the "boundary between what is known and
that which is unknowable." Making that journey was supposed to deepen in
the student a sense of ignorance "such as his teacher was not ashamed to
avow."[58]

V

It was ironic, considering Tucker's scholarly hopes, that his most successful
piece of writing in these months was a sentimental romance he serialized in
the *Southern Literary Messenger*. Beginning in the fall of 1844 and continuing through the entire next year, Tucker's story, called "Gertrude," traced
the fortunes of a "poor country girl" from a cottage in rural Virginia to a
townhouse that was the hub of social life in nearby Washington. Readers
followed the tale eagerly. When the pressures of Tucker's work and a bout
with illness prevented his sending off installments to Richmond, the editor
of the magazine and a former Tucker student, Benjamin Blake Minor, wrote
that subscribers clamored for more. Its appeal encouraged Minor's hope that
he could increase circulation of the literary journal.[59]

On one level at least, "Gertrude" was a love story. Just before the girl
leaves for the city, where she will be less a burden on her financially strained
family, she realizes that she is in love with her stepbrother Henry, a handsome youth whom Tucker portrays as honorable, virtuous, and "bred to the
bar." Though the lovers make plans to marry, Gertrude's mother, Mrs. Austin,
has other ideas. She is a coldly practical, mercenary figure whose aim is to
wed her daughter to money, ease the plight of the family, and continue her
spendthrift habits. Soon after Gertrude establishes herself in Washington,
and despite her steadfast loyalty to Henry, she inadvertently charms the
most attractive of all bachelors in the city. This Colonel Harlston, congressman from South Carolina and a well-to-do planter, brings a glitter to Mrs.
Austin's eyes. Excitedly she promotes the one-sided relationship, while
working like a witch in a fairy tale to undermine and frustrate Gertrude's
discovered love for Henry.

At first what Minor termed the "principle to be enforced" in the story
puzzled him, but no doubt before long he saw that "Gertrude" was closely
allied to Tucker's more serious work. For one thing Tucker took advantage
of his readers' interest to remind them of the temptations one found at the
seat of federal power. It was conspicuously in Washington that virtue was

most in want, where Gertrude found herself "continually exposed to influences" that threatened to transform her. Writing at a time when memories of depression were fresh, Tucker also made "Gertrude" a parable on banking. Gertrude's stepfather, the kindly Dr. Austin, had held to the common belief that investing in bank stock was the most dependable means of a regular cash income. Austin's bank collapsed—apparently as a result of overspeculation, but in his words because the capital was "embezzled"—and the hapless country doctor was left holding worthless paper. Tucker's message was not antibank altogether; only a few years before he had tried to help the Tyler administration plan its policy on a national bank. Tucker used Dr. Austin's bad luck to harp on the evil effects of loosely chartered, badly administered "wildcat" banks. Banks were complex. They often promised too much. Dr. Austin, "no politician nor political economist," could have benefited from the counsel of wiser men like Tucker, whose plan for a federated system would have prevented many banking excesses.[60]

Most noticeably, however, "Gertrude" was a discussion of womanhood—a homily on the value of simplicity, sentiment, and Christian character in what most nineteenth-century Americans saw as quite obviously the weaker sex. Tucker had begun this lesson in the two novels he published in 1836. Especially in *George Balcombe,* he called on Virginia women to reject the "ologies" of female radicals like Fanny Wright; there were, he said, "secrets in heaven and earth not dreamed of in their philosophy." The noblest of God's works was a *"right woman,"* Balcombe insisted, *"a genuine unsophisticated woman"* in whose heart great truths displayed themselves to learned and unlearned alike. The "march of mind" ruined women. Their business was to do plain housewifely duties, read the Bible, darn stockings, and as Tucker put it, "boil their bacon and greens together." Like Mrs. Balcombe and the Trevor women in *The Partisan Leader,* Gertrude was delightful in her ordinary honesty. She conquered Washington society because she was free from fashionable affectation. "The beautiful and graceful need no such sophistication," Tucker explained, "and the cheerful, amiable, and intelligent, gifted by nature with acuteness and tact, are at once at home in every society."[61]

Tucker provided reasons for his audience to see in his treatment of simple female virtues a celebration of weakness, daintiness, and lilting deference. Women in his romances, as in the plantation novels of other writers like John Pendleton Kennedy and William Gilmore Simms, were seemingly fragile beings, utterly subservient to men. In Balcombe's phrase, a wife ought to reflect the character of her husband, to be a "moon" to his brightness. Woman, said Tucker in "Gertrude," was "passive, yielding, and accommodating from the necessity of her position" and dependent therefore on the men who "regulated her destiny." Tucker's doting on the simple beauty of Gertrude placed him in the company of Northern writers in these decades whose portrayals of Southern women could easily leave the impression of fawning aloofness or shielded delicacy.[62]

Still, these references and similar ones only spoke to one side of a dynamic relationship and underplayed Tucker's awareness of the real power women naturally exercised. Important to his argument, and another index of his agreement with other writers, was that women were "generous, devoted, trusting, tender, and weak" because God intended them to be so. Simple and heart-centered, women were for that reason likely repositories of God's grace; they were Christlike because of their part in the family. It gave Tucker great joy—and had moved Upshur to rhapsodize on the Williamsburg household—that Lucy as a mother exuded just this virtue. Like Horace Bushnell, the Hartford minister whose *Views of Christian Nurture* in 1847 made an appeal for a Godly homelife that would raise young Americans steeped in holiness, or like the anonymous writer of a long sermon on domesticity that a Richmond Presbyterian paper, *The Watchman of the South,* reprinted in these years, Tucker saw God's hand in the "established order of the universe." Habit formed virtue, and therefore the mother of the Christian family was central to the work of teaching pure and virtuous conduct: she hastened "the universal reign of domestic happiness." A teacher, the woman was also an object lesson. Gertrude's sweet simplicity, like a simple faith, promised to baffle and triumph over the "ways of this bad world."[63]

Women honored and obeyed their husbands. But if they were silent, they were also strong, playing in God's domestic plan the part of moral prompters, moral energizers, who loved, scolded, and exalted men to do better, to be better, and to do them honor. Balcombe told his wife that he owed all honor to her, having guided himself by "'the confident unerring instinct of *woman's love'*"; Henry's commitment to Gertrude elevated his sentiments and gave his life an extra moral dimension. "To your service will I devote all my powers," he swore to her, making the same pledge Tucker once had made to Lucy. "I will seek distinctions. I will win honors and you shall wear them as a garland." From that night, Tucker told readers of "Gertrude," the young man's "views were loftier, his purposes more definite, his measures bolder, his spirit more enthusiastic, and his whole character roused to a new energy." He developed a force of mind that he had not before suspected in himself. He rushed into life with "vigor and mission."[64] Tucker's attention to womanhood in his writings served to emphasize the hope he placed in the family as the best promoter of evangelical faith and through it of social strength.

VI

Indeed here was the theme that united Tucker's discussions of various topics in the mid-1840s. God's benevolence and men's boldness went together:

Southern institutions generated moral men fit for the tasks ahead of them. Just as women braced and prepared men for providential work, it was the responsibility the black man imposed on the master that gave slavery its moral value. Because the master was a tutor of Christianity, slavery worked "great moral improvement" on the slaveholder as well. Slaves were part of the family; like the family, they were a means to grace. While it was easy for white men to lord over blacks their position as superiors, wrote Tucker, to do so "stifled sympathy, nourished false pride, engendered false appetites, and stimulated indulgence and excess. . . ." The slave was a moral responsibility, testing a man's moral fiber, shaming the "proud, self-seeking, restless, discontented, thankless master."[65]

Even Tucker's essay on the principles of pleading, which Harvard law professor Simon Greenleaf welcomed and helped Tucker get through its Boston printing in 1846, had as an implicit larger purpose the preservation of a legal institution that helped to mold men. The common law was more than the sum of experience in a practical, adversary system of justice. It was a reflection of common sense, order, and tradition, impressing its students with these virtues; it "consecrated" freedom of thought, speech, and action. "It is the honour of the Common Law," Tucker told one of his later law classes, "that he who studies it presently acquires a habit of doubting whether what is unjust can be law, and whether that which is unaccountable can be true."[66] By training young Virginia lawyers to respect the common law, Tucker tempered in them the same steel of resistance that Burke had attributed to revolutionary readers of Blackstone.

No doubt there was much wishful thinking here, just as there was in Tucker's fictional discussions of pliant western Virginians. He hoped that his training of young men in the law would make them tribunes of common liberties. He prayed that the domination of whites over blacks would not arouse those "appetites" and promote the "indulgences" by which, he admitted, "the moral and intellectual man is transformed from the image of his God to that of a beast."[67] Tucker may have intended his homely portraits of Southern women to persuade them to be more as he pictured them than as they were, though actually Fanny Wright could count on few followers among them. In emphasizing the moral tutelage women provided, Tucker may have betrayed a worry that Southern women were inclined to use that moral mandate against slavery, though again there was scant evidence that the women of the South were on the whole more likely than the men to identify morality with antislavery.[68] Tucker's strictures on womanhood did draw on the fanciful memories of one who, tragically early in life, had lost his maternal tie. He did exaggerate Southern ways that he hoped would underscore cultural differences between North and South and thereby further the cause of separate nationhood.

True too that all this talk of fortifying the Southern gentleman—husband, slaveholder, lawyer—spoke as directly as Tucker ever did to the anguish he felt as changes in American life continued to undermine the authority men of talent and training once had exercised. In his *Lectures* he made the decline of the English ruling aristocracy an allegory of development he either had experienced or saw coming. England, he wrote, had lost herself worshipping mammon. Men newly wealthy had replaced the traditional nobility, whose peerage rested on military prowess, and thus had elevated "the gilded crest of the *millionaire* above the coronet of the noble." Men of commercial or industrial wealth bought out landowners and spurned chivalry, he said; such wealth knew neither stability nor locality. Nor did it know honor, in the sense of playing by established rules. Instead of fox chases in the English countryside, there were now slaughters on well-stocked game preserves. Instead of well-bred four-mile racers, horses were now scrawny creatures unable to run past a milepost. The generous hunter and the gallant saddle horse, it seemed, had gone the way of the country gentleman—gone with the military spirit, the taste for danger, the love of "hardy sports and vigorous exercises that 'toughen manhood.'" No reader could have missed the message that the Virginia gentleman could disappear as surely as was the English gentry, and there were real reasons for these apprehensions.[69]

Tucker, besides being subject to such special interests and private anxieties, had never developed the cast of mind that suggested he try to stand outside his society and judge it. Yet his society did differ markedly from social patterns emerging elsewhere, and he—unusually sensitive to such changes, losing "control" in several ways at once—was in a position to offer stinging commentaries on them. Tucker argued for the community he believed to be part of God's plan for men and therefore crucial to their well-being. Everyone needed personal relationships that gave assurances of social position and continuity with the past, that raised expectations no higher than could be fulfilled, that promised control over the immediate affairs of life, and that were based on trust—a mutual sense of responsibility—in dealings with others. Losing this simplicity and facing the unknown, frightening developments of factories, wage earning, and moneymaking at noteworthy human cost alarmed Northerners and Southerners alike—leading, for one thing, to the concern for womanly piety and family strength as a domestic counterweight to social change.[70] Old-fashioned women ensured warmth and structure in the family and the passing down of sturdy values. Slavery more than any other topic was the pivot on which debates over the direction of American life turned because it was the ultimate bond, at least the ultimate power relationship, between one person and another.

It was indicative of Tucker's view of the way the world should be that land was crucial to it. The folksy trust that was so much a part of community, and also of the Christian life, was easiest to maintain in a rural setting where men and women knew one another and their forebears. The framework of "Gertrude" was the attempt of the girl's parents to hold onto their land, to save the family farm from the brokers and creditors who in distant cities laid paper claim to it; the two examples of wretchedness and corruption Tucker drew in the romance were characters owing their troubles to rootlessness. Since unlanded wealth could change the character of the South as it had that of England and was changing Northern society, it was important to Tucker that in this country there was plentiful land in the West. Though the opening of new lands caused social upheaval, as he knew first-hand, he thought these problems only temporary. In his commentaries on Tocqueville, Tucker wrote that, as soon as men had claimed all usable land, its possession would probably once more become a distinction, and then "its effect in giving permanency & locality to the affections and stability to society" would be "decidedly advantageous." Living on the land, whether as owner or tenant, promoted a "sort of family tie" by which ordinary af-fections ensured moderate duties and ready compliance. When the relation of landlord and tenant was exchanged for that of debtor and creditor, heredi-tary ties gave way to sharp practice and ill feeling.[71]

Even without Tucker's finished notes on *Democracy in America,* readers could see in his writings the outline of a therapeutic proposal. It represented good intentions, the sincerity of a kindly man whose adherence to heart could indeed mean warmth and affiliation. Where every person participated in a free-for-all after wealth and position, people became isolated and com-petitive and binding institutions were undermined. His answers to these dif-ficulties was not to withdraw from the world into experimental laboratories, as Northerners apparently did in forming utopian cells, but to forge again the links between man and his woman, master and his servant, to find "anchorage" in land and law. To Tucker it appeared providential that all these means were at the disposal of the South. The uniqueness of the Southern social order only made him more certain of that Providence, just as the wilderness his own voice cried in convinced him that he was part of a plan far larger than he was given to understand. A "chosen one" himself, Tucker believed that the South could in the same way be the agent of God's work in this world, that Southerners were the chosen people of the Ameri-can testament. The South was destined to be the exemplar of God's moral government, the place where community and those natural ties "by which the mind is informed, and the heart made better" persisted despite the in-trusions and temptations of modern life.[72]

A large number of eastern Virginians, most of them gentlemen perhaps, shared the discontent that helped Tucker see in traditional life a tonic for a distressed world. Few of them, however, drank more deeply of it than did Tucker. In fact his therapy was a sickness itself, an evasion of realities he would not accept, a protest of trust issued from fear. He was willing to inflict injury in order to impose community. The struggle to obtain Texas, he wrote, expecting Mexico to resist that move, would prompt the belief among Southerners that *"to a stout heart and strong will in a good cause nothing is impossible."* Expanding Southern territory into Texas would bring both the land so critical to the stable society and a contest for that land, raising the blood of the Southern gentleman and uniting society behind him. War, he said in his *Lectures,* had strengthened the natural ties of old English society. The wife who rushed out of her cottage to greet her returned warrior fully devoted herself and their children to him; in the grim fellowship of the campaign against a common enemy there arose a "community of feeling" between officer and soldier by which the private could share in the glory his leaders won. Asleep in England, the military spirit, wrote Tucker, could animate a whole people. Foreign war was an evil, but not the worst. Who, he asked, "would purchase peace abroad by discord and insurrection at home?"[73]

CHAPTER EIGHT

"Thro' the Lips of Madmen"

WHILE TUCKER'S late-winter letter to Bet Bryan was dismal enough to be catching, this favorite niece and friend of more than twenty years did her best to cheer him. His wife and their children were healthy and comfortable, she wrote. Tucker's position was honorable, the work of teaching was congenial, and "the opportunity of doing good to others thrown your way," so important to a man of his temper, was a "crowning blessing." By the standards of most men Tucker could view his life as a commission fulfilled. He had told his students that they were his "testament to the rising generation," and many of them were busy in politics, successful in law, and devotedly loyal to him. He remained active, providing essays and reviews for the *Southern Quarterly Review,* which William Gilmore Simms edited from his home outside Charleston; Tucker planned a biography of John Randolph and had begun a textbook on the law of Virginia. Bet was puzzled that her uncle had let anything "real or imagined" mar his happiness. "As for enemies," she reported in this warm letter, "as far as I know you have none."[1]

But in February 1850 Tucker was a prophet whose prophecies had failed and whose enemies were multiplying in his mind. He was ignored, his voice lost and message unheeded. "What unprofitable waste of breath" it was, he now declared to incoming law students, "trying to sway the minds of others." Why was it that the experience of age was lost to men, he asked them; why were the "teachings of the old, the grave, the austere, the devout so often thrown away on the young, the joyous, and the inconsiderate?" The last three years, he told Bet, had been "disheartening." He felt betrayed. Persons from whom he had every right to expect friendship and gratitude had paid him in "treachery and wrong." He collected these injustices no less eagerly than he displayed them for his few listeners. "If my friends were only as active as my enemies I should not care," Tucker wrote later that year; "but friends are often neglectful, enemies never." He protested that he suffered such unfairness without complaint, "opposing only passive resistance to wrong, and bearing the evil as I may." Depressed and apprehensive, Tucker may once again have felt like the English poets Lord Byron and William Cowper, with whom he had loved to compare himself while mourning the deaths of two wives in Missouri many years before. If he was

mad it was a "reasoning madness," he had said then, and when "God conde-
scends to communicate with men, he does it thro' the lips of madmen."[2]

I

It was the first week of September 1846. As had become Tucker's habit, he
was spending the month resting at the White Sulphur Springs resort near
Warrenton, a place Richmond newspapers described as "a charming retreat
from the Summer and cares of life," a "sovereign remedy for *ennui* and low
spirits."[3] This season there was a special reason to seek such escape. The
country was at war with Mexico and the conflict had widened considerably
since late spring. With American military help, California had revolted against
Mexican rule; in mid-August United States forces entered Santa Fe and ab-
solved all inhabitants of their allegiance to Mexico. That same month, David
Wilmot, a Pennsylvania congressman, expressed widespread Northern disap-
proval of the war by submitting as an amendment to a military appropriations bill the proviso that slavery would be prohibited in all territory won in
the war.

But at the Springs, it was the tournament season, a romantic pageant that
helped make this resort one of the most popular in the region. There were
knights in bright silks with titles like "the Knight of the Rappahannock"
and "the Black Knight of Hiawatha"; beneath an ornate reviewing stand
"fair Ladyes" from Richmond, Baltimore, and Washington eagerly awaited
the competition. By spearing brass rings at a full gallop, each rider sought
to make his lady queen of the fancy ball that climaxed the festival. As
heralds sounded a brass fanfare, the contestants and their horses arrayed
themselves before the stand to hear the "Gentleman Judge," Beverley
Tucker, read the invocation. It was an original sonnet that beckoned his
hearers to a happier, simpler day; it spoke of nymphs, crowns of love and
beauty, of the goddess whose instruments the lads were and whose purpose
they fulfilled. Strive boldly, Tucker abjured the "knights"—in a charge that
echoed his less whimsical lectures and addresses—"strong in the consciousness of your own faith and truth." Forward to the lists, he chanted:

> Bright eyes are upon you;
> And love's warm breath shall lend its rich perfume
> To the applause that waits upon your triumph.

After the tournament the sunset along the upper Rappahannock was striking, the sun lowering behind a dark cloud that seemed to rest on the crest of
the Blue Ridge mountains in the distance. Bright flashes of heat lightning
played around and above smaller clouds of every variety and hue. The scene
would have challenged the brush of the most sensitive artist, reported a correspondent for the Richmond *Enquirer;* it was sublime and impressive, and
"such another sun-set may not be again seen."[4]

The 1846 season at Fauquier Springs was, by at least one account, the best the resort ever had. Hundreds of guests, including high officers of government and "learned professors and literary men," wiled away time with old friends. There were abundant opportunities to make new acquaintances. Tucker made a showing at the evening music and dancing functions; he walked with other visitors along the paths that led down to the river and through the hillside meadows. A dinner given at Warrenton in honor of Polk's vice-president, George M. Dallas, was a highlight of the 1846 season and brought Tucker to table with Virginia senator John Y. Mason, cabinet members Robert J. Walker and George Bancroft, and the young Illinois congressman Stephen A. Douglas. A reporter for a local newspaper described the dinner as "ordered and decorous," though there were thirteen prepared toasts at the affair and some forty more volunteered from the tables. One of these salutes hailed Tucker as among Virginia's "most learned and loyal sons."[5]

With such notice Tucker might have broadened his friendships, but for the most part he let these opportunities slip by. Temperamentally unsuited for the business of getting to know people, caring little for the ceremonies of introduction, and taking pride in being an "old fashioned body" uninterested in elbow-rubbing, Tucker stuck largely with old Springs acquaintances. He found the elderly John Buckner Thruston, judge of the United States Circuit Court in Washington and a Virginia-born veteran of the Revolution, a delightful companion until his death in 1845; Judge John Scott of the Virginia General Court and earlier a conservative delegate to the 1829-30 constitutional convention was a regular at the resort and another Tucker favorite.[6]

Except perhaps for George Bancroft, with whom the Virginian may have exchanged a few words at the Warrenton dinner, Tucker's few Northern friends at the waters were generally not the sort to twit him or to test his assumptions. Vice-President Dallas came down from Pennsylvania each summer to the springs and fully agreed with Tucker that abolitionists, "in their career of fanaticism," regarded slavery as a precipice over which they could tumble all institutions. Adam Waldie, a Philadelphia publisher whom Tucker always looked forward to seeing at Fauquier, was a literary patron of Tucker and Upshur in the early 1840s. A self-proclaimed aristocrat, Waldie read *George Balcombe* three times, found the romance a fertile source of "imaginings and cogitations," and saw in Tucker the "magnanimity of a great mind."[7]

By the 1840s a series of misunderstandings and perceived rebuffs had broken Tucker's few links with minds more active than Waldie's. Tucker's correspondence with Francis Lieber, at first so promising in its candor and mutual good feeling, closed coolly. Having offered to write a review of the *Political Ethics*, Tucker learned that his friend at South Carolina College

cared only for reviews done by the "hand of a master." Clumsily, Lieber
then declined to write a notice of Tucker's Randolph-Macon address.
Tucker so doubted the interest of outsiders in his ideas that, when asked
in 1844 to choose for his planned National Institute address a subject less
sensitive than slavery, he had decided against appearing at all. Preparing
Pleading for its Boston publisher, Tucker's strenuous and self-conscious
effort to gain the good offices of Simon Greenleaf at Harvard suggested
once again his uncertainty of his own intellectual standing. Of limited help,
though encouraging, Greenleaf chided the Virginian for his "quite lover-
like" protests of neglect when Greenleaf fell behind in his writing. Apparently surprised to find *Pleading* dedicated to him, the New Englander was tardy
in his thanks for this honor and remiss in helping Tucker get his book a
review in the *Law Reporter*. After November 1846, he too dropped from
Tucker's list of correspondents.[8]

Never were the consequences of such isolation more serious, for no act
of state in Tucker's lifetime rivaled the Mexican War in the momentous
problems it raised. Politicians in 1846 quarreled over the cloudy origins of
the conflict and over what was to be done with the territory gained and the
people conquered as a result of it. Northern opponents of the war objected
not merely because it would extend the boundaries and prolong the life of
slavery. James Russell Lowell, poking bitter fun at Anglo-Saxon claims to
superiority over the Mexicans, suggested American artillerymen wrap their
shot in leaves from the New Testament so that they would be "shooters as
well as *fishers* of men." When a whole country was unjustly overrun and
conquered by a foreign army and subjected to military law, it was "not too
soon for honest men to rebel and revolutionize," wrote Henry David
Thoreau, particularly when "ours is the invading army."[9]

Had Tucker made contact with the antislavery and antiwar writers of the
Concord circle, he might have been surprised at the points on which they
could have agreed. Besides having roots in generational differences, the
impulses of Tucker and the transcendentalists were both reactions to the
rude dislocation of contemporary change. Thoreau wrote of the disgusting
materialism of mid-nineteenth-century America. Tucker in Williamsburg
complained of "habits of luxury & the prevailing taste for ostentation."
While Emerson dismissed New England politicians as a sorry lot with "saucy
village talents," Tucker described their Southern counterparts as "empty
bags" incapable of standing up. Like Thoreau, for whom the Walden experience was a ritual of renewal, of purification through simplicity and a return
to first principles, Tucker saw his part as one of regeneration: if Thoreau saw
in the wilderness of the West the "tonics and barks which brace mankind,"
for Tucker the prairies of Texas and the frontier beyond carried the challenge
that made manhood. In Emerson's "self-reliance"—the moral independence
that pleaded "trust thyself"—there were similarities to Tucker's "heroic"
willingness to challenge the car of destiny.[10]

But while the failings and superfluities of American life led the New England transcendentalists to an activist nonconformity, a heightened self-consciousness, and an urge to form the future, Tucker's sense of corruption led him to an escapist chivalry, a fear of self-criticism, and a wish to recapture the past. While Tucker found meaning for man only in society and its institutions, Emerson called society an enemy of manhood. Emerson's transcendentalism recognized the equal participation of all creatures in homeostatic Nature; Tucker's Burkean organicism explained, to the contrary, the natural inequality of men. Transcendentalism tried to raise man's awareness by searching for an overarching, intuited unity. Tucker's intuition was the deadening awareness of common sense, the submerging of consciousness into the lowest common denominator of every man's feeling. For Tucker, history was the key to natural and right relationships and values; Emerson believed that the centuries were "conspirators against the sanity and authority of the soul." As Tucker tried to revitalize Virginia on the basis of selected values of past ages, Emerson, who was calling for an American Scholar, dismissed a "foolish consistency" as the "hobgoblin of little minds."[11]

These intellectual differences, making all the more apparent the fairyland of Tucker's medieval tournament, led the Virginian to a very different view of the Mexican War. While Thoreau, Lowell and others saw it as a moral outrage, a departure from peaceful principles and a perversion of mission, Tucker justified the contest with Mexico as a matter of racial strength and holy crusade. God did not "visibly lay bare his almighty arm to fight the battles of the just," he wrote, but he taught "their hands to war and their fingers to fight." For Tucker the deity was, ambiguously, "always present to help those who will help themselves."[12]

II

Tucker was isolated, but not alone. Lucy and their children, always a source of warmth and pride, were especially important to him now—so important, in fact, that there was a plaintive quality to Tucker's expressions of both. Several years before, when Lucy and the young ones made one of their visits to the Smith family in Missouri, Tucker had yearned for their return, his heart, he wrote, "withering away for want of something to love." True, his sojourns to the Springs were often alone; he was, as Lucy put it, "a natural lover of peace and quiet" and she encouraged her husband to free himself as much as possible from household cares. But he was not one for the "awful solitude" of life without wife or family.[13]

Lucy Tucker, now thirty-five, had borne her husband six children by 1847. One daughter, her mother's namesake, had died in the fall of 1844. Tucker was fond of pointing out that the remaining five youngsters were

BEVERLEY TUCKER, c. 1846

robust and promising. His oldest son, St. George, was eight in 1847 and
making rapid progress in reading; Thomas Smith, six, was Tucker's favorite,
for reasons his father did little to hide. Hasty, violent, "but the most generous and affectionate creature that ever lived," Tommy was always ready
"to fight an injury and then to plead for the person that injured him," was
willing to fight Goliath himself in defense of his older brother. A visitor to
the Tucker home in these years described Cynthia, fifteen in 1847, as a
"graceful, slender" young woman of "dark sparkling eyes and rich raven
hair" whose beauty was "most refined and spirituelle."[14] Making Tucker's
discussions of feminine character in *Balcombe* and "Gertrude" partly the
lessons of a dutiful father, Cynthia helped in the household by caring for
her two younger sisters: Frances, only four, and Henrietta, born in January
1846. It was a sign of Tucker's clan pride, and of his persistent need to
make clear his position in the family, that each of the children received the
additional name Beverley. When yet another son was born into the family
in the spring of 1848, he, like his brothers and sisters, carried a title—really
a burden—touting his father. He was Berkeley Montague Beverley Tucker.
    Such fertility was not physically remarkable in a man of Tucker's age,
and for a Southerner of his temperament and station expressing love was

more than easy—it was necessary: he could be exceedingly tender toward persons in his charge, as he was with many of his students and was with Cynthia who, it was said, he "petted and idolized without spoiling." Nonetheless, for one so anxious about his lack of power in society and politics, siring children late in life was expressive in more ways than one. It demonstrated power in the quarter that was of heightened importance to him. Tucker felt the need to establish his domestic potency for many of the same reasons he spoke firmly of domestic authority in his writings. Aware of his inadequacy on a broader scale, he would at least prove himself capable of satisfying his younger wife. The sad truth was that Tucker doubted himself on this score as well. If we believed novelists and poets, he wrote Lucy in 1843 after reading Gustave Flaubert's *Madame Bovary,* "we should suppose it impossible for a young woman to love an old man." He quickly berated himself for such worries, for doubting Lucy's love even momentarily. While *Bovary* was a "powerfully written" story, and regardless what others might decide on bare facts, he was sure none of Flaubert's questions entered the minds of anyone who knew Lucy and him.[15]

In wanting "something to love" Tucker suggested how badly he himself wanted to be loved, and as his isolation and self-doubt increased so did the urgency of his need for sympathetic listeners. In the late summer of 1846 he reached out for the appreciative notice of the English conservative Carlyle, whose dim view of popular government and of wage-earning "freedom" Tucker had cited in his *Lectures on the Science of Government.* He sent along a copy of this work, which the Scotsman politely acknowledged in October as written in a "candid, ardent and manful spirit." Encouraged, Tucker wrote more letters for the packet to London, asking Vice-President Dallas to endorse and forward them and including Sir Robert Peel on his list of possible friends. Though Carlyle did carry on a regular correspondence with Emerson, he proved too busy to keep up an exchange with the Virginian; Peel never replied.[16]

Tucker's search for an intimate who shared his ideas and passions ended in December when he reopened his long-dormant friendship with James Henry Hammond. Now in his late thirties, having retired from public life after a term as South Carolina governor and a scandal that tied him to sexual liberties with the daughter of a friend, Hammond was tending to his Silver Bluff plantation, which, he said a bit unhappily, was "far from the great line of travel." Tucker's short note was rewarded with a lengthy message from Hammond regretting their silence of ten years, testifying that only recently he had opened Tucker's 1836 letters and read them again with the "keenest interest"; the law professor answered with an even more effusive letter that set the tone the two men maintained for several years. He was overjoyed at recapturing this onetime friend, certain that Hammond would provide the reassurance he was looking for. Tucker found it comforting that the younger man was willing to submit to his wisdom. "I wish to become one of your pupils," wrote Hammond, who was just as glad as Tucker to collect injustices and plot vengeance, "and will be thankful for all the time you can bestow upon me."[17]

The quick coziness of this rekindled friendship was symptomatic of the marginality of men like Tucker and Hammond, whose calls for disunion and separate culture received only occasional public response in the South. Tucker described himself as a man who was often made to feel "like an outlandish animal in a strange land." But his exchanges with Hammond were symphonies of harmonic thinking, dances that called for mutual back-scratching. Hammond lost no time praising the judge for his constancy and hailing him as a reasoner "bold & searching." "To hold communion with such a mind," was Tucker's reply ". . . is a high privilege in these days of drivelling corruption & coward[ly] compromise." Complaining of the lack of printing establishments in the South, the Virginian asked Hammond for extra sheets of his public letters to the British abolitionist Thomas Clarkson, which Tucker planned to use in his course on government; partly to recip-rocate, but mostly to draw from Hammond some of the same sustenance that he offered the Carolinian, Tucker sent off a bundle of his own essays and lectures. Hammond read everything the law professor sent him with what he said was "great & increasing pleasure," insisting that Tucker pro-duce a volume of his collected works.[18]

Offering to help in this effort was Hammond's bookish comrade William Gilmore Simms, whose publishing contacts in the North Hammond talked of enlisting in Tucker's behalf. Simms's origins hardly had marked him for much influence. His father, an unsuccessful Scotch-Irish shopkeeper, had run off to the Mississippi frontier when his son was still young, leaving him to the care of his maternal grandmother. Educated in the law, Simms's real love was journalism and fiction, fields that brought him pleasure but little pay. Like Hammond, he had eventually married well and become a junior member of the planter gentry in South Carolina. Earlier an opponent of nullification, Simms by the late 1840s had put that episode behind him. As the editor of the *Southern Quarterly Review*—a journal making a rigorous case for Southern culture—and a prolific writer of romances mostly glorify-ing Carolina history, he had become painstakingly correct in everything he said, wrote, and did.[19]

Though Simms had yet to meet Tucker, in the spring of 1847 he remem-bered *George Balcombe* as "an excellent & thoughtful novel" and said he esteemed its author as "a sound man, an able thinker and a charming writer." He was more than willing to contribute what he could to the preparation of a Tucker textbook on government. Neither he nor Hammond had seen the Virginian's *Lectures on the Science of Government*. But even after Tucker sent them a copy, they seemed so bent on flattery that they failed to see in

WILLIAM GILMORE SIMMS
at about the time of Tucker's death

it the very book they spoke of publishing. Simms and Hammond combined
to assure Tucker that only he could undertake the project; not even Calhoun
was as well qualified. "The cast of your mind, your historical, political, &
legal information, your long & close observation of the action of our Government . . . & your clear, vigorous & brilliant style of writing" all came together, purred Hammond, to make Tucker the writer who should supply
Southern statesmen with a manual of politics. It would, he said, place Tucker's
name "first on the roll of American political philosophers."[20] Such superla-
tives greatly pleased Tucker. It helped to have close friends who shared their
fears and aired their grievances.

It also helped to have intellectual "sons" who expressed filial affection
and proved their mentor's potency by carrying on the fight, spreading the
word, making converts. Tucker did indeed boast increasingly of the way he
"infused"—he used the word—his ideas into the minds of his students. Forgetting his earlier denials of indoctrinating them, he wrote Hammond proudly that not one of them had ever left him "without being, *for the time,* a
Southern man in feeling and a States-rights man in conviction." Tucker's
students in the mid and late 1840s made reports to Williamsburg that at first
gave him every reason to cheer. Powhatan Robinson in Petersburg wrote of
having been too "thoroughly imbued" with the truth of states' rights principles ever to renounce them. Joseph Carrington spoke of sound republican
doctrines as a "beacon light" warning Virginia of approaching danger. Robert
Ould in Washington often sent his love to Tucker, thanked him for molding
his opinions, and spoke of the pride he had in the correctness of the princi-

ples he learned at Tucker's feet. "Freedom from the hauntings of the spectre, Doubt," he said, "is a rare blessing." In 1847 Ould referred to his former professor lovingly as the *"pater"* of the states' rights creed.[21]

A number of Tucker's "progeny" were in a position to act on the principles he had labored to teach them. When in February 1847 the Virginia Assembly adopted resolutions condemning the Wilmot Proviso, Tucker claimed that this stand was indirectly his own work. The resolves, passing with a heavy majority, originated with a militant states' rights faction in the House of Delegates. First organized to support Calhoun for the 1844 Democratic presidential nomination, the group was also committed to the overthrow of the "old Hunker" party leadership in the state, which centered about the Ritchie family and the Richmond *Enquirer*. Former Tucker students were among the leaders of this insurgent Southern-rights faction from its earliest formation. In Richmond William W. Crump, a successful young lawyer who grew to be Tucker's close friend, was prominent among the "young fogies," as was Washington Greenhow, a William and Mary law graduate of 1839. Walter D. Leake was an active states' rights Democrat in Goochland County and a state legislator who kept in contact with his former mentor. In Tucker's own James City County, William S. Peachy worked in the radical Democratic cause; James B. Jones did so in Petersburg. Robert L. Montague, an ambitious young lawyer and a member of the prominent Middlesex County family, consulted often with Tucker and soon became well known in the tidewater as a Southern radical.[22]

Even through his students, however, Tucker's bid for effectiveness was none too firm in the spring of 1847, for these followers were not altogether successful in controlling the Virginia Democracy. Calhoun's criticism of the Mexican War and his break with the Polk administration that February caused division among radical Democrats in Virginia. Crump, Greenhow, and others who saw the Carolinian as the foremost Southern-rights spokesman found themselves at loggerheads with militants who were willing to drop him for the more aggressive standard of the anti-Wilmot resolutions. Crump and his friends sat out the spring elections, ineffective in councils and at least momentarily in disrepute. Because of the party disunity that Calhoun had worsened, Leake lost badly in the Richmond area congressional district to Tucker's archenemy John Minor Botts, who as a House member in 1842 had leveled charges of sedition against Tucker, Upshur, and William and Mary. Tucker could write his former students that he had told them so: the consequences of identifying themselves with Calhoun was paying the price of his blunders; winning control of political machinery was tricky business for men who prided themselves on being independent of party.[23]

III

The hardest lessons of the past year, though Tucker was no longer able to benefit much from them, were his own. Having wrapped himself in medieval romance and fawning friendship, he was more susceptible than ever to the pressure of time and the effects of disruption. The commencement address he delivered at William and Mary in July 1847 reflected this vulnerability. Still saddened by the death of Dew the preceding summer and now mourning the loss of William Harper in South Carolina, Tucker made his valedictory the production of one taking final stock. The great probability, he told students in the Wren Building, was that his voice would "now be heard for the last time within these walls"; he implored listeners to hear him as one "standing on the verge of time." He also made final charges, issuing a moving plea for continuity at the college. "Virginia *continues* what she is," he told graduates, "in part because the spirit of her ancient chivalry *continues* to act on her through William and Mary." Tucker called the college the "ark of Virginia's safety."[24]

In the fall William and Mary became instead a listing barge of discontent and infighting. Dew's death, removing an important source of leadership, permitted suppressed faculty jealousies and ill feeling to surface. After first trying to secure the services of John Johns, the assistant Episcopal bishop of the Virginia diocese, the Board of Visitors asked the interim president, Robert Saunders, who was professor of mathematics, to head the college. The board also chose George Frederick Holmes, a highly recommended young Englishman then teaching in Richmond, to handle the offerings in political economy, history, and elementary government. Finally, the Visitors named Archibald Peachy, a former Tucker student and a member of an old Williamsburg family, to teach moral philosophy, metaphysics, belles lettres, and logic.[25]

But the Peachy appointment rankled several faculty members, who considered the young man's appointment a matter not of academic credentials, which were slim, but of favoritism and political jobbery. President pro tem Saunders resigned his office in protest against it, and other faculty murmured angrily. Tucker, who greeted Holmes as a sturdy states' rights, free-trade man and who had helped engineer Peachy's selection, objected strongly but politely to the faculty "insurrection." Soon Tucker became engaged in an unfortunate quarrel with humanities instructor Charles Minnegerode, the German scholar whom he had helped attract to the college several years before. When Peachy discovered why Saunders had resigned, there were additional exchanges.

Everyone took sides. Early in the morning of November 23 Tucker was called out of his house in nightshirt and unbuckled shoes to help Peachy, who was armed and threatening to shoot, disperse a mob of students—faces blackened—blasting horns and rattling cow bells outside his bedroom window. There were rumors, fanned by gossips in Williamsburg and reported in the Richmond *Enquirer,* of a Saunders-Peachy duel that a student was

involved in negotiating; there was simultaneous talk in Richmond of making
William and Mary a state institution and moving it elsewhere, perhaps to
the capital. In January 1848 Holmes resigned his professorship in disgust.
Not long afterward the Board of Visitors in special session called for the
resignation of all faculty members pending a full review of the controversy
at the regular July meeting. Never had the fortunes of William and Mary
dipped so low.[26]

The very air in Williamsburg seemed poisoned. Earlier certain that the
whole affair would resolve itself, Tucker by the time Holmes left had pronounced his position at the college "almost intolerable." The controversy
angered him; Holmes's letter of resignation, describing William and Mary
as "a disorganized and sinking Institution" suffering an "inevitable decline,"
gnawed at him. Although his former students rained letters on the Board of
Visitors praising his capabilities and begging successfully for his reelection
to the faculty, the mass resignations caused Tucker much worry. At the close
of the academic year the number of graduates had dropped from forty-seven
the year before to thirty-two. In 1849 the total fell to a mere seven. Professors Millington and Holmes refused reelection and departed Williamsburg;
Minnegerode and Saunders went to other institutions. The Rector of Bruton
Parish, also involved in the furor, left the village in the summer of 1848. Of
the earlier college professors, only Tucker and his young friend Peachy remained. Fathers of prospective students wrote Tucker that the commotion
in Williamsburg gave them no choice but to send their sons to a more secure
academy, and Bet Coalter Bryan found the "disjointed state of Society" in
Williamsburg a baneful influence on Tucker's children, for whom the "carping tone of unkindness" was dangerously contagious.[27]

The tumult in Williamsburg that summer left Tucker highly sensitive to
the larger instabilities of 1848. He looked with morbid fascination on the
rash of revolutions convulsing Europe. News reached Williamsburg in March
of violent outbursts in Paris as workers, students, and the lower middle class
united in the depths of an economic depression to demand a more representative government and a wider suffrage from Emperor Louis-Phillipe. Though
the disturbance in France may have been—as Karl Marx observed from London—a farcical reenactment of the great Revolution of 1789–93, for Tucker
this latest social and political upheaval was much too similar to that earlier
one. The "giddy multitude" dominated the forces of order and law. Leaders
used "neat epigrams and specious paradoxes" to generate mob support. In
Lamartine, the revolutionary leader and literary figure who played a critical
part in the 1848 French upheaval, Tucker saw once again the malignity of
political abstraction, doubting that this "sky-scraping poet" for whom he
had reserved admiration would fare any better than the metaphysicians of
the first revolution. The brutality General Cavaignac used to put down
demonstrators during the chaotic "June Days" aroused in Tucker appre-

hensions of another reign of Napoleonic military despotism.[28]

Worst of all, the disorder in France raised the specter of wider revolution. Like Hammond, Tucker feared the speed of change the French upheaval symbolized; he was scarcely able to think of affairs there without holding his breath. "Before you look an event in the face," the South Carolinian complained, "it is elbowed off by a dozen new comers, each more worthy of your scrutiny." "Does it not seem to you sometimes that the world must be approaching some grand catastrophe?" he asked. Later in the year, when similar revolutions broke out in Italy, Hungary, Germany, and Ireland, Tucker answered with a question of his own: "Has Hell opened all her mouth?"[29]

In truth, revolution of a kind was brewing in Virginia as well. The movement for another constitutional convention had quietly continued throughout the 1830s and '40s. Complaints recurred of multiple voting by landowners in several counties, of city dwellers' controlling elections in nearby counties, and of the murkiness of the "householder" voting qualification. Since at least 1843 the *Enquirer* had been calling for what, in Tucker's mind, was that most horrid of possibilities—universal manhood suffrage. Most observant politicians in the state agreed that news of the 1850 census figures would bring support for a convention to a head. In the counties west of the Shenandoah Valley, where inequities of representation and taxation were especially marked, public meetings clamored for reform.[30]

Western agitation was partly a result of interest in the internal improvements that an eastern-dominated legislature had neglected and partly a consequence of political strategy on the part of Whigs, whose greatest strength was in the western counties. But it most alarmed Tucker for the antislavery sentiment it concealed. Providing basis for this concern was an *Address to the People of West Virginia* that Henry Ruffner, president of Washington College in Lexington, published in late 1847. In the booklet Ruffner, like other Virginians, lamented the "fallen condition of 'The Old Dominion.'" Unlike Tucker and most easterners, he laid blame for that lean and haggard condition on "the consuming plague of slavery." Slavery drove out free labor, argued the *Address,* and had a ruinous moral effect on whites. Ruffner went on to outline a slave emancipation plan which, if necessary, westerners could put in effect after separating from the rest of the state. In part calculated to win redress of sectional inequities, the pamphlet threatened to tie a white belt around the eastern counties of Virginia and leave them to their own devices; Ruffner included sharp words for the "chivalry and nullifiers" who meanwhile tried to justify slavery. "[W]hile we are gazing in astonishment & stupor at Europe," Hammond need not have reminded Tucker, are not "cunning men busy here preparing us for a catastrophe as much worse as our fall will be from a greater height to a lower depth[?]" "[T]here is no disguising the fact," concluded Tucker's congressman Thomas H. Bayly, "that we have traitors among us."[31]

Further unsettling to Tucker was the warming sectional battle over Mexican War spoils. Although the Senate defeated all efforts to pass the Wilmot Proviso, the problem of congressional power over slavery in the territories would not down. Organizing a territorial government for Oregon—where, for the time being, local laws prohibited slavery—Congress kept the issue alive throughout the early and summer months of 1848. The question of free-soil or slave territory in the West divided Democrats and embarrassed Whigs in the presidential campaign, and the openly sectional character of the new Free Soil Party confronted Southern slaveholders with an undisguised threat. Tucker agreed with Hammond that a military hero might "succeed in purging our rapidly increasing distempers" and for that reason thought the Whig candidate, the uncomplicated, apolitical General Zachary Taylor, a "God-send." Tucker rejoiced in Taylor's election, but together with Hammond worried over the advice the new President would have and planned on writing a series of open letters to Taylor. Meanwhile the threat of the Wilmot measure was distracting in the extreme. Hammond wrote in November that disunion was freely discussed in Carolina, old Union men of the nullification crisis participating in it; he spoke of "writhing under the passage of the Proviso." When in December an Ohio congressman offered a resolution in favor of restricting slavery in New Mexico and California, Tucker's nephew Beverley, now in Washington, saw "in effect" the success of the Proviso. "God be our Deliverer," he wrote his uncle; he for one was ready to put on his armor.[32]

Annus mirabilis was the term Tucker later used to describe 1848. A year of frightening European events, disturbances in Williamsburg, and important turns in federal politics, it was also the year of a sad family loss, for in August, after a long illness, Henry Tucker died at his home in Winchester. Henry's death left Beverley the sole survivor of St. George Tucker's family, both removing a chastening source of criticism and confirming the younger brother's sense of peculiar mission. The effect of these events, within and outside the circle of Tucker's private influence, was to hasten the decay of mind that had begun much earlier. Not that Tucker's view of the world was utterly illogical or his thinking disjointed or episodic; certainly for Tucker, and for any Southerner whose emotional investments were in the same system and style of life, developments in 1848 were causes for worry. But Tucker's estimate of what he could do about events jibed ever worse with reality. His sense of the present and of his possibilities in it grew duller and duller, enlarging fancy and encouraging escapism. For one thing he firmly believed that he could shape the course Zachary Taylor, whom he had never met or written, chose to follow as President.[33] After Tucker learned that no Washington newspaper would carry the advisory articles he had hoped to compose for Taylor, he traveled there in March to put the new chief executive straight.

By the trip, Tucker explained to Bet Coalter Bryan, he aimed to see "whether reckless exposure may not bring about what care and nursing have failed to accomplish." His guide in Washington was young Beverley, Henry's son, who took pride in being a clever businessman there and a prodigy in capital intrigue. With Beverley by his side, Tucker plunged into the hoopla of Taylor's inauguration, satisfied that many important people—"Pendletons and Danridges & such"—discovered him to be "the *gamest* old man they ever saw" and especially pleased to come across an old friend, the Kentucky judge and former treasury secretary George M. Bibb, who agreed to introduce Tucker to the President. When Bibb and Tucker and Beverley appeared at the postinauguration White House reception, Taylor—who surely was at that point more interested in the punch bowl than in any conspiracy against Southern rights—proved more difficult to buttonhole than Tucker had expected. Convinced despite these unlikely circumstances that he could win Taylor over, Tucker later reported that he would have succeeded except that "Jonathan after Jonathan pushed up," introduced himself or his wife to the President, and then whisked him away. Three times, he insisted, Taylor had tried to hear what he had to say. So angry was Tucker when he left the crowded party that in August he was still stewing about the "impudent yankeys" who had thwarted him.[34]

When the present bore heavily, pondering the Virginia past offered the same refuge Tucker took in mock-medieval jousting matches. In November, when the budding illustrator David Hunter Strother visited Williamsburg and with his uncle, a Randolph, spent an evening with the Tuckers, his impression was not only one of generous hospitality but also of the pressing weight of the past. He left "steeped in dreamy traditions." Much of this ambience belonged to the Tucker house itself—its portraits of family members "in the quaint costumes of past generations," its parquetted oaken floors with semicircles worn in them by the swinging of the heavy doors, its furniture "solid, dark, and ancient." Certainly Strother's impression was the mellower because of the hot whiskey punch Tucker called for, and the gray-headed servant Ganymede took care to keep the guests' silver goblets filled.[35]

But mostly it was Tucker who left this "dreamy" impression of graceful decadence. After one or two students had joined him and his guests in the sitting room, and after Cynthia had come in and wished everyone a good night, Tucker spoke exuberantly of the past glory and great men of Virginia. "Mortified by the decrepitude of his native State," as Simms noted not long after Strother's account, Tucker was capable of the "noblest appeals to the slumbering patriotism and virtues of his countrymen." That evening, with the young artist, his uncle, and the students gathered around, Tucker doubtless made the same comparison between old Virginia and old England that had appeared so often in his letters and that he had made implicit in a review of Thomas Macaulay's *History of England* written that spring for Simms's *Quarterly*. The country gentleman, unlettered and un-polished though he may have been—Tucker pointed out—was all the same a gallant and genial fellow. Surrounded by men who were his equals or by others "confessedly his subordinates or dependents," he was proud of family, jealous of rights, and familiar with arms. An old clock on the fire-place mantle "tingled its silver bells unheeded," recalled Strother, as his host, increasingly eloquent, explored such "mellow and engaging themes" and told of his own brushes with destiny—of shaking hands with Washing-ton and sitting down to table with John Hancock. Tucker's charming con-quest of Strother only underlined his failures outside the frame house in which, he admitted, he showed "to more advantage than anywhere except on paper. . . ."[36]

Like many other Southerners, Tucker was not pleasantly surprised when Taylor in the first year of his administration depended more on high-tariff and antislavery Whigs than on the counsel of states' rights, proslavery men in the party or out of it. But Tucker, believing himself a prime candidate for advisor and having earlier praised Old Zach for his "simplicity, integrity, fidelity, moderation, prudence, magnanimity, and . . . every thing necessary to constitute true greatness," was particularly out of sorts. One solution was to add perversity to Taylor's list of qualities. When in October Cali-fornians organized themselves and adopted an antislavery constitution, Tucker concluded that the chief executive—and the emissary he sent there inviting them to go ahead with a convention—had conspired to bring about the result. That gathering, he later charged, was a mob headed by a military governor appointed by the President. By late November Tucker had de-cided that he was a vindicated counselor now secretly pined after. Having heard "quite authentically," he was sure that Taylor was tired of being guided by false lights; having seen a letter Tucker had sent him before his recent three-month tour of the North, the President supposedly had spoken of it in a way suggesting that "he felt the want of such information as I gave him. . . ."[37]

More than anything else, however, Tucker tried to put the wayward course of the Taylor administration out of mind. From August to early December, Hammond heard nothing from his usually effusive correspon-dent. When Tucker finally did sit down with a pen, he told the Carolinian he had lacked the heart to write. "I have been so disgusted with the doings of the administration," he explained, "and so baffled in my attempt to let old Z. hear one word of truth, that I shrink from the topic of politics."[38]

IV

Tucker had nothing to do with calling the Nashville Convention. He nonetheless took full advantage of it as a means of proving himself the truly prescient Southern leader. The work of Calhoun supporters using contacts in Mississippi, the convention was set for the first Monday in June, 1850. Calhoun, again in the Senate, thought the meeting of delegates in the Tennessee capital would present the North with an unbroken Southern front and the alternative of dissolving the Union or of recognizing Southern interests within it—especially as they now involved questions of fugitive slaves, slavery in the District of Columbia, and slavery in the new western territories. Governors of Georgia, Alabama, and South Carolina asked their legislatures to support the convention; the governor of Virginia, John Floyd, whose father had held that office during the nullification crisis twenty years before, sent a message to the assembly in December 1849 endorsing the Nashville plan with enthusiasm. Tucker believed it promising in spite of Calhoun. Calhoun was too weak for the work Tucker wanted to do, too timid, too tainted—a secretary of state who had bargained for Texas and then a senator who had obstructed the effort against Mexico. Too radical for the frightened, Calhoun was too mercurial for the courageous. "The man I most dread," Tucker wrote Hammond in December, "is Calhoun."[39]

While Calhoun's thinking seemed fickle to Tucker, his own mind was mercurial in another way, quickly making the shift from melancholy withdrawal and mutterings of betrayal to strident activism. Here, he sensed, was his last opportunity to incite the rebellion he had so long hoped to see. If words could bring it about, Tucker had them ready. Each dispatch he dashed off to Hammond surpassed the preceding one in frantic patriotism. Were he in Congress, he said, he would agitate for Southern departure until he succeeded or the rascals expelled him. "The blood of martyrs is the seed of the church," he explained to his fellow disciple; was the South out of seed? When a man ought to fight, he continued, "and will not fight until he is kicked, I want to see him kicked." He would support the strongest measures Hammond would propose at the convention, or move the strongest the Carolinians would support. "Agitate! Yes, I would agitate," he wrote feverishly, but no one would listen to him or print what he had to say. Why do we cling with a death grip, asked this aging revolutionary, to hopes and plans that disunion would make irrelevant? "Why does not Ambition look forward to the high rewards which popular favor is eager to bestow, at the end of any revolutionary movement, on those who begin it[?]"[40]

Anxious as Tucker was to appear in Nashville, he had no assurance that he would attend officially. William Gilmore Simms—for whose *Southern Quarterly Review* Tucker had recently written a blistering indictment of French radicalism—assured the professor that because of the glory of his forebears his right to go to the convention was "unquestionable." Unlike the South Carolina legislature—which had chosen representatives, including Hammond, in caucus—the Virginia assembly seemed more likely to make the choice of delegates part of the regular spring elections. Tucker saw little chance of his success in a popular canvass. Traveling to Richmond in late January to confer with his friend Governor Floyd and finding several leaders keen on sending him to Nashville, the professor encouraged friends and former students in Richmond to push his selection as a specially appointed delegate. He announced his intention of traveling to Nashville on his own if need be.[41]

In long, laboriously statesmanlike passages, Tucker urged Hammond and the South Carolina delegation to Nashville to steer a firm public course. The popular mind, he correctly counseled in early February, was unprepared for blatant disunionism; the militants who tried to shape opinion had to be "careful not rashly to break the cord by which they would lead it." By Tucker's strategy the Nashville Convention would recommend certain constitutional amendments to Southern legislatures. Framed so that Southerners would see them as indispensable to their *"complete security,"* the amendments were to be written so that the requisite number of Northern states would *"surely not"* accept them. Under this cloak of reasonableness, Tucker wanted to "keep the thing simmering" until 1852, when Southerners could unite on a favorite son and thus prevent the selection of a President in the electoral college. Next, to forestall an election in the House, the South would withdraw its congressional delegation from Washington. The Union would be left without a government, peacefully dissolved.[42]

Tucker spent the weeks from late January to early March torridly working to maintain public interest in the convention. Using the voice of "A Son of Virginia" in a series of articles for the sympathetic *Richmond Semi-Weekly Examiner,* he managed for a time to balance explosive words with apparent good sense. Shrewdly protesting a love for the Union, seeking to calm the fears of men who were frightened at the word "convention," Tucker first excited and then cautioned his readers. When he glowingly described for Virginians the economic benefits of a Southern confederacy, he did so, he wrote, principally to persuade Northerners against "throwing away" their relationship with the bountiful South. He assured his readers that delegates were assembling in Nashville merely "to consult and advise," and in fact would have no authority to vote on secession. To suppose that deputies to Nashville were disposed to hasten breakup of the Union, Tucker wrote emphatically in his February 5 installment, was an "extravagant assumption." From what Tucker could learn, and because of what he wanted to believe, his strategy of suggestion was working. Crump reported that Richmonders read his articles with "avidity"; antiunion opinion was quietly gaining in Virginia.[43]

Tucker deceived himself. Early in March, in a strong address Tucker had believed Calhoun incapable of risking—in a message many men expected to be the feeble senator's last—the Carolinian made an ominous case for

Southern grievances and a plea for Northern concessions that marked the beginnings of a sectional reconciliation. On March 7, after conferring with Calhoun in the sick man's chambers, Webster angered Northern militants by denouncing emotionalism, deploring the Wilmot Proviso, and calling for a tougher fugitive-slave law. Less dramatically, younger Democrats like Douglas of Illinois and Foote of Mississippi and older ones like Thomas Ritchie maneuvered to close ranks, secure compromise, and place the onus of crisis on the Taylor administration.[44] By mid-March the weight of public feeling shifted away from sectional confrontation.

With tensions eased somewhat, Tucker's frustration became unbearable. Like "a full black bottle" turned upside down, he was "full to the throat" with rage. He saw enemies on both sides; Northerners were insolent and knavish, Southern spokesmen cowardly and imbecilic. He blasted party professionals for seeking security in the federal government. When men talked of disunion, their only question was where they would go. "Go to the Devil" was Tucker's crisp reply. "If you will not lead, fall to the rear and give place to them that will." In his last newspaper appeal to Virginians on March 19, Tucker wrote that he would happily blow the golden land of California to the moon if "half the scheming, self-seeking politicians who pass among us for great men went with it." He would have paid a thousand dollars to speak for only a few hours on the floor of the Senate, he told Hammond. But that theatre was barred to him. He would gladly have spoken out. But his powers of speech were puny. "Oh that I had the voice of John Randolph," he cried to his friend in South Carolina—the harp of Randolph's voice instead of the "Jews-harp" of his own.[45]

Rather than a bottle turned upside down Tucker was a man turned inside out, meshing deeply felt needs with events outside him, attributing to others the instability and duplicity he could not find in himself. He imputed to Northern enemies the evils he would have denied in pro-Texas and Mexican War Southerners. "In the history of human wrong," he wrote of the plan to admit California as a free state, "it would be hard to find such a combination of rapacity, fraud and violence." Long-festering wounds and now impatience enabled Tucker to perceive what less-troubled men did not. Yet his rhetoric in 1850, like his thought, was a mix of the shrewd, the questionable, and the self-deceiving. The "Omnibus" compromise proposals that Henry Clay introduced in the Senate in January did admit coveted California as a free state while leaving the question of slavery open in territories for which, as Tucker pointed out, "no man cares a straw." But the compromise was hardly a "surrender." Although an 1807 law forbidding unauthorized settling of public land remained in force at mid-century, the military governor of California could scarcely have appealed to it convincingly in throwing out Yankee "intruders." When the Clay measures were made known they did disappoint many Virginians. But Tucker convinced himself that in the hearts of

Southerners lay secret secessionist sentiments "long cherished in silence."[46] The peculiar sensitivity Tucker took to his political analysis also gave evidence of the ravages such feeling worked on his thinking.

If Tucker sensed the unsteady quality of his own mind, he preferred not to face it. Was he talking nonsense, he wrote Hammond, or the stuff of wise men? Did his letters "smell of the palsy?" He asked Hammond not to reply. Tucker preferred to believe that the Lord was on his right hand. He saw with a "prophetic vision," and though the grave was the only place left for an old man, he wrote Hammond eerily, "mine may yet be a bloody one."[47]

V

On the last day of March 1850, Calhoun died in Washington, and soon, as if the Lord did indeed sit on Tucker's right hand, events began to occur as they did in the dreams Tucker said were his sustenance. Early in May a joint Democrat-Whig caucus in his congressional district met according to the instructions of the General Assembly, elected Henry A. Wise delegate to the Nashville Convention, and named Tucker alternate. Wise, who was more interested in the upcoming constitutional convention, cleverly deferred to Tucker. "We *must* be represented," he wrote the old law professor, "& *you are the man.*" Without leaving the house, "without a shadow of personal popularity, without being known by sight in half the counties of the district," boasted Tucker, he had been elected to the Nashville Convention.[48] A dream had come true.

Tucker eagerly outfitted himself for this long-awaited task, busily preparing for the Tennessee excursion and happily writing Hammond of his plans. Late in May he bade his family and Williamsburg friends farewell and climbed into the westbound coach. Sleepless but too excited to feel tired, he spent many hours on rough roads and wooden-plank turnpikes before arriving in Wheeling on the twenty-eighth. The delegate quickly boarded a downriver steamboat, and when he awoke the following day he was alongside the Cincinnati wharf.[49]

Self-conscious of his office, beyond Virginia for the first time since 1843, and in the presence of strangers, Tucker drew himself up into a properly sober and observant figure. He was anxious to see how others reacted. On the boat he conducted himself with "great reserve and mildness" and thought Lucy would be pleased at the news that only one man had guessed his furtive mission. When a former member of the New York legislature laughed about the Nashville meeting, Tucker took delight in surprising him and calling him down. Confronted with the seriousness of the Virginian, perhaps frightened by him, the Yankee quickly grew silent, by Tucker's report, "exceedingly deferential, and deeply interested in the whole matter."

If most Northerners were as responsive as this New Yorker, Tucker concluded, the convention might indeed have an impact on the opinion in that section. He did not find anything in Cincinnati, where he strolled about part of the day, to improve his opinion of Yankees. He thought the city on the Ohio crude, impersonal, and confusing. Everyone had something to do and did it neither thinking nor caring about anything else, he wrote home after returning on board. Even the women, whom he refused to call ladies, had "the genuine business look." Rude Irish and Germans had so overrun the place that Tucker claimed he heard barely a word of English spoken there.[50]

When on the evening of June 2 Tucker finally arrived in the Tennessee capital, he could scarcely have found it much more civilized. Nashville offered diversion every bit as raucous as river towns in free states. But Tucker was not one to seek out such temptations, and it must have suited his taste that the most popular entertainment that night was a concert given by a touring band of Swiss bell ringers. In any case, the political charms of Nashville pleased him most. Excitement there even surpassed that of legislative sessions. Hundreds of delegates and onlookers crowded streets and hotels, spreading highflown talk everywhere they went. Reporters scurried about gathering news stories that a newly opened telegraph office would flash to the waiting country when the convention opened the next day.[51]

Within an hour Tucker was caught up in the drama. Locating Hammond, in whose tavern room he and two other Virginians lodged that first night, he stayed up for hours talking strategy. He discovered the Carolinian, though not physically imposing, to be perfectly engaging, intelligent and dignified; he had, according to another visitor in Nashville, a "conservative, pale, intellectual aspect, with a high forehead, white and polished as marble." Hammond later recalled that his impression of Tucker was mixed: if "vain as a peacock & without solid judgment or discretion," the older man was all the same a jolly companion who, besides being informed, was loyal to country and friends. Exhausted from this late night caucus, Tucker had summoned extra energy by nightfall of the second day in Nashville, when, at a lavish supper, Hammond introduced him to other delegates from South Carolina. Together with the pomp of the convention, the praise of these elegant Carolinians dizzied Tucker, who now prayed for the strength needed to do his duty in the great work before the delegates, to show himself "worthy to be the Son of Virginia," and a source of pride as husband and father. "I am already sensible that I am much looked to," he wrote home the night the convention opened; "as much depends on me here as on any other man."[52]

The convention gathered at a time when sectional tempers had cooled markedly, but it deserved and received the serious attention of political observers. Just a few days before Tucker learned that he would travel to Nashville as a delegate, a select Senate committee under Clay's chairmanship presented a report it had been preparing since mid-April on the prickly issues before Congress. Southerners denounced the report because it allowed the admission of California as a free state without observing the 36°30' Missouri Compromise line and offered no guarantee that slaveowners could take their laboring property into all territory acquired in the Mexican War; militant antislavery spokesmen attacked the plan because it failed to apply the Wilmot Proviso to the territories and, in an accompanying provision, proposed a strengthened fugitive-slave bill. Also arousing administration opposition, the bills excited protracted debate, almost countless amendments, and, by early June, stalemate. A strong Southern stance at Nashville might tip the scales against compromise, and perhaps do more.

Tucker intended to point the way to such a militant position. Earlier in letters to Hammond and now in informal sessions with radical delegates, he pressed for an address to the people of the South setting forth in lawyerlike fashion Southern rights, Southern grievances at Northern wrongs, and remedies in the form of constitutional amendments. Second, in an accompanying address to the North, Tucker would have been "temperate, but earnest and stern," warning that the South would remain in the Union only with the adoption of the amendments proposed. Next he wanted Southerners to elect a provisional government which, while in no way supplanting the sovereign powers of the states, would have authority to dissolve Southern membership in the Union. To this general Congress, said Tucker, each state should send "every man who ought to be consulted in great affairs." He was ready for anything, as long as it was radical. Sitting in Williamsburg, he had proclaimed in January, he had "done enough to make myself *participi criminus* in any *treason* that may be committed." He was now sitting in a latter-day Stamp Act Congress.[53]

In the hectic day or two after Tucker's arrival in Nashville, he and Hammond focused their attention on the constitutional amendments. Working closely with the two men was Robert Barnwell Rhett, a talented and politically experienced member of the Carolina delegation; Tucker's two friends among the Virginians, William O. Goode and William F. Gordon, probably worked on drafts of the proposed amendments as well. The first would have repealed the "general welfare" clause of the Constitution and have expressly limited congressional taxing and spending power. Another would have bound Northern sheriffs and other local constables to cooperate with officers of the federal government in the arrest, safekeeping, and return of fugitive slaves; dereliction in these duties would have placed them in contempt of United States District Courts. Tucker intended these amendments to solidify the South, as he had explained earlier to Hammond, and to create enough opposition in the North to open the way for more decisive Southern action.[54]

Passage of the amendments depended, of course, on the support of many more convention members than there were militant delegates from South

Carolina and Virginia. Tucker and the radicals looked in vain for that support. When the Nashville congress convened on June 3, first in the Odd Fellow's hall and then the next day in the larger McKendree Methodist Church, it soon became clear that sober leadership was in control. In an organizational coup, moderates succeeded in electing as president of the convention William Sharkey, a former chief justice of Mississippi and a sound Whig whose early support for the gathering had disguised his fundamentally cautious temper and confidence in regular political processes. Tucker must have shifted restlessly while the Mississippian assumed the chair with an innocuous reminder to the delegates that their object was the perpetuation of the Union in its original purity. In other developments Tucker detected the same moderate message. By Wednesday evening the convention had entrusted the all-important business of considering and preparing resolutions to a committee made up of two men from each state, selected within the state delegations. Except for Hammond, Rhett, and a few others, the committee was hardly a group of firebrands. Cave Johnson, who reported on the convention for his friend James Buchanan, described the Nashville meeting as "less ultra and factious" than he had expected.[55]

Controlled by moderates, the convention was inundated with mediocrities. The method of selecting delegates in the nine states that sent them was irregular. In many cases local conventions sent men of merely local prominence. There were governors of Tennessee and Alabama, one or more ex-governors, and a host of colonels and majors of militia.[56] Senators and congressmen remained in Washington, curious but wary. Other men of wider reputation declined attending because of the drop-off in popular feeling for the meeting. The delegates seemed to Cave Johnson composed mostly of old nullifiers and young disciples of the dead Calhoun. Langdon Cheves of South Carolina, quite old by this time, was also a heavy drinker, Johnson had heard, "and of course useless except [for] his name." A young Northern woman, governess at a nearby plantation and as "Kate Conynham" a contributor to the *Model American Courier,* thought that General Gideon Pillow of Tennessee, the Mexican War veteran, was principally conspicuous for his white military vest; William H. Polk, brother of the late President, caught her eye because "bearded like an Ottoman chief." Parliamentary squabbles, though seeming to lend an air of dignity and solemnity, were nearly comic in their complications and in the time they consumed. There was even something lacking in the galleries, where gentlemen and ladies, whether because divided of mind, impartial, or fickle, cheered anti-Northern and pro-Union utterances alike.[57]

Tucker was beyond noticing such absence of distinction. Were not Washington, Patrick Henry, and Nathaniel Greene unknowns before the great events of the Revolution called them forth? The convention was "a very able body," he wrote Lucy on June 8 and he, presumably among the most able, was doing "perspiring work" that gave him great satisfaction. A resolution he and a Virginia colleague presented, one of dozens that the chair referred routinely to the resolutions committee, he said had been "well received." Twice that week he had spoken on incidental occasions—once saying a few words that cleared up "some confusion and unpleasant altercation about a trivial matter"—and he believed these good impressions would win him a favorable hearing at another, more important time. All members, he wrote home, wished to hear what he had to say on the main topic for discussion. He had prepared an address on the California question which, he learned, Cheves thought a "most lucid analysis" and an "unanswerable argument." Here was the theater Tucker had always seen himself acting in and the central role he was just as happy to believe he played. People told him that he reminded them of John Randolph. Newspaper reporters made special requests that, when he spoke, he stand where they could hear every word. "My position is one for which I have long wished," he declared. "My great fear is that I may disappoint expectations."[58]

When at last Tucker was able to deliver his address, the main issue was no longer in doubt. In a clever procedural maneuver, moderates had succeeded on the eighth in passing, without amendments, the basically conciliatory statement of the resolutions committee. The multitude of changes suggested on the floor afterward did little to alter the substance of the official convention position. The delegates declared that the federal government should ensure the right of citizens to take their property—as defined in any state—into all jointly held federal territory. If it did not, they said, the South was "ready to acquiesce" in the extension of the Missouri Compromise line to the Pacific. The convention threatened nothing if Congress failed to enact such a measure, and it seemed doubtful that the resolutions were strong enough to prevent passage or change the substance of the Senate compromise bills. The minority report of Rhett, Hammond, and the other radicals on the Gordon committee, the "Address to the Southern People" that Tucker earlier had envisioned, was the only major topic still under discussion on Wednesday the twelfth, the only thing keeping the tired delegates from their homeward journey.[59]

With the choir loft of the McKendree Church crowded with spectators, Tucker arose from his pew that afternoon as an elder whose youthful fire, he said, time had quenched, whose imagination age had chilled. Privately he had worried about his weak voice and trouble enunciating, and he now mentioned them: with his shortcomings he could neither bellow tempests of eloquence, shaking the walls of the building, nor call down the plaudits of the galleries, leading captive the hearts and minds of men. He could only speak "words of truth and soberness."[60]

Unlike other convention orators, said Tucker, he did not shrink from the question how best to redress Southern wrongs and provide security against

danger. While zealous for harmony in the convention, he was glad that objections to the minority "Address," generally credited to Rhett, had opened
discussion of the larger topic of disunion. Tucker aimed to ease the excitement of the public mind by speaking freely and reasonably of crisis. "Vague
and undefinable apprehension" of danger was so much the worse because
mysterious and hushed. He was one of the brave men for whom danger
stiffened the sinews and summoned up the blood, whose exultation at the
prospect of battle was contagious and therapeutic.[61]

In explaining the forces behind the compromise plan, Tucker spoke of
sinister conspiracies. In a lengthy and tedious philippic, he described the
agreement of Clay, Webster, and Cass in favor of the Senate compromise
measure as more than "a marvelous coincidence of opinion . . . among men
who so rarely think alike"—it was an "ominous conjunction," "full of meaning," and, Tucker insisted, "this precise number three is not fortuitous." In
the triple league of Clay, Webster, and Cass, Tucker saw Caesar, Pompey,
and Crassus—Augustus, Antony, and Lepidus; he foresaw the interlude of a
Roman triumvirate or a French consulship followed by a military despotism.[62]

"With words of encouragement, in accents of hope, full of joyful expectations," Tucker tried to persuade listeners that the North would let the South
go in peace. Boldness would preclude bloodletting. Webster's Massachusetts
would have to lose her sense and "be prepared to rush on self-destruction,"
believed the Virginian, before she and the North would make war on seceded
Southern states. The cotton of this region was too important to the New
England economy. Factories would tumble into ruins during such a war,
ships rot at wharves; the valuable Southern market would be lost. Northern
manufacturers and shippers, like the merchant princes of Venice, would
finally skulk in the corners of their marble palaces and "live meagerly on
contributions levied on the curiosity of travellers." Unemployed "free labor"
would be forced within a week of such a civil war to beg, rob, or starve. England, without a West where restless workers might flee, was even more
dependent on the richness of the South. While there were real evils in Union,
the evils of disunion were purely imaginary, Tucker assured his audience.
Peaceful secession was virtually a certainty.[63]

Thus the path to the formation of a new nation lay clear but for the will
to travel it. As within an hour Tucker's voice began to grow hoarse, he
brought his rambling oration to a hasty climax. If only a tier of the lower
South withdrew from the Union, he proclaimed, slave states of the upper
South would soon join them. With a modest, economical government,
serving as a mere central agency for independent states, the confederation
would require merely a revenue tariff and could share in the flourishing
international free trade among commercial and agricultural nations. Pennsylvania, on the border of a free-trade confederation, would then choose to
join it and become its workshop rather than compete with European manu-

facturing for the Southern market. Illinois—whose downstate citizens clamored for slavery—Indiana, and even Ohio could very possibly become members of the confederacy because of their natural transportation ties to the Southern mouth of the Mississippi.[64]

The excitement of the convention permitted Tucker to fly into worlds entirely of his own building. The league he envisioned would stretch southward into the Caribbean, he prophesied, embracing, in due course, Cuba and Santo Domingo. It would include Jamaica too, for England would recognize the economic error of emancipation and gladly allow the staple-growing island to join the prosperous Southern confederacy. From the Chesapeake to the Gulf, from the Atlantic to the Rio Bravo, the new nation would embrace all the things needed for agriculture, manufacture, and commerce; the Mississippi, James, Potomac, and Ohio would "bind together the three great interests of civilization with a cord twisted by the bands of Nature, in a union like that of the sexes—a union of congenial, not conflicting interests."[65]

Tucker finally gave up. "I have come here with my mind charged to bursting with thoughts that vainly struggle for utterance," he explained to his listeners. To unpack his heart and to voice all that he wished to say was as useless as trying "to drain Lake Erie through a goose quill." He took his seat.[66]

Apparently Tucker's greatest forensic effort changed few votes. The convention passed Rhett's Address, though not without dissents, as a relatively harmless sop to the radicals and then adjourned. After cheers for the convention officers, Hammond worked his way over to congratulate Tucker—though privately he concluded that the Virginian, with his "bad voice," was not a good speechmaker—and with Hammond the tired and now voiceless orator walked out of the hall. The two friends returned to their rooms to pack. Tucker was pleased with himself.[67]

When the reporter for the *Richmond Examiner* looked at his notes that evening, he discovered that he had lost the thread of Tucker's argument. Having followed the Virginia delegate's remarks in detail through his discussion whether to support Clay's compromise and into the sarcastic comments on Clay, Webster, and Cass, the newspaperman, unmoved, dismissed Tucker's labored and impassioned appeal for independence in a single laconic sentence: "He discussed the question of disunion, and showed that if the event should come to pass, the South could sustain itself."[68]

VI

"Alas for Virginia!" declared Tucker in an essay he wrote in the spring of the next year; the monarch's roar no longer shook the forest there. He believed it was different in South Carolina, where gentlemen were still treated as such. "Let her continue thus to honour merit, and reward service, and she will never be left without a prophet." Tucker's comparison was based in part on experience. After the Nashville Convention—as a guest of Hammond, who had decided that the old professor was so fine a companion that he should come home with him to Silver Bluff for a few weeks—the Virginian was at last able to visit this fabled country of Rutledge, Pickney, Lowndes, Hayne, McDuffie, and Harper. On the sixteenth of June Tucker and Hammond were fifty miles outside Nashville, and five days later they reached Augusta, "weary and travel soiled" but thankful to be in the healthy sand hills and pine woods of Georgia.[69] Shortly afterward they reached Hammond's estate.

Tucker's stay at Silver Bluff was gentlemanly indeed. He worked as hard as he could enlarging on the Nashville speech, which he wanted to publish immediately, and when the heat was too stifling to write or to get into the sun, he and Hammond played billiards. "I have no wish to be made a Lion of," he wrote Lucy of the social schedule Hammond and friends planned for him, "but I do not think it will be right to slight the attentions which are prepared for me." So he happily followed the dictates of conscience. At festivities in the hamlet of Barnwell Court House, not far from Hammond's plantation, Tucker was a guest orator on the Fourth of July—a holiday he did not ordinarily observe, but enjoyed in this instance.[70] No doubt he used it as an excuse to deliver a revised version of the Nashville address, embroidered as appropriate for his receptive audience.

Buoyed as Tucker was to be courted by these esteemed persons, his visit to Carolina was not flawless. His Barnwell address and even his conversations while there moved Hammond to repeat his comment that a defect in Tucker's voice rendered him practically unable to "speak at all. . . ." Part of the trouble was that Tucker's hosts were just as high-strung and eager to be the center of attention as he was and were trying just as hard to be impressive. Alfred Proctor Aldrich and Samuel Wilds Trotti, the Barnwell men who invited the Virginian to stay with them after the fourth, were glad to have him, but something mysteriously marred the visit. Hammond later described the families at Barnwell as a "factious set" and admitted that Tucker "was not treated with much distinction" there. Moreover, Tucker wanted badly to see Simms while in the South. The editor had been unable to join Tucker and Hammond at Barnwell and was supposed to meet the Virginian visitor on the train headed downcountry and then to show him about Charleston. But Simms, who earlier had spoken of a "prejudice" he believed Virginians always had against South Carolinians, now missed Tucker because of a sudden attack of diarrhea. He wrote an elaborate apology. Hammond meantime had 500 copies of Tucker's Nashville speech printed and 25 sent to him in Charleston in Simms's care, but they also arrived too late. "I fear," Hammond wrote Simms in late July, that Tucker "went off in disgust with all of us. . . ."[71]

If so, worse disgust followed his return to Williamsburg. Select friends did praise the Nashville speech. John Moncure Daniel of the *Richmond Examiner* said that it "laid the knout on those rascals in the Senate with apalling severity," and Crump called it a "gem—clear, cogent, Classic & unanswerable." But Senator Foote of Mississippi, now an enemy of extremism, used Tucker's Nashville address to flay Southern radicals and to discredit their cause. Richmond opinion on the speech was mixed. Radical sentiment elsewhere died in September as the Clay bills separately passed the Congress and the country heralded another sectional compromise. The second session of the Nashville Convention in mid-November, attracting neither Tucker nor Hammond, was poorly attended and virtually ignored. Although it called yet another convention for Montgomery, Alabama, late in 1851, not many Southerners were excited about it. "*Here* all is *peace & harmony,*" Virginia Senator James Mason reported from Washington before Christmas, "the surface as smooth as a tranquil sea."[72]

Further disgusting Tucker, and causing anger that stretched his nerves during all the winter months, were the sessions of the constitutional convention in Richmond. There the tide of numbers he so terribly feared at last washed away the foundations of the Virginia he wished to preserve. Besides recommending universal manhood suffrage and providing for a western majority in the House of Delegates, the convention abolished the old system of county-court justices that Tucker had praised in his law classes as distinctively Virginian and "absolutely devoid of all tendency or disposition to usurpation." He cursed convention delegates as a "rabble of low ignorant demagogues" and reserved special venom for Henry Wise—who, he said, proposed changes in the governor's authority over the militia in order to render the state powerless to counter the movement of federal troops. Wise, he wrote caustically, stood in the convention "like an auctioneer, winking at the West and nodding at the North," accepting bids from all quarters. "We are betrayed and sold," he wrote when the convention adjourned in mid-March; reformers had set up over him without his consent "a tyranny which," he told Hammond angrily, "I know will prove at once insolent and base, which will delight to dominion [*sic*] over all that is wise and brave and true, and at the same time surrender the Sovereignty of brave old Virginia to her enemies, persecutors & revilers."[73]

Our only hope, said Tucker in a phrase he now used more than ever and often to refer to different things in the same breath, is in "rashness." If only South Carolina would act, he repeated again and again to his sympathetic friends in that state. If only South Carolina would act the South would be saved and its saviors vindicated. For but a brief time did events there offer any hope of action. In December 1850 the South Carolina legislature had made provisions to elect delegates to the Montgomery Convention late the following year and also planned a year hence to call a state convention, unless the governor called it earlier, with power to consider separate secession. Too, the Southern Rights associations of the state scheduled a May 1851 general meeting in Charleston, and these committees of concerned citizens might mobilize support for separate state action despite the misgivings of other Southern states.[74]

Tucker's capacity to test his impulses and ideas against the reality outside him, never strong and growing weaker over the past few years, now parted him altogether. He encouraged Hammond to send South Carolina emissaries to European courts soliciting aid and friendship for the state, and urged Hammond himself—recently defeated for the Senate—to travel to England, where, the Virginian continued to believe, the South could find allies in Carlyle and other conservatives. When the British minister in Washington and South Carolina officials exchanged letters on the statutes discriminating against black seamen on vessels visiting Charleston, Tucker saw an opportunity for exploratory negotiations; when the letters were published Tucker suspected an abolitionist conspiracy to embarrass South Carolina at a delicate point in these proceedings. He suggested to Hammond and to James Means, secretary of state in Columbia, that South Carolina amend the law so as to exempt British ships, thus showing that Carolina was "ready to meet her more than half-way," and acquainting Britain with the idea, "to which her mind is now open, that S.C. is a power to be treated with." The preamble to the law would lay the basis for British cooperation in South Carolina autonomy and make clear to the world the divinely appointed role the South filled in bringing the sons of Ham into the fold of Christ. Tucker believed such a law with such a preamble would cause a stir equal to the Declaration of Independence. "This is my stake in the game in which honour is to be won," he declared, "and I would not, at this moment, exchange it for all the tinsel that glitters around the name of Henry Clay."[75]

Bickering among leaders, questions of expediency, and simple inertia frustrated Tucker's plans for South Carolina just as they always had. Hammond, who considered himself every bit as noble as Tucker told him he was, had fallen into competition with Rhett for the place Calhoun's death opened in the political hierarchy of the state. The preceding fall he and Rhett had delivered rival eulogies on the late senator, and after the legislature selected Rhett for the Senate, each man and their friends divided. Hammond grew so morose and vengeful that even Tucker could do little for him. Besides, Tucker had miscalculated Hammond's willingness to bring on immediate secession in South Carolina. Though protesting that he was a disunion man, Hammond had doubts that South Carolina could secede successfully alone, that it could be done peacefully, and that Europe would help the state in either case. In late February, when Southern-Rights men elected delegates to the May meeting, Hammond found these secessionists objectionable both because most of them were immediatists and because they were, he believed, under the control of Rhett. Hammond and Simms denigrated "Rhett & the Violents" as foolish, premature, and demagogic. Hammond complained of the "folly & madness" of Rhett's extremism; his followers were so young, unknown, inexperienced, laying all their confidence in God and the sword. "[M]anagement, intrigue, and the game of petty and selfish factions," Simms agreed, had pushed able and independent men off the shelf.[76]

Complaining of sickness, weariness of body and mind, and anxiety about both South Carolina and Hammond, Tucker by mid-April had begun helping Hammond with a plan the Carolinian had devised to place his state neither in the Union nor quite out of it. Hammond, who petulantly had declared his public career over and had removed his household across the Georgia border, thought his scheme would influence the May gathering of Southern-Rights men despite his absence. He proposed recalling South Carolina senators and congressmen, disfranchising Carolina citizens who acted as federal agents, taxing the property of Northerners within the state to the point of confiscation, refusing federal appropriations for South Carolina, and ignoring presidential elections. The state in Hammond's plan would have bided her time, waited for cooperation from other Southern states, and in the meantime placed herself on a war footing. Tucker would have chosen a less equivocal stance.[77]

He was obsessed with the hope that something, anything, would happen. Writing an essay for Simms and the *Quarterly*—though he began it as a review of the Hammond and Rhett orations on Calhoun, Hammond's touchiness on the subject caused a change in plans—Tucker gleefully added contributions of his own to Hammond's scheme. Avoid all legislation that might embroil Carolina in the federal courts, advised Tucker in comments he sent Hammond as he wrote the article. But by all means discharge state officials of their oath to uphold the federal Constitution and make aiding federal forces sent to subjugate the state a crime, without calling it treason, punishable by death. Tucker's ideas were as extreme as his outrage. He called for the hanging of all abolitionists and the reenslavement of all free blacks who did not immediately leave South Carolina and suggested that the state make escaping slavery across her borders a capital offense. Slaveholders might then demand escapees as fugitives from justice rather than merely as runaway servants. Finally, Tucker moved that South Carolina avoid the problem of war powers in a system of constitutional restraints by establishing an authority—a convention of the people—above and beyond them. This convention would appoint executive officers as necessary and would resemble a council the Romans had used to muster the energies of the state in times of crisis. Tucker believed that such a body would at the return of peace permit the state constitution "to go on, as if nothing had happened."[78] No one seconded the motion.

The louder Tucker shouted—the more bizarre he became—the less men seemed to listen. In late May, after hearing from Simms that the convention in Charleston had met but decided to do nothing for the time being, Tucker described his mind as "packed to bursting," thoughts and words "crowding for utterance." The way they spilled out formed a pattern that helped demonstrate, to anyone who might have tried to help him, why he was so "bottled up." Tucker spoke of the peaceful end of Southern oppression in the Union but hoped out loud for the violent dissolution that would bind men to their natural leaders, for the "threat to the fireside" that moved men to act. They had to be placed in desperate circumstances. But to do so he had to win over men in political leadership, most of whom he despised for their success; placing men where they might act required leadership, maneuvering, persuasion. Yet he admitted privately to Simms and publicly in his piece for the *Quarterly* that men could not be *"reasoned up to"* this realization that action was necessary when their feelings were less extreme than his. Tucker thought of this awareness as a matter of "resolute heart"—a sense of danger and the "wisdom" to meet it with boldness. Yet Hammond and Simms spared nothing in attacking the arrogance and rashness of Rhett in his "violents."[79]

Patriotism, indignation, the "heart" to act were all important in fomenting rebellion. But so were an intolerable mound of grievances, organization, consensus among leaders with a claim to legitimacy, a reasonable assurance of success, and an occasion sufficient to move men to support it. Tucker thought of himself as a hero who made events or as a healer who made the most of them. In fact, badly out of touch with the real possibilities of the situation, he was a victim at the mercy of them. *"The state will not secede,"* Hammond finally had to tell Tucker later in May. "Nine tenths of the men having any pretense to Statesmanship have come out against Separate secession & the great body of the people, tho keen for disunion," he believed, "are shrinking from the hopeless sacrifices of separate action as they become more & more apparent." Powerless as usual to bring many men to see the flow of events with the fear he did, Tucker surely found no blow as devastating as these words of surrender. "I know that I will 'die unheard,'" continued this younger man in whom Tucker had invested so much confidence. "This I am aware has been your apprehension life-long."[80]

Hammond did not exaggerate by much, and he must have known that he worsened those apprehensions. When he and Tucker had reestablished their friendship Tucker had written to him of passing on the "truncheon" of states' rights which, as a "banner" in the earlier days, the older man believed he received from John Randolph. If Hammond failed Tucker, Tucker had failed his own mentor, and certainly Randolph was very much on Tucker's mind in these months. While courage slackened everywhere and imposters tampered with the constitutional structure of the state Tucker loved, incompetents presumed to write about the half brother he idolized. He had for years toyed with the idea of writing his own biography of Randolph. By doing so he would have answered the earnest pleas of many friends, Simms included; until he began it, he was determined to keep the field clear. In a few contemptuous paragraphs for the *Messenger* in the spring of 1844, he had dismissed Lemuel Sawyer's frankly partisan life of Randolph as a libel on the man. During the early months of 1851 he wrote for the *Quarterly* a lengthier review of Hugh Garland's two volume biography. Garland, a Virginia native who researched much of the book in Washington, took the precaution of writing Tucker that he had studied Randolph's views thoroughly. "I think I understand and appreciate them," he assured his subject's brother, asking for anecdotes and sidelights. He offered to show Tucker the sheets of the book before it appeared. The author had carefully avoided everything, he said, that might give offense.[81]

Garland could have saved himself the trouble. Of little avail it was to enlist Tucker's help or to seek his approval in a project he considered a family affair. Had Garland been ten times as well prepared for the work, Tucker commented dryly, he would have realized that he was still not half qualified to undertake it. His mistake was in expecting to sound the depths of the ocean with a mere fishing line. Besides, his factual errors were legion, his understanding of political and constitutional history meager. Garland must have shuddered on reading these remarks, but he may also have realized that castigating his book gave Tucker an opportunity he needed to sing in praise of Randolph; Tucker wrote at a time when these songs came easily. During the second Jefferson administration, he reminded readers of the July issue of the *Quarterly*, all Randolph's friends had deserted him, yielding to the President's popularity or the wiles of patronage until he stood alone, "surrounded on every side by deadly foes, denounced by the press and reviled by the many-voiced clamour of the multitude. There he stood," Tucker wrote lovingly, "amid 'the host of Hatred,' dealing blows on every hand, from which the boldest of his assailants shrank."[82] Instead of shrinking, Tucker's enemies were laughing.

So resonant with meaning was Tucker's view of Randolph's life that his biography, had he managed to write it, would have been virtually an autobiography in reverse and ideal self-images. What Tucker did say of Garland's volumes was revealing enough. A man of marvel, mystery, and might was Randolph, whose listeners found his words so true and his sentiments so just that they "caught the contagion of all his feelings." To minds deficient in acuteness, his thought looked like paradox; sensitive, fastidious, haughty, and scornful, he took no pains to conciliate men who differed with him. "Though not envious, though courteous to equals and enthusiastically deferential to all true greatness, it was impossible not to see that there was an instinct in the man, which would never let him rest below the topmost pinnacle of fame and power." "Who would not have been John Randolph?"

Tucker asked rhetorically. "Who would have been?" was the more searing question for one who on countless occasions had compared himself to Randolph in his feeling and mission. Tucker now pronounced that comparison foolish and beyond reach. "It is impossible to *imitate* ORIGINALITY," he pointed out in what he remembered as one of Randolph's sayings, and he said it was an undeniable truth: "We recommend it especially to all imitators of Mr. Randolph."[83] Tucker never really began his autobiography because he could not take measure of the man whose measurements he had failed to fill.

With warmer weather Tucker's spirits rose even as his health declined. Relieved when the academic year ended, he paid a July visit to the Bryans' Gloucester County estate for salt baths, which seemed to ease his aching body, and for a "fortnight's 'discharge from care.'" He returned to Williamsburg later that month, not much better but fortified enough to write Hammond a few words of rueful encouragement. "There is Hope in Desperation," he declared in words he repeated in one of his pieces for the *Quarterly;* "in despair none." Cheer up, then, he advised. "Cheer up: and give yourself, in mind and heart, to the great interests now at stake." Men of the truest hearts were needed, men with the feeling to face danger with boldness. Tucker had done all he could, said all he was able. The time was late. All he asked was that Hammond remember his debt to him, and that he hurry to bring on the secession crisis. "Of the practicability and ultimate success of our plan of operation I have no shadow of a doubt," he assured Hammond. "But for God's sake let *us try* to *give it* a *fair trial.*" His own sons being too young to understand fully the crusade their father wanted to lead, Tucker relied on Hammond's heart to leap at the notes he sounded. What were old men for, he asked finally, "but to lead forlorn hopes," to fill trenches with their bodies, "to be marched over by younger men who may live to profit by it?"[84]

It was now late July and Simms was headed for New York to see publishers. Always interested in doing the things professional writers did, he kept a notebook of his journey and mailed home installments to the Charleston *Evening News*. This time he successfully negotiated a rendezvous with Tucker, taking a sidetrip from Richmond down the peninsula to Jamestown and Williamsburg and in that disheveled setting enjoying the hospitality his friend had so long held out for him. Though the visit exhausted Tucker, within a few days he and Simms were off together for a brief visit to Washington, then on to Harpers Ferry and Warrenton, arriving finally at the Capon Springs, where Tucker hoped to regain his failing strength. The excitement of the place weakened him further; when Simms left for the north on August 19 he described Tucker as seriously ill and "very feeble."[85] Members of Henry St. George Tucker's family soon moved the sick man to their home nearby. Tucker died there on the twenty-sixth, perhaps in his brother's own deathbed, on the eve of the tournament season.

The week before, Simms's readers had seen the Virginian identified in the *Evening News* as John Randolph's half brother, "without his eccentricities" but with all his talents, "a living record of all that was great and noble, in men and events, in the history of the Old Dominion. . . ."[86] Eager to please and romantic in his perception, Simms saw only the surface. He would have come closer had he pointed out that at the end of Tucker's life he was much like his hero in "Gertrude": a well-meaning man whose effort to save a runaway carriage and the woman inside it left him—body broken and mind tormented—helpless to prevent the treachery that separated him forever from the one thing he loved most.

Afterword

TUCKER'S FAMILY and Williamsburg friends buried him in the yard of Bruton Parish Church, near the door, in a grave marked by a small obelisk protruding high above the wall surrounding the cemetery. Before his death Tucker himself may well have composed the inscription that went on the monument, for it commemorated him as a judge and professor "descended from the best blood of Virginia" and a gentleman who valiantly defended her rights and the liberties of her citizens. When the college opened that October the president, Benjamin S. Ewell, enlarged on this tribute, expressing deep regret at losing a man whose best eulogy, said Ewell, was to be found "in the results of his able teachings" among his pupils.[1]

In the troubled decade that followed Tucker's death, those students and others in his small circle remembered him as a champion of independence. Henry A. Washington, a young professor at the college who married Cynthia Tucker in 1852, used Tucker's lessons on Virginia history in an address he made that same year before the Virginia Historical Society. One of Tucker's law graduates saluted his memory in May 1854 by offering a toast to the anniversary of Virginia independence at a banquet in Hinds County, Mississippi. The next year, when William Lamb published a life of Upshur, the passages in praise of Tucker as displaying "powers of intellect unsurpassed by any of his countrymen" appeared with commentary in the Williamsburg paper. Simms ensured that Tucker was included in Duyckinck's *Cyclopoedia of American Literature,* an important contemporary reference book, and named one of his children Beverley Hammond.[2]

As Tucker's disciples celebrated his memory in the 1850s, they must have reflected often on the old man's sagacity. There was, after all, good sense in some of his secessionist message. As Tucker believed probable, the North did grow in population and power in the 1850s. The compromise of 1850 failed to quiet antislavery agitation or to persuade abolitionists of their constitutional obligation to return fugitive slaves; the compromise did nothing to protect against the rising clamor in favor of free soil in the western territories. Tucker had said often that Northern presses and Northern books were potent instruments in the sectional struggle, that the South should hammer her own literary weaponry. *Uncle Tom's Cabin* proved him correct, and the South was unable to produce anything as effective as Stowe's novel. As

Tucker believed possible, even probable, Northerners crossed into the South and attempted to foment slave insurrection; John Brown's 1859 raid on Harpers Ferry in fact took place on ground Tucker had described in *The Partisan Leader*. The issues of slavery and the power of the slave states in the Union did provide the organizing principle for a distinctly antislavery party in the North during the mid-1850s, and, as Tucker predicted, it eventually won the presidency. Tucker may also have been correct in his belief that peaceful secession was possible in 1850; certainly by 1861 Northerners had much clearer reasons for maintaining "nationhood" and much greater resources to apply against Southern "rebellion." In the secession winter of 1860 South Carolina finally proved to be "a theatre where a man can act," as Tucker said it was, and the war, if not the guerrilla action he predicted in *The Partisan Leader,* was for the South primarily a defensive struggle.[3]

Yet it would be a mistake to decide that Tucker was quite the prophet he believed himself to be. For one thing, his predictions of British help in the Southern bid for independence only previewed the mislaid hopes of Southern leaders in 1861. The British never broke the Northern naval blockade that Hammond and Simms rightly feared; they hardly provided the South conspicuous military aid. Of course the situation in London was different in 1861 than it was at Tucker's death, but there is little reason to believe that Lord Palmerston as foreign secretary in 1851 would have proven more willing to help the South than he was as prime minister in the early 1860s. Tucker assumed that British reliance on Southern cotton and the clout of conservatives like Peel and Carlyle would, after independence, soon bring about an Anglo-Southern alliance. He misread the signs. True, writing in October 1850 a letter that Tucker described as "full of encouragement," Carlyle said that he sympathized with Southern slaveholders and agreed with Tucker that immediate abolition was no remedy for the Southerners' dilemma; he looked forward with scant joy to the time when, as he said, "all mastership and obedience whatsoever" would disappear and render "Society impossible among the Sons of Adam." But Carlyle confessed that his power to halt these changes was negligible. Besides, the British conservative had doubts about the racial oppression that was central to servitude in the South. "My notion," he told this admiring Virginian, "is that the relation of the White man to the Black is not at present a just one according to the Law of the Eternal."[4]

Tucker was correct that the political strength of the North and its small farmer–wage earner ideal threatened the South. But the votes of Southern states to leave the Union in 1860–61 grew out of political circumstances that Tucker did not foresee and brought results he seriously misgauged. For many years he had tried to break down the party loyalties of Southern leaders, believing that a nucleus of sound men could "awaken" the Southern people to the higher loyalty of love for the South and regard for its interests. After Tucker's death, when Whigs and then Democrats split over the issue of slavery, this dissolution did hasten secession. But in the end secession in each state had almost as much to do with internal issues and factional maneuvering as with slavery or national issues,[5] and in a few cases came about nearly by political accident. Nor did secession result from, or bring, the consciousness of Southern peculiarity that Tucker believed would unite the section through a long struggle. The glue Tucker thought crisis would supply even proved insufficient to hold Virginia together, and while Southerners did fight and sacrifice in defense of their homes and out of love of locale, they never became the People he believed they were. Indeed his own provincial loyalties foretold the serious divisions within the Confederacy—the jealousies among states and between state governments and the Confederate administration in Richmond—that hampered the war effort.

In short, Tucker's historical interest lies less in the prescience he insisted was his than in the impression he provides of his society, of the ideas that sustained it, and of the stresses the nineteenth century imposed on it. In his formative years, eastern Virginia was for the most part a rural society, relatively homogeneous and stable, a land that supported a reliance on tradition: the habits and beliefs of forebears continued serviceable because their setting remained much the same. It was possible in such a society to know personally most of the people with whom one treated from day to day, to identify them by their families and the station they had occupied in the past. Individual achievement was less important than accrued attributes and responsibilities: one's membership in a family, roots in locale, and certainly one's color were important determinants of personhood. Men and women were thus subject to qualifiers, the carriers of subjective social baggage; people dealt with one another, for better and worse, as subjects of interest rather than as objects of little matter or, as in a more fluid situation, of fleeting importance. This subjective mode of interpersonal dealings promoted affective ties among people. It inculcated a sense of belonging that imposed strict codes of behavior, developed an awareness of place in time, and defined one's honor as the integrity of an individual who above all had position in hierarchy.

A sense of who was superior to whom was indeed the dominant feature of the world Tucker and other young Southerners of his day grew into. Thin as the evidence is on Tucker's early life, it does form a pattern suggesting how fathers in the early republican South tried to build in their sons, especially in eldest sons, strong male personalities, to produce "commanding" figures who would be prepared for the tasks of public and domestic authority. Men of means—while subscribing to an ideal of self-sacrifice for the common good—were to assume political leadership. In the absence of rich diversity, this vision conformed well enough to reality; as long as most issues could be settled on the local or state level, men who were deferred to there might convincingly manage conflict as surrogates for the whole. On another level, men were to make the decisions that involved matters outside the family and to impose discipline within it, while women were subordinate, helpful, the principal source of affection and the focus of home life. Finally, though only a minority of Virginians held slaves in 1800, that form of property carried special domestic or "fatherly" responsibilities, buttressing male authority and promoting distinctions through the entire social order. Black servitude thus blended well with attitudes toward the poor and toward work; slavery and the discriminatory social attitudes it encouraged merged smoothly with Anglo-Scotch definitions of sex roles and of male prowess and with the persistent ideals of English rural independence.[6]

For a young man at the onset of the nineteenth century, this system of tradition and ranking, so warmly supportive of deserving males, justified great expectations. Tucker's narrative demonstrates the impact that changes in the pace of life, quality of politics, and structure of Southern society had on such dancing images. The economic decline of the state made the traditional elite apprehensive and even ashamed. Competition at the bar rudely announced the increasing "openness" of society. Egalitarianism in Missouri made a mockery of old pretensions. Party loyalties in politics created linkages between local and federal issues, served the needs of career politicians, and (so it seemed to a Tucker) deadened perceptions of "real" issues while debasing the quality of leadership. The development of western Virginia exacerbated sectional tensions in the state and undermined long-standing eastern control; internal improvements in the commonwealth and throughout the country shortened distances, brought different people together, "speeded up" the passage of events by quickening the rate of news, and subverted local peculiarities. Growing Northern political power promised majoritarian attacks on slavery.

Crying of his neglect and foretelling ruin unless crisis intervened, Tucker thus fought a rearguard action against the forces that elbowed him and men like him out of their preferred place as public leaders. Men of fixed principles, deep convictions, and steadfast purpose are called fools nowadays, Tucker wrote Hammond in late 1850, "and I am not sure that they are of any more use than fools." When Henry Wise, whom Tucker considered an opportunist and democrat of the worst variety, tried to ingratiate himself to the older man, he shrewdly wrote that he, like Tucker, had little interest in selfish political gain; *"truth,"* he told Tucker, "has too much power over you & me for the public arena." Never having had the chance to attempt anything great, mused Tucker offstage, and never stooping to anything small, he had done nothing. "Patriotism!" he exclaimed in his later years; only if he *"had a country"* could he prove himself a patriot, and though he said he had none, secession would change all that. Just as secession would keep South Carolinians "alive to the value of 'her prophets'—to the value of integrity and stability," the Virginian wrote Hammond, so would this climactic venture lift Tucker from the obscurity he bitterly complained of. He was certain that immortality awaited the man who was foremost in advancing the independence of the South.[7]

The circle of friends Tucker drew around him helped make clear how much he wanted to find that handle on power. In Virginia his closest friends, Upshur and Ruffin, were like him in their background, anguish at decline, and anger at attempts to enlarge the scope of federal authority. Both Waddy Thompson and Duff Green could claim Virginia forebears of middling distinction and complain with Tucker of an entire "new order of things" in which "second rate men" controlled everything. In South Carolina Tucker drew additional support from men like William Campbell Preston and William Harper, who, like him, had felt the sting of egalitarianism in Missouri. Tucker was willing to accept help from almost any quarter. In later life he found warmest succor in the friendship of Simms and Hammond, neither of whom were the men of breeding Tucker considered himself to be. Tucker, Hammond, and Simms each had peculiar reasons for feeling offended; they shared bitterness at the neglect society paid them and took turns consoling one another in their "disappointments & misfortunes." Tucker worked hard to convince Hammond that he was the man on whom the destiny of the South depended; Hammond for his part testified to Simms's greatness at the same time that Simms stroked Tucker and asked the Virginian to fortify Hammond.[8] While Tucker took help from almost anyone who offered it, all his friends expected secession to place them where they deserved to be.

In these straits, especially sensitive to the changes around him, Tucker was in one sense an exception to his society; he belonged to a fading elite. Nonetheless it is possible to see him as an expression of that social order, to see in his writing evidence of the things most important to the culture he saw as failing. Tucker's story illuminates the tie between ideas and social elements for the very reason that he believed these connections dissolving. For one thing his political expectations help us to understand how well—until qualitative changes overtook Virginia—republican canons of local rule, self-sufficiency, and simplicity could align with life circumstances there. Slavery, Edmund Morgan has noted, made Southerners in the second half of the eighteenth century particularly conscious of dependence or tyranny; Tucker's story makes clear, further, that a regard for personal liberty and for weakness and frugality in government made sense to a people who had erected few formal community institutions and who, at least in parts of the state, therefore neither expected nor wanted much of government services. Subjective social ties, while tending to keep the focus of life on local affairs and people, also contained elements of distrust of "outside" persons who did not belong in this immediate scheme of things; in the antebellum South-east the republican principle that local government was most dependable had a cultural corollary in the view that distant people were least trustworthy, and it was a belief that figured prominently in Tucker's political teachings. The republican maxim that parties were a bane to free government carried particular currency in a system that long had encouraged the informal settling of affairs. The commonwealth view that representatives ought to be truly selfless and concerned only for the good of the whole held appeal longer than elsewhere in a social order based on distinctions; in it slavery helped to identify the men whom Tucker, hoping to prolong such gradation, called "the few gentlemen whose circumstances and character place them above suspicion of any personal designs."[9]

Too, Tucker's citations of Highland courage against overwhelming odds and his repeated references to English country life highlighted the stable features of Southern society and the self-view of its elite. Tucker lionized the British gentry and the order of things comfortable to it. "We too are English," he was fond of saying, hesitating not for a moment to assert the superiority of the Anglo-Saxon race; in Virginia no less than in England were the thoughts of the country gentleman distracted by his love for corn-fields, dairy, cider press, his greyhounds, fishing rod, gun, ale, and tobacco. Simms wrote of "genuine Briticism among us" and in 1851 Tucker wrote Hammond happily that an English visitor to Williamsburg had seen "more here to remind him of what England was than anywhere else." Nothing in England, another traveler once had told him, was "'so much like *old* England.'"[10]

More than the musings of an odd man out, Tucker's critique of emerging "modern" miseries brought to the surface the assumptions Southern society was based upon. His concern for the social setting and purpose of economic endeavor, more than merely a celebration of slave society, helps us to understand how a Southerner of his ilk might have expected subjective social ties—a cooperative, affiliative tone—to "soften" socioeconomic dealings. Tucker was not opposed to moneymaking, as one might expect of a spokesman for a traditional society. He did, however, detest the crassness, materialism, and cruel dishonesty that he portrayed in figures like Gertrude's mother or, in the same story, the banking shark he named McScrew and who he said was "one of those sagacious men of cool heads and cold hearts." Colonel Harlston was especially attractive to Gertrude because, though wealthy, he took no interest in money for its own sake. Similarly, Tucker in no way opposed merchandising or commerce as a walk of life. He praised the commercial successes of New England in a talk to Richmond merchants in 1841 and criticized those Jacksonians who wanted only gold and silver coin to circulate as money; to destroy the credit system, he wrote, would be as foolish "as to kill the nightingale for his voice." Yet like those many antebellum Americans who were distrustful of banks and paper money,

Tucker hoped very much to hold onto a social order in which such devices were accountable, "humane," and aimed at the common good. Credit had to be based on *"prudence, integrity,* and *faith inviolable,"* he told those merchants; commerce should not simply be regarded "as the art of getting rich at the expense of others."[11]

Tucker's brief on behalf of slavery, besides suggesting that the proslavery argument emerged for different reasons in various parts of the South, contained the message he thought most critical of his age and its drift. He brought it into the open when Northern "assaults" on the South called for Southern spokesmen, and Tucker was eager to serve. Even so, his view of slavery is more interesting for what it says of his social expectations and moving ideas. An evangelical who had read his Burke and Carlyle, Tucker made the best case he could for the organic wholeness, the affiliation rather than competition, which seemed divinely ordained. Men had to keep in touch with their feelings, honor the past, feel a part of their locale, know their place on the social scale and their part in the cross-thatch of community responsibilities. Slavery was instrumental in this design. Writing an addendum for the published version of his Nashville speech, and in several letters to Hammond, Tucker went so far as to foresee in the distant future black freedom as part of this providential scheme; "the salutary pupilage of the race of Ham" would be prolonged until, Christianized and trained for self-government, Southern freedmen would establish colonies on the banks of the Amazon and would eventually return as missionaries to Africa.[12] Tucker believed himself caught up in this divine project, but he could write of eventual slave manumission only because other features of Southern life like family, landholding, and local networks of trusting friends embodied the same values and would presumably endure afterward. Meanwhile slavery was a preservant of republican government, freeing citizens to concern themselves with lofty purposes at a time when disinterestedness seemed in short supply. Slavery was a homely duty in a period when to Tucker's mind domestic hierarchy was giving way to autonomy and disorder.

It helps us to take Tucker's commentary seriously to keep in mind that it partook of widely shared apprehensions. In truth, his edition of the proslavery-secession argument was a kind of reform effort. As such it resembled quite different reform movements outside the South in that it grew out of a concern for qualitative changes in American and northern European society. While abolitionists in England and the North, as David Brion Davis has argued, saw slaves as commodities, as objects, as the ultimate victims of exploitation and thus as indirect evidence of contemporary social evils, Tucker reacted to the same specter and thought along the same lines. Only the direction was different; he saw the slave as the quintessence of subjectivity, the ultimate dependent person or subject of responsibility, a symbol of an older, simpler way of life that God did not intend to pass away. Together with Northerners like Catherine Beecher, Tucker preached temperance, womanly piety, and family strength as counterweights to the vice and worldly competition he saw about him. Like founders of utopian communities outside Boston, Tucker found professional politics, loose living, materialism, artificiality, overcrowding, and perfunctory human relationships alarming, and his effort to forestall these dangers contained the same nostalgia, apocalyptic fervor, and suspicion of the federal government so marked among romantic reformers in the North.[13] Slavery for Tucker worked to sustain an uncomplicated, godly way of life; secession would establish a moral quarantine, ensuring that simple morality would endure in the South if nowhere else.

Understandable though Tucker's message is in view of its social roots, his sense of what he was doing permits us to reach deeper into the tangled impulses that produced him and his work. Standing aside the rush for success in public life, contemplating developments that apparently placed worthy men on the outside, Tucker and the friends he attracted believed themselves in a morally prominent position in American life. Just as they comforted themselves as overlooked political leaders, so they took solace in their own peculiar virtue and intellectual purity, trying to afford one another the sustenance they missed in an altered society. No doubt the wishes Tucker could not fulfill elsewhere gave his moralizing, especially by his last years, concentrated force. The "'Gospel of enlightened selfishness' which calls itself utilitarian," he wrote for Simms's *Review*, ". . . denies the importance of any considerations, the value of which cannot be estimated in dollars and cents. . . ." Like Tucker, Hammond and Simms referred often to their peculiar moral delicacy, which, they assured each other, qualified them mightily for the leadership they longed to exercise. Indeed passing moral review on Jacksonian society was itself a lifting experience, the very pause heightening the ethereal feeling of being divorced from the ordinary. Adam Waldie—the Philadelphia publisher who met Tucker at the Virginia springs, found him intoxicating, and eventually went insane—discovered that the mere act of writing his friend left him "elevated for the time above the grovelling and miserly cares of the grubs around me." Waldie helps to illustrate how uniquely Tucker and his coterie could view themselves and their message. "Since our acquaintance was formed," Waldie wrote Tucker, "I feel, as it were, a spark of intellectual desire, newly created—a love of the purely moral and intellectual, unmixed with the grossness of common pursuits, and never before [have I] had such a *yearning* after that kind of society."[14]

Tucker did hold himself above venality and in many of his students set off the sparks that Waldie described. Tucker considered himself a man of ideas. In certain respects he was, for he thought at length about life around him; wrote fiction, public letters, essays, and sermons; taught at a major place of higher learning in the Old South; and invited his understudy Hammond to "'ponder boldly' on any subject." That ideas were important to him no one could deny. In his adherence to the political principles he learned from his father, he testified to the importance of those categories of thought to the generation that followed the "founding fathers" and tried to carry on their work. He did indeed see his world and problems in it in terms of the patterns that imbibed beliefs suggested, and though we must treat these frames of references in connection with social realities or needs, they also carried their own imperatives, providing language that influenced his interpretation of events and urging him to look for certain patterns in them.[15] As a set of intellectual forms or a frame of reference, republicanism, for example, brought into focus issues that Tucker saw as worth speaking to and thereby acted on its own as a shaping influence: republicanism brought expectations of temporal decay in self-government; Tucker and men like him saw threatening changes as "corruption" and faced them with all the energy such danger called for.

What makes Tucker's life especially interesting is that intellectual modes, or ways of thinking and knowing, shifted in his youth from a rationalist to a romantic "style." Again, he was in this instance more illustrative than exceptional; his romantic sensibility offered a good example of the impact romanticism made on his generation of Southerners, and in the details of his growth he suggested how circumstances in Virginia could make the newer romantic mode more satisfying than the old. Like many other students at William and Mary, Tucker drew from Scottish common-sense philosophy a suspicion of the "abstraction" and "pretension" that repelled him at the college in the 1790s and that later he found so repugnant in Northerners. From Burke and Blackstone he gathered a sense of the security and stability social institutions could provide, even as they were challenged and ridiculed in the "excesses" he witnessed in youth and maturity. By converting to evangelical Protestantism, as did so many other Americans of his day, Tucker gained a warmth of mood, a belief in divine providence, an assurance that active striving could bring about moral improvement, and a sense of sin and goodness that merged well with republican concepts of virtue and time. Holding together this confidence in intuition, faith in tradition, and emotional piety was a romantic emphasis on "heart," on feeling; the impulses of the heart hastened and lent shape to the melancholy, dejection, nostalgia, and belief in decay that was so common among eastern Virginians in Tucker's day, and that he epitomized. The romantic mode of mind suggested a cathartic solution to the misery he felt and even indulged in.

Being powerless makes for frustration; marginality can lead to sensitivity. Neither necessarily brings one to creative detachment. Tucker, with Waldie, may have seen himself as a lover of the purely moral and intellectual. But Tucker was an intellectual failure, and really not an intellectual at all. His

writing on public issues recognized little distinction between objective inquiry and special advocacy; he sometimes said he aimed at universal truths,
but he mounted particular apologies. In his fiction he demonstrated neither
sense of humor nor irony. He had no feel for the complexities, the contradictions, in human nature—no taste for ambiguity, no dramatic depth.

Indeed the inability of Southerners like Tucker to produce scholarship
or writing as enduring as that of Emerson, Thoreau, or Melville—or of the
South to produce men like them—points to the need for a comparative study
of antebellum intellectual culture. Clearly Tucker was too isolated, too
provincial in his experiences, and too much of a prisoner of his society for
any of the "distance" or nonconformity that a few intellectuals even in his
own day cultivated. His friendships were too limited in number and too
fawning in quality for the rigor that men and women, by contrast, took to
their work in the Concord circle; Tucker, Hammond, Simms, Upshur, and
the rest were preposterously uncritical of each other's writing. Except for
a brief correspondence with Poe, Tucker made contact with no writers or
critics whose theories of literature permitted one to transcend the confines
of his culture. Lacking ties that might have proven stimulating, Tucker
failed to gain by those he did have. If he explored epistemological issues
that natural scientists at William and Mary might have raised, he never
reflected on them in writing. In other respects Tucker's intellectual life suffered from institutional weaknesses stemming from the simplicity of his
society. He enjoyed, for example, none of the visibility or exposure to vary-
ing opinion that frequent lyceum meetings might have provided him and that
did benefit his Northern counterparts; he profited from no critical exchanges
in the few magazines the South produced and enjoyed none of the literary
acclaim or intellectual demands that a wide readership would have brought
him.[16]

Tucker's mode of thought itself helps to account for his intellectual shortcomings. Waldie, enchanted with Tucker's disdain for commonness, con-
gratulated the Virginian because his "head and heart beat in such exquisite
harmony." The fact was that Tucker's heart carried the tune in the music he
composed, and this dominance of impulse over analysis stunted his intellectual growth, satisfying him with subjectivity, illusion, and timidity. For one
thing Tucker's theology acted to inhibit clear thinking and critical acuity by
assuring him of absolutes, prompting a vision of the world that made for
simple splits between good and evil, heightening suspicions of persons not
in league with him—helping thereby to personify evil—and closing his mind
to alternative interpretations of men and events. Evidence of this closedness
abounded in his later writings: he advertised his essays as voicing "absolute
conviction" rather than "mere opinion"; he convinced himself that political
rivals like Rhett in South Carolina were the "Devil's ministers on earth."
Moreover Tucker, like other eastern Virginians in the early nineteenth

century, used the melancholy mood and exotic escape of romanticism to blur unpleasant realities. Just as the example of knights and talk of old England shaped Tucker's behavior, so did the dictates of the heart and language of fancy color his thinking. He never trained a sharp eye on these influences in his own life. He did unwittingly write an intellectual self-commentary while writing one of his review essays for the *Southern Quarterly*. He had been reading a romance, he said, "in which what little truth there may be is indistinguishably blended with falsehood, and the whole, seen through a delusive medium, is so presented as to pass for the moment as unquestionable truth. We are thus deceived."[17]

Fervency of faith and the "delusive medium" of romantic fantasy set only modest objectives for one's thinking. Tucker and his friends never developed a yen to extend the limits of consciousness, to heighten awareness. The thread running through all his thought was the limitation of mind. St. George Tucker had pressed for the powers of reason, had strived for something we might call objectivity—measuring his thoughts against a standard of reasonableness other learned men shared or nearly agreed on—and had been prepared to live with doubt. His son relied on intuition, common-sense feeling, guides to truth that turned him inward and comforted him with the belief that few things were really knowable. "The most valuable truth that discovery makes known to the philosophic mind," he wrote, commenting on an address Hammond made at the College of South Carolina in late 1849, "is the depth of its former ignorance." Such breakthroughs, he cautioned, should sober men "into a steadier pace with the thought that all that the limited faculties of man can *ever* discover, may still be as nothing in comparison with that which man in the flesh shall never know." Tucker might have confronted the issue of how one tested for truth and knew it when it surfaced, but he was content to let his "native sense of right and wrong" judge; he might have used his intellect to plumb the unreason that is so much a part of human life. He did recognize that not all "ideas and influences" reach men through the "bodily senses." But the point of the observation was that the mind was finally "inscrutable."[18]

Probing Tucker's intellectual softness returns us to his place in society and to the changes he noticed in it. His style of thought, as much as his ideas, was responsible for his intensity and direction, but his ultimate purposes were integrative and restorative rather than critical or intellectual. At the intersection of his social anxiety and his intellectual diffidence was the sensibility a traditional elite developed as gaps yawned among roles that earlier had been united. Tucker was keenly aware that, as antebellum society grew more complex, political leader, moral steward, amateur writer, armchair philosopher, and social luminary broke apart as a set of things defining the better sort of men. The "gentleman" represented in Tucker's mind the unity of these social roles: the gentleman was one who, when not busy with the public work that Tucker prescribed as the burden of the Dardenne clan in Missouri, had "due intervals for study, reflection, and day dreaming and repose of mind," and Tucker was confident that the gentleman's realm was shrinking. Thus he reflected and shared with others a concern deeper than the frightening prospects of industrial squalor and ruthless moneymaking. He worried about the locus of authority in antebellum society, the problem of moral control and who prescribed it, the "fact" of disappearing delicacy or sensitivity among cultural spokesmen.[19]

Tucker feared social fluidity, but beyond it, doubt, the suspension of judgment, the very act of questioning. Authority seemed everywhere to be in jeopardy, the wheels of society and intellect whirring out of control. In these circumstances, the beauty of slavery was its certainty, the promise of control it held out. Authority was the master's essential quality, standing virtually unquestioned, and such authority carried particular consolation when, as Tucker saw it, "innovation is shaking the foundations of all recognized right and revolution is assailing all its bulwarks." Control was at the very bottom of slavery, supposedly testifying to a slaveholder's self-control and insuring the control of one's immediate affairs of life; slavery confirmed the control of "truths" in a setting that made the circulation of "untruths" manifestly dangerous and provided some of the assurances that were so necessary when, in what Tucker mockingly called the "age of discovery," "fixed principles" were losing their persuasive force. Slavery was earthy; its day-to-day contacts were fundamentally human, emotional, even familial in Tucker's experience. Master-slave relations confounded the contemporary rejection of "all arguments drawn from the inner consciousness of man."[20]

It might be enough to say that Tucker's own psychological experiences rendered him especially vulnerable to his "age of speculation" and the social flux of antebellum America. His life did offer a case study in the effects of childhood trauma, for the death of his mother and the disturbance it caused contributed noticeably to his idealization of women and longing for the past with its "wholeness" and security. His rivalry with his brother and his rebellious affinity for John Randolph go far to explain the roots of his character and the grudges that lent force to his beliefs. Too, the uneasy truce Tucker arranged with his father and his father's doctrines helps to account for the fervency of the son's adherence to one feature of paternal orthodoxy while he destroyed another; this father-son conflict helps to explain Tucker's highly-charged attitude toward authority, his overweening conscience, his search for a faith in which God was loving, and his groping for the "certainty" that would vindicate him as his father's replacement.[21]

Yet the peculiar features of Tucker's psychological development and decay were also suggestive of his society and generation. His ambivalent feelings for his father recapitulated what seems a persistent theme in human life, the tension that develops as sons vie for attention and compete for place in what at first is a father's world; such generational conflict is deserving of close attention in the aftermath of revolution, as orthodoxy is passed on and undergoes changes of emphasis. Tucker vividly illustrated issues of authority, nostalgia, and adequacy that were of general concern in the antebellum South. Moreover, the difficulties he had making adjustments to antebellum life demonstrated strikingly how changes in social structure and popular conceptions could render personalities superfluous in early-nineteenth-century America: trained in the forms of the gentlemen, schooled in the responsibilities of republican leadership, Tucker like many of his friends offered an example of identity confusion and dysfunction of role. As his sense of self left him badly fitted for the needs of his society, as he discovered that the "audience" of nineteenth-century Virginia was neither responsive nor respectful, Tucker fashioned parts for himself that he hoped events would make viable: he thought of himself alternately as prophet, hero, social healer, and founding father. Such fantasies so embellished his reputation in Virginia as a cranky old man that, when David Campbell wanted to emphasize how outlandish were the ideas of a political rival, he described him as almost as "reckless" as Beverley Tucker.[22] By 1850 few men paid serious attention to Tucker because there was little left of him that was credible; he, like so many other antebellum American gentlemen in a romantic age, had given himself up to empty performances, and in one sense his anger was appropriate to his felt irrelevance.

Tucker struggled with all his might to bring on a crisis that would cleanse. "The only hope that Virginia can ever again recover her place in her own respect, and in the respect of the world, is in disunion," he wrote Hammond, hoping South Carolinians would take the lead in seceding. "It is when men are aroused by dangers that threaten the fireside that they learn to know and appreciate their truly great men." Mercifully, Tucker's death spared him secession and Civil War, for surely they would have been every bit as bitter for him as was the Confederate defeat that led Ruffin to suicide. War led to the death of his favorite nephew, and the secessionist impulse did little if anything to bring to the fore the kind of men Tucker wanted to lead the new nation. The "mind" of Southern society, as opposed to what Tucker called the "brute mass," never rose to the surface as he had expected. In state after state, heading the secessionist cause were the "upstarts," the democratic leaders whom Tucker called demagogic, or the ordinary political professionals who he said made faro dealers look like conscientious statesmen. Hammond and Simms discovered that opposing the 1850 compromise encouraged men like Robert Barnwell Rhett to make rash and arrogant popular appeals.[23] The excitement of secession and the needs of war accelerated this tendency, ironically leaving them on the same wayside they had found so lonely in the prewar period. Never having to hear the historical verdict on his hopes, Tucker liked to think of himself as the messiah of radical restoration, as a tragic hero.

He really was a pathetic figure. His feeling enabled him to see the real differences between North and South better than most Southerners in his day, but the dictates of his "heart" urged him away from any but a cataclysmic solution to those differences. The way Tucker held ideas and sought converts to them left him in the end unable to test his beliefs against the realities of worlds outside Virginia; his fear of developments rendered him at last incapable of the critical self-consciousness that to some degree at least had marked his father's generation. In that sense he lost the life of his mind and embodied the anxieties of the Old South. Eastern Virginia society, growing less deferential at the same time it boasted of its heroic past, had produced a man as unadaptive as Southern hierarchy, as divided himself as Virginians were fearful of internal divisions. Tucker was bent on stability yet proud of his impulsiveness. Concerned with power, he was unsure of his self-control. He spoke loudly of his loyalty to fatherly precepts but boasted that the uprising of his generation would overtake and set aside the glory of the revolutionary fathers. He preached love but acted on bitterness that showed how desperately he competed for recognition in a society he wanted to be without competition. Though he detested expediency, he was willing to forego nothing to bring about secession.

Though Tucker's influence may be difficult to measure exactly, Virginians remembered him and thought of men like him at the outbreak of war. Neglected during his lifetime, attacked for his extremism, Tucker provided channels public opinion could flow into when secession became a plausible political course. While his states' rights principles were important to that influence, so was the heart he asked his students to take to the task of defending those principles. "The desire of some for change, the greed of many for excitement, and the longing of more for anarchy and confusion," wrote a hapless Virginia moderate in 1861, "seems to have unthroned the reason of men, and left them at the mercy of passion and madness."[24] Tucker would have been proud of the part he played in that revolution.

Guide to Abbreviations Used

AgHist	*Agricultural History*
AHR	*American Historical Review*
AmJLH	*American Journal of Legal History*
AmJurist	*The American Jurist and Law Magazine* (1829–43)
AmQ	*American Quarterly*
APU	Abel Parker Upshur (1791–1844)
BDAC	*Biographical Directory of American Congresses*
BPL	Boston Public Library
CBT	Cynthia Beverley Tucker (1832–1908)
CHS	Charleston Historical Society, Charleston, South Carolina
CW	Colonial Williamsburg Foundation, Williamsburg, Virginia
DAB	*Dictionary of American Biography*
DG	Duff Green (1791–1875)
Duke	William R. Perkins Library, Duke University
EC/ECB	Elizabeth Coalter Bryan (1805–56)
ER	Edmund Ruffin (1794–1865)
FBT	Francis Bland Tucker (1742–88)
FTC	Francis Tucker Coalter (1779–1813)
GFH	George Frederick Holmes (1820–97)
GT	George Tucker (1775–1861)
HL	Huntington Library, San Marino, California
HLW	Hugh Lawson White (1773–1840)
HStGT	Henry St. George Tucker (1780–1848)
JC	John Coalter (1769–1838)
JHH	James Henry Hammond (1807–64)
JHI	*Journal of the History of Ideas*
JP	*Journal of Politics*
JR	John Randolph of Roanoke (1773–1833)
JSH	*Journal of Southern History*
LC	Library of Congress
LST	Lucy Smith Tucker (1812–67)
MCT	Mary Coalter Tucker (? –1827)
MHR	*Missouri Historical Review*
MHS	Missouri Historical Society, Saint Louis
MVHR	*Mississippi Valley Historical Review*
NBT	Nathaniel Beverley Tucker (1784–1851)
NYHS	The New York Historical Society
PHF	The Historical Foundation of the Presbyterian and Reformed Churches, Montreat, North Carolina
PSQ	*Political Science Quarterly*

SAQ	*South Atlantic Quarterly*
SHC	Southern Historical Collection, University of North Carolina, Chapel Hill
SHSM	State Historical Society of Missouri, University of Missouri Library
SLM	*Southern Literary Messenger* (1834–64)
SQR	*Southern Quarterly Review* (1842–57)
StGT	St. George Tucker (1752–1827)
TAS	Thomas A. Smith (1781–1844)
T-C	Tucker-Coleman Collection, Swem Library, College of William and Mary
TR	Theodorick Bland Randolph (1771–92)
TTT	Thomas Tudor Tucker (1752–1828)
TWW	Thomas W. White (1788–1843)
USC	South Carolina Library, University of South Carolina
UVa	Alderman Library, University of Virginia
VHS	Virginia Historical Society, Richmond
VMHB	*Virginia Magazine of History and Biography*
VSL	Virginia State Library, Richmond
WCP	William Campbell Preston (1794–1860)
WGS	William Gilmore Simms (1806–70)
WHMC	Western Historical Manuscript Collection, University of Missouri Library
WM	Swem Library, College of William and Mary
WMQ	*William and Mary Quarterly*
WT	Waddy Thompson (1798–1868)

Notes

Preface

1. *Congressional Globe,* 31st Cong., 1st sess., 1850, Appendix, pt. 2, p. 1391; Vernon Louis Parrington, *The Romantic Revolution in America, 1800–1860,* vol. 2 of *Main Currents of American Thought,* 3 vols. (New York: Harcourt, Brace & World, 1927, 1930), p. 34.

2. *Petersburg* (Va.) *Intelligencer,* quoted in *National Intelligencer,* August 1, 1850; William W. Crump to NBT, November 14, 1849, T-C; George H. Reese, ed., *Proceedings of the Virginia State Convention of 1861,* 4 vols. (Richmond: Virginia State Library, 1965), 3:12.

3. Louis Hartz, *The Liberal Tradition in America: An Interpretation of American Political Thought Since the Revolution* (New York: Harcourt, Brace & World, 1955), p. 147.

4. Winthrop D. Jordan, *White Over Black: American Attitudes Toward the Negro, 1550–1812* (Chapel Hill: University of North Carolina Press, 1968), p. 429.

Chapter One

1. NBT, *Southern Convention: Remarks of the Hon. Beverley Tucker of Virginia* ([Richmond]: Colin, Baptist and Howland, [1850]), p. 16.

2. [NBT,] *George Balcombe: A Novel,* 2 vols. (New York: Harper & Brothers, 1836), 1:22–23. See also "Edward William Sidney" [NBT], *The Partisan Leader: A Tale of the Future,* 2 vols. ("Printed for the publishers by James Caxton, 1856" [Washington: Duff Green, 1836]), passim, but especially "Dedication." All my citations of *The Partisan Leader* will refer to the recent reprint, with an introduction by C. Hugh Holman, which was published in 1971 by the University of North Carolina Press as part of the Southern Literary Classics Series, C. Hugh Holman and Louis D. Rubin, Jr., gen. eds.

3. Nathaniel Tucker, "The Bermudian," in Frederick Charles Hicks, *Bermuda in Poetry, 1610–1908* (Hamilton, Bermuda: The Colonial Press, 1915), pp. 31–40. On the Tucker family background, see St. George Tucker's autobiograhical sketch—written for John Adams, who called the Tucker family of Virginia "one of the most sentimental and accomplished" in the country—in "Randolph and Tucker Letters," *VMHB* 42 (July 1934): 211–23 (hereafter cited as StGT autobiographical sketch; Adams's opinions quoted in Richard Rush to StGT, December 2, 1813, T-C). Beverley Tucker mentioned "The Bermudian" in a letter to his family, December 10, 1809, T-C. For an engaging account of the Tucker family of Bermuda, focusing on St. George Tucker's brother Nathaniel, see Lewis Leary, *The Literary Career of Nathaniel Tucker, 1750–1807,* Historical Papers of The Trinity College Historical Society, series 29 (Durham, N.C.: Duke University Press, 1951).

4. StGT autobiographical sketch, p. 213. Charles T. Cullen, "St. George Tucker and Law in Virginia, 1772–1804" (Ph.D. dissertation, University of Virginia, 1971), pp. 10–12; Jack P. Greene, *The Quest for Power: The Lower Houses of Assembly in the Southern Royal Colonies, 1689–1776* (Chapel Hill: University of North Carolina Press, 1963), pp. 28–29, 369–71.

5. StGT autobiographical sketch, pp. 213–15.

6. Ibid., pp. 215–16; Edward M. Riley, "St. George Tucker's Journal of the Seige of Yorktown, 1781," *WMQ,* 3d ser. 5 (July 1948): 375–95; and Charles Washington Coleman, Jr., "The Southern Campaign, 1781 . . . ," *Magazine of American History* 7 (July, September 1881): 36–46, 201–16.

7. Responsible for the compliment to Frances was Hugh A. Garland, *The Life of John Randolph of Roanoke,* 2 vols. (New York: D. Appleton and Company, 1850), 1:4. StGT autobiographical

sketch, pp. 215-16; William Cabell Bruce, *John Randolph of Roanoke, 1773-1833: A Biography Based Largely on New Material*, 2 vols. (New York: G. P. Putnam's Sons, 1922), 1:29-34. The painting of Frances Bland Tucker now hangs in the Tucker house in Williamsburg.

8. TTT, Charleston, South Carolina, to StGT, December 23, 1784, T-C. Bruce, *John Randolph of Roanoke*, 1:35-37; Tucker genealogical chart, oversize box, T-C.

9. JR to ECB, November 1, 1828, and December 22, 1830, Bryan Papers (3400), UVa; Bruce, *John Randolph of Roanoke*, 1:37-41. After visiting the Matoax ruins at mid nineteenth century, Garland lamented the steady encroachment of the wild pine and broom sedge, the wilderness that had replaced the fruitful fields, and the symbolic trespass of "factory boys" who, with their dogs, chased rabbits over the same hills "where once the proud sons of a proud race pursued the same lightfooted game." Garland, *Life of John Randolph*, 1:5-6.

10. Benjamin Watkins Leigh's comment on Frances Tucker's voice quoted in John Randolph Tucker, "The Judges Tucker of the Court of Appeals of Virginia," *Virginia Law Register* 1 (March 1896):797. JR to ECB, November 1, 1828, and December 30, 1830, Bryan Papers (3400), UVa; NBT, notes for an autobiography, Stories, Anecdotes, and Sketches, box 83, T-C.

11. StGT to FBT, October 3, 1787, T-C. StGT autobiographical sketch, pp. 217-18; StGT to FBT, April 19, October 17, and October 27, 1787, T-C. Governor Patrick Henry commissioned Tucker to attend the Annapolis Convention partly on the basis of his pamphlet *Reflections on the Policy of Encouraging the Commerce of the United States and of Granting them Exclusive Privileges in Trade* (Philadelphia: Mathew Carey, 1785); see also "Ms. proposals for the improvement of the Union," dated September 1786, T-C.

12. StGT to FBT, October 4, December 1, December 3, and December 5, 1787, T-C; Neill Buchanan's memorial to Frances Tucker quoted in Bruce, *John Randolph of Roanoke*, 1:32; Philip Francis, trans., *A Poetical Translation of the Works of Horace . . . In Four Volumes*, ninth ed. (London: Printed for T. Payne and Son . . . , 1791), 1:92-93. Tucker borrowed the first lines of Ode 24, Book I. See also StGT, autobiographical sketch, p. 218.

13. StGT autobiographical sketch pp. 218-19; StGT to TR and JR, June 29, 1788, Bryan Papers (3400), UVa; StGT to John Page, January 13, 1789, CW. On postwar Virginia court reorganization, see Cullen, "St. George Tucker," chap. 5.

14. NBT, untitled poem dated Williamsburg, April 1828, in NBT Poems, box 83, T-C. NBT, notes for an autobiography, Stories, Anecdotes, and Sketches, box 83, T-C. On the psychic shock loss of mother, strange people, and puzzling events can bring young children, see "Note on Psychological References."

15. Jedidiah Morse, *The American Geography; Or A View of the Present Situation of the United States of America . . .* (Elizabeth Town: Printed by Shepard Kollock, 1789), p. 383. See also Isaac Weld, *Travels Through the States of North America . . . During the Years 1795-1796 and 1797*, 2 vols. (London: John Stockdale, 1799), 1:95-96.

16. StGT, *A Letter to the Rev. Jedidiah Morse, A.M., Author of the "American Universal Geography," by a Citizen of Williamsburg* (Richmond: Thomas Nicholson, 1795), reprinted in *WMQ*, 1st ser. 2 (January 1894):194-96n.

17. St. George Tucker kept nearly a dozen bound volumes of scientific and other notes which, with numerous folders of his poems, are preserved in boxes 62-64, T-C. See also John Page to StGT, November 17, 1784; and Jeremy Belknap, Boston, to StGT, December 28, 1795, May 18, 1796, and February 8, 1798, all in T-C. St. George's semaphore experiments received attention in the *Virginia Gazette and General Advertiser*, December 24, 1794. For a note on Tucker as poet, with selections from his work, see William S. Prince, ed., *The Poems of St. George Tucker of Williamsburg, Virginia, 1752-1827* (New York: Vantage Press, 1977).

18. StGT, *Liberty, A poem On the Independence of America* (Richmond: Printed by Aug. Davis, 1788). StGT, Poems, boxes 80-82, T-C. On Tucker's circle, see Richard Beale Davis, *Intellectual Life in Jefferson's Virginia, 1790-1830* (Chapel Hill: University of North Carolina Press, 1964), especially pp. 281-82, 319-30. Tucker's plan was to collect his several pieces, with titles like "The Genius of American Liberty" and "Secular Ode to the 4th of July, 1803," to form a book of verse that would inspire the younger generation.

19. StGT, *Liberty*, p. 20.

20. John Page to StGT, July 23, 1789, and June 3, 1793, T-C; TTT to StGT, May 13 and September 15, 1789, T-C; StGT to John Page, January 11, 1795, CW.

21. [StGT,] *The Probationary Odes of Jonathan Pindar, Esq. A Cousin of Peter's and Candidate for the Post of Poet Laureate of the C. U. S. In Two Parts* (Philadelphia: Benj. Franklin Bache, 1796), pt. 1, pp. 18, 16, 39; pt. 2, p. 71. "Jonathan" was supposed to be the American cousin of "Peter Pindar," a figure British satirist John Wolcott created in the 1780s as mock poet laureate of England.

22. Cullen, "St. George Tucker," pp. 174–85. For the issues Tucker discussed in his lectures, see David Watson's notebook for the 1796 term, Watson Papers (530), UVa.

23. StGT, *A Dissertation on Slavery: With a Proposal for the Gradual Abolition of It in the State of Virginia* (Philadelphia: Mathew Carey, 1796), title page. See also ibid., pp. 3–12. In Tucker's proposals, black females freed at birth were to serve as indentured servants until age twenty-eight—a compensation for the childhood sustenance their masters provided—and were then to receive a modest dowry to help them begin a free life. In a letter to Robert Pleasants, June 29, 1797 (a copy of which appears in StGT Notebooks, volume not numbered, p. 38, T-C), Tucker explained his decision in the *Dissertation* to "accommodate" himself to prejudice rather than "to encounter it."

24. StGT, *Dissertation on Slavery*, "To The Reader" [a foreword without pagination] and pp. 105–6; note to poem "The fourth of July 1803," dated January 15, 1804, folder 4, box 80, T-C. Surely the representatives of a free people, Tucker wrote the assembly, "cannot disapprove an attempt to carry so incontestable a moral Truth into practical Effect." StGT to Speaker, House of Delegates, November 30, 1796, T-C. The legislature tabled the manumission proposal; Ludwell Lee to StGT, December 5, 1796, T-C.

25. Randolph and Tucker genealogies, T-C; StGT to John Page, January 24, 1791, CW; TTT to StGT, July 14, 1792, T-C; George Tucker (a cousin of St. George who also left Bermuda in the late eighteenth century and settled in Virginia) to StGT, January 31 and August 14, 1800, T-C.

26. Tucker genealogical chart and family letters of the period, T-C.

27. NBT, notes for an autobiography, Stories, Anecdotes, and Sketches, box 83, T-C; Maria Rind to StGT, n.d., 1790s box, T-C. See also StGT to JC, July 20, 1790, Bryan Papers (3400), UVa. In the first letter Beverley ever wrote his father, he referred to "that depression of spirits" he thought, was "generally the forerunner of sickness." NBT to StGT, August 4, 1799, T-C. For the likely impact these recurrent family deaths had on young Tucker, see "Note on Psychological References."

28. NBT, notes for an autobiography, Stories, Anecdotes, and Sketches, box 83, T-C. On Beverley's trials as suggestive of a psychosocial "failure" at an important step in his life, see "Note on Psychological References."

29. StGT to JC, July 20, 1790, Bryan Papers (3400), UVa; "Garrison Articles to be observed by the Officers and Privates Stationed at Fort St. George in Williamsburg," n.d. (c. 1790), box 16, T-C; JR to Theodorick Tudor Randolph, December 13, 1813, typescript copy, Grinnan Papers (2118), UVa; ECB Diary, January 8–June 1, 1853, with a biographical sketch of JC, VHS. "The first blow I ever received," John Randolph tersely wrote his nephew in the letter noted above, "was from the hand of this man, and not a week after his union with my mother." St. George Tucker, while praising a stepson's "sense of honor & independence," warned the young man to correct his impetuosity, to remember that "a passionate man is a scourge both to his friends and himself." StGT to TR, June 19, 1788, Bryan Papers (3400), UVa. See also StGT to TR and JR, August 13, 1788, and August 30, 1789, Bryan Papers (3400), UVa; StGT to TR and JR, June 12, 1787, and to Alexander Campbell (Tucker's ward), December 10, 1809, T-C.

30. Eliza Tucker, Bermuda, to StGT, July 30, 1802, T-C. See also Henry Tucker to StGT, December 1, 1795, May 6, 1800, January 10, 1802, and January 1, 1806, T-C.

31. HStGT to StGT, February 5, 1806, T-C.

32. Maria Rind to StGT, n.d., T-C; StGT to JC, July 20, 1790, Bryan Papers (3400), UVa. See also TTT to StGT, July 14, 1792, December 19, 1801, and January 28, 1802, T-C; Frances Tucker, Bermuda, to StGT, September 16, 1802, T-C; Eliza Tucker, Bermuda, to StGT, March 21, 1803, and November 23, 1804, T-C. For studies of sibling rivalry, see "Note on Psychological References."

33. HStGT to StGT, August 11, 1799, T-C. See also HStGT to StGT September 7, 1796, August 19, 1797, August 18 and October 13, 1798, August 4, July 21, and September 1, 1799, T-C; NBT to StGT, September 13, 1800, T-C.

34. HStGT to "Citizen" StGT, September 7, 1796, T-C; I[saac] A. Coles, Amherst, to HStGT, July 20, 1799, "Original Letters," *WMQ*, 1st ser. 4 (October 1895):106. HStGT to StGT, June 16, 1799, T-C, includes a summary of the address. Comments on Henry as a student are found in

Joseph S. Watson to David Watson, November 4, 1799, and October 26, [1800,] Watson Family Papers, LC. These letters and others that David Watson's friends at William and Mary sent him during these years appear in "Letters From William and Mary College, 1798-1801," *VMHB* 29 (April 1921):129-79; "Letters to David Watson," *VMHB* 29 (July 1921):255-86; and "Letters From William and Mary, 1795-1799," *VMHB* 30 (July 1922):221-49. Hereafter my references to these published letters will be to the volume and page where they appear.

35. Robert Polk Thompson, "The Reform of the College of William and Mary, 1763-1780," *Proceedings of the American Philosophical Society* 115 (June 1971):187-213, especially pp. 206-13. St. George Tucker spoke of the promise of the college in his *Letter to the Reverend Jedidiah Morse.*

36. Weld, *Travels,* 1:95; Thomas Jefferson, *Notes on the State of Virginia* (New York: Harper Torchbook edition, 1964), p. 146; Morse, *American Geography,* p. 382. For an account of the aeronautical exploits of William and Mary students at the turn of the nineteenth century, see Joseph Watson to David Watson, May 7, 1801, *VMHB,* 29:167-69.

37. Samuel Miller, *A Brief Retrospect of the Eighteenth Century, Part First; in Two Volumes: Containing a Sketch of the Revolution and Improvements in Science, Art, and Literature During That Period* (New York: T. and J. Swords, 1803), 2:503; Thomson, "Reform of the College of William and Mary," pp. 206-11; Davis, *Intellectual Life in Jefferson's Virginia,* pp. 52-53; Joseph S. Watson to David Watson, September 7, 1796, February 11, 1798, November 4, December 9, and December 24, 1799, *VMHB,* 29:131-37, 145-54. College records for this period are incomplete; exact information about student enrollment is unavailable. I cannot even determine exactly when Tucker began the college course. *The History of the College of William and Mary From Its Foundation, 1690 to 1874* (Richmond: J. W. Randolph and English, 1874), published before a fire that destroyed many college records, lists Beverley Tucker as a student in 1801-2. But this publication—its author unknown—is unreliable, and Tucker may very well have begun one or two years earlier.

38. Years later, Benjamin Watkins Leigh, who became a successful lawyer and United States senator, recalled "the real instruction . . . in literature, in professional learning, in manners, in morals, in true honor" he gained in the society of the Tucker household. Leigh to NBT, March 26, 1839, T-C. For St. George Tucker's library, see Davis, *Intellectual Life in Jefferson's Virginia,* pp. 94-96, and Jill M. Coghlan, "The Library of St. George Tucker" (M.A. thesis, College of William and Mary, 1973).

39. Miller, *Brief Retrospect,* 2:503. Adam Smith, *An Inquiry Into the Nature and Causes of the Wealth of Nations,* ed. Edwin Canaan, Introduction by Max Lerner (New York: The Modern Library, 1937), pp. 734 ff. For the attention Americans paid Smith and other theorists of economy and society in these years, see Drew G. McCoy, "The Republican Revolution: Political Economy in Jeffersonian America, 1776-1817" (Ph.D. dissertation, University of Virginia, 1976).

40. Besides *Wealth of Nations,* Miller in *Brief Retrospect* lists as texts used at the college Samuel Rutherford and Jean-Jacques Burlamaqui in natural law, Emerie de Vattel and Georg F. Von Martens in the law of nations, and Locke, Rousseau, and Montesquieu in politics proper.

41. On readings in politics and the politicized atmosphere at William and Mary, see Joseph Watson to David Watson, December 24, 1799, October 26, [1800,] January 17, March 2, and April 1, [1801]; Chapman Johnson to David Watson, December 19, 1799, May 18, and October 27, 1800, and February 20, 1801, *VMHB,* 29:151-66, 265-76. See also "Letters of Rev. James Madison, President of William and Mary College, to Thomas Jefferson," *WMQ,* 1st ser. 5 (April and July 1925):77-95, 145-58, and passim; and Charles Crowe, "Bishop James Madison and the Republic of Virtue," *JSH* 30 (February 1964):58-70.

42. Chapman Johnson to David Watson, December 19, 1799, *VMHB,* 29:265; Joseph Watson to David Watson, October 26, [1800,] and March 2, [1801,] *VMHB,* 29:155, 164. See also Joseph S. Watson to David Watson, February 9, [1799,] *VMHB,* 29:138-39; Chapman Johnson to David Watson, May 18, 1800, *VMHB,* 29:270; John W. Tomlin to David Watson, January 14, 1798, *VMHB,* 30:236; Joseph C. Cabell to Dr. William B. Hare, January 4, 1801, and Thomas L. Preston to Andrew Reid, Jr., January 7, 1802, in "Glimpses of Old College Life," *WMQ,* 1st ser. 8 (April 1900): 215-16. In 1779 the college Board of Visitors withdrew faculty commons eating privileges and ended fixed salaries, so that professors depended on students' fees for income—originally a thousand pounds of tobacco per student per year. Thomson, "Reform of the College of William and Mary," p. 210.

43. Examples of religious skepticism at William and Mary during this period abound. See, for example, William Brockenbrough to David Watson, January 14, 1798, *VMHB*, 30:237–39; Isaac Coles to David Watson, March 21, 1798, ibid., pp. 240–42, contains an account of the church attack. For a glance at this infidelity from the vantage point of the mid-nineteenth century, see John Tyler, "Early Times of Virginia—William and Mary College," *De Bow's Review* 27 (August 1859):136–49.

44. William Godwin, *Enquiry Concerning Political Justice and Its Influence on Morals and Happiness,* critical introduction and notes by F. E. L. Priestley, 3 vols. (Toronto: University of Toronto Press, 1946). The debate on Godwin at William and Mary, which ended in a divided issue, was mentioned in J. S. Watson's letter to David Watson, November 4, 1799, *VMHB*, 29:146–47. For a contemporary reference to the influence of Godwin in Virginia, see William Wirt, *The Letters of the British Spy; to which is prefixed A Biographical Sketch of the Author,* introduction by Richard Beale Davis ([1st ed., Richmond: Samuel Pleasants, Jr., 1803;] reprint ed. Chapel Hill: University of North Carolina Press, 1970), pp. 203–5.

45. William Paley, *The Principles of Moral and Political Philosophy* (Philadelphia: printed by Thomas Dobson, 1794), pp. 73–75, 421, 48–49, xii–xiii. For secondary treatments of moral philosophy as taught in early-nineteenth-century colleges, see "Essay on Sources."

46. William Duncan, *The Elements of Logic. In Four Books . . . Designed Particularly for Young Gentlemen at the University; And to Prepare the Way to the Study of Philosophy and the Mathematics* (New York: printed by L. Nichols, & Co. for Evert Duyckinck, bookseller, 1802); Thomas Reid, *Essays on the Intellectual and Active Powers of Man,* 2 vols. (Philadelphia: printed by William Young, 1793); Dugald Stewart, *Elements of the Philosophy of the Human Mind* (Philadelphia: printed by William Young, 1793); Hugh Blair, *Lectures on Rhetoric and Belles Lettres,* 2 vols. (Philadelphia: From the Press of Mathew Carey, 1793). Dismissing Descartes' need to prove the existence of material things "by philosophical arguments," Reid concluded "that philosophy must make a very ridiculous figure in the eyes of sensible men, while it is employed in mustering up metaphysical arguments, to prove that there is a sun and a moon, an earth and a sea" (*Essays,* 1:220; see also "Opinions of Philosophers about Universals," 1:467–87). While Stewart was not as representative a reactionary figure as Reid, he opened *Elements* complaining of the "frivolous and absurd discussions which abound in the writings of most metaphysical authors . . ." (p. 9).

47. For a recent treatment of the connection between slavery and republicanism in eighteenth-century Virginia, see Edmund S. Morgan, *American Slavery, American Freedom: The Ordeal of Colonial Virginia* (New York: W. W. Norton & Co., 1975), pp. 363–87.

Chapter Two

1. Barraud to StGT, February 22, 1802; NBT to JR, February 21, 1802, both in T-C. Incomplete and undated draft of essay on the power and influence of the press, folder 7, NBT Papers, WM. The quality of Tucker's handwriting in a pupil's notebook suggests the approximate date and likely purpose of the piece. On the wide impact of these disorders, see "An Inhabitant of Williamsburg," in *The Virginia Argus,* May 5, 1802, reprinted in "William and Mary College in 1802," *WMQ,* 2d ser. 5 (January 1925):61–62.

2. NBT to JR, February 21, 1802, T-C.

3. StGT to Alexander Campbell, July 7, 1809 and to TR and JR, June 12, 1787, T-C. StGT to Mr. Hettrick [Campbell's tutor in Winchester], March 5, 1806, and Tucker's "Sketch of a Plan for the endowment & establishment of a State University in Virginia," in StGT to William Hening, January 4, 1805, both in T-C.

4. JC, Williamsburg, to his father, April 20, 1789, typescript copy, Bryan Papers, group 1B, folder 1, VSL; StGT, *Blackstone's Commentaries: With Notes of Reference, to the Constitution and Laws, of the Federal Government of the United States; and the Commonwealth of Virginia,* 5 vols. (Philadelphia: Wm. Young Birch, and Abraham Small, 1803), 1:xiv; NBT to JR, February 21, 1802, T-C. In the letter noted above, Coalter also wrote that the statesman who zealously served his country found in "duty done" the happiness that was the "constant attendant of virtue."

5. See "Essay on Sources" for secondary works on American legal training in the early nineteenth century. The reliable standard is Alfred Zantzinger Reed, *Training for the Public Profession of the Law: Historical Development and Principal Contemporary Problems of Legal Education in*

the United States with Some Account of Conditions in England and Canada, bulletin no. 15 of the Carnegie Foundation for the Advancement of Teaching (New York: [The Foundation], 1921); see pp. 110–12 for Blackstone and the Revolution.

6. StGT, *Blackstone's Commentaries,* 1:iv, xviii; Julius S. Waterman, "Thomas Jefferson and Blackstone's Commentaries," 27 *Illinois Law Review* 629 (1933).

7. StGT, *Blackstone's Commentaries,* 1:vii–viii *et seq.*; Cullen, "St. George Tucker," pp. 223–32; Elizabeth Kelly Bauer, *Commentaries on the Constitution, 1790–1860* (New York: Columbia University Press, 1952), pp. 175–77, 260–64, 280–83, 340–42.

8. StGT, *Blackstone's Commentaries,* 1:vii–viii *et seq.*

9. Ibid., vol. 1: "Appendix," pp. 140 ff., 170, 278–89.

10. Ibid., vol. 1:39, n. 18; "Appendix," pp. 140 ff., 171, 314–16, and passim.

11. On the ambiguities of Tucker's constitutional commentary, see ibid., vol. 1: "Appendix," pp. 3–4, 7–21, 73–77, 173, 348–50, 367, 376–77.

12. Ibid., vol. 1: "Appendix," p. 63, and passim; for a discussion of Blackstone's treatise as a piece of conservative scholarship, see Daniel Boorstin, *The Mysterious Science of the Law: An Essay on Blackstone's Commentaries, Showing How Blackstone, Employing Eighteenth-Century Ideas of Science, Religion, History, Aesthetics, and Philosophy Made the Law At Once a Conservative and a Mysterious Science* (Cambridge, Mass.: Harvard University Press, 1941).

13. StGT, *Blackstone's Commentaries,* 1:8–10, 29–32, and passim. Blackstone's contention that the law was the proper domain of "gentlemen of bright imaginations" (1:29) led him to recommend a sound scholarly foundation before one undertook legal study. Thus, preparation at one of the universities was preferable to mere study at the desk of an attorney as an apprentice. Despite these warnings, most American law students in the early nineteenth century trained for the law as they had in the eighteenth—by reading texts with a practicing attorney. While St. George Tucker echoed Blackstone on the importance of "liberal education" as a basis for law schooling, publication of his William and Mary lecture notes eased apprenticeship training by making a wealth of well-organized material now widely available. Reed, *Training for the Law,* p. 117.

14. NBT to JR, February 21, 1802, T-C; Chapman Johnson to David Watson, January 24, 1802, *VMHB,* 29:280; Joseph C. Cabell to David Watson, June 7, 1799, *VMHB,* 29:262. See also Joseph Watson to David Watson, February 9, 1799, *VMHB,* 29:139; and Cullen, "St. George Tucker," pp. 185–94.

15. NBT to StGT, July 29 and December 6, 1802, T-C. JC to StGT, January 14 and June 22, 1804, T-C; NBT to StGT, January 27, 1803, July 6, 1804, T-C. Coalter biographical sketch in ECB Diary, VHS.

16. NBT to JR, January 20, 1806, T-C. See also NBT to StGT, July 6, 1804, July 25, 1805, and June 24, 1808, T-C.

17. NBT to StGT, August 29, 1805, T-C. See also NBT to StGT, December 2, 1802, T-C; on Belsham, see Herbert Butterfield, *George III and the Historians,* rev. ed. (New York: The Macmillan Company, 1959), pp. 58–59, 67–68, 233–34.

18. FTC to Frances Davenport (mother of Coalter's deceased second wife), February 28, 1803, Bryan Papers (3400), UVa; NBT to FTC, October 22, 1804, T-C. See also NBT to StGT, December 2, 1802, August 29, September 5, 1805; George Tucker to StGT, March 5, 1806, and JC to StGT, January 3, 1806, all in T-C. Hay was famous for his role in defending James Callender, in whose 1800 sedition trial St. George Tucker had intervened, and as the prosecuting attorney in the Aaron Burr conspiracy case in the summer of 1807; Mary Newton Stanard, *Richmond: Its People and Its Story* (Philadelphia: J. E. Lippincott Company, 1923), pp. 95–98, and Samuel Mordecai, *Virginia, Especially Richmond, in By-Gone Days* (Richmond: G. M. West, 1856), pp. 63–105.

19. JR to StGT, September 13, 1787, quoted in Bruce, *John Randolph of Roanoke,* 1:81; NBT to StGT, June 4, 1802, and JR to NBT, June 24, 1802, both in T-C. See also Charles Carter to StGT, June 4, 1802, and NBT to StGT, June 11, 1802, T-C. The death of Randolph's older brother Richard in 1796 had left him sole male heir to the Randolph lands but also saddled him with Richard's debts and those of the family estate; Bruce, *John Randolph of Roanoke,* 1:127–55.

20. Judith Randolph to StGT, May 30, 1800; Nancy Randolph to StGT, December [n.d.], 1801; JR to NBT, June 24, 1802; all in T-C. "Yours are talents of a very inferior stamp," Randolph once wrote the younger man. "Of this I know you must be sensible as well as myself, but this knowledge can neither modify you nor render you less dear to me" (JR to NBT, June 21, 1801, T-C). St.

George Tucker's plan to send Beverley to Staunton for further reading cast a "gloom" over Randolph, who believed it "the commencement of a separation which is to be final" (JR to NBT, June 24, 1802, T-C). See also FTC to StGT, August 11, 1799; HStGT to StGT, August 24, 1800; and Judith Randolph to StGT, March 10 and September 16, 1805; all in T-C. On the Randolph-Maria Ward love affair, see Bruce, *John Randolph of Roanoke*, 2:325 ff.

21. Judith Randolph to StGT, February 19, 1804, T-C. NBT to StGT, July 10, 1802, March 27, April 29, May 11, and June 1, 1804, T-C; NBT to FTC, April 21, 1805, T-C; NBT to JR, April 21, 1805, and April 29, 1806, T-C. See also Judith Randolph to StGT, June 4 and September 4, 1803, and July 26, 1806, T-C.

22. A pungent contemporary account of Randolph came from John Quincy Adams who, after listening to him willingly for between three and four hours, wrote: "His speech, as usual, had neither beginning, middle, nor end. Egotism, Virginian aristocracy, slave-scourging liberty, religion, literature, science, wit, fancy, generous feelings, and malignant passions constitute a chaos in his mind, from which nothing orderly can ever flow. . . . It was useless to try to call him to order; he can no more keep order than he can keep silence." Allan Nevins, ed., *The Diary of John Quincy Adams, 1794–1845: American Diplomacy, and Political, Social, and Intellectual Life, from Washington to Polk* (New York: Charles Scribner's Sons, 1951), p. 229. See also "Essay on Sources."

23. *Annals of Congress*, 8th Cong., 2d sess. (1804–1805), 17:1024. Randolph may have derived the name of his faction from the "Quis? Quo? Quid?" limericks that St. George Tucker, family, and friends circulated among themselves in the 1790s, or from the Latin phrase used in medieval scholastic philosophy, *quid tertium est?*–thereby considering his politics the third line, or logical conclusion, of a syllogism containing Federalists and Jeffersonian Republicans. The Quids comprised a coterie of conservatives, mostly Southerners, who stood for decentralized government, limitations on executive discretion, a small military and naval force, gentlemanly rule, an agricultural rather than an industrialized America, and later, opposition to the War of 1812. They considered themselves the guardians of the faith Jefferson as President was willing to abandon as circumstances dictated.

24. NBT, "Garland's Life of Randolph" [pub. 1850], *SQR* 20 (July 1851):46; NBT to JR, January 31, 1807, T-C. See also NBT to JR, December 31, 1807, T-C. For Randolph's injunction "above all" to read Burke, see *Letters of John Randolph to a Young Relative: Embracing a Series of Years from Early Youth to Mature Manhood* (Philadelphia: Carey, Lea & Blanchard, 1834), p. 191. Hugh Blair Grigsby reported after Randolph's death that the congressman's library included "not only the great historical works of the language in all their ample proportions, but the tracts and essays which the contest about Whig and Tory for a century had called forth." "The Library of John Randolph," *SLM* 20 (February 1854):76–79.

25. Increasingly Tucker thought of himself, too, as one whom Byron alone could portray; Tucker believed himself a gentleman of private woes and secret thoughts, unsung in his brilliance, tenacious in his lonely defense of truth. In his early twenties in these years, he clearly found in this older half brother one whose color and power were especially appealing and after whom he could pattern his own personality. For more on this process in young persons—on the need to formulate an identity that partakes of a view of the world and that therefore can be highly suggestive of his or her society —see "Note on Psychological References." Tucker's feelings for Randolph and Byron surfaced in NBT to EC, July 30, 1825, T-C, and will receive treatment in chapter 4, below. Later Tucker spoke of Randolph and Byron as "of the same order" and wished that each man could have been the biographer of the other; undated, unpublished piece on the proposal that Washington Irving write a life of Randolph, Stories, Anecdotes, and Sketches, box 83, T-C.

26. NBT to JR, April 2, April 15, April 29, and December 20, 1806, T-C. Tucker's phrase, "the Sin of heresy," referred to attacks on Randolph in the Richmond *Enquirer*.

27. Beverley spoke of taking his "degrees as a man" in a letter to JR, April 29, 1806, T-C. See also NBT to StGT, September 20, 1805, and NBT to JR, November 18, 1805, January 20, March 10, and April 29, 1806, all T-C; HStGT to StGT, December 3, 1805, and June 17, 1806, T-C.

28. County courts, local magistrates presiding, sat once a month at the county seats and dispatched minor judicial and administrative business in the state court system Tucker knew as a beginning lawyer. Higher courts, known as district or superior courts, sat in the spring and fall of each year at a location central to five adjacent counties and heard both appeals from county courts and original cases of a serious nature. The Supreme Court of Appeals, to which St. George

Tucker had been appointed two years before his son's qualification at the bar, sat twice a year in Richmond and was the court of last resort unless a cause could be shown to involve a federal question. Tucker expected district courts at Staunton and Prince Edward, together with nearby county courts, to provide most of his practice. William Waller Hening, comp., *The Statutes at Large; Being a Collection of all the Laws of Virginia . . .* , 13 vols. (Richmond: George Cochran [and various printers], 1809-23), 12:730-63; 13:11-17, 427-67 (hereafter referred to as Hening); StGT, *Blackstone's Commentaries*, vol. 4, "Appendix," pp. 3-30; vol. 5, "Appendix," pp. 53-60; and Cullen, "St. George Tucker," chap. 5 and passim.

29. NBT to FTC, October 25, 1806, T-C. See also NBT to StGT, June 22, June 30, July 24, 1806, and January 23, 1807, T-C. According to Charlotte County, Va. Order Book 15, p. 181, Tucker passed his licensing examination August 5, 1806. I am indebted to Ms. Gene McKinney, resident of Charlotte Court House and a member of the Association for the Preservation of Virginia Antiquities, for her generous help in locating and copying pertinent county records there.

30. NBT to StGT, February 8 and May 17, 1807, T-C. See also NBT to StGT, June 30 and July 24, 1806, January 23 and March 22, 1807, T-C.

31. NBT to StGT, February 16, February 19, February 28, March 22, and June 20, 1807, T-C; NBT to JR, February 19, 1807, T-C. In this letter to Randolph, Tucker wrote, "Could I remember the days of my mother, there might be a period to which I could look back with pleasure, but as it is, all is a dead blank, or worse."

32. NBT to JR, April 21, 1807, T-C. Tucker crossed out the word "best" before mailing the letter. See also NBT to StGT, February 28, 1807, T-C.

33. NBT to StGT, May 17, 1807, T-C. See also NBT to JR, April 21, 1807; FTC to StGT, November 4 and December 16, 1803; and JC to StGT, June 14, 1805; all in T-C.

34. NBT to StGT, [c. July 23, 1807,] T-C. See also NBT to JR, [Randolph dated the note July 25, 1807,] T-C.

35. StGT to NBT, July 28, 1807, T-C.

36. NBT to StGT, December 26, 1807, T-C; NBT to JR, February 28, April 6, and January 19, 1808, T-C. For corroborating testimony on the "urgency of the times" for lawyers in Virginia, see GT to StGT, July 31 and October 19, 1808, T-C. In a letter to Randolph of June 30, 1808 (T-C), Beverley castigated himself for his "supineness and inactivity," and these words became vessels of deeply felt emotion that he later applied to the South. His affairs in 1808, he told Randolph, were "like those of the nation," and he implied that the nation—the Jefferson administration and the federal government—might be to blame for his ills.

37. NBT to StGT, September 5, 1805, T-C. See also NBT to StGT, October 4, 1807, T-C. For references to romantic oratory at the bar in this period, see Wirt, *Letters of the British Spy*, pp. .132 ff. and John Pendleton Kennedy, *Memoirs of the Life of William Wirt, Attorney-General of the United States* (2 vols. [Philadelphia: Lea and Blanchard, 1849], 1:57-58, 362 ff.)—where Kennedy includes Wirt's interesting letter to Francis Walker Gilmer of November 16, 1813 ([1812], from Gilmer Letterbook, UVa). See also Perry Miller, *The Life of the Mind in America: From the Revolution to the Civil War* (New York: Harcourt, Brace and World, 1965), pp. 112-13, 151-55. After attending a district court session in the spring of 1808, Tucker reported that Wirt had "effected an entire monopoly of praise and admiration at this term. . . ." NBT to StGT, April 7, 1808, T-C.

38. NBT to JR, March 12 and March 26, 1808, T-C. At one point, the elder Tucker sharply remarked that it would have been better had Beverley "been born a day labourer, than become the prey of despondency and care from repeated disappointments and vexations." NBT to StGT, April 21, 1808, T-C. See also NBT to JR, May 15, 1806, and to StGT, June 24, 1808, both in T-C. Later Tucker wrote his father that he could "never bear to think of the injustice that I have done you, and can never forgive myself the unhappiness which I fear I have caused you." NBT to StGT, November 11, 1808, T-C.

39. The frame of government that the revolutionary Virginia assembly adopted in 1776 left many features of the colonial government untouched. During the early decades of the nineteenth century it worked as a system of checks on popular rule and a preservant of eastern power. The General Assembly chose the governor annually; it appointed intermediate and supreme court judges, who served for life. An eight-man executive council, a vestige of the colonial governor's privy council, advised the state executive on matters of veto and pardon. The suffrage lay only with freeholders—men who owned twenty-five settled, or fifty unsettled, acres of land—and even if liberally

interpreted, these requirements gave precedence to landholders, many of them slaveholders as well, over owners of other property and allowed many eastern Virginians with land in several counties a multiple vote. Legislative apportionment was notoriously weighted toward the eastern counties. For secondary sources on the Constitution and government of Virginia in the early republic, see "Essay on Sources."

40. Robert Sutcliff, *Travels in some Parts of North America, in the Years 1804, 1805, and 1806* (New York: C. Peacock for W. Alexander, 1811), p. 95; Augustus John Foster, *Jeffersonian America: Notes on the United States of America Collected in the Years 1805-6-7 and 11-12*, ed. with an introduction by Richard Beale Davis (San Marino, Calif.: The Huntington Library, 1954), p. 151; Society of Virginia for Promoting Agriculture, "Memoirs," 1818, VSL, quoted in Charles W. Turner, "Virginia Agricultural Reform, 1815-1860," *AgHist* 26 (July 1952):83; StGT to Alexander Campbell, July 7, 1809, T-C. See also JR to Josiah Quincy, March 22 and July 1, 1814, in Edmund Quincy, *Life of Josiah Quincy of Massachusetts* (Boston: Ticknor and Fields, 1868), pp. 350-55; Richmond *Enquirer*, November 25, 1806; William Strickland, *Observations on the Agriculture of the United States of America* (London: W. Bulmer and Co., 1801), pp. 45 ff.; George Redd, *A Late Discovery extremely Interesting to Planters and Farmers, Relative to Fertilizing Poor and Exhausted Lands . . .*, (Winchester: J. A. Lingan, 1809), pp. 3-4, 15-16; and "Essay on Sources."

41. Richmond *Enquirer*, December 5, 1806. See also legislative petitions for these years, VSL, and for secondary references to Virginia politics and society, see "Essay on Sources."

42. Calls for more accessible justice were frequent in Virginia in the early nineteenth century. See, for example, material from Amherst County, December 1802, and from Albemarle County, December 15, 1806, and December 28, 1807, legislative petitions, VSL; Richmond *Enquirer*, January 11, 1805, December 20, 1806, December 6 and December 27, 1810; and Chapman Johnson to David Watson, January 24, 1802, *VMHB*, 29:280-81. On attempts to make courts in early-nineteenth-century America adequate to the needs of a growing and spreading citizenry, see Richard E. Ellis, *The Jeffersonian Crisis: Courts and Politics in the Young Republic* (New York: Oxford University Press, 1971). Also valuable are Charles T. Cullen, unpublished paper on the Virginia court system, and Christopher S. D'Angelo, "Judicial Reform in Virginia, 1800-1829; The Call for Decentralization" (Unpublished Honors Essay, University of Virginia, 1975). Major statutes altering the court structure are found in Samuel Shepherd, comp., *The Statutes at Large of Virginia . . .*, 3 vols. [n.s.] (Richmond: Samuel Shepherd, 1835-36), 3:357-62 (hereafter referred to as Shepherd); *Acts Passed at a General Assembly of the Commonwealth of Virginia* (Richmond: [various printers, 1785-]): *1808*, pp. 5-10, *1809*, pp. 9-16, *1810*, pp. 11-12, and *1811*, pp. 5 ff. (hereafter referred to as *Acts of the General Assembly*). For the concern many of these changes caused members of the bar, see HStGT to StGT, December 12, 1807, November 3, 1808, January 14 and February 19, 1809, January 20 and March 1, 1810, February 27, 1811, and March 21, 1812, T-C; George Tucker to StGT, January 12, 1811, T-C; Peyton Randolph to Joseph Carrington Cabell, December 28, 1800, and StGT to Cabell, December 25, 1808, Cabell Deposit (38-111), UVa, Archibald Stuart to Creed Taylor, December 20, 1809, Creed Taylor Papers (1232), UVa; Richmond *Enquirer*, January 13 and December 12, 1807, January 14 and 16, 1808, and January 27, 1809.

43. N[athaniel] H. Claiborne, *Sketch of a Speech, Delivered in Session of the House of Delegates, 1810* (Richmond: John O'Lynch, n.d.), pp. 3-4, 8; "Another Citizen," in Richmond *Enquirer*, December 20, 1806; Wirt, *Letters of the British Spy*, p. 163. See also Thomas Jones[?], *An Address To The People of Virginia. In two parts. Showing the danger arising from the unbounded influence of Lawyers, and the impolicy of confiding To them the Legislation of our State* (Winchester, Va.: Isaac Collette, 1808); remarks of Thomas Gholson, Jr., in the House of Delegates, Richmond *Enquirer*, December 12 and 22, 1807, and January 12, 1808. On popular antagonism toward the bar and common law in this period, see Ellis, *Jeffersonian Crisis*, pp. 111-22, 250-66, and Miller, *Life of the Mind in America*, pp. 105-85, 223-38. Suspicion of attorneys in Virginia was scarcely peculiar to the early nineteenth century; in 1745 (5 Hening 345 [1819]), the assembly restricted the fees lawyers could charge their clients.

44. Judith Randolph to StGT, January 29, 1808, and HStGT to StGT, March 3, 1808, both in T-C. See also HStGT to StGT, February 3, 1810, and April 4, 1811, and NBT to JC, September 24, 1814, T-C; Creed Taylor to "some gentlemen of the bar," January 22, 1808, and John Minor to Creed Taylor, November 30, 1809, Creed Taylor Papers (1232), UVa; StGT to Joseph Carrington Cabell, December 25, 1808, and enclosed notes of Judge William Nelson, Cabell Deposit (38-111),

UVa; "Camden" in Richmond *Enquirer*, January 27, 1809; StGT, *Blackstone's Commentaries*, vol. 4, "Appendix," "Of the Trial by Jury in Virginia," pp. 64–74. In handbooks designed to aid justices of the peace, many of whom were untrained in the law, members of the Virginia bar sought to inform and standardize their judgments. See Humphrey Smith, *The Magistrates's Monitor and Judge's Remembrance, being a treatise on the nature of Justice in a series of letters addressed to a Justice of the Peace* (n.p., 1803), and William Waller Hening, *The New Virginia Justice, comprising the office and authority of a Justice of the Peace* (Richmond: T. Nicholson, 1795; Johnson & Warren, 1810; S & G Cochran, 1820; Shepard & Pollard, 1825). In this vein see also John Robinson, *A Collection of the most useful and approved forms of process, judgments, and orders, used in the county courts and late district courts of law, in Virginia* (Richmond: Seaton Grantland, 1809). For more comments on the decline of civic spirit in Virginia in these years, see Wirt, *Letters of the British Spy*, pp. 191–94, 244; Foster, *Jeffersonian America*, pp. 157–60; and "To the People of Virginia from A Son of a Soldier of '76," Richmond *Enquirer*, February 14, 1809.

45. StGT, *Blackstone's Commentaries*, 1:11; NBT to StGT, May 8, 1814, T-C. See also Creed Taylor to William Branch Giles, March 22, 1808, and Giles to Taylor, March 27, 1808, Creed Taylor Papers (1232), UVa; Richmond *Enquirer*, March 22, 1808.

46. Wirt, *Letters of the British Spy*, p. 260; NBT to JR, April 21, 1807, T-C; NBT to StGT, September 5 and April 25, 1805, T-C. See also NBT to StGT, June 25, 1809, March 16, 1811, May 4, 1812, and April 15, 1814, T-C. Prerevolutionary Virginia statutes divided the bar into upper and lower divisions—though how closely lawyers adhered to this distinction is open to question. A law of 1732 (4 Hening 360 [1819]), aimed to reduce "the number of unskilful attorneys practicing at the county courts," while expressly not extending "to any counsellor or barrister at law"; a 1786 measure (12 Hening 339 [1823]) forbade counsel or attorneys practicing before county, city, or borough courts to practice before the high court of chancery or the general court in Richmond. In 1788 legislators eliminated the formal gradation between "country" and Richmond practitioners but nonetheless stipulated that an attorney who lost a case in a lower court could not himself appeal it to the next higher court. Revising a 1745 law that prescribed licensing procedures for attorneys, the Assembly in 1792 (1 Shepherd 13 [n.s. 1835]) established rules for admission to the bar by which an applicant for license produced before three judges of the superior courts a certificate from the county court where he resided, attesting to his honesty and proper age; superior court judges then examined the applicant and, if he qualified, granted him a license to practice before all state courts. Since superior court judges found standards difficult to establish and virtually impossible to maintain with any uniformity, requirements for law practice in these years probably did decline somewhat. For a hint of the way the system worked in practice, see J. J. Monroe to Creed Taylor, September 19, 1806, and T. B. Robertson to Creed Taylor, October 15, 1806, Creed Taylor Papers (1232), UVa. A rule that lawyers practicing before the Supreme Court of Appeals take an oath against dueling touched off an interesting newspaper debate on distinctions within the legal profession and the status of lawyers in the judicial structure: see Richmond *Enquirer*, November 30 and December 4, 1810. On long-standing English gradations at the bar, see Reed, *Training for the Public Profession of the Law*, pp. 108–9.

47. NBT to StGT, February 26, 1815, T-C. See also NBT to StGT, May 8, 1814, and March 25, 1815, T-C; Charles T. Cullen, unpublished paper on the Virginia court system. For a treatment of the effects of circuit riding on the Tennessee bar at about the same time, see Daniel H. Calhoun, *Professional Lives in America: Structure and Aspiration, 1750–1850* (Cambridge, Mass.: Harvard University Press, 1965), especially pp. 71 ff.

48. Young Tucker recited paternal lessons in letters to his father, January 29, 1810, and November 14, 1807, T-C. Judge Tucker advised his sons more than once to "check every Emotion of passion or disgust, & avoid every possible subject of Altercation or disagreement"; StGT to TR and JR, August 13, 1788, Bryan Papers (3400), UVa. As a novice lawyer, Beverley spoke of having no enemies among his colleagues except where he "chanced to meet with that swollen empty pride to which I can not render the homage it expects . . ." (NBT to StGT, May 5, 1810, T-C).

49. NBT to StGT, January 21, 1809, and May 11, 1807, T-C. See also NBT to StGT, March 22 and October 4, 1807, August 13, 1808, May 5, 1810, and January 30, 1814; NBT to JR, September 12, 1807; all T-C.

50. NBT to StGT, February 28, 1807, T-C. NBT to StGT, August 13, 1808, T-C.

51. NBT to StGT, December 10, 1809, and January 10, 1811, T-C. See also NBT to JR, January

12, 1807, T-C. Accompanying Tucker's self-doubt and sense of pedigree was a crude nativism. The country, he declared, was becoming an "asylum for the refuse of every other nation, a receptacle for the filthy sweepings of the other quarters of the globe." NBT to JR, April 15, 1806, T-C.

52. NBT to JR, January 31 and November 4, 1807, and February 16, 1808; NBT to StGT, March 11, 1808; all in T-C. Noting that Randolph's opponents in the 1808 canvass forced him to exert himself, and that "his health, spirits, and popularity" were all the better for it, Tucker spoke of a tonic that worked for him as well. NBT to StGT, August 18, 1808. He elaborated on this "political mania" in letters to Randolph January 6 and March 3, 1808, and to his father, July 11, 1807, February 9, September 25, and October 22, 1808, and March 29, 1812, all in T-C; and in NBT to FTC, August 2, 1807, Bryan Papers (3400), UVa.

53. The travail of opening law practice in Virginia was scarcely unique to Tucker during these years. See, for example, Chapman Johnson to David Watson, August 14, 1800, *VMHB,* 29:272-73; Peyton Randolph to Joseph Carrington Cabell, December 28, 1800, and May 25, 1802, Cabell Deposit (38-111), UVa. "I had been taught to hope for better things," Tucker wrote in despair, "—but hope and I have bid adieu for some time past." NBT to JR, April 6, 1808, T-C.

54. JR to Judith Randolph, April 19 [and draft of the same letter, dated April 20], 1800, Bryan Papers (3400), UVa; NBT to JR, July 19, 1807, and March 20, 1808, T-C; HStGT to StGT, June 17, 1806, T-C. See also JR to Judith Randolph, April 19, 1800, Bryan Papers (3400), UVa; JR to John St. George Randolph (eldest son of Richard Randolph), September 6, 1806, Randolph Papers, Duke; NBT to StGT, March 11, 1808, T-C; NBT to JR, January 12, 1807, and March 3, 1808, T-C. Beverley's "intuitive love of virtue & hatred of vice," believed Henry, was "a far better protector of the purity of our principles than any cold reasoning whatsoever." But he noted that Beverley's "impetuosity" could also lead him astray. HStGT to StGT, June 17, 1806, T-C. For similar comments on the younger Tucker's "purity of heart & delicacy of feelings," see HStGT to StGT, October 13, 1805, April 30, 1808, and July 30, 1811, T-C.

55. William T. Barry to his brother, February 15, 1804, in *WMQ,* 1st ser. 13 (October 1904):113. William Wirt, writing Dabney Carr, June 8, 1804, discussed the limits of reason as "the proper channel of conviction" (see Kennedy, *Wirt,* 1:33-34). For other evidence that Tucker's nostalgia and sense of decay only accentuated a mood many Virginians shared in the early nineteenth century, see Wirt, *Letters of the British Spy,* and student baccalaureate addresses listed in William and Mary College Faculty Minutes for these antebellum years. "Remove me to the scene where my mother lived and died," Beverley wrote of his personal anguish, "where I have sported around her, hung on her hand, and slept in her bosom." NBT to JR, January 12, 1807, T-C.

56. NBT to StGT, May 8, 1814, and October 4, 1807; NBT to JR, March 20, 1808; all in T-C. See also NBT to JR, January 19, 1808, and NBT to StGT, March 11 and November 11, 1808, T-C.

57. NBT to JR, March 10, 1806, and March 3, 1808, T-C. Tucker cursed "his majesty" Jefferson and his embargo policy in letters to JR, January 31 and December 30, 1807, January 24 and February 16, 1808, T-C.

58. NBT to StGT, September 14, 1811, T-C. See also NBT to StGT, October 16 and October 30, 1808, February 15, April 9, April 12, May 27, June 18, October 15, November 12, and December 10, 1809, May 5 and October 21, 1810, T-C; NBT to JR, April 22, 1809, StGT to NBT, December 19, 1808, and MCT to StGT, July 15, 1810, all in T-C. NBT to JR, January 9, 1810, Bryan Papers (3400), UVa. Charlotte County, Va., Deed Book 11, pp. 162, 170. In a letter Randolph apparently left as a housewarming note when Tucker and Polly moved into the Roanoke cabin, the older man committed it to the future comfort of the newlyweds. "But my dear Bev," he concluded, "can you ever want whilst I have any thing left in the world!" JR to NBT, [c. June 1, 1808,] T-C.

59. NBT to StGT, September 16, 1810, T-C. Joseph Wood's miniature of Tucker is now in the possession of Dr. Janet C. Kimbrough, Williamsburg; a life-sized copy hangs in the Tucker-Coleman Room, WM.

60. NBT to StGT, March 16, 1811, and endorsement in Randolph's hand to a note signed "N.B.T." and intended for Randolph, undated, in 1811 folder, T-C. See also [NBT] to JR, undated, but written after the birth of Tucker's son in June 1811; NBT to StGT, March 16, October 27, and November 24, 1811; and HStGT to StGT, June 10, 1812, all in T-C.

61. NBT to StGT, March 16, 1811, and JC to StGT, May 18, 1812, both in T-C. See also NBT to StGT, January 11, 1811, and HStGT to StGT, June 12, 1812, T-C.

Chapter Three

1. HStGT to Governor James Barbour, July 6, 1812, Tucker Family Papers (2605), SHC. For Henry's wartime experience, see HStGT to Barbour, July 25 and July 26, 1814, SHC; TTT to StGT, September 27, 1814, and letters after that date from Henry to his father, T-C. Letters of the period describe Beverley's contrasting exploits, but see especially NBT to StGT, July 3, 1813, and May 8, 1814, and NBT to JC, February 8, 1814, T-C; and NBT to FTC, February 28 and September 11, 1814, Bryan Papers (3400), UVa.

2. NBT to StGT, August 24, November 7, and December 15, 1813, December 18, 1814, February 26 and May 8, 1815; NBT to JC, September 24, 1814, and March 24, 1815; all in T-C. See also HStGT to StGT, December 3, 1814; Philip Barraud to StGT, January 17, 1814; GT to StGT, May 23, 1815; all T-C. Tucker claimed that General Winfield Scott himself promised to recommend him to the War Office for a permanent post.

3. NBT to JC, November 22, 1815, T-C. NBT to StGT, November 24, 1815, T-C. See also a note Tucker drew on John Coalter for $300, November 25, 1815, Grinnan Papers, VHS. The move west saddened Henry St. George and Thomas Tudor, Beverley's uncle in Washington; both men lamented what Henry called the "dispersing and diminished" fortune of the clan. TTT to StGT, May 31, 1815, and HStGT to StGT, November 17, 1815, T-C.

4. For these and other details of the winter journey, see NBT to StGT, December 6, 1815, T-C. Tucker spoke of Phillis, possibly the mammy of his boyhood, as a "treasure beyond all price" in a letter to his father, January 14, 1810, T-C.

5. MCT to StGT, January 9 and March 25, 1816; MCT to JC, January 29, 1816; NBT to StGT, March 18 and May 17, 1816; all in T-C. While Tucker was sick, his friend Dr. Pryor Quarles, a Virginian serving as an army surgeon in Saint Louis, tended to business matters for Tucker, who in March made one last visit to Southside Virginia to put his affairs in order.

6. NBT to StGT, June 7 and June 23, 1816, T-C. HStGT to StGT, June 12, October 5, and December 10, 1816, T-C; MCT to JC, June 16, 1816, Grinnan Papers (2118), UVa.

7. NBT to StGT, February 23, 1812, May 13, 1813, January 30, 1814, and May 8, 1815, T-C. MCT to StGT, October 23, 1814, T-C. As Tucker would want it, given his own weakness in public speaking, the boy talked a "great deal, very plain and sometimes to purpose" and, the father repeatedly observed, Jack "hardly ever" cried or fretted. NBT to StGT, May 13, 1813, and February 9, 1812, T-C.

8. NBT to StGT, September 24, 1816, T-C.

9. Ibid. Tucker's growing spirituality will receive treatment in the following chapter.

10. NBT to JC, February 19 and July 16, 1817, T-C. See also Theophilus McPheeters and NBT to JC, December 29, 1816, Grinnan Papers, VHS; NBT to StGT, July 13, 1817, T-C. Tucker's speculative purchases were mostly in the Saint Charles region north of Saint Louis and are recorded in Saint Charles County Deed Books C, p. 413, D, pp. 214–15, G, pp. 354–55, and H, pp. 382–84, County Records Office, Saint Charles, Missouri. Judging from these records and from letters to friends in Virginia, Tucker in these years before the panic of 1819 bought or contracted for extensive holdings in the Big Calument River area, in the Marias Croche section, and in the vicinity of the village of Saint Charles; land he claimed at times exceeded 10,000 arpents (about 8,000 acres), and he purchased much of it for as little as thirty cents an acre. But see below, chapter 4, note 29.

11. NBT to StGT, July 13, 1817, T-C. For another account of political and social confusion in Missouri at this time, see Timothy Flint, *Recollections of the Last Ten Years . . . in the Valley of the Mississippi . . .* (Boston: Cummings, Hilliard, and Company, 1826; reprint ed., New York: DeCapo, 1968), pp. 179–81 and passim. My page references will be to this recent reprint.

12. NBT to JC, February 19, 1817, T-C. See also NBT to StGT, February 20, 1817, and January 5, 1818, and NBT to Carter Coupland, May 1, 1816, T-C. For a discussion of the braggadocio the frontier and its conditions encouraged, see Kenneth S. Lynn, *Mark Twain and Southwestern Humor* (Boston: Little, Brown and Company, 1959). The sycamore story and other matters in a lighter vein are discussed in John F. McDermott, "Nathaniel Beverley Tucker in Missouri," *WMQ*, 2d ser. 20 (October 1940):504–7. See also Lilburn A. Kingsbury, "The Missouri Span in the Life of Beverley Tucker," an unpublished address to the Saline County Historical Society at Arrow Rock, July 24, 1939, MHS.

13. NBT to StGT, September 8 and November 16, 1817, T-C. Tucker's rude home probably

resembled the structure that he described in *George Balcombe*, 1:15, the romance of Missouri life published in 1836.

14. Flint, *Recollections*, pp. 197-98.

15. NBT to StGT, January 5 and April 2, 1818, T-C.

16. NBT to StGT, April 2 and August 13, 1818, T-C. Tucker shared memories of service on the Missouri bench in "Charlot Tayon," *SLM* 2 (January 1836):71-74. See "Essay on Sources" for secondary accounts of the legal profession in frontier Missouri.

17. "Memorial of the Citizens of Missouri Territory," in appendix 1 of Floyd C. Shoemaker's *Missouri's Struggle for Statehood, 1804-1821* (New York: Russell & Russell, 1916). NBT to StGT, August 13, 1818, T-C. *Laws of a Public and General Nature . . . of the Territory of Missouri and the State of Missouri, Up to the Year 1824* (2 vols., [Jefferson City: W. Lusk & Son, 1842]), 1:345-50, 444-49 (hereafter referred to as *Laws . . . of Missouri*). From 1816 to 1820, nineteen counties were organized in Missouri. While the congressional act of April 29, 1816, authorized the Missouri territorial assembly to establish circuit courts, it by no means required the abolition of the county courts or the dismissal of justices of the peace.

18. NBT to JR, September 21, 1817, T-C; Phillip S. Paludan, "The American Civil War Considered as a Crisis in Law and Order" (*AHR* 77 [October 1972]:1013-34), discusses the effect the frontier experience had on western attitudes toward government, order, and community.

19. The Saint Louis *Missouri Gazette & Public Advertiser*, April 7, 1819, noted that "The importance of the country west of the Mississippi, and its rapid growth, have become subjects of the deepest interest to the whole nation."

20. The Saint Louis grand jury on April 5, 1819, made the first antirestriction presentment; grand juries in Saint Charles and Washington counties, also on Tucker's circuit, made similar protests in July. *Missouri Gazette & Public Advertiser*, July 14 and August 4, 1819; Franklin *Missouri Intelligencer*, July 30, 1819; *St. Louis Enquirer*, August 4, 1819. For the presentment and Tucker's endorsement, see *Missouri Gazette & Public Advertiser*, April 14, 1819, and NBT to James Monroe, April 8, 1819, Dalton Collection, MHS. See also NBT, St. Louis, [to James Monroe,] August 4, 1819, T-C. The grand jury for the superior court—the territorial grand jury—called the May antirestriction rally while sitting for Tucker's northern circuit. *Missouri Gazette & Public Advertiser*, May 12, 1819.

21. "Hampden," *Missouri Gazette & Public Advertiser*, April 7, 21, and 28, May 5 and 19, and June 16, 1819. John Hampden was a seventeenth-century English champion of traditional liberties against royal usurpation. In letters to John Coalter, April 11 and April 19, 1819 (Grinnan Papers [2118], UVa.), Tucker urged republishing the "Hampden" pieces in the Richmond *Enquirer;* writing Thomas A. Smith, May 15, 1819 (T-C), he acknowledged that numbers 2 and 4 were his own. The fifth in the series appeared later and bore his stylistic and logical marks. Bates spoke of the articles in a letter to Tucker from Saint Louis, May 14, 1848 (T-C). In 1819 Bates was district attorney for the northern circuit. "Sydney" remains unidentified, but judging by the name he took and the way his articles "paralleled" those of "Hampden," Tucker probably had enlisted his help. "Sydney" took the lower road generally, addressing minor points, answering paltry criticism, and impugning the credibility of the prorestrictionists.

22. "Hampden," *Missouri Gazette & Public Advertiser*, April 7, 21, and 28, 1819.

23. "Hampden," *Missouri Gazette & Public Advertiser*, May 5, 1819. "A Farmer of St. Charles County," ibid., April 7, 1819, ridiculed legal rights to unrealized property by reciting a fable about an innkeeper who sold a traveler a plate of fried eggs, and then charged him for all the chickens that might have been hatched of those eggs to the end of time. For other anti-Hampden arguments, see "Pacificus," ibid., May 19, 1819.

24. "Hampden," ibid., June 16, 1819.

25. "A Farmer of St. Charles County," ibid., April 7 and May 19, 1819; "A Citizen of Missouri," ibid., April 28, 1819. All parties to the debate agreed that the Constitution (Art. IV, Sec. 4) obliged Congress to provide every state with a republican form of government; whether one permitting black bondage was republican led to bitter divisions. Tucker himself refused to become involved in the discussion. "Sydney" (ibid., April 14, 1819), and Bates in one of the "Hampden" essays simply noted that in the Constitution the word "republican" referred to slave and free states alike. "Pacificus," who may very well have been Timothy Flint, nonetheless wrote in the *Missouri Gazette & Public Advertiser*, June 2, 1819, that it was "problematical whether a good Christian or a genuine

practical republican can consistently sanction the introduction or continuance of slavery. . . ." For the problems some Southerners had with the ideal of republicanism in this debate, see Philip F. Detweiler, "Congressional Debate on Slavery and the Declaration of Independence, 1819-1821," *AHR* 73 (April 1958):598-616.

26. "Pacificus" in the *Missouri Gazette & Public Advertiser,* May 26, 1819, invoked St. George Tucker; see also "A Farmer of St. Charles County," ibid., May 19, 1819, for a reference to Jefferson's *Notes on the State of Virginia.*

27. "Hampden," *Missouri Gazette & Public Advertiser,* June 16, 1819; NBT to JC, February 8, 1814, and to StGT, July 24, 1814, T-C; NBT to TAS, May 15, 1819, T-C. For earlier references Tucker made to slaveholding as a way of life, see NBT to JR, February 12, 1806, and to StGT, August 21, 1807, T-C.

28. *McCulloch* v. *Maryland,* 4 *Wheaton* 316 (1819); *Annals of Congress,* 15th Cong., 1st sess., 1816, 2:1318-39.

29. "Hampden," *Missouri Gazette & Public Advertiser,* April 7, April 21, May 5, and June 16, 1819. For secondary references to the ideology of Hampden, Sidney, and other English political thinkers of the late seventeenth and early eighteenth centuries, see "Essay on Sources."

30. "Hampden," *Missouri Gazette & Public Advertiser,* April 21, 1819; NBT to TAS, May 15, 1819, T-C.

31. "Hampden," *Missouri Gazette & Public Advertiser,* April 21, 1819, passim. "A Citizen of Missouri," ibid., April 28, 1819, noted—with insight missing the point—that several persons who had written on the Tallmadge amendment had "allowed themselves to be swayed by their feelings. I fear that an effect may be produced directly opposite to what is intended," he said, "—that it will not produce conviction, but indignation."

32. NBT, Saint Louis, [to James Monroe,] August 4, 1819, T-C.

33. Flint, *Recollections,* pp. 200-201; NBT to JR, September 21, 1817, T-C. Flint's vantage point was Saint Charles, where he first saw Tucker in the fall of 1816. Two years before the Dardenne plan materialized, Tucker was there with other "respectable strangers from Virginia, the Carolinas, and Kentucky" (pp. 197-98), exploring tracts of ground and confirming Flint's view of the intoxicating effect Missouri had on easterners.

34. NBT to StGT, August 11, 1816, and September 26, 1819, T-C. See also NBT to StGT, January 19, 1819, and November 14, 1820; NBT to John Coalter, January 8, 1819; MCT to StGT, April 28, 1819; all T-C. For evidence that Tucker began speculating in the Saint Charles area as early as August 1816, and for records of the extensive landholdings he and his friends accumulated in the years 1819-23, see Deed Books E, pp. 410, 426-27, 429, F, pp. 185, 299; G, pp. 36-37, 84-85, 223-24, 230-31, 246-48, 351, 354-55, 551; and H, pp. 434-35; all in County Records Office, Saint Charles, Missouri.

35. Flint, *Recollections,* p. 198. NBT to StGT, January 19, 1819, and November 14, 1820; NBT to JC, January 8, 1819; all T-C.

36. NBT to StGT, January 19, 1819, and November 14, 1820; MCT to StGT, April 28, 1819, all in T-C. Harper and Preston should need no introduction here; the *DAB,* 4:286-87 and 8:207-8, offers sketches of them. On Lacy, who became a pillar of the Presbyterian church in Missouri, and on the Dardenne congregation, see Missouri Presbytery Records, vol. 1 (1817-31), PHF; Mrs. George W. McElhiney, comp., "A History and Record of the Presbyterian Church at Dardenne, Saint Charles County, Missouri, 1819-1871," box 847, 28757, PHF; and Session Book of the Dardenne Presbyterian Church, PHF. The College of South Carolina professors were B. R. Montgomery and Edward D. Smith; Smith died on reaching Missouri in August 1819. M. LaBorde, *History of South Carolina College* . . . (Charleston: Walker, Evans and Cogswell, 1874), pp. 86-91. On Nott's father, see John Belton O'Neall, *Biographical Sketches of the Bench and Bar of South Carolina,* 2 vols. (Charleston, S.C.: S. G. Courtenay and Company, 1859), 1:121-24.

37. NBT to StGT, January 19, 1819, T-C.

38. The stark contrast between Tucker's vision and the more prevalent "yeoman ideal" helps to make concrete the contrasting images of the West Henry Nash Smith derived mostly from literary sources in his classic *Virgin Land: The American West as Symbol and Myth* (Cambridge, Mass.: Harvard University Press, 1950). Too, Tucker's experience—his hope to recreate in the West old forms of society and the emphasis he gave selected themes in republicanism—provides a case study in the failure of Southern conservatives to make the adaptations Rush Welter explores in "The

Frontier West as Image of American Society: Conservative Attitudes before the Civil War" (*MVHR* 66 [March 1960]:593-614) and suggests the limitations of the Democrat-Whig framework developed in his *The Mind of America, 1820-1860* (New York: Columbia University Press, 1975).

39. NBT to StGT, September 26, 1819, T-C.

40. [NBT,] "From Missouri. Extract of a Late letter from this interesting country to a Virginian," Richmond *Enquirer*, December 11, 1819; NBT to JC, January 8, 1819, T-C.

41. "Letter from a Missourian to Virginia," *Missouri Gazette & Public Advertiser*, January 26, 1820. Internal evidence points to Tucker as the author of the "Letter" and his brother Henry as its addressee. Its tone, phraseology, and references compare strikingly to letters Tucker sent his father and John Coalter during this period. The "Letter" contained a wish that its recipient were still a member of Congress, and Henry Tucker had resigned at the conclusion of the fifteenth Congress in March 1819. Tucker may have intended the letter as a promotional brochure—at least as much of it as appeared in the *Enquirer*—and therefore asked Henry to send it to Ritchie. I have not found the letter among Henry's papers.

42. *Missouri Gazette & Public Advertiser*, January 26, 1820. Charless's political sentiments, which were somewhat secretly sympathetic to restriction, certainly did nothing to soften his charges against the Virginia patrician.

43. An anecdote appearing in W. V. N. Bay, *Reminiscences of the Bench and Bar of Missouri* (Saint Louis: F. H. Thomas and Company, 1878), p. 279, and almost surely relating to Tucker, suggests the response his concern for ancestry could call forth even from other men of high standing in the West. According to the story, David Barton, seated in a crowded tavern in Franklin, Missouri during these years, grew tired of a Virginia judge's "fluent" and tedious recitation of his pedigree. Barton—Tennessee-born and later a United States senator—turned to a nearby friend, and in a stage voice loud enough for everyone to hear, asked drily, "W., do you know my horse Pomp?" "Oh, yes," replied W. "Well, sir," continued Mr. Barton, imitating the judge's peculiar tone and manner, "he is the finest horse in the United States. I have tried him under the saddle, and I have tried him in the carriage; I have tried him in the plow, and I have tried him in the wagon; and in none of these places is he worth a d——m! But he is the finest horse in the United States. *It is in the blood, sir; it is all in the blood!*"

44. See letters from "A Farmer of St. Charles County," *Missouri Gazette & Public Advertiser*, April 7, May 5, and June 9, 1819. Charless, commenting on the "Letter from a Missourian to Virginia," made a number of oblique references, usually with key words italicized, hinting that the author must be "a member of *some Bible society*" (Tucker was elected president of the Missouri Auxiliary Bible Society in December 1818); that he must be in a lucrative position (i.e., on the government payroll); that he must be busy, "probably going from county to county" (on circuit). How would Congress prevent South Carolinians from bringing slaves to Missouri? We do not know, chided Charless, but "we are no *judges of law*." He said "backing out Yankees" had to be a new invention of "a learned man of the Dardenne prairie." "Hampden, Jun." was no more merciful. See *Missouri Gazette & Public Advertiser*, January 26 and February 16, 1820. One defender who came to Tucker's assistance recognized him as an upholder of the rights of Missouri, as "the man who had done most to disseminate the knowledge of her injuries, and her demands for redress. The writer cannot for a moment be mistaken . . . ; the writings of Hampden, Sydney and others will remain immortal monuments of his talents, his zeal, and his patriotism." See "No Yankee," *Missouri Gazette & Public Advertiser*, February 23, 1820.

45. NBT to JC, January 8, 1819, and NBT to StGT, November 10, 1821, T-C. See also NBT to StGT, September 26, 1819, July 5, 1820, and January 20, 1822, T-C.

46. NBT to Frederick Bates, February 29, 1820, Bates Collection, MHS. In Tucker's letter of resignation he described the judicial workload as too heavy for him; see also NBT to StGT, January 31, 1820, T-C. Another reason for Tucker's parting was his need, he said, to return to the east on business. He never made clear why this trip was necessary, but in letters Tucker hinted that there were problems with his title to the Dardenne lands—trouble that he may have tried to clear up in Washington. Charless took a dig at this embarrassing possibility in his footnotes to the "Letter of a Missourian to Virginia," *Missouri Gazette & Public Advertiser*, January 26, 1820. See also ibid., February 9, 1820; Flint, *Recollections*, pp. 198-99; and NBT, Saint Louis, to William Wirt, Washington, January 1, 1822, Smith Papers (1729), UVa. Either immediately before leaving for Virginia or on the way there Tucker heard of the Missouri Compromise measures Congress passed in March

1820. In May, at Henry's home near Winchester, Tucker learned that he would not stand as a delegate to the convention.

47. "To the People of Missouri Territory," undated essay in Tucker's hand, Public Letters and Resolutions, box 83, T-C. McNair was a former antirestrictionist, whom Tucker had known through church work and as register of the Saint Louis land office. By an act of January 1822, Tucker's third circuit included Saint Louis, Franklin, Washington, Saint Francis, and Jefferson counties. 1 *Laws . . . of Missouri* 682, 860 (1842). "Address of Judge Tucker to the St. Louis Grand Jury," *St. Louis Enquirer,* December 23, 1820. Tucker's remonstrance came before Congress had seated Missouri representatives, so that at the time the state truly was "independent." Now we must "learn to submit to the severe but necessary discipline of wholesome institutions," said Tucker, and "to set that example of deference to the sovereign will of the law . . . which it is so much easier to follow than to originate. . . ."

48. 1 *Laws . . . of Missouri* 760, 778 (1842). Dorothy B. Dorsey, "The Panic of 1819 in Missouri," *MHR* 29 (January 1935):79–91; William J. Hamilton, "The Relief Movement in Missouri, 1820-1822," *MHR* 22 (October 1927):51–92. NBT to StGT, September 26, 1819, T-C.

49. *Missouri* v. *Lane, Missouri Gazette & Public Advertiser,* February 20, 1822, involved payment of court costs after defendant was found guilty of assault and battery; Tucker declared loan-office certificates unacceptable. In *Glasscock* v. *Steen,* Saint Charles *Missourian,* April 4, 1822, Tucker denied extension of the due date on defendant's debt and then, under existing statute, ordered Steen confined. Tucker received support from other circuit judges in later decisions, and the Missouri Supreme Court upheld all these opinions in *Baily* v. *Gentry and Wife,* 1 *Missouri Reports* 102 (1870). See also *Brown* v. *Ward,* 1 *Missouri Reports* 127 (1870), and *Craig* v. *Missouri,* 4 *Peters* 410 (1830).

50. Saint Charles *Missourian,* May 2 and 30, 1822. See also, ibid., March 7 and May 16, 1822; *Missouri Gazette & Public Advertiser,* March 6, 13, 20, and 27, and April 9, 1822; Dorsey, "Panic of 1819 in Missouri," pp. 88–90.

51. Hamilton, "Relief Movement in Missouri," pp. 80–92. The 1820 Missouri Constitution allowed for the adoption of amendments after two successive general assemblies passed the proposal by a majority vote of two-thirds. All the amendments noted did pass the legislature that expired in early 1822. Judges therefore considered relief legislation under these threats.

52. "Necker," Saint Louis *Missouri Republican,* March 20, April 17, May 8, May 15, and May 20, 1822. "It has sometimes moved my gall," wrote Tucker, "to be cavilled at by those who profess to know nothing about the matter [of state finance]; but whenever any of it has flowed into my pen I have dashed it out. I have a better purpose in view than to provoke impertinence." (*Missouri Republican,* May 29, 1822.)

53. Tucker's opinion in *Missouri* v. *Lane, Missouri Gazette & Public Advertiser,* February 20, 1822; NBT, Saint Louis, [to James Monroe,] August 4, 1819, T-C.

54. Tucker's opinion in *Missouri* v. *Lane, Missouri Gazette & Public Advertiser,* February 20, 1822.

55. NBT to StGT, March 10 and May 13, 1822, T-C. It pleased Tucker to tell his father of the strides the bar had made while he was on the bench; more than once he had "to conceal a tear of pride" while presiding at court. NBT to StGT, January 31, 1820, T-C; see also letters of the period, ibid.

56. NBT to StGT, May 18, 1822, T-C. For a discussion of the election and its results, see Hamilton, "Relief Movement in Missouri," pp. 89–92. In 1822 the Kentucky Supreme Court struck down relief legislation there and moved the assembly to establish another, more sympathetic, tribunal. Judicial anarchy reigned in that state for several years after.

57. NBT to StGT, March 10, 1822, T-C. See also NBT to StGT, January 20, May 13, May 18, August 28, and September 29, 1822, and January 12 and October 17, 1823, T-C.

58. NBT to StGT, July 2, 1825, T-C.

Chapter Four

1. Blair, *Lectures on Rhetoric and Belles Lettres,* 1:75–76; NBT to JR, December 30, 1807, T-C. Edmund Burke, "A Philosophical Inquiry Into the Origins of Our Ideas of the Sublime and Beautiful," in *The Works of Edmund Burke,* 3 vols. (New York: George Dearborn, 1837), 1:33–98. Burke

thought the causes of the sublime sensations were pain and danger; Blair saw the feeling arising from the confrontation with mighty force or power. Machiavelli, whose influence on English republican thought was considerable and whose work Tucker knew from his readings at William and Mary, wrote that when catastrophe came, virtuous men renewed the first principles of liberty and restored the state. Caroline Robbins, comp., *Two English Republican Tracts* (London: Cambridge University Press, 1969), pp. 52 ff. See also Boorstin, *Mysterious Science of the Law,* pp. 88–91.

2. NBT to StGT, November 11, 1825, T-C. See also NBT to StGT, September 24, October 3, and November 28, 1825, January 13 and May 22, 1826; NBT to EC, December 25, 1825, T-C.

3. NBT to StGT, May 22, 1826; NBT to EC, December 26, 1826, T-C.

4. NBT, notes for an autobiography, Stories, Anecdotes, and Sketches, box 83, T-C.

5. Religious Essays, Bryan Papers (3400), UVa; Tucker's postscript to EC, [April 28, 1826,] T-C. Apparently Tucker's tract was never published. He referred to it in letters to EC, August 16, October 31, and December 26, 1826, and March 3, 1827, T-C. For evidence of Tucker's developing piety and growing involvement in church work, see Sermons and Religious Writings, folder #325, box 85, T-C; William S. Lacy to NBT, January 3, 1839, T-C; NBT to StGT, January 30, 1814, December 12, 1816, and September 26, 1819, T-C; *Missouri Gazette & Public Advertiser,* January 8, 1819; Session Book of the Dardenne Presbyterian Church, PHF.

6. Sermon on John 1:7–8, Religious Essays, Bryan Papers (3400), UVa; sermon no. 2, May 28, [1826,] Sermons and Religious Writings, folder #325, box 85, T-C; dialogue recalled after crossing the mountains in May 1825, Stories, Anecdotes, and Sketches, box 83, T-C.

7. NBT, notes for an autobiography, Stories, Anecdotes, and Sketches, box 83, T-C; sermon on John 1:7–8, Religious Essays, Bryan Papers (3400), UVa; sermon on 1 Cor. 14:40, Sermons and Religious Writings, folder #325, box 85, T-C; NBT to StGT, April 19, 1826, T-C. See also NBT to StGT, December 11, 1824, T-C; piece entitled "Do our pleasures chiefly lie in the Pursuit or in the Enjoyment of the objects of our desires?", sermon on 1 Cor. 2:4, and sermon no. 3, 1 Cor., dated May 31, [1826,] all in Sermons and Religious Writings, folder #325, box 85, T-C. For the persistence of St. George Tucker's naturalist piety, see "There is a God! All nature cries!" dated August 31, 1817, folder 5A, box 80, T-C.

8. NBT to StGT, April 19 and May 22, 1826, T-C. On Chamberlin and his relationship with Tucker, see William J. Harding, *Ancestry in the Line of Her Father Adelia Chamberlain Harding . . .* (Salem, Mass.: The Salem Press, 1907), pp. 22–26; Chamberlin to Secretary, United Domestic Missionary Society, March 22, 1826, in William Warren Sweet, *Religion on the American Frontier,* vol. 2, *The Presbyterians 1783–1840: A Collection of Source Materials* (New York: Harper & Brothers, 1936), pp. 654–56; MCT to EC, January 23, 1827, T-C; NBT to Chamberlain, August 2, 1827, and Chamberlin to NBT, April 3 and June 12, 1828, T-C. It was likely Chamberlin who made flattering comments on Tucker's religious reflections. "I have been laboring ten years to qualify myself for the ministry; I have travelled more than a thousand miles to bring the light of the gospel to you," Tucker reported hearing from a missionary; "and you have given me clearer views of its essential truths than I ever had before." NBT to EC, March 3, 1827, T-C. *The Quarterly Christian Spectator, Conducted by an Association of Gentlemen* (New Haven: Howe and Spaulding, 1819–29; New York: John P. Haven, 1829–38). In a letter to Bet Coalter (January 17, 1830, Bryan Papers [3400], UVa), Tucker singled out for special praise the "Review of Taylor and Harvey on Human Depravity" (*Christian Spectator* 1 [June 1829]:343–84). Among Taylor's important tracts were *Concio ad Clerum: A Sermon Delivered in the Chapel of Yale College, September 10, 1828* (New Haven: Hezekiah Howe, 1828) and "Application of the Principles of Common Sense to Certain Disputed Doctrines" (*Christian Spectator* 3 [n.s.] [September 1831]: 453–76). The publisher of the *Spectator,* March 8, 1830, T-C, acknowledged Tucker's interest in the journal; see also Chauncey Allen Goodrich, New Haven, to NBT, April 20, 1831, T-C.

9. "Desultory Reflections at the Close of the Year," *The Literary and Evangelical Magazine* 9 (December 1826):643–45; sermon on Matt. 10:29, Religious Essays, Bryan Papers (3400), UVa. On Tucker's affection for the Reverend Rice, see William S. Lacy to NBT, January 29 and February 28, 1832, and NBT to Mrs. S. B. Penn, September 13, 1833, T-C.

10. Sermon dated May 19, 1826, No. 1, Sermons and Religious Writings, folder #325, box 85, T-C. NBT to EC, March 3, 1827, T-C.

11. NBT to EC, December 26, 1826; NBT to JR, May 16, 1825, T-C. Elizabeth Coalter, whom

Tucker called Bet, was the only surviving daughter of John Coalter and Tucker's older sister Fanny, who had died in 1813. In Bet's late teens Tucker, now childless, took her as a kind of foster daughter. Doting over her, he told her of the polish expected of an elegant, accomplished Virginia lady and lectured her on the value of her breeding; he thought of her, himself, and John Randolph as a trio of similarly endowed family members who alone could understand and appreciate one another. Such concern, fortified during brief visits Tucker made to Virginia in the 1820s, evoked from Bet a devotion that was a constant delight to her uncle. He found her letters—which George Bibb, a friend of Randolph, admired as "chaste, beautiful, & touching"—a mainstay in these years. She soon became Tucker's confidant, an affectionate, supportive woman to whom—as in a diary, or to a mother—he could disclose his innermost thoughts. Bibb to NBT, August 7, 1844, T-C. For letters representative of Tucker's special feeling for Bet, see NBT to EC, January 20, 1823, January 4, May 14, and July 30, 1825, January 20 and October 31, 1826, T-C. See also ECB to NBT, February 7, 1829, and October 25, 1830, T-C.

12. NBT to EC, January 20, 1826, and NBT to JR, May 16, 1825, T-C. Tucker believed that local attachments were peculiar in owing their strength to "images of the past which the *eye* awakens in the *mind*." While he advised Bet to try not to arouse them too often—for they were painful—he nonetheless doubted that any human power could "exorcise those phantoms"; they emanated from the warmest and purest reaches of the heart. See NBT to EC, January 20, 1826, T-C. For nostalgic references to Virginia, which in their piquancy suggest that Tucker may well have begun this romance in Missouri, see *George Balcombe*, 2:84–85, and NBT to JR, March 22, 1825, T-C.

13. NBT to StGT, August 7, 1826, T-C. See also NBT to StGT, May 23 and October 17, 1823, April 19 and August 7, 1826, T-C. Tucker's sense of loss extended beyond the dissolution of the Dardenne clan—and beyond the relocation of the Missouri capital, which in 1826 was moved from nearby Saint Charles to Jefferson City farther west. He deeply lamented the loss of men in the state whom he considered equals in patriotism. Joshua Barton, Bates's law partner, and a United States Attorney whom Tucker described as an "extraordinary man," was killed in 1823 over an allegation he made against a notorious land official; Alexander Gray, a Kentuckian and circuit court judge in Missouri, died in 1825 committing the care of his memory to Tucker—a gesture that greatly moved the Virginian. We *have had* among us men who could do much," said Tucker, and if assassins with dirk and pistol had wreaked havoc on the best leaders, he considered it "remarkable that almost everything that is done in that way is the work of men who are fed from the federal treasury." NBT to StGT, October 23, 1823, and August 7, 1826, T-C. Someone calling himself "Revenge and at defiance of all Law" threatened Tucker's own life; see note dated June 17, 1830, T-C.

14. NBT to JR, March 25, 1827, T-C. See also NBT to JR, March 22 and October 31, 1826, February 13 and February 26, 1827, and October 7, 1828; NBT to EC, May 25 and October 31, 1826; HStGT to NBT, April 11, 1826; all in T-C.

15. "I trust I may thank God," Tucker wrote in his only surviving reference to St. George Tucker's death, "that there is one in heaven on whose mind I was providentially enabled to shed the light of truth." NBT to EC, March 3, 1827, T-C.

16. NBT to EC, August 14, 1828, T-C. NBT to JR, March 23, 1829; NBT to EC, March 23, 1829; JC to NBT, February 27, 1829, all T-C. On the divisions Tucker's marriage to Eliza Naylor caused within the Dardenne Church, see Missouri Presbytery Records, 1:155 ff., PHF, and George R. Pitts to Meredith M. Marmaduke, January 29, 1829, Sappington Papers, MHS.

17. NBT to JR, March 23, 1829, T-C; NBT to EC, May 13, 1829, Bryan Papers (3400), UVa. See also NBT to EC, July 13 and September 3, 1829, January 17, 1830, Bryan Papers (3400), UVa; EC to NBT, April 20, 1829, and JC to NBT, May 5, 1829, T-C; NBT to Philip Barraud, April 24, 1829, Barraud Papers, WM.

18. Sermon dated May 19, 1826, No. 1, Sermons and Religious Writings, folder #325, box 85, T-C; NBT to EC, April 3, 1829, ibid. See also NBT to EC, March 23, 1829, T-C; NBT to EC, May 13, 1829 and January 17, 1830, Bryan Papers (3400), UVa.

19. NBT to TAS, February 10, 1830, T-C. On Smith's background, see "Genealogy of the Smith Family of Essex County, Virginia," *WMQ*, 1st ser. 6 (July 1897):41–52.

20. The Reverend Thomas A. Ware recounted Christian Witt's description of Tucker in the mid-1820s while introducing a Civil War reprint of *The Partisan Leader*, in this case subtitled *A Novel, and an Apocalypse of the Origin and Struggle of the Southern Confederacy; by Judge Beverley Tucker, of Virginia. Originally Published in 1836* (Richmond: West & Johnson, 1862), p. vi. Just

before the wedding and, as Tucker said ruefully, *"in Lucy's presence,"* his face took on another scar when a horse kicked him and cut through his upper lip. NBT to ECB (Bet herself married John Randolph Bryan in January 1830), May 5, 1831, Bryan Papers (3400), UVa. William P. Cochrane to NBT, December 28, 1830, T-C, expressed some of the pain Tucker's new habits brought his *"true friends"* in the church.

21. NBT to ECB, October 3, 1830, Bryan Papers (3400), UVa.

22. NBT to ECB, October 3 and May 5, 1831, Bryan Papers (3400), UVa. According to legend in the Tucker family, Lucy's parents were surprised and at first not entirely pleased with her choice of a mate; though surely they gave their assent to the marriage, they supposedly lingered in the back room during the wedding reception in the front parlor. Conversation with Dr. Janet C. Kimbrough, Williamsburg, Va., spring 1972. On Tucker's self-examination in these days of new marriage and old frustrations as a crisis of middle age, turning on his view of his own generative powers, see "Note on Psychological References."

23. NBT to StGT, July 2 and September 24, 1825, T-C; NBT, notes for an autobiography, Stories, Anecdotes, and Sketches, box 83, T-C. The death of Connecticut-born Rufus Pettibone in July 1825 had created the supreme court vacancy. Though one Missourian that year had remarked that if Tucker lived he would "probably be appointed," the judicial workload had demanded an immediate replacement. Charles S. Hempstead, Saint Louis, to William Lucas, Cotes sans Dessein, August 19, 1825, Lucas Collection, MHS. Tucker's friend Robert Wash, a William and Mary graduate, received the place on the high Missouri court.

24. On the 1830 Missouri campaign, see, for example, Columbia *Missouri Intelligencer,* June 26 and July 10, 1830; Fayette *Western Monitor,* June 2, July 21, August 25, September 6 and 15, 1830; *St. Louis Beacon,* May 13, July 8, 20, 29, and August 5, 1830.

25. *Missouri Intelligencer,* September 4, 1830. NBT to StGT, July 2, 1825, and NBT to JR, October 7, 1828, T-C; "Lycurgus," *Missouri Intelligencer,* May 4, 1830; "Another People," ibid., July 17 and July 24, 1830; "A Citizen," ibid., July 3, 10, 17, and 24, 1830; ibid., September 4, 1830.

26. "A Friend to State Rights," *Western Monitor,* November 3, 1830. See also articles of August 25, September 15, and December 1, 1830, ibid. "I wish you every possible success in your defence of State rights," Miller wrote of Tucker's newspaper series, "and hope before you close your numbers, you will be able to *rouse* our Citizens from the lethargy into which they have fallen. . . ." Miller to NBT, October 28, 1830, T-C; also see Miller's letter of February 8, 1831, T-C.

27. "Friend to State Rights," *Western Monitor,* October 13, 1830. A rough draft of this essay can be found in Public Letters and Resolutions, box 83, T-C. See also *Western Monitor* articles of October 28 and November 24, 1830. Tucker contended that the people of the states were the "rightful owners" of public lands in their state. We cannot secure our property from the hand of the oppressor, he said in a fiery passage, "but we have a right to anticipate that a day of justice and retribution will come. . . ." *Western Monitor,* December 1, 1830.

28. Ibid., October 13, November 3, 1830. Also see the November 24 piece, a rough draft of which appears in Public Letters and Resolutions, box 83, T-C. On Tucker's quarrel with the Presbyterian elders, see minutes of September 1831 meeting in Saint Charles, Missouri Presbytery Records, vol. 1, PHF. See also NBT to Hiram Chamberlin, February 23, 1831; Chamberlin to NBT, January 19 and February 20, 1831, January 11, 1836; and William S. Lacy to NBT, March 12 and September 14, 1831; all in T-C. Tucker was charged with dancing Christmas Day 1830, thereby "bringing reproach on the church—injuring the cause of Christ and shewing contempt for the disciples of the church. The above charge and specifications," Tucker learned, were "taken upon the ground of general rumor." Thomas Parkes, clerk of the Booneville Church, to NBT, September 22, 1831, T-C. Tucker commented on the worldliness and showy rhetoric of itinerant preachers in *George Balcombe,* 1:160-65, and in a letter to Hiram Chamberlin, August 2, 1827, T-C.

29. MCT to EC, June 3, 1824 [1825], T-C. Two years after Tucker arrived in Missouri he reported that "a pack of yankee Swindlers" broke the bank in which he had made investments; NBT to StGT, May 28, 1818, T-C. In the aftermath of the Panic of 1819, he was forced to borrow from his father—$3000 in 1821 because he was unable to collect on earlier land sales; another $1200 in the fall of 1823. NBT to StGT, June 11, 1821, and October 17, 1823, T-C. Acknowledging this second amount, Tucker wrote that "perhaps it is wisely ordered that the heart should less engage itself about the happiness and welfare of the preceding than of the rising generation, but . . . it is

nevertheless hard to bear the inadequate returns which the old receive for their affection. . . ."

30. "Friend to State Rights," *Western Monitor*, October 13, 1830; NBT to StGT, August 7, 1826, T-C; undated piece, Essays, Lectures, and Fragments, box 83, T-C. For a response to Tucker, see "An Original Jackson Man," *Western Monitor*, November 3, 1830. Though Tucker's antagonism for "Yankeys" resembled the prejudice later American agrarians felt toward bankers and other elements in the market economy—whom they often referred to as "Jewish interests," the Virginian himself was a "chosen one" who at one level seems to have felt a certain affinity for Jews. When the Roman Empire stamped out local attachments and corrupted simple virtue, Tucker wrote in an undated sermon, the Jews—"oppressed and despised"—tried "to comfort themselves under persecution and contempt by cherishing . . . an opinion of peculiar holiness," countering—as was Tucker himself—the "insolence of worldly power, by the insolence of spiritual pride." Undated essay, Sermons and Religious Writings, folder #325, box 85, T-C.

31. John Miller to NBT, February 8, 1831, T-C; *Missouri Intelligencer*, November 30, December 4, and December 11, 1830; *Niles' Weekly Register* 39 (December 25, 1830):302. The *St. Louis Beacon*, September 15, 1831, warned that "the Federalists will spare no trick, no strategem, no fraud, no invention, no falsehood to create division and animosity among the Jackson men." Tucker was named to the Democratic state central committee in October. Testifying to his growing prominence was the bitterness he provoked. One Missourian, in the midst of the "Friend to State Rights" series, warned Colonel M. M. Marmaduke to be on guard "against the machinations & deeply laid stratagems of Judge Tucker," and wondered what would be the "*ultimate* of his truly singular & extraordinary career." George R. Pitts to Marmaduke, October 11, 1830, Sappington Papers, MHS. Mering, *Whig Party in Missouri*, pp. 20-21.

32. Draft of a letter [to Governor James Hamilton, Jr.] regarding states' rights in South Carolina, September 1, 1831, Public Letters and Resolutions, box 83, T-C. Calhoun's "Fort Hill Address" appeared in the *St. Louis Beacon*, September 8, 1831.

33. NBT to Miller, September 25, T-C. *St. Louis Beacon*, September 1, September 8, and September 15, 1831; *Missouri Intelligencer*, September 24, 1831. Alphonso Wetmore to NBT, September 7, 1831, and John Miller to NBT, September 20, 1831, T-C.

34. Jefferson City *Jeffersonian Republican . . . Extra*, March 24, 1832, folder #352, box 86, T-C. Miller agreed with Tucker; "the sooner we get rid of worthless and unsound members," he wrote Daniel Dunklin, "the better." Miller to Dunklin, March 8, 1832, Dunklin Papers, WHMC, quoted in Randolph Eugene Forderhase, "Jacksonianism in Missouri, From Predeliction to Party, 1820–1836" (Ph.D. dissertation, University of Missouri, 1968), p. 368. Results of the convention appeared in the *St. Louis Beacon*, October 13, 1831.

35. B. E. Ferry (editor of the *Western Monitor*) to NBT, November 1, 1832; T. C. Batte to NBT, October 8, 1831; W. S. Lacy to NBT, February 28, 1832; all in T-C. See also John Miller to NBT, October 19, 1831; Alphonso Wetmore to NBT, February 12, 1832; Gray Bynum to NBT, February 29, 1832; all T-C. On the state of the Missouri Democracy in the last months of 1831, see "A Friend to Jackson's PRINCIPLES," *St. Louis Beacon*, November 17, 1831; *Missouri Intelligencer*, December 3, 1831.

36. *Missouri Intelligencer*, April 7, 1832; NBT to LST, April 21, 1832, T-C; "Communicated . . . extract from a Speech Delivered on the 24th of April last, at Saint Louis, Missouri, by Beverley Tucker, Esq.," Richmond *Enquirer*, February 7, 1833. See also John Miller to NBT, March 13 and March 27, 1832; Neill Sebree to NBT, March 14, 1832; and John Strite to NBT, May 5, 1832; all in T-C. The April 10 Saint Louis *Missouri Republican*, quoted in Forderhase, "Jacksonian Politics in Missouri," p. 369, described Tucker as a "whole hog eleventh hour Jackson man"; on April 7 the *Missouri Intelligencer* also advised Tucker "to go to Washington, (not as our Representative, however), take up his abode in the *President's* house, and *there* preach his doctrine to his heart's content, and there receive his *reward*."

37. NBT to LST, March 2 and May 20, 1832, T-C. See also NBT to LST, April 14, April 21, April 2[2], May 11, 1832, and undated letters, c. April and June 1832, T-C.

38. For the collapse of Tucker's campaign, see John Strite to NBT, May 19 and May 26, 1832; Eli Bass, chairman, state central committee, to NBT, July 11, 1832; John Miller to NBT, June 18 and July 22, 1832; William Wright to NBT, July 23, 1832; all T-C.

39. Draft of a letter [to Governor James Hamilton, Jr.] regarding states' rights in South Carolina, September 1, 1831, Public Letters and Resolutions, box 83; NBT to LST, May 11, 1832; both in

T-C. Several years before Tucker's run for Congress he had advised against John Coalter's entering politics. "There is no trade that requires so regular an apprenticeship," he had written, "with the help of which a fellow becomes an expert in his evolutions as one of your tumblers whose joints seem to work both ways at pleasure." NBT to EC, May 25, 1826, T-C. For recent studies of changes in the political culture of early-nineteenth-century America, see "Essay on Sources."

40. Alphonso Wetmore to NBT, August 25, 1832, T-C. Among these letters assuring Tucker that he had lost with his honor intact, were John Miller to NBT, June 18 and September 18, 1832; Thomas C. Batte to NBT, July 27, 1832; W. Clarkson to NBT, August 22, 1832; B. E. Ferry to NBT, November 6, 1832; and H. G. Harrison to NBT, September 6, 1832; all in T-C.

41. JR to NBT, October 26–November 3, 1832, T-C.

42. "To The People of Missouri," Saint Louis *Free Press*, January 10, 1833 [dated December 26, 1832]. Reprinted, with an introduction, in *The Richmond Whig and Public Advertiser*, February 8, 1833. Copy of *Whig* version in NBT Scrapbook, T-C.

43. Pertinent sections of Jackson's December 10 proclamation appear in William W. Freehling, ed., *The Nullification Era: A Documentary Record* (New York: Harper and Row Publishers, 1967), pp. 153–63. "The President not only denies that it is right for a State to secede without good cause," Tucker wrote his brother Henry, "but he denies that she is the judge of the sufficiency of the cause. But he goes still further, & maintains that an act of secession would be a mere *brutum fulmen,* which [w]ould leave the people of the State subject to the laws of the Union, and to the pains & penalties of Treason. There is Consolidation. The history of the Tariff shows what sort of thing a consolidated Government would be, and the annunciation of this doctrine by authority, and the immediate concentration of the ambitious, the greedy, and the servile in support of it, convince me that we must take decisive measures to meet the emergency." NBT to HStGT, January 23, 1833, HL. For a contrasting analysis of Jackson's position in 1832-33, see Richard B. Latner, "The Nullification Crisis and Republican Subversion," *JSH* 43 (February 1977):19–38.

44. "To The People of Missouri," Saint Louis *Free Press*, January 10, 1833.

45. Richard K. Crallé, ed., *Works of John C. Calhoun,* 6 vols. (New York: D. Appleton and Company, 1854–59), 6:1–59, 59–94. Hereafter referred to as Calhoun, *Works*. St. George Tucker's *Blackstone's Commentaries*, vol. 1, "Appendix," Note D, passim.

46. "To The People of Missouri," Saint Louis *Free Press*, January 10, 1833. Tucker said that the South Carolinians had "embarrassed a plain question by mixing it up with the jargon of nullification" that "bewildered him" (NBT to HStGT, January 23, 1833, HL). Madison's position during the nullification crisis, and his opinion of nullification as an outgrowth of the doctrines contained in the Virginia Resolutions, can be seen in the *Niles' Weekly Register, Supplement to Volume XLIII* (Baltimore: Franklin Press, May 1833). The Virginia Resolves of December 21, 1798, and the Report of the Assembly, adopted in the 1799–1800 session as an answer to criticism of the original papers, asserted the obligation of a state to protect its citizens from untoward federal legislation. Because of the nature of the federal Union, each state had the ultimate right, should it see the terms of the contract of 1789 broken, to declare it dissolved. While Jefferson's Kentucky Resolutions of November 1798 proclaimed the Alien and Sedition Acts "NOT LAW . . . altogether VOID and OF NO FORCE," Madison's Virginia Resolves expressed a vaguer hope that other states would agree on the unconstitutionality of the acts in question and take "necessary and proper measures" to maintain the rights reserved in the Tenth Amendment to the states and the people. Tucker, basing his constitutionalism on the Virginia position, was able at once to deny nullification and to defend secession, quite correctly showing that Madison disclaimed anything like state veto power and then urging a more radical course.

47. "To The People of Missouri," Saint Louis *Free Press*, January 10, 1833; StGT, *Examination of the Question, "How Far the Common Law of England is the Law of the Federal Government of the United States?"* (Richmond: John Dixon [1800]); StGT, *Blackstone's Commentaries,* vol. 1, "Appendix," Note E. For a discussion of this movement and the political awareness that gave it immediacy, see William Winslow Crosskey, *Politics and the Constitution in the History of the United States,* 2 vols. (Chicago: University of Chicago Press, 1953), 1:597–98, 634–38.

48. "To The People of Missouri," Saint Louis *Free Press*, January 10, 1833. For more on Tucker's view of sovereignty, see "A Friend to State Rights," *Western Monitor*, December 1, 1830, and "Communicated . . . extract from a speech delivered on the 24th of April last, at St. Louis, Missouri, by Beverley Tucker, Esq.," Richmond *Enquirer*, February 7, 1833.

49. "To The People of Missouri," Saint Louis *Free Press,* January 10, 1833. Of course nullification did not strike many observers outside South Carolina as particularly conservative, nor, in fact, were all nullifiers interested in remaining in the Union. But for Calhoun's frame of mind, see Calhoun to James Hamilton, August 28, 1832, a public letter that appears in Calhoun, *Works,* 6:144–93.

50. "To The People of Missouri," Saint Louis *Free Press,* January 10, 1833. For the roots of this view of dissolving the federal Union, with the numerous qualifiers that Tucker's father insisted upon, see StGT, *Blackstone's Commentaries,* vol. 1, "Appendix," 73–77, 140 ff., 315.

51. HStGT to NBT, January 20 and January 24, 1833, T-C. Printed in "Correspondence of Judge Tucker," *WMQ,* 1st ser. 12 (October 1903):90–92. See also HStGT to NBT, September 22, 1831, and November 14, 1833; HStGT to JR, December 24, 1832; all in T-C.

52. HStGT to NBT, March 13, 1833; "To The People of Missouri," Saint Louis *Free Press,* January 10, 1833. See also "Friend to State Rights," *Western Monitor,* December 1, 1830. "Am I then for war?" Tucker asked Virginians in a piece Ritchie printed; "No. I am for avoiding war by prudent boldness." "A Friend of States Rights," Richmond *Enquirer,* February 19, 1833.

53. "I need not ask what a soldier's daughter would have her husband do," Tucker wrote his wife from Louisville, January 1, 1833, T-C. See also NBT to LST, January 9, 1833, T-C. He sent the second letter from Greenbrier, Virginia.

54. NBT, Roanoke Plantation, to LST, January 24, 1833, T-C. See also NBT to LST, January 18 and January 31, 1833, T-C. With Tucker acting as his brother's amaneusis, Randolph sent off letters describing the principles of Jackson's December 10 proclamation as "detestable doctrines; of which it is hard to say, whether they exceed in atrociousness or folly." JR to Peter Browne, January 21, 1833, item 9506, UVa.

55. NBT to HStGT, Richmond, January 29, 1833, and William Brodnax, Richmond, to NBT, February 19, 1833, T-C.

56. "Charlotte Court House, February 4th, 1833," Richmond *Enquirer,* February 9, 1833. James Hamilton, Jr., to NBT, February 6, 1833, T-C. In another letter, February 23, 1833, T-C Hamilton referred to Tucker's messages of February 2 and 14: "Your Brother's [Randolph's] Charlotte Resolutions have been read and admired here with great enthusiasm," reported Hamilton. "They are dignified, polished & . . . the sentences draw blood at every thrust." He overlooked for the time being Tucker's dismissal of nullification.

57. NBT to LST, February 21, 1833, T-C. When Benton received his copy of the Charlotte resolves he acknowledged them, regretting the impasse to which South Carolina had brought the states' rights cause; he mentioned the futility of attacking Jackson, given the popular belief that the Union was under attack and the general was its savior. "He ought to be here now," Benton wrote of Randolph. "'One blast on *his* bugle horn is worth a thousand men.'" Benton, Washington, to NBT, February 11, 1833, T-C. Printed in "Correspondence of Judge Tucker," pp. 86–87. "A True Friend to Andrew Jackson," Washington, D.C., *United States Telegraph,* February 23, 1833; "A Friend of State Rights Because a Friend of Union" [title varied], Washington, D.C., *United States Telegraph* March 6, 7, 12, 13 and 14, 1833; draft of Tucker's letter, apparently to Jackson, dated March 1, 1833, T-C.

58. NBT to LST, February 21, 1833, T-C. Tucker offered no detailed account of his discussion with the President, but several years later told his older brother that his message to Jackson had been simple: "if a government of opinion was to be exchanged for a Government of force," Tucker "prayed God that the people might lose no time, in bringing to the only arbitrament the question 'whether they can be governed by force.'" NBT to HStGT, copied in NBT to LST, September 7, 1837, T-C. A few days after Tucker's impromptu visit to the White House, he and Randolph attended a "half formal, half family dinner" with Jackson, which passed off, Tucker thought, a bit uneasily. NBT to LST, February 26 and 28, 1833, ibid.

59. The Virginia Assembly supported the compromise tariff bill and, in resolutions passed in late January, called on the nullifiers to avoid any act that might "disturb the tranquility of the country, or endanger the existence of the Union." Richmond *Enquirer,* January 29, 1833. See also Benjamin Watkins Leigh to Governor John B. Floyd (with enclosures), February 6, 1833, George Frederick Holmes Papers, LC. One Virginian wrote Tucker that, whatever argument he made against the Force Bill, "Jackson's a Republican. Hurra for Jackson's the reply. . . ." George Boswell, Petersburg, to NBT, January 31, 1833, Tyler Scrapbook, WM. Another states' rights supporter considered the role of Virginia as temporizer in the crisis "disgraceful to the State." William Brodnax, Richmond, to NBT, February 19, 1833, T-C.

60. NBT, Washington, to LST, February 21, 1833, T-C. See also NBT to LST, February 26 and 28, 1833, and Dixon H. Lewis to NBT, March 8, 1833, T-C.

61. NBT to LST, February 13, 26, and 28, 1833, T-C. Jackson, exclaimed Tucker one day after the president had successfully avoided another chat with him, "knows me to be the author of papers which will *shake his throne.*" NBT to LST, March 9, 1833, T-C. "You can do so much good, in arousing the Spirit of Old Virginia, as well as the rest of the [South]," William Harper wrote Tucker in the spring of 1833. "Every thing that is valuable to Southern interests and human liberty depends upon it. There is something in what you write that men will read." William Harper, Fairfield, South Carolina, to NBT, August 12, 1833, T-C.

62. NBT to LST, February 26 and 28, 1833, T-C. See also NBT to LST February 13, 1833, and NBT to Thomas Hart Benton, February 6, 1833, T-C. "If South Carolina at this moment listens to the Syren Song of peace," Tucker wrote the nullifiers after he and Randolph had returned to Virginia, "she will surrender her independence and that of the whole South." The Force Act was the most important point at issue now, he pointed out; permitting the state convention then in session to nullify that act would only embarrass the states' rights cause. Scorn the compromise tariff and wait patiently for the federal government to enforce this obviously unconstitutional measure, advised Tucker, then call a convention of other aggrieved states. "Such a convention is all that Jonathan [i.e., the North] dreads, because in it he knows that the right to secede (the only sanction to the limitations of federal power) will be affirmed." Postponing the convention until after the end of Jackson's presidential term would, believed Tucker, help ensure its outcome and increase the likelihood of western support. NBT to James Hamilton, Jr., March 22, 1833, T-C.

Chapter Five

1. NBT to John Crittenden, March 9, 1838, Crittenden Papers, LC. William and Mary Faculty Minutes, 1830-36 volume, pp. 45-46. See also NBT to Daniel Call, March 14, 1835, Tucker Family Papers (2605), SHC; Joseph Martin, comp., *A New and Comprehensive Gazetteer of Virginia and the District of Columbia* . . . (Charlottesville: Published by Joseph Martin, Joseley and Tomins, Printers, 1835), p. 200; and the Albany, New York, *Argus,* November 15, 1833, in College Papers, WM.

2. NBT to John Crittenden, March 9, 1838, Crittenden Papers, LC.

3. NBT to LST, June 15, 1835, T-C; Richmond *Enquirer,* July 14 and August 11, 1834; *Address of Joseph C. Cabell to the Citizens of Richmond on the 10th of December 1834 on the Expediency of a Liberal Subscription to the Stock of the James River and Kanawha Canal* (Richmond: n.p., 1835); Martin, *Gazetteer of Virginia,* pp. 143-44, 194-95; Edmund Ruffin, *Essay on Calcareous Manures* (Petersburg: J. W. Campbell, 1832). For secondary references to Virginia economy and society in this period, see "Essay on Sources."

4. United States Census Office, *Fifth Census; or, Enumeration of the Inhabitants of the United States. 1830. To Which is Prefixed a Schedule of the Whole Number of Persons within the Several Districts of the United States Taken According to the Acts of 1790, 1800, 1810, 1820* (Washington: Duff Green, 1832), pp. 10-13, 84-89; United States, Bureau of Census, *Historical Statistics of the United States: Colonial Times to 1957* (Washington: Government Printing Office, [1960]), p. 693; Fletcher Hewes and Henry Gannett, *Scribner's Statistical Atlas of the United States; Showing by Graphic Methods their Present Condition and their Political, Social, and Industrial Development* (New York: Charles Scribner's Sons, 1883), p. xliv, plates 18, 19, 21.

5. Expressions of eastern apprehension and sectional feeling were common in the Richmond *Enquirer* immediately before the Convention met; see as examples published letters in the January 24 and 27, 1829, issues. Hugh R. Pleasants, "Sketches of the Virginia Convention of 1829-30," *SLM* 17 (March 1851):147-54; Hugh B. Grigsby, *The Virginia Convention of 1829-30: A Discourse Delivered Before the Virginia Historical Society. At Their Annual Meeting, Held in the Athenaeum in the City of Richmond, December 15th, 1853* (Richmond: MacFarlane and Fergusson, 1854). *Proceedings and Debates of the Virginia State Convention of 1829-30 to Which are Subjoined the New Constitution of Virginia and the Votes of the People* (Richmond: Samuel Shepherd and Company for Ritchie and Cook, 1830), especially pp. 51, 54-55, 58, 84-85, 225, 413. See also "Essay on Sources."

6. NBT to StGT, June 26, 1825, and C. A. Swoope to NBT, [c. January, 1832,] both in T-C.

For more on Tucker's treatment of his slaves—evidence on this score is disappointingly thin—see NBT to TAS, February 10, 1830, and W. S. Lacy to NBT, March 12, 1831, T-C. For speeches on slavery during the 1831-32 debate, see the Richmond *Enquirer,* especially January 19, 26, and 31, February 14, and April 24, 1832; Richmond *Constitutional Whig,* March 28, 1832. A number of addresses during this session appeared as pamphlets: *The Speech of Charles Jas. Faulkner (of Berkeley) in the House of Delegates of Virginia, on the Policy of the State with Respect to Her Slave Population. Delivered January 20* [sic], *1832* (Richmond: n.p., 1832), pp. 14–15; *Speech of James M'Dowell, Jr. (of Rockbridge), in the House of Delegates of Virginia, on the Slave Question: Delivered Saturday, January 21, 1832,* 2d ed. (Richmond: n.p., 1832), p. 15. Selections from these and other pertinent addresses are found in Joseph Clark Robert, *The Road From Monticello: A Study of the Virginia Slavery Debate of 1832,* Historical Papers of the Trinity College Historical Society, series 24 (Durham, N.C.: Duke University Press, 1941).

7. Littleton Waller Tazewell, *A Review of the Proclamation of President Jackson, of the 10th of December, 1832, in a series of numbers originally published in the "Norfolk and Portsmouth Herald," under the signature of "A Virginian"* (Norfolk: J. D. Ghiselin, 1888); Agricola [pseud.], *The Virginia Doctrines, not Nullification* (Richmond: Samuel Shepherd and Company, 1832); *Speech by John Thompson Brown (of Petersburg), in the House of Delegates of Virginia, in Committee of the Whole, on the State of Relations Between the United States and South Carolina. Delivered January 5, 1833* (Richmond: T. W. White, 1833). Claude H. Hall, *Abel Parker Upshur, Conservative Virginian, 1790-1844* (Madison: State Historical Society of Wisconsin, 1964), pp. 89–94.

8. Speech of Samuel McDowell Moore (Rockbridge County), Richmond *Enquirer,* January 19, 1832. See also Robert, *Road From Monticello,* p. 64.

9. Peachy to NBT, July 7, 1834, WCP to NBT, October 16, 1834, Bates to NBT, August 11, 1834, and DG to NBT, December 23, 1833, all in T-C; *Richmond Whig and Public Advertiser,* July 11, 1834, copy in College Papers, WM. *Farmers' Register* 2 (September 1834):239. See also NBT to LST, July 8, 1834; DG to NBT, October 3, 1834; George E. Boswell to NBT, August 18, 1834, APU to NBT, February 14, 1839; all in T-C.

10. NBT to TAS, July 9, 1834, T-C.

11. William and Mary Faculty Minutes, 1830-36 volume, pp. 209–11. Tucker received a salary of $600 per year and an additional $20 or $30 (the record varies) per student registered for his courses. Thomas G. Peachy to NBT, May 30 and July 7, 1834, T-C. "Indeed it has been a pleasure to me to return to study," Tucker wrote Lucy's father, "and as I wish, from time to time, to prepare written lectures on particular topics, I shall never be in want of employment." NBT to TAS, October 2, 1834, T-C. Rogers, after teaching at the University of Virginia, helped to establish the Massachusetts Institute of Technology in 1861.

12. Robert Stevens, "Two Cheers for 1870: The American Law School," in *Perspectives in American History,* ed. Donald Fleming and Bernard Bailyn (Harvard University: The Charles Warren Center for Studies in American History 1967-), vol. 5, *Law in American History* (1971), p. 413. See also Reed, *Training for the Public Profession of the Law,* pp. 94–98, 117, 128-33.

13. In 1800 only William and Mary and Transylvania University in Lexington, Kentucky, had provided academic instruction in the law. Tucker apparently supported a state statute which, for seven years after 1842, exempted graduates of law courses at William and Mary and at the University of Virginia from standing examination before judges. See Bill 175, dated February 28, 1842, College Papers, WM, folder 16. For more on antebellum legal training, see the Essay on Sources.

14. For Story's inaugural lecture of August 1829, see Perry Miller, ed., *The Legal Mind in America: From Independence to the Civil War* (Garden City, N.Y.: Doubleday and Company, 1962), pp. 177–89; "Harvard Law School: Its Advantages," a contemporary advertisement in Charles M. Haar, ed., *The Golden Age of American Law* (New York: George Braziller, 1965), pp. 65–67.

15. Stevens, "The American Law School," p. 418; Reed, *Training for the Public Profession of the Law,* pp. 151, 154-59.

16. Maxwell Bloomfield has developed this interpretation of the social direction of the bar in *American Lawyers in a Changing Society, 1776-1876* (Cambridge, Mass.: Harvard University Press, 1976), pp. 32-58, 136-90. *The American Jurist* (vol. 11 [April 1834]: 365-408) published a review article that treated Joseph Story's *Conflict of Laws*—a text that aimed to make the common law systematic and accessible to the practitioner—with much enthusiasm.

17. Nathan Dane, in his 1829 proposal to establish a chair in law at Harvard, specified that lectures and publications of the occupant should address themselves to that law and equity "equally in force in all parts of our Federal Republic," to place emphasis on state laws "the most important and most national," thus making these lectures useful in more states than one and clearly distinguishing from "that state law which is in force, and of use, in a single state only." Quoted in Charles F. Warren, *History of the Harvard Law School and of Legal Conditions in America,* 3 vols. (New York: Lewis Publishing Company, 1908), 1:418-19.

18. NBT, "A Lecture on the Study of the Law; being an introduction to a course of lectures on that subject, in the College of William and Mary . . . ," *SLM* 1 (November 1834):148. The lecture also appeared in pamphlet form. My citations will refer to the *Messenger* printing.

19. "Lecture on the Study of the Law," pp. 150-51. See also Reed, *Training for the Public Profession of the Law,* pp. 154-57; Anna Haddow, *Political Science in American Colleges and Universities, 1636-1900,* ed. with an introduction and concluding chapter by William Anderson (New York: D. Appleton-Century Company, [1939]), pp. 157-58.

20. "Lecture on the Study of the Law," pp. 145-46. See above, chapter 2, note 46. Tucker enlarged on this view of the legal profession as "truly fraternal" in the valedictory address that he gave his first graduating law class and that appeared in the *SLM* 1 (July 1835):597-602.

21. TWW to NBT, January 15, 1835, T-C. LST to her mother, November 6, 1834; Nathaniel Macon, Buck Spring, [N.C.,] to NBT, February 12, 1835; Wyatt Cardwell to NBT, January 29, 1835; ECB to NBT, January 10, 1835; Calvin L. Perry, Charlottesville, to NBT, November 20, 1834; all T-C. David Holmes Conrad, an old friend of Tucker, twitted him for his "grave and philosophical" first lecture. Conrad, Martinsburg, to NBT, December 9, 1834, T-C.

22. Tucker listed his readings in the yearly August or September advertisements the college placed in prominent regional newspapers, copies of which can be found in the William and Mary Faculty Minutes. For some of the rough notes he used in preparing for class, and for a notebook entitled "Proceedings of the Moot Court," see Essays, Lectures, and Fragments, box 83, T-C. Henry John Stephen, *A Treatise on the Principles of Pleading in Civil Actions: Comprising a Summary View of the Whole Proceedings in a Suit of Law,* 3d American ed., with large additions (Philadelphia: R. H. Small, 1837); John Mitford, *A Treatise on the Pleadings in Suits in the Court of Chancery by English Bill,* 2d ed. (Dublin: printed by P. Byrne, 1795); Thomas Starkie, *A Practical Treatise on the Laws of Evidence, and Digest of Proofs, in Civil and Criminal Proceedings . . . With References to American Decisions by Theron Metcalf* (Boston: Wells and Lilly; Philadelphia: H. C. Carey and I. Lea; 1826); John Tayloe Lomax, *Digest in the Laws Respecting Real Property, Generally Adopted and in Use in the United States; Embracing, More Especially, the Law of Real Property in Virginia . . .* (Philadelphia: J. S. Littell, 1839); Benjamin Watkins Leigh, ed., *Supplement to the Revised Code of the Laws of Virginia: Being a Collection of all Acts of the General Assembly, of a Public and Permanent Nature, Passed Since the Year 1819 . . .* (Richmond: S. Shepard and Company, 1833); Henry St. George Tucker, *Commentaries on the Laws of Virginia, Comprising the Substance of a Course of Lectures Delivered to the Winchester Law School, . . .* 2 vols. (Winchester: Printed at the Office of the Republican, 1836-37). Demanding intensive reading of his students, Tucker scorned shortcuts. A review of Samuel Warren's *Popular and Practical Introduction to Law Studies* (London: A. Maxwell, 1845) in the *Law Reporter* (8 [February 1846]:433-39) denounced such books as "unsafe inventions to overcome the difficulties of an arduous profession in some illegitimate manner— as sort of patent medicines for chronic illness." A former student of Tucker's wrote him to be sure to see this review, "as the ideas of the writer correspond with those I have frequently heard you express in relation to textbooks in general." Powhatan Robinson to NBT, February 23, 1846, T-C.

23. "Lecture on the Study of the Law," pp. 146-47.

24. Tucker identified William and Mary with the states' rights "school" often and his students absorbed this lesson, but see especially *An Address Delivered Before the Society of the Alumni of William and Mary College, Upon the 5th of July, 1842* (Richmond: P. D. Bernard, 1842), pp. 9-10, and Joseph M. Carrington to NBT, June 17, 1844, T-C.

25. W. S. Peachy, Williamsburg, to APU, March 9, 1842, T-C. Tucker listed his texts in the periodic public notices mentioned in note 22 above. See also Essays, Lectures, and Fragments, including the "Proceedings of the Moot Court," box 83, T-C, and notebook of law lectures, James Henry Rawlings Papers (6436), UVa.

26. Joseph Story, *Commentaries on the Constitution of the United States.* 3 vols. (Boston:

Hilliard, Gray, and Company, 1833). Together with the earlier legal treatises of Nathan Dane and Kent's *Commentaries on American Law* (4 vols. [New York: O. Halstead, 1826-30]), Story's *Commentaries* made up an authoritative body of scholarship supporting the federal supremacy interpretation of the Constitution and challenging St. George Tucker's view at every turn. The Constitution, wrote Story—and he said on subjects of government "metaphysical refinements are out of place" (1:viii)—was neither made nor ratified by the states as sovereignties or political communities; it did in fact create a national government. Story's argument that American nationhood antedated state government bolstered this position. Tucker spent the spring and early summer of 1835 upbraiding Bancroft, first through a friend in New York, Francis L. Hawkes, and then in a review of Bancroft's *A History of the United States, from the Discovery of the American Continent to the Present Time* (10 vols. [Boston: Charles Bowen, 1834-74]) in the *Messenger* (1 [June 1835]:587-91). Hawkes to NBT, May 1 and October 26, 1835, T-C. For Tucker's comments on Kent during the 1839-40 academic term, see notebook of law lectures, James Henry Rawlings Papers (6436), UVa.; on the continuing threat Story posed the South, see an anonymous review of his work in *SQR* 2 (October 1842):416-22.

27. "Lecture on the Study of the Law," p. 146; NBT, *A Series of Lectures on the Science of Government, Intended to Prepare the Student for the Study of the Constitution of the United States* (Philadelphia: Carey and Hart, 1845), pp. 59-60. Hereafter referred to as *Lectures*. The discussion in the following pages draws on material that Tucker did not deliver in formal lectures until 1836, when Dew assumed the presidency of the college and Tucker took on responsibility for the "philosophy of government" as well as constitutional law; it nonetheless seems safe to assume that he began reading in this subject, putting his thoughts together, and passing them on to students as early as 1834-35.

28. NBT, "A Lecture on Government," *SLM* 3 (April 1837):209-216; *Lectures*, pp. 32-34. In the *Lectures*, p. 55, Tucker said, "I am aware that this account of the primitive origins of government is at variance with all the theories of social compact which have been put forth." But if these theories contradicted all we know of the early history of the human race, he asked, "shall we reject the testimony of history, or shall we permit ourselves to doubt the justice of these theories and endeavor to take a view of human nature as shall reconcile philosophy to history [?]"

29. "The Primary Form of Incipient Government," *Lectures*, pp. 52-65.

30. Ibid., p. 37. But see also "The Body Politic. What is it?" ibid., pp. 65-80; 37 ff.

31. Ibid., p. 145. Henry St. George Tucker, in a text that he published a decade after Beverley assumed the William and Mary chair, made his own remonstrance against "the metaphysical subtleties of the schools" but came down strongly for natural law "as that *rule of rectitude which is prescribed to us by the author of our being and pointed out by our reason;* and which lies at the foundation of all wise and salutary systems of positive law." Henry St. George Tucker, *A Few Lectures on Natural Law* (Charlottesville: James Alexander, 1844), p. 2.

32. *Lectures*, p. 145. See also, ibid., pp. 66-67, 126-29. Tucker's viewing the right of property as a human construct avoided the possibility that Lockean natural-rights theory might somehow be turned for radical purposes: if the concept of nature provided the real foundation of private property, it was a simple step to the revision of "artificial" inequities in its distribution. To Tucker's mind, Blackstone, by arguing that property in some sense existed independently of society, failed to stress strongly enough the social significance of property. Man needed society; society needed property. Boorstin, *Mysterious Science of the Law*, pp. 160-61, 169-80; C. P. Courtney, *Montesquieu and Burke*, in *Modern Language Studies*, ed. J. Boyd, J. Seznec, and P. E. Russell (Oxford: Basil Blackford, 1963), pp. 162, 182-83; J. G. A. Pocock, *The Ancient Constitution and the Feudal Law: A Study of English Historical Thought in the Seventeenth Century* (Cambridge: at the University Press, 1957), pp. 30-55 and passim.

33. *Lectures*, pp. 146 ff. Cf. StGT, *Blackstone's Commentaries*, vol. 1, "Appendix," p. 3. According to St. George Tucker's view of natural law, unbalanced material rewards did nothing to change the equal status of men in the abstract, nothing to alter their essential worth. Beverley Tucker, by rejecting that abstract plane, those ideas of inherent, ideal equality, was able to take unequal conditions and work toward a view that things in no way "ought" to have been different.

34. *Lectures*, p. 147.

35. [NBT], "Note to Blackstone's Commentaries, Vol. I Page 423. Being the Substance of Remarks on the Subject of Domestic Slavery, delivered to the Law Class of William and Mary College,

December 2d, 1834," *SLM* 1 (January 1835):227; StGT, *Dissertation on Slavery*, p. 96.

36. "Note to Blackstone's Commentaries," pp. 227-28.

37. John Wickliffe Dew Notebook, box 2, Dew Family Papers, WM; Thomas R. Dew, *Lectures on the Restrictive System, Delivered to the Senior Political Class of William and Mary College* (Richmond: Samuel Shepherd & Co., 1829). Stephen Mansfield, "Thomas Roderick Dew at William and Mary: A Main Prop of that Venerable Institution," VMHB 75 (October 1967):429-42.

38. Thomas R. Dew, *Review of the Debate in the Virginia Legislature of 1831 and 1832* (Richmond: T. W. White, 1832); reprinted in Chancellor [William] Harper, Governor [James Henry] Hammond, Dr [William Gilmore] Simms, and Professor [Thomas R.] Dew, *The Pro-Slavery Argument; As Maintained by the Most Distinguished Writers of the Southern States . . .* (Charleston, S.C.: Walker, Richards and Company, 1852), p. 324. My references are to this later edition. For examples of the closeness of Dew's thinking to Tucker's, see pp. 294, 309-11, 324-25, 414-20, 447, 451-62, 490.

39. "Note to Blackstone's Commentaries," pp. 227-28. Cf. Dew, "Review," pp. 309-11, 321.

40. Burke quoted in "Note to Blackstone's Commentaries," pp. 230-31. See also *Lectures*, pp. 109-110, 160-61, 345-46; Dew, "Review," pp. 461-62. For the address Tucker referred to, delivered in March 1775 and a favorite with other antebellum Southerners, see Burke, *Works*, 1:222-50, particularly 229-30. Tucker mentioned it in his "Lectures on the Study of the Law," p. 152.

41. "Note to Blackstone's Commentaries," p. 230.

42. [NBT], "Slavery," *SLM* 2 (April 1836):336-39.

43. Ibid., p. 338.

44. Ibid., p. 337.

45. "Note to Blackstone's Commentaries," p. 227. But see also Courtenay, *Montesquieu and Burke*, p. 151; Boorstin, *Mysterious Science of the Law*, pp. 63-64; Pocock, *Ancient Constitution and the Feudal Law*, pp. 36-37.

46. For examples of the dissonance between new developments and old verities, see the arguments of Abel P. Upshur, Benjamin Watkins Leigh, John Randolph, and John S. Barbour in *Proceedings and Debates of the Virginia State Convention of 1829-30* and proslavery selections in Robert, *Road from Monticello*, pp. 66-112 *inter alia*. Also see notes 4 and 5 above.

47. StGT, *Dissertation on Slavery*, pp. 5, 8, and 74. Though close friends and members of the Coalter family cheered Tucker's proslavery essay on Blackstone, he made so much of the opposition it ignited that White in Richmond felt the need to write reassurances. A Richmonder who asked the editor of the *Messenger* how he "could have been so much off [his] guard as to give place" to the piece was, said White, but a "quondam" friend anyway. He had to admit that the author of a stinging reply to Tucker, which White sent him for examination before publishing it, was "very much a gentleman—one of good and kind feelings and excellent temper"; yet as if trying to ease Tucker's mind—and probably failing—White wrote a week later to say that the anonymous critic's style marked him as being "of an earlier generation" and one who was "now and then supercilious appearing . . ." (TWW to NBT, February 16, March 12, March 19, and March 28, 1835, T-C; see also St. George Coalter to NBT, February 17, 1835, and JC to NBT, June 1, 1835, T-C). "Remarks on a Note to Blackstone's Commentaries, Vol. I, Page 423." *SLM* 1 (February 1835):266-70, and "From the Author of the 'Note to Blackstone's Commentaries,'" ibid., (March 1835):388.

48. NBT to StGT, May 23, 1807, T-C. See also NBT to JR, January 12, 1807, T-C.

49. "Note to Blackstone's Commentaries," p. 230; "Slavery," pp. 336-37, 339. In his writings, Tucker never drew a formal connection between his religious beliefs and his view of perfectionism and its dangers; nonetheless his objections to perfectionism did resemble those made on one side of the squabble which, in 1837, led to a split between Old- and New-School Presbyterians and the exclusion of antislavery congregations from the church General Assembly. After 1832 Tucker kept his distance from the church. Otherwise in 1837 he might have considered the ambiguity of his position: theologically he was closer to the New School and New Haven; temperamentally he was closer to the Old School and its unwillingness to meddle with slavery.

50. "Slavery," p. 339. Tucker's filiopiety surfaced frequently, but there are good examples in his "Note to Blackstone's Commentaries," pp. 227-28, Lectures, Essays, and Fragments, box 83, T-C, and in his [review of] *"The History of England*, from the accession of James II; by Thomas Babington Macaulay," *SQR* 15 (July 1849):408 and passim.

Chapter Six

1. NBT, "Lecture on Government," *SLM* 3 (April 1837):213-15. NBT to Hugh Lawson White, March 2, 1837, John Overton Papers (571), SHC.

2. NBT to LST, November 16, 1835, and April 23, 1843, T-C. See also NBT to LST, October 27 and 29, 1835, November 2 and November 5, 1835; Roscoe Cole, Columbus, Mississippi, to NBT, April 9, 1836; John M. Speed, Lynchburg, to NBT, August 9, 1836; Thomas Meaux, Amelia, to NBT, October 5, 1836; Vincent Witcher to NBT, February 9, 1837; William S. French to NBT, December 12, 1837; N. W. Burton, Murfreesboro, Tennessee, to NBT, February 10, 1838; all in T-C; and Tucker's "Introduction to Lecture on Law Of N[ature] and N[ations]," Essays, Lectures, and Fragments, box 83, T-C.

3. Of 153 bachelors of law (who earned the early L.B. degree) at the college between 1834 and 1851, only 14 were from outside Virginia. Even non-Virginians were Southerners. About 9 out of 10 Virginia students of law were from tidewater counties with heavy black populations. Except for 8 students from Richmond, 5 from Norfolk, and a few from other cities, virtually all of Tucker's students were products of rural or small-town Virginia. By comparison, half of the Virginians who attended Harvard Law School between 1820 and 1860 were from the Piedmont or mountain areas of the state; a third came from cities or towns of more than 5,000 population by the 1850 census. *History of the College of William and Mary,* pp. 124-42; Harvard University, *A Catalogue of the Officers and Students of the University in Cambridge* (1820-1860). Tucker's interest in teaching a select group was paralleled in his evangelical impulse. Though we send missionaries out to the loathed and despised, Tucker wrote in a discussion of Christ's command to preach to the poor, what about the "enlightened, the refined, the elegant, & accomplished," he asked, "the men whose wisdom and integrity are the best hope of their country . . . for the maintenance of order, for the defence of public and the protection of private right . . . ?" Piece on Luke, 7:22, Sermons and Religious Writings, folder #325, box 85, T-C.

4. T. Robinson to NBT, March 17, [1837]; and Littleton Waller Tazewell to NBT, January 16, 1838, T-C. See also Fortunatus Syndor, Lynchburg, to NBT, November 10, 1836; Richard K. Crallé [related to John M. Speed, a Tucker student 1835-37] to NBT, April 17, 1838; H. Haralson, LaGrange, Georgia, to NBT, May 17, 1841; all T-C.

5. Sermon on Matt. 10:29, "Are not two Sparrows sold for a farthing? And one of these shall fall on the ground without your father." Religious Essays, Bryan Papers (3400), UVa.

6. [NBT,] "Christian Education," *SLM* 1 (April 1835):432-35.

7. The teacher of the great questions, Tucker believed, could hardly be expected to "stick too close to the text." All these questions from his abstract of theological tract, in NBT to EC, [April 28, 1836,] T-C. See also NBT to St. George Coalter, May 13, 1835, T-C, and sermon on Prov. 19:27, "The instruction that causeth to err," Religious Essays, Bryan Papers (3400), UVa.

8. "Lecture on the Study of the Law," pp. 150, 152-53; HStGT, *Lectures on Government* (Charlottesville: James Alexander, 1844), pp. 208-9. See also *Address Delivered Before the Society of Alumni,* pp. 10, 13-14, 16-17.

9. HLW, Washington, to NBT, December 7, 1834, and February 17, 1835; J. T. Brown, Petersburg, to NBT, March 27, 1835; Littleton Waller Tazewell to NBT, December 7, 1834; all in T-C.

10. NBT to LST, May 2 and 3, June 6 and June 15, 1835; WCP, Columbia, to NBT, June 14, 1835; all in T-C. Tucker's regard for the Tennessean, see NBT to HLW, Washington, January 25, 1840, Hugh Lawson White Papers, LC, and [NBT,] note "Copied from a Western Paper," n.d. [early 1840], Thomas A. Smith Collection, SHSM.

11. JC to NBT, June 1, 1835, T-C. Littleton Waller Tazewell, Richmond, to NBT, December 7, 1834; James Semple, Richmond, to NBT, December 10, 1834; DG to NBT, January 12, 1835; WCP, Washington, to NBT, February 10, 1835; James Hamilton, Jr., Charleston, to NBT, February 19, 1835; John Taliaferro, Fredericksburg, to NBT, February 24, 1835; all T-C.

12. *Register of Debates in Congress . . . ,* 24th Cong., 1st sess., 1836, 12, pt. 2:1967, 2456.

13. NBT to JHH, February 17 and February 18, 1836, Hammond Papers, LC.

14. NBT to JHH, February 18, 1836, ibid. See also NBT to JHH, March 15, 1836, ibid.

15. *Congressional Globe,* 24th Cong., 1st sess., 1836, 3:228-29, 401-2; see also Van Buren to Nathaniel Macon, February 15, 1836, Macon Papers, Duke.

16. NBT to LST, January 10, 1836, T-C. JHH to NBT, June 5, 1836, T-C. On Hammond's

torment, physical and emotional, see his diary entries for April 12, 17, and 19, 1836, Hammond Papers, LC. Among Tucker's anonymous pieces were "Western Scenery: Extract of a Letter from a Western Traveller," *SLM* 1 (December 1834):139; "The Romance of Real Life," *SLM* 1 (February 1835):271-72; "Original Literary Notices," ibid., pp. 307-12; "The Beauties of the Court of Charles the Second . . ." ibid., pp. 312-14; "Extract From Reminiscences of a Western Traveller," *SLM* 1 (March 1835):336-40; and "Charlot Tayon" [a sketch of an important figure in early Saint Louis], *SLM* 2 (January 1836):71-74. The publisher of the *Messenger* wrote Tucker often in these years; see especially TWW to NBT, November 11 and November 17, 1834, February 16, February 19, and June 13, 1835, February 6, 1836, and January 24, 1837, all in T-C.

17. DG to NBT, January 12, 1835, T-C. See also DG to NBT, December 23, 1833, and January 12, 1837; NBT to LST, April 28, 1835; WCP to NBT, September 22, 1835; Ruffin to NBT, July 9, 1836; APU to NBT, March 17 and June 14, 1837, and June 30, 1840; all T-C. DG to Richard Crallé, September 10, 1832, and March 4, 1836; Green Papers, LC. APU to DG, February 23 and March 17, 1836, and August 4, 1837; Crallé to DG, May 1, 1836; and Memorandum, dtd. Columbia, [S.C.,] December 8, 1836; all in Duff Green Papers (993), SHC. For more on Green's exploits as a Southern publicist, see John S. Ezell, "A Southern Education for Southrons," *JSH* 17 (August 1951):303-27.

18. [NBT,] "The Pickwick Papers," *SLM* 3 (September 1837):532; [NBT,] "Literary Notices," *SLM* 1 (May 1835):520; [NBT,] "Bulwer's New Play," *SLM* 3 (January 1837):90. In the *Messenger* Tucker voiced frequent objections to what (in "Bulwer's New Play," p. 90) he called the "corrupt taste of a corrupt society"; see also his reviews of [Charles Dickens,] *The Public Life of Mr. Tulrumble, Once Mayor of Mudfrog* and *Oliver Twist, SLM* 3 (May 1837):323-25, and of [Benjamin D'Israeli,] *Henrietta Temple: A Love Story,* ibid., pp. 325-31. Thomas White of the *Messenger* took much pleasure in Tucker's attacks on the "coxcomb literati both at home and abroad," partly for the attention they drew to his magazine. TWW to NBT, June 13, 1835, and January 19, June 13, and June 23, 1837, T-C.

19. Besides the unlikelihood that Tucker could write two novels and keep up with teaching at the same time, *Balcombe* carried the marks of fresh experience and a refugee's longing for home. (See chapter 4, section II.) Senator Preston of South Carolina recognized in Tucker's *Balcombe* Missouri characters and scenes familiar to both men from the Dardenne days of the 1820s and praised the work for its fully American quality—"neither holding the skirts of Bulwer [and] only the little finger of Scott." WCP to NBT, November 6, 1836, T-C. Harper & Brothers printed 2,200 copies of *Balcombe,* reported having 700 copies left on inventory in 1838, and three years after the book appeared paid Tucker a net profit of $112.17. Robert French to NBT, May 31, June 14, November 28, and December 27, 1836; Harper & Brothers to NBT, May 13, 1838, and October 1, 1839; all T-C. See also Edgar Allan Poe's review of *Balcombe* in the *Messenger* (3 [January, 1837]: 49-58). After a long summary, Poe criticized Tucker's characterization as unoriginal, made only a few objections to style, refrained from commenting on Balcombe's "philosophy," and then pronounced the book "upon the whole . . . *the best* American novel." Poe thought the portrait of Balcombe "an unmistakable transcript" of Tucker.

20. William Campbell Preston, who in Washington arranged publication of *The Partisan Leader,* read the manuscript in the spring of 1836, finding "inherent difficulties" in the attempt at once to do fiction and prophecy. (WCP to NBT, March 22, 1836, T-C.) Undaunted, Tucker wrote Green that if the work proved popular he would continue it indefinitely, writing "a volume every month of my life." (NBT to DG, April 20, 1836, Green Papers, LC.) Green published 2,000 copies of a two-volume edition and put them on sale at about a dollar a volume. He criticized Tucker for making "the tariff the prominent idea when I think you should make the slave question the basis of your supposed separation." (DG to NBT, September 13, 1836, T-C.) Abel P. Upshur's review of the tale, more a political than a literary commentary, appeared with Poe's review of *Balcombe* in the January 1837 issue of the *Messenger.* Upshur and Tucker collaborated on the review, which they hoped to publish in at least one Northern journal. APU to NBT, June 17 and November 27, 1836, and January 21, 1837, T-C. See also WCP to NBT, April 16, and May 24, 1836, and DG to NBT, May 2, 1836, T-C; NBT to DG, September 23, 1836, Duff Green Papers (993), SHC; NBT to WCP, May 18, 1836, folder 9371, UVa. *The Partisan Leader* reappeared during the Civil War, published in Richmond as the prophecy of independence and in New York as a blueprint for treason. My page references are to the 1971 reprint in the Southern Literary Classics Series. See chapter 1, note 2.

21. John P. Kennedy, *Swallow Barn, or A Sojourn in the Old Dominion,* 2 vols. (Philadelphia:

Carey & Lea, 1832), and *Horseshoe Robinson: A Tale of Tory Ascendency,* 2 vols. (Philadelphia: Carey, Lea & Blanchard, 1835); William Alexander Caruthers, *The Kentuckian in New York, Or, the Adventures of Three Southerns,* 2 vols. (New York: Harper & Brothers, 1834) and *The Cavaliers of Virginia, or The Recluse of Jamestown: An Historical Romance of The Old Dominion,* 2 vols. (New York: Harper, 1834-35). William R. Taylor, *Cavalier & Yankee: The Old South and American National Character* (New York: Harper and Row, 1969) offers the standard discussion of Northern and Southern literature of this period as part of efforts at cultural definition and as a reflection of social anxiety. For more on studies of the plantation novel, see "Essay on Sources."

22. "The great art, and the great charm of Sir Walter Scott," wrote Tucker in a review, "is that he never *describes* his characters. He brings us *into their society,* and makes us *know* them." "The Romance of Real Life," *SLM* 1 (February 1835). The Virginian also praised Cooper for his "dilineations of characters," which, he said, were "among the most distinct and vivid that we remember to have seen." Review of [Robert Montgomery Bird], *Nick of the Woods, SLM* 3 (April 1837):254-57. For a recent treatment of Tucker's attempt to make characters and societies known to readers, see Arthur Wrobel, " 'Romantic Realism': Nathaniel Beverley Tucker," *American Literature* 42 (November 1970):325-35.

23. Poe, whose early contributions to the *Messenger* included the horror tales "Berenice" and "Morella," moved from Baltimore to assist White in editorial duties in the late summer of 1835. That fall, when White relayed to Tucker Poe's compliments on some of the law professor's poetry, Tucker responded with a letter that began a brief exchange on literary and critical theory. Tucker disclaimed great originality in his prose or poetry. But to Poe, he wrote, original thoughts "come thronging unbidden, crowding themselves upon him in such numbers as to require the black rod of that master of ceremonies, Criticism, to keep them in order." Remember, he cautioned, "fancy must be the servant, not mistress. It must be made the minister of higher faculties." (NBT to TWW, November 29, 1835, Griswold Papers, BPL.) Tucker's interest in Poe, who like the older man had lost his mother early in life, was warmly received—"the want of parental affection," Poe wrote Tucker, "has been the heaviest of my trials." (Poe to NBT, December 1, 1835, Poe Papers [6012], UVa.) It was probably Tucker's high regard for Poe's work that helped White decide to keep the young assistant as long as he did; White's complaints of Poe's bad work habits and melancholy began almost as soon as he reached Richmond and in December 1836 forced White to dismiss him. See also NBT to Poe, December 5, 1835, Griswold Papers, BPL; TWW to Lucian Minor, September 21, 1835, White Papers, Duke; NBT to TWW, January 26, 1836, T-C; TWW to NBT, December 3 and December 27, 1835, and April 26, 1837, T-C.

24. See, for example, the Mary Scott seduction tragedy, *Balcombe,* 1:46 ff., and Douglas Trevor's romance and unconsummated marriage, *The Partisan Leader,* pp. 78-87, 107, 276-78. On early American criticism, see William Charvat, *The Origins of American Critical Thought, 1810-1835* (Philadelphia: University of Pennsylvania Press, 1936).

25. *Balcombe,* 1:88, 270, 273-79; 2:79 ff., 259. *The Partisan Leader,* pp. 39, 64-67, 150, 169 ff., 323.

26. *Balcombe,* 1:22-23, 25, 71, 84; 2:245-46.

27. Ibid., 1:77, 130, 2:68-69. *The Partisan Leader,* pp. 15, 268.

28. *Balcombe,* 1:78, 2:70; *The Partisan Leader,* pp. 254-55.

29. *The Partisan Leader,* p. 256. For Schwartz's "impertinent" questioning, see ibid., p. 19.

30. Ibid., pp. 274, 257.

31. Ibid., pp. 44-46.

32. Ibid., pp. 57, 108, 177.

33. Ibid., pp. 45, 36, 43, 46, 56.

34. NBT to JHH, March 15, 1836, Hammond Papers, LC. For comments on Green's handling of *The Partisan Leader* and its wide unavailability, see WCP, Washington, to NBT, January 15, 1837; APU to NBT, June 14, 1837; William M. Robinson to NBT, July 8, 1837; and William S. French, Vicksburg, to NBT, February 26, 1838; all in T-C. See also NBT to DG, November 20, 1836, Green Papers, LC.

35. NBT to St. George Coalter, May 13, 1835, T-C. See also *History of the College of William and Mary,* p. 166; *The Partisan Leader,* pp. 108-9.

36. APU to NBT, March 8, 1836, T-C.

37. ER to NBT, December 6, 1836, T-C; see also TWW to NBT, May 18, 1837, T-C. The fruits

of Ruffin's labors on old Virginia were *The Westover Manuscripts* . . . (Petersburg: E. and J. C. Ruffin, 1841).

38. NBT, "Political Science; A discourse on the questions, 'What is the seat of sovereignty in the United States, and what the relation of the People of those States to the Federal and State Governments respectively,' read before the Petersburg Lyceum on the 15th of May, 1839," *SLM* 5 (August 1839):566. Crallé, Washington, to NBT, April 1, 1837; Wyndham Robertson, Richmond, to NBT, April 1, 1837; William W. Moore, Washington, to NBT, April 24, 1837; all in T-C.

39. NBT to LST, May 19, 1839, T-C; "Political Science," pp. 559-66. This address substituted for the book of Virginia revolutionary documents Tucker had planned to publish. See also NBT to LST, April 28 et seq., 1839, and APU to NBT, March 8 and April 9, 1836, T-C.

40. [NBT,] "The Writings of George Washington," *SLM* 1 (June 1835):592. See also "Washington's Writings," *SLM* 4 (May 1838):328-35, especially 329-30. *Address Delivered Before the Society of the Alumni*, pp. 16-18. See also Tucker's later review of Macaulay's *History of England, SQR* 15 (July 1849):374-78. Tucker's moral view of history typified themes in early American historiography, but he stoutly rejected the common use of historical literature to shape and give voice to American nationalism. See George H. Callcott, *History in the United States, 1800-1860: Its Practice and Purpose* (Baltimore: The Johns Hopkins University Press, 1970).

41. "Lecture on the Study of the Law," pp. 145-46; *Address Delivered Before the Society of Alumni*, pp. 5 ff. See also Joseph C. Mayo to NBT, December 10, 1845, T-C and, for a theoretical discussion of the cultural function Tucker was serving in his effort to raise up old Virginia, see Anthony F. C. Wallace, "Revitalization Movements," *American Anthropologist* 58 (April 1956): 264-81.

42. "Lecture on the Study of the Law," p. 145; *Balcombe*, 1:22-23, 251, and passim; *Partisan Leader*, pp. 8-9 and passim.

43. William L. Rudd, Lynchburg, to NBT, January 27, 1838, T-C. John M. Speed to NBT, October 18, 1838, and April 15, 1839, T-C.

44. NBT, "A Discourse on the Genius of the Federative System of the United States," *SLM* 4 (December 1838):761-69, especially 762-63. The "genius" Tucker talked about was the separation of powers between state and central government. Where matters of diplomacy, armies, navies, large revenues, and commercial regulations were at issue, the temptations of avarice and the allurements of ambition were considerable. By contrast, the political apparatus of Virginia carried no "principle of corruption," preached Tucker, nothing to disturb the balance of its powers or to unsettle the "harmony of its action."

45. Ibid., pp. 768-69.

46. Ibid., pp. 767-68. *Partisan Leader*, pp. 205, 246, 250.

47. *Lectures*, p. 25; NBT, *A Discourse on the Dangers That Threaten the Free Institutions of the United States, Being An Address to the Literary Societies of Hampden Sidney College, Virginia* . . . (Richmond: John B. Martin & Company, 1841), pp. 7-9. Tucker's Randolph-Macon address, republished in *Lectures*, pp. 5-30, appeared earlier as *A Discourse on the Importance of the Study of Political Science, as a Branch of Academic Education in the United States* . . . (Richmond: Peter D. Bernard, 1840). Commending Tucker's scholarly "freedom and elegance," the Boston reviewer nonetheless noted a tendency toward "loose and discursive talk," and in the Virginian's "pride of country" found characteristically Southern provincialism. "Tucker's Discourse," *North American Review* 43 (July 1841):269-71.

48. *Partisan Leader*, p. 249; message of Wyndham Robertson to the General Assembly, Richmond *Enquirer*, December 8, 1836. During the 1830s and the early 1840s Tucker received honorary memberships from literary and "moral improvement" societies at Randolph-Macon College, Wake Forest College in North Carolina, Hampden-Sidney, and Marshall College in Huntington, Virginia. Soil conservation practices and crop rotation, leading to diversified farming, lessened somewhat the impact of the 1837 Panic in Virginia, but as late as 1842 Tucker spoke of the financial distresses of the lower counties.

49. *Address Delivered Before the Society of the Alumni*, p. 10; John J. Jones to NBT, September 4, 1840, T-C; Richard I. Cocke to NBT, January 1, 1840, T-C. See also Robert Ould to NBT, December 31, 1843, T-C.

50. John M. Speed to NBT, February 25, 1839, T-C; William L. Rudd, Lynchburg, to NBT, January 27, 1838, T-C. If Bernard Trevor had not imbued his children "with opinions, or changed

their minds with the arguments by which he was accustomed to support them," Tucker wrote in his romance of Southern independence, "he had made them full partakers of his feelings." *Partisan Leader,* p. 57. See also D. H. Conrad to NBT, September 24, 1840, and September 20, 1847, T-C.

51. "The Literary Messenger," signed "Humanity," Richmond *Enquirer,* February 9, 1837; "The Southern Literary Messenger: A Peep into the Review of the 'Partizan Leader,'" ibid., February 16, 1837; *Georgetown Metropolitan,* n.d., quoted ibid., March 18, 1837. On February 25 the *Enquirer* carried extracts from the *Charleston Courier* and the Lynchburg *Virginian* attacking the book, and even after White's public regrets for the Upshur review in the *Enquirer* of March 9, the paper carried unfriendly comments on March 11 and 18. See also Hall, *Upshur,* p. 233, n. 37.

52. HStGT to NBT, September 26, 1837; HStGT [to NBT], enclosed with LST to NBT, September 2, 1837; NBT to HStGT, copied in NBT to LST, September 7, 1837; Richard Crallé to NBT, April 1, 1837; all in T-C. TWW to NBT, January 31 and February 7, 1837; ECB to NBT, March 24, 1837; APU to NBT, March 17, 1837; and DG to NBT, January 12 and July 4, 1837; all T-C. *Richmond Whig and Public Advertiser,* January 31, 1837. Outside Williamsburg that fall, Lucy overheard that *The Partisan Leader* was "the poorest most indifferent t[hing (o]f the novel kind) that has appeared for some time and that none of the booksellers in Washington would *own* that they had ever seen it." LST to NBT, September 5, 1837, T-C. On the rift within the Tucker family *The Partisan Leader* caused, see also St. George Coalter to NBT, January 14, 1837; NBT to LST, September 17, 1837; ECB to LST, October 5, 1837; Beverley Tucker to NBT, October 12, 1840; all T-C.

53. Thomas R. Dew, "An Address. Delivered before the Students of William and Mary, at the Opening of the College, on Monday, October 10, 1836," *SLM* 2 (November 1836):760–69.

54. "N," "Review of President Dew's Address," *SLM* 3 (February 1837):130–35. John M. Speed to NBT, July 15, 1837, T-C. The notoriety of William and Mary as a states' rights Whig institution was understandable. With Tucker and Dew on the faculty, the college also received direction from a board of visitors that included Ruffin, Upshur, and John Tyler.

55. [NBT,] "To Our Readers." [Reply to the] "Review of President Dew's Address," *SLM* 3 (April 1837):269; NBT, "A Lecture, Delivered to the Law Class of William and Mary College, June 17, 1839, being the last of a course of Lectures on the Philosophy of Government and Constitutional Law," Richmond *Enquirer,* July 2, 1839. In asking Tucker's permission to publish the address, a committee of students gave as their purpose "doing justice" to him and "acquitting this College of the charge, which has gone abroad, that she is but a hotbed of party prejudice in which we are manufactured the zealous advocate and blind party bigot." Their published letter to the editor of the *Enquirer* thereupon spoke of preparing the public mind "for the reception of truth." Tucker's address also appeared in *SLM* 5 (September 1839):587–92. For evidence of Tucker's special affection for the law class of 1839, see NBT to LST, June 16 and 17, 1839, T-C.

56. "Lecture . . . the last of a course on the Philosophy of Government and Constitutional Law," pp. 590–92.

57. Ibid., p. 592; "Discourse on the Importance of the Study of Political Science" [June, 1840], *Lectures,* pp. 28–30.

58. *Address to the Literary Societies of Hampden Sidney College* [September, 1841], p. 13.

Chapter Seven

1. Alexis de Tocqueville, *Democracy in America,* The Henry Reeve Text as Revised by Francis Bowen; Now Further Corrected and Edited With a Historical Essay, Editorial Notes, and Bibliographies by Phillips Bradley, 2 vols. (New York: Alfred A. Knopf, 1945). All my page references will be to the Vintage paperback edition.

2. APU to NBT, February 14, 1839, T-C. Philip Rieff, *The Triumph of the Therapeutic: Uses of Faith After Freud* (New York: Harper and Row, 1966), especially chapter 3, "Community and Therapy," deals with Tocqueville's social thought.

3. Tucker's notes on Tocqueville are contained in folder #324, box 84, T-C. See in particular the conclusion to 2[d] R[eading, foolscap sheet] 17.

4. [Abel Parker Upshur,] *A Brief Enquiry Into the True Nature and Character of Our Federal Government: Being a Review of Judge Story's Commentaries on the Constitution of the United States,* "By a Virginian" (Petersburg: Edmund and Julian C. Ruffin, 1840).

5. NBT to JHH, April 24, 1847, Hammond Papers, LC. Northern spokesmen like Kent and Story—Tucker wrote in his collaborative review—had tainted the rising generation and the legal pro-

fession with the notion that, but for elections, "the United States differed in nothing . . . from the consolidated kingdoms and empires of Europe." "Liberal and Strict Construction of the Federal Constitution," *The Southern Magazine and Monthly Review* 1 (February 1841):129–47. Despite the support of Tucker, Upshur, and Green, Ruffin's magazine—partly for reasons of his own limited talents in writing and editing, but mostly because he could find only about eighty subscribers—failed after two issues. APU to NBT, March 17, 1837, September 24 and December 14, 1840, and February 1 and March 1, 1841; ER to APU, September 26 [enclosure, APU to NBT, October 8] and October 24, 1840; ER to NBT, January 24, February 5, and April 14, 1841; all in T-C. See also APU to DG, September 16, 1840, Duff Green Papers (993), SHC.

6. *Partisan Leader*, pp. 169–70, 323; [Upshur,] *Enquiry*, p. 124. See also *Partisan Leader*, p. 150.

7. NBT to John Tyler, February 4, 1836, Misc. Mss. Tucker, NYHS; Tyler to NBT, October 29, 1837, T-C; *History of the College of William and Mary*, p. 12.

8. APU to NBT, February 1, 1841, T-C. See also NBT to LST, April 6, 1841, T-C; Lyon Gardiner Tyler, *The Letters and Times of the Tylers*, 3 vols. (Richmond: Whittet and Shepherson, 1884–85; Williamsburg: n.p., 1896), 2:11–12.

9. WCP to NBT, April 9, 1841, T-C. APU to NBT, April 10, 1841, and ER to APU, October 24, 1841, both T-C.

10. Nevins, ed., *Diary of John Quincy Adams*, p. 520. For a secondary account of Clay and the bank issue during Tyler's administration, see Glyndon G. Van Deusen, *The Life of Henry Clay* (Boston: Little, Brown and Company, 1937), pp. 344–54.

11. NBT to Tyler, April 11, 1841, T-C. See also NBT to Thomas Ritchie, July 12, 1845, Tyler Scrapbook, WM; NBT to JHH, December 9, 1848, Hammond Papers, LC. Tucker had some reason to expect Clay's support of the plan. Before the December 1839 Whig nominating convention, the Kentucky senator had written Tucker a friendly letter which, besides denouncing the damages of federal patronage, emphasized the common constitutional ground he and Tucker occupied. Clay to NBT, October 10, 1839, in Tyler, *Letters and Times*, 1:601–2. See also Clay, Richmond, to NBT, February 24, 1840, and from Washington, December 11, 1840, T-C.

12. Draft of bank bill, apparently enclosed with Tucker's letter to Tyler, April 11, 1841, T-C.

13. NBT to Tyler, April 11, 1841, T-C; "A State Rights Man" [NBT], "To John Tyler, President of the U.S.," Richmond *Enquirer*, August 17, 1841. See also NBT to Thomas Ritchie, July 12, 1845, Tyler Scrapbook, WM; NBT to JHH, December 9, 1848, and January 30, 1849, Hammond Papers, LC; Tyler to NBT, July 28, 1841, and June 16, 1842, in Tyler, *Letters and Times*, 2:43–54, 168–69.

14. Wise to NBT, May 5, 1841, and APU to NBT, April 10, 1841, T-C; Clay to NBT, April 15, 1841, and Tyler to NBT, April 25, 1841, in Tyler, *Letters and Times*, 2:30, 32. See also NBT to Clay, April 3, 1841, and WT to NBT, May 22, 1841, T-C. In a letter to Clay, the President reminded him that antibank sentiment among radical "locofoco" Democrats was strong, and that premature legislative action might make capitalization of the bank difficult. Having learned from Tucker that the senator had in hand a sketch of Tucker's state association plan, the President chose not to mention it, and in fact renounced any intention of submitting bank legislation to Congress that summer. Tyler to Clay, April 30, 1841, in Tyler, *Letters and Times*, 3:92–94. To Wise it seemed that Clay supporters were simply unwilling to yield the constitutional point, unprepared "to get or take a National Bank from any other source than Congress." Wise to NBT, May 5, 1841, T-C.

15. "To John Tyler, President of the U.S.," Richmond *Enquirer*, August 10 and 13, 1841. See also Tucker's articles, all of them over the signature "A State Rights Man," ibid., August 17, 24, and 31, and September 3, 1841. On readying the letters for the press and for sympathetic comments on them, see Wise to NBT, June 27, July 11, July 24, July 31, August 5, August 11, and August 17, 1841; William W. Crump to NBT, August 17, 1841; APU to NBT, August 28, 1841, all in T-C.

16. APU to NBT, August 7 and September 10, 1841, T-C. Upshur correctly quoted Tyler in his letter of September 10. See also APU to NBT, August 28, 1841; J. B. Christian to NBT, September 11, 1841; Wise to NBT, September 11, 1841; NBT to LST, September 13, 1841; WT to NBT, September 13, 1841; all in T-C. In October, when Tyler briefly visited Williamsburg and Gloucester County, Upshur prepared Tucker for the President's arrival. "Do not let him escape you without some wholesome lessons on the use of his patronage," Upshur wrote from Washington. "He will confer freely with you, & you know how to improve the occasion for the advancement of the true faith." APU to NBT, October 19, 1841, T-C.

17. John Murdaugh to NBT, September 18, 1841, T-C. Botts's remarks appeared in the *National*

Intelligencer, a Whig organ predictably hostile to what Murdaugh in the above letter called the "Williamsburg influence," February 5 and 8, 1842. See also "The Abstractionists," *Richmond Whig and Public Advertiser,* August 31, 1841, and "Judge Upshur," ibid., September 10 and 21, 1841. In "Timeleon," Richmond *Enquirer,* September 21, 1841, Upshur spoke warmly enough of the college to defend it against recent and anticipated attacks. Newspapers unfriendly to Upshur early in 1842 accused him of writing *The Partisan Leader;* Botts, knowing who had, created such a stir against Tucker that Upshur decided his cause and that of the college required a public reply. To this end he asked former William and Mary students to compose open letters on Tucker's loyalty to the Union and the soundness of his lessons in constitutional law there. APU to NBT, October 2, October 11, October 19, October 30, and November 10, 1841, and February 9, March 13, and March 28, 1842, T-C. See also WCP to NBT, February 13, 1842, and WT to NBT, February 13, 1842, T-C. Students' testimonials were enclosed with APU to NBT, April 2, 1842, T-C.

18. John Murdaugh to NBT, September 18, 1841, T-C. On Tucker's peculiar despair, see APU to NBT, December 23, 1841, T-C. Tucker rehearsed his disappointment in Tyler in letters to LST, May 25, 1842, and to CBT, January 9, 1850, T-C, and to JHH, March 28, 1849, Hammond Papers, LC.

19. APU to DG, May 1, 1842, Green Papers (993), SHC; Notes on Tocqueville's Commentaries, 1st R[eading, foolscap sheet] 2, folder #324, box 84, T-C. See also APU to NBT, March 28, April 20, and June 6, 1842, T-C.

20. Adin Ballou, *History of the Hopedale Community, From Its Inception to Its Virtual Submergence In The Hopedale Parish* (Lowell, Mass.: Thompson & Hill—The Vox Populi Press, 1897), p. 29. For the "Constitution of the Fraternal Communion" and the declaration required of all members, see ibid., pp. 27–37. See also Tocqueville, *Democracy in America,* 2:210.

21. NBT, "Temperance. An Address read before the Temperance Society of William & Mary College . . . ," *SLM* 8 (July 1842):440–43.

22. Tucker viewed Lieber's *Letters to a Gentleman in Germany* as a "pure money making affair— yet as a composition possessing some merit." TWW to NBT, April 9, 1835, T-C. Frank Freidel, *Francis Lieber: Nineteenth Century Liberal* (Baton Rouge: Louisiana State University Press, 1947), p. 132, refers to Lieber's contributions to the *Messenger.*

23. NBT [to Lieber, May-June, 1840], and Lieber to NBT, June 15, 1840, T-C. Francis Lieber, *Manual of Political Ethics, Designed Chiefly for the Use of Colleges and Students at Law,* 2 vols. (Philadelphia: J. B. Lippincott and Company, 1875); all my page references will be to this later, more widely available edition.

24. Lieber, *Political Ethics,* 1:173–76, 223 ff. Lieber's assurances that this sovereign was not a force that should be "directly and absolutely brought into play in politics" gave Tucker little comfort. Lieber to NBT, June 19, 1840, T-C.

25. [NBT,] "An Essay On the Moral and Political Effect of the Relation between the Caucasian Master and the African Slave," *SLM* 10 (June and August 1844):329–39, 470–80; *Lectures,* pp. 290–350. My page references will be to the *Messenger* installments, the second of which bore a slightly varied title.

26. "Moral and Political Effect of the Relation between the Caucasian Master and the African Slave," p. 473. See also, ibid., pp. 477–78; "Note to Blackstone's Commentaries," p. 230; *Lectures,* pp. 330–37, 346–50; NBT to JHH, February 17, 1836, Hammond Papers, LC. George Bibb, a Kentuckian serving as Tyler's secretary of the treasury, sent Tucker's essay to Peel. Bibb to NBT, August 20 and October 28, 1844, T-C.

27. "Moral and Political Effect of the Relation between the Caucasian Master and the African Slave," p. 476. *Lectures,* pp. 536–37.

28. Tocqueville first saw democratic men as agents of endless change that formed and dissolved associations and kept "public spirit" high. By the appearance of his more theoretical discussion in the second volume, he had decided instead that freedom brought about an isolation, a self-preoccupation that meant competition rather than affiliative public spirit, an inwardness that restricted one's moral view to the immediate, personal concerns of business and self-comfort. See Rieff, *Triumph of the Therapeutic,* pp. 69–70, and Seymour Drescher, "Tocqueville's Two Democracies," *JHI* 25 (April-June 1964):206–7.

29. Thomas Carlyle, *On Heroes, Hero-Worship, and the Heroic in History* and *Past and Present,* vols. 5 and 10 of the Centenary Edition, *The Works of Thomas Carlyle* (London: Chapman and Hall, 1897). See especially *Past and Present,* pp. 143–50, 174, 209 ff., and 286–87. Tucker spoke

glowingly of Peel and Carlyle as "radically conservative, willing to amputate to save life," in a letter to JHH, May 29, 1849, Hammond Papers, LC. See also Gerald M. Straka, "The Spirit of Carlyle in the Old South," *The Historian* 20 (Autumn 1957):39–57.

30. "Moral and Political Effect of the Relation between the Caucasian Master and the African Slave," p. 480. *Lectures,* pp. 348–49.

31. Harper, "Memoir on Slavery," in *The Pro-Slavery Argument,* p. 23. See especially pp. 19–27 for commentary based on Wakefield. George Fitzhugh, *Sociology for the South: or, The Failure of Free Society* (Richmond: A. Morris, 1854) and *Cannibals All! Or, Slaves Without Masters* (Richmond: A. Morris, 1857).

32. NBT to LST, May 26, 1839, T-C. In later years the Reverend Stringfellow was probably best known for "The Bible Argument: or, Slavery in the Light of Divine Revelation," in E. N. Elliott, ed., *Cotton Is King, and Proslavery Arguments: Compromising the Writings of Hammond, Harper, Christy, Stringfellow, Hodge, Blesoe, and Cartwright . . .* (Augusta, Ga.: Pritchard, Abbott & Loomis, 1860). The notice Tucker received for his slavery essay came from friends with whom he was already in contact. George M. Bibb to NBT, August 20 and October 28, 1844, and APU to NBT, September 30, 1844, T-C.

33. "Note to Blackstone Commentaries," pp. 230–31. See also "Moral and Political Effect of the Relation between the Caucasian Master and the African Slave," p. 474; *Lectures,* p. 331.

34. Francis Markoe, Jr., to NBT, February 22 [and 23], 1844, T-C. See also APU to NBT, February 22, 1844, and NBT to APU, March 1, 1844, T-C; note to Tucker from the Institute Speaker Committee, February 20, 1844, folder 8, NBT Papers, WM.

35. APU to NBT, March 13, 1843, T-C. See also APU to NBT, March 28 and October 25, 1842, October 26, 1843, and January 25 and February 3, 1844, T-C. For a view of Tyler's interest in Texas annexation as a slaveholders' conspiracy, see Frederick Merk with the collaboration of Lois Bannister Merk, *Slavery and the Annexation of Texas* (New York: Alfred A. Knopf, 1972). Charges of Southern deviousness are not entirely in order. Certainly in the minds of Tucker, Tyler, Duff Green, Waddy Thompson, Robert J. Walker, and other Southerners involved in Texas plans, it was important that the republic, once in the Union, would add Southern weight on the federal scales; true, slavery and sectional interests were frankly guiding motives for Secretary of State Upshur. But no informed American could have seen British designs on the Southwest as innocent. And by early 1844 pro-Texas sentiment in the Tyler circle was anything but secret. That winter the administration paper in Washington, the *Madisonian,* had argued for annexation, and Green, who at this time was Upshur's London emissary for Texas affairs, had published letters in a Boston paper no less explicit. So open was American talk of acquiring Texas in 1843 that in November the Mexican minister in Washington had warned American officials of such an affront to his government.

36. W. P. Gray, Houston, to NBT, May 6, 1841; Burnley to NBT, October 27 and June 21, 1841, all in T-C. See also NBT to LST, June 15 and 22, December 25 and 28, 1835, January 10 and January 23, 1836, and May 26, 1839, and APU to NBT, February 25 and March 28, 1839, all in T-C. Draft of a contract between Tucker and Burnley dated October 20, 1838, folder 8, NBT Papers, WM. Burnley made periodic reports to Tucker on Texas affairs, opportunities there, and British interest in the region; see especially Burnley to NBT, November 1, 1838, January 2 and April 10, 1839, May 25 and October 2, 1841, and December 3, 1843, T-C.

37. Thompson exercised himself to win Tucker's favor, finally sending his son to Tucker for legal training early in 1842. WT to NBT, May 22, October 5 and October 14, 1841, and January 12, 1842, T-C; WT to NBT, September 13 and November 10, 1841, Tyler Scrapbook, WM. Henry Wise heard from Tyler that Thompson was being pushed for the mission to Mexico solely out of the President's regard for Tucker's confidence in him. Neither Wise nor Upshur regarded Thompson as highly as did Tucker. Wise to NBT, January 8 and January 15, 1842, and APU to NBT, January 28, 1843, T-C.

38. APU to NBT, October 10 and December 4, 1843, T-C. Upshur, who himself daydreamed of retiring to a Texas plantation, kept in close touch with Tucker throughout the year; see also, APU to NBT, February 25, 1839, March 13, July 15, October 3 and October 26, 1843, and NBT to APU, March 1, 1844, T-C.

39. APU to NBT, December 4, 1843, T-C. [Robert J. Walker,] *Letter of Mr. Walker, of Mississippi, Relative to the Annexation of Texas . . .* (Washington: Globe Office, 1844). NBT [to Walker], May 6, 1844, Misc. Mss. Tucker, NYHS.

40. For details on the effort to obtain Texas by treaty, see Merk, *Slavery and the Annexation of Texas,* pp. 44 ff.

41. NBT [to Walker], May 6, 1844, Misc. Mss. Tucker, NYHS. Tucker reminded the Mississippi senator that *The Federalist,* no. 14, had explained as one of the immediate objects of the Constitution the union of the thirteen states—which the founders knew practicable—and, quoted Tucker, the addition of "such other States as might arise in their own bosoms, *or in their neighborhoods,* which, we cannot doubt to be equally practicable" (his emphasis).

42. NBT to Calhoun, December 12, 1844, in J. Franklin Jameson, ed., *Correspondence of John C. Calhoun,* in the *Fourth Annual Report of the Historical Manuscripts Commission, American Historical Association* (Washington, D.C.: [Government Printing Office,] 1900), pp. 1008-10. In Tucker's May note to Walker he spoke highly of his friend Seth Barton's "Randolph of Roanoke" letters in the Richmond *Enquirer.* These articles, which many Southerners attributed to Tucker, accused President Adams and Secretary of State Clay of the "unwarrantable and perfidious alienation of Texas." (Richmond *Enquirer,* April 18, 1844.) See also, ibid., April 16 and 23, 1844; NBT [to Walker], May 6, 1844, Misc. Mss. Tucker, NYHS; JHH to NBT, January 24, 1847, T-C; NBT to JHH, February 6, 1847, Hammond Papers, LC.

43. NBT to JHH, March 28, 1849, Hammond Papers, LC. Tucker quite possibly "coached" Bayly in this business—judging from later references Tucker made to him and from the texture of Bayly's speeches. But the evidence is only circumstantial. See also speech of Thomas H. Bayly, January 7, 1845, in *Congressional Globe,* 28th Cong., 2d sess., 1845, 14:144-45, and appendix, pp. 122-28; "Meeting in Williamsburg," Richmond *Enquirer,* May 10, 1844.

44. Even South Carolinians discovered constitutional flexibility on the Texas issue. George McDuffie declared in the Senate that the power to acquire territory was not set down in the Constitution "by any express grant." Robert Barnwell Rhett, in an exchange with Joseph Ingersoll of Pennsylvania, said he "did not feel very scrupulous as to the particular means, provided Texas was got; and have it they would." *Congressional Globe,* 28th Cong., 2d sess., 1845, 14:334-35, and appendix, pp. 55-58.

45. Robert Ould, Georgetown, D.C., to NBT, December 31, 1843, and Clay to NBT, January 11, 1845, T-C. *Congressional Globe,* 28th Cong., 2d sess., 1845, vol. 14, Appendix, pp. 326-30; William S. Archer, *Speech of Mr. Archer, of Virginia, Delivered in the Senate of the United States, May, 1844* (Washington: Gales and Seaton, 1844), copy in T-C Room, WM.

46. *The Liberator,* November 26, 1841, cited in John L. Thomas, *The Liberator: William Lloyd Garrison, A Biography* (Boston: Little, Brown and Company, 1963), p. 328.

47. *Prigg v. Pennsylvania,* 16 Peters 539 (1842). For more on the Prigg case, Story's decision, and the problem of fugitive slaves in federal relations, see Thomas D. Morris, *Free Men All: The Personal Liberty Laws of the North, 1780-1861* (Baltimore: The Johns Hopkins University Press, 1974).

48. APU to NBT, April 20, 1842, T-C. Tucker probably learned of Adams's remark through this letter. See also APU to NBT, January 25 and February 3, 1844, T-C, and William Goodell's antislavery *Views of American Constitutional Law, in its Bearing upon American Slavery* (Utica, N.Y.: Jackson & Chaplin, 1844).

49. HStGT, *Lectures on Government,* pp. 183, 186, 190; HStGT, *Lectures on Constitutional Law, for the use of the Law Class at the University of Virginia* (Richmond: Shepherd and Colin, 1843), p. 210. Henry's son John Randolph absorbed his father's faith in constitutional government; see the "Valedictory delivered by J. R. Tucker to the [University of Virginia] Law Class—July 3, 1844," Tucker Family Papers (2605), SHC. William Cabell Rives, a member of the Charlottesville bar and a close friend of Henry, echoed his sentiments during the Texas annexation debates in Congress. "What would it profit us should we gain Texas," he asked the Senate, "if thereby we lost our regard for that sacred instrument which was the bond of our national union, the pledge and palladium of our liberty and happiness." *Congressional Globe,* 28th Cong., 2d sess., 1845, vol. 14, appendix, pp. 178-79.

50. *Lectures,* pp. 113 ff., 126, and passim; Municipal Law of Virginia draft, pp. 9-10, Essays, Lectures, and Fragments, box 83, T-C; Lieber, *Political Ethics,* 1:228-38. See also NBT to Daniel Call, March 14, 1835, Tucker Family Papers (2605), SHC, and a "Review of Judge Story's Inaugural Address," *Christian Spectator* 2 (March 1830):43-61—a piece that Tucker likely saw and that equated codification with "headlong innovation and blind enactment."

51. NBT, *The Principles of Pleading* (Boston: Charles C. Little and James Brown, 1846), p. 27. See also, ibid., pp. 28, 48, 54–56, 62–71, 97–99; "Professor Beverley Tucker's Valedictory Address to his Class," pp. 598–99. On the technical features of pleading, see William E. Nelson, *Americanization of the Common Law: The Impact of Legal Change on Massachusetts Society, 1760–1830* (Cambridge, Mass.: Harvard University Press, 1975), pp. 72 ff.

52. *Pleading*, p. 2. See also, ibid., pp. 30, 49–61, 76, and Notebook of Law Lectures, James Henry Rawlings Papers (6436), UVa.

53. *Pleading*, pp. 1–2, 9–10.

54. W. B. Napton to NBT, July 29, 1847, and Edward Bates to NBT, November 7, 1848, T-C, wrote of the need for pleading reform. "Rights of Slaveholding States, and of the Owners of Slaves" (*AmJurist* 23 [July 1840]:346–47), argued that the writ of *replegiando* as a means of recovering runaway servants was "well known to the laws of the several states [before 1789] and was in constant use for that purpose, except so far it had been superseded by local legislation. The object of the framers of the constitution [in the fugitive slave provision], therefore, was not to provide a new mode by which the master might be enabled to recover the services of his fugitive slave, but merely to restrain the exercise of a power which the state legislature would . . . have possessed, to deprive the master of such preexisting right of recaption." On the writ *homine replegiando* as an antislavery device, see Morris, *Free Men All*, pp. 11 ff., 74–79, and passim. Abolitionists like Charles Sumner could hold with Lord Mansfield in the 1772 Sommersett decision that only positive statute could support slavery; a Michigan lawyer, Thomas Cooley, based his antislavery position on the common-law guarantees of personal liberty. David Donald, *Charles Sumner and the Coming of the Civil War* (New York: Alfred A. Knopf, 1960), p. 231; Phillip S. Paludan, "Law and the Failure of Reconstruction: The Case of Thomas Cooley," *JHI* 33 (October–December 1972):597–614. See also Goodell, *Views of American Constitutional Law*, pp. 3–5.

55. NBT to Daniel Call, March 14, 1835, Tucker Family Papers (2605), SHC. For a discussion of the common law as the law of Virginia "in her capacity as a Sovereign State," see Municipal Law of Virginia draft, pp. 10, 17 ff., Essays, Lectures, and Fragments, box 83, T-C.

56. HStGT to NBT, November 13, 1843, T-C. Tucker referred to the deal with Green in NBT to LST, May 2 and May 10–11, 1835, T-C. On the William and Mary–University of Virginia rivalry, see NBT to LST, October 27 and November 2, 1835; HStGT to NBT, August 15 and October 30, 1841, September 16, 1842, all in T-C. Hugh Trevor, in *The Partisan Leader*, pp. 38, 46, had brought himself to believe "that *union, on any terms*, was better than disunion, *under any circumstances*." See too NBT to JHH, May 29, 1849, Hammond Papers, LC.

57. *Lectures*, frontispiece; E. S. Dorsey to NBT, January 25, 1845, T-C. See also NBT to Dorsey, December 31, 1844; NBT [to Francis Lieber, May–June, 1840]; NBT to LST, May 26, 1839; all T-C.

58. *Lectures*, frontispiece and passim. "The character of all great things in the world is durability," Tucker asked the printer to insert in one of his pages; and in the moral as in the physical world durability was what man found it "hardest to maintain." NBT to Dorsey, December 31, 1844, T-C. *Lectures*, ignored by reviewers, was not the enduring work that Tucker had wanted to write.

59. B. B. Minor to NBT, May 11, June 25, and September 14, 1844, and March 1, March 31, July 28, and October 4, 1845, T-C. [NBT], "Gertrude; An Original Novel," *SLM*, vol. 10 (September 1844) through (with interruptions) vol. 11 (December 1845). Former congressman James Henry Hammond later praised "Gertrude"; Phillip Pendleton Cooke, a Virginia writer, claimed to have read it at one sitting. JHH to NBT, January 24 and 26, 1847, and Cooke to NBT, March 29, 1847, T-C.

60. Minor to NBT, June 25, 1844, T-C; "Gertrude," *SLM*, 10:644, 11:181–84.

61. *Balcombe*, 1:45, 70, 88, 273–79, and 2:48–52, 160–63; "Gertrude," *SLM*, 10:642–44, 11:707 ff. See also Tucker's review of Manzoni's *I Promessi Sposi*, *SLM*, 1:520–21, and of Bulwer's *Duchess de la Valliere*, *SLM*, 3:90–91. Private letters conveyed this same regard for feminine warmth and simplicity; NBT to LST, June 27, 1835, February 1, 1836, and August 18, 1844, T-C.

62. *Balcombe*, 1:27–374; "Gertrude," *SLM*, 10:645, and 11:690. Wilson Flagg's *Analysis of Female Beauty* (Boston: Capen & Lyon, 1834) was part of Tucker's library; see also "The Belle of the White Sulphur," chap. 11 of "The Virginia Springs," *Putnam's Monthly* 7 (January 1856):44–45. In 1849 Tucker completed a play that doubtless extolled the same virtues "Gertrude" portrayed; "Viola" was lost before being published—perhaps in the mails between Williamsburg and South Carolina, where William Gilmore Simms read it in manuscript. WGS to NBT, September 6, 1849, in Mary C. Simms

Oliphant, Alfred Taylor Odell, and T. C. Duncan Eaves, eds., *The Letters of William Gilmore Simms*, 5 vols. (Columbia: University of South Carolina Press, 1953), 2:553-56.

63. *Balcombe*, 1:273-74, and 2:165; "Appropriate Sphere of Women," *The Watchman of the South*, September 21, 1837; "Gertrude," *SLM*, 10:647. Stephen Hempstead to TAS, June 9, 1839, and APU to NBT, July 18, 1842, both T-C. Horace Bushnell, *Views of Christian Nurture, And of Subjects Adjacent Thereto* (Hartford: Edwin Hunt, 1847). Commending the *Watchman* to Tucker, the editor called it "an old-fashioned Virginia Presbyterian Paper"; William Plumer to NBT, August 30, 1837, T-C. See also Tucker's "Christian Education," and Dew's Dissertation On the Characteristic Differences between the Sexes, and on the Position and Influence of Women in Society," *SLM* 1 (May 1835):493-512, (July 1835):621-32, and (August 1835):672-91.

64. *Balcombe*, 2:48-49; "Gertrude," *SLM*, 10:543, and 11:259, 691.

65. "Moral and Political Effect of the Relation between the Caucasian Master and the African Slave," pp. 333, 331, 334.

66. Municipal Law of Virginia draft, pp. 23-24, Essays, Lectures, and Fragments, box 83, T-C. Greenleaf, Cambridge, to NBT, February 18, and April 24, 1846; Little & Brown, Boston, to NBT, February 20 and March 2, 1846; all T-C. Though *Pleading* was a volume principally of local interest, wrote a reviewer in *The Law Reporter* (10 [October 1847]:278-82), it was an "able defense" of a "time-honored system."

67. "Moral and Political Effect on the Relation between the Caucasian Master and the African Slave," p. 331.

68. Cf. Taylor, *Cavalier & Yankee*, pp. 175-76.

69. *Lectures*, pp. 208, 198. But see, ibid., pp. 194-213 and passim, and also Tucker's review of Dickens's *Pickwick Papers*, *SLM*, 3:530; NBT to JHH, Hammond Papers, LC; Richard K. Crallé to NBT, June 29, 1837, and WGS to NBT, January 30, 1850, T-C.

70. The point I am arguing here is that proslavery and antislavery grew out of similar social apprehensions. See my afterword, and for more on the connection between social change in Tucker's lifetime and reform movements, including the cult of domesticity, see in particular William E. Bridges, "Family Patterns and Social Values in America, 1825-1875," *AmQ* 17 (Spring 1965):3-11; John L. Thomas, "Romantic Reform in America, 1815-1865," ibid., pp. 656-81; David Brion Davis, *The Problem of Slavery in the Age of Revolution, 1770-1823* (Ithaca, N.Y.: Cornell University Press, 1975), as well as Davis's "Some Themes of Counter-Subversion: An Analysis of Anti-Masonic, Anti-Catholic, and Anti-Mormon Literature," *MVHR* 47 (September 1960):205-24 and "Some Ideological Functions of Prejudice in Ante-Bellum America," *AmQ* 15 (Summer 1963):115-25.

71. Notes on Tocqueville's Commentaries, 1st R[eading, foolscap sheet] 1 and 2[d] R[eading, foolscap sheet] 1, folder #324, box 84, T-C. See also *Lectures*, pp. 283, 338-39; Essay on Texas annexation, n.d. [c. June 1844], Essays, Lectures, and Fragments, box 83, T-C.

72. "Moral and Political Effect of the Relation between the Caucasian Master and the African Slave," p. 480.

73. Essay on Texas Annexation, n.d. [c. June 1844], Essays, Lectures, and Fragments, box 83, T-C; *Lectures*, p. 202.

Chapter Eight

1. ECB to NBT, February 21, 1850, T-C.

2. Parting address to students, n.d. [c. 1850], Essays, Lectures, and Fragments, box 83, T-C; NBT to ECB, February 15, 1850, T-C; NBT to JHH, October 18, 1850, Hammond Papers, LC; NBT to EC, [April 28, 1826,] T-C.

3. Richmond *Enquirer*, September 2, 1845.

4. Ibid., September 11, 1846. See also "The Virginia Springs," *Putnam's Monthly* 6 (November and December 1855):482-90, 589-94, and 7 (January 1856):42-49.

5. *Warrenton* (Va.) *Flag of '98* quoted without date in Richmond *Enquirer*, August 18, 1846; *Enquirer*, September 1 and 11, 1846. NBT to LST, August 21, 1837, T-C.

6. NBT to LST, September 2, 1837, T-C. See also NBT to LST, August 24 and September 5, 1837, T-C; NBT to JHH, August 20, 1849, Hammond Papers, LC. William Gilmore Simms later described Tucker as having "morbid caprices" and being "distrustful of new persons." WGS to JHH, July 15, 1847, in *Letters of William Gilmore Simms*, 2:330.

7. Dallas to NBT, May 22, 1847; Waldie to NBT, November 3, 1840, April 27 and August 21, 1841; all in T-C. Condy Raguet, the free-trade publicist, was another Philadelphian on friendly terms with Tucker. See, for example, Raguet to NBT, May 31, 1841, T-C.

8. Lieber to NBT, June 15 and October 29, 1840; Greenleaf to NBT, February 24, 1846; all in T-C. See also NBT to APU, March 1, 1844, T-C, and *Pleading*, pp. iii–v. Greenleaf's opinion of Tucker as a student of pleading remained high. See Beverley Tucker to NBT, June 26, 1847, and Henry C. Semple's testimonial letter, March 30, 1848, T-C.

9. For Lowell's bitterly funny satires, "The Biglow Papers," see *The Poetical Works of James Russell Lowell*, 4 vols. (Boston: Houghton and Mifflin Company, 1894), especially 2:43–50, 55, 58–64, 89–97. Thoreau's view of the immorality of the war appeared in the 1847 essay "Civil Disobedience." The war was the work of a "Satanic Genius," declared Ralph Waldo Emerson from Concord, proceeding calculatedly on the basis of "how much crime the people will bear." William H. Gilman, et al., eds., *The Journals and Miscellaneous Notebooks of Ralph Waldo Emerson*, 12 vols. to date (Cambridge, Mass.: The Belknap Press of Harvard University, 1960–), 9:412, 426–27, 444–45, and passim.

10. NBT to JHH, March 13, 1847, Hammond Papers, LC; Gilman et al., eds., *Journals and Miscellaneous Notebooks of Ralph Waldo Emerson*, 9:444; NBT to JHH, March 13, 1847, Hammond Papers, LC; Thoreau, "Walking," in Walter Harding, ed., *The Selected Works of Thoreau* (Boston: Houghton Mifflin Company, 1975), p. 672; Emerson, "Self-Reliance," in *Essays: First and Second Series*, vol. 2 of *The Works of Ralph Waldo Emerson*, 6 vols. (Boston and New York: The Jefferson Press, 1920 [?]), p. 49. For more on Thoreau's critique of shopkeeping stodginess and acquisitive competition, see Bradford Torrey and Francis H. Allen, eds., *The Journal of Henry D. Thoreau*, With a foreword by Henry Seidel Canby, 14 vols. (Boston: Houghton Mifflin Company, 1949), 1:367–68, 387–90, 395–96, and passim.

11. Emerson, "Self-Reliance," *Works*, 2:66, 58. See also "History," ibid., pp. 9–43, and "The American Scholar. An Oration Delivered Before The Phi Beta Kappa Society, At Cambridge, August 31, 1837," *Works*, 4:81–115. "The Chivalrous Don Quixotes of Conservatism," observed Lowell in "The Biglow Papers," as if to comment on the festivities at the Virginia Springs, "still encumber themselves with the clumsy armor of a bygone age." Lowell, *Works*, 2:91.

12. Essay on Texas annexation, Essays, Lectures, and Fragments, box 83, T-C.

13. NBT to LST, April 20, 1843; LST to NBT, August 9, 1844, T-C. See also NBT to LST, June 9, 1839, and August 19, 1844, and NBT to CBT, December 7, 1847, all T-C; NBT to ECB, January 24, 1848, Bryan Papers, VSL.

14. NBT to ECB, January 26, 1844, T-C; David Hunter Strother's description of Cynthia appears in Cecil D. Eby, Jr., " 'Porte Crayon' in the Tidewater," *VMHB* 67 (October 1959):444.

15. Eby, " 'Porte Crayon' in the Tidewater," p. 444; NBT to LST, April 13, 1843, T-C.

16. NBT to LST, April 20, 1843, and Carlyle to NBT, October 25, 1846, T-C. George M. Dallas to NBT, May 22, 1847, T-C.

17. JHH to NBT, December 19, 1846, and January 24, 1847, T-C; NBT to JHH, December 2 and December 29, 1846, and February 6, 1847, Hammond Papers, LC. See also Hammond Diary, February 6, 1841, January 31, July 2, and November 17, 1844, Hammond Papers, LC.

18. NBT to JHH, December 29, 1846, and February 6, 1847, Hammond Papers, LC; JHH to NBT, March 2, April 14, and May 12, 1847, T-C.

19. For examples of Simms's deliberate play in the game of winning friends, see his notes to Tucker, in *Letters of William Gilmore Simms*, May 6, 1849, 2:510–12, and March 12, 1851, 3:98–101. On Simms, see Jon L. Wakelyn, *The Politics of a Literary Man: William Gilmore Simms*, Contributions in American Studies Number 5 (Westport, Conn.: Greenwood Press, 1973) and John Higham, "The Changing Political Loyalties of William Gilmore Simms," *JSH* 9 (May 1943):210–23.

20. JHH to NBT, May 12, 1847, T-C. See also JHH to NBT, March 2, 1847, T-C; WGS to JHH, April 1, [April 4], and June 4, 1847, *Letters of William Gilmore Simms*, 2:299 n., 297–301, 322. The Carolina writer heaped further praise on Tucker's romances in writing Evert Augustus Duyckinck, a New York publisher compiling an American encyclopedia, December 6, 1851, *Letters of William Gilmore Simms*, 3:344–45.

21. NBT to JHH, March 13, 1847, Hammond Papers, LC; Powhatan Robinson, Petersburg, to NBT, August 13, 1844, T-C; Joseph M. Carrington, Richmond, to NBT, June 17, 1844, T-C; Robert Ould, Georgetown, D.C., to NBT, December 31, 1843, June 16, 1845, and November 27, 1847,

T-C. See also NBT to JHH, December 29, 1846, and April 24, 1847, Hammond Papers, LC.

22. By these Virginia resolves the state refused to bind herself to the Wilmot measure and reasserted the right of any citizen to reside with his property of any description in all the territory the country acquired. Richmond *Enquirer*, February 19, 1847. On the day they appeared in the *Enquirer*, Calhoun introduced in the Senate a set of four nearly identical resolutions that Tucker believed were inspired by, if not copied from, those adopted in Richmond. NBT to JHH, March 13, April 24, 1847, Hammond Papers, LC; *Enquirer*, May 10, 1844. Leake to NBT, February 15, 1844; Crump to NBT, May 5, 1844; Montague to NBT, August 5, 1845, all in T-C. The activities of Greenhow, Leake, Peachy, and Jones received notice in the *Enquirer*, March 24 and 26, 1847. Tucker's nephew Beverley organized Jefferson and Berkeley counties for the pro-Calhoun Democrats; see R. M. T. Hunter to [?], February 23, 1843, Charles Henry Ambler, ed., *Correspondence of Robert M. T. Hunter, 1826-1876, Annual Report of the American Historical Association for the Year 1916*, 2 vols. (Washington: [Smithsonian Institution,] 1918), 2:60-62. For more on the "young fogies," see Henry T. Shanks, *The Secession Movement in Virginia, 1847-1861* (Richmond: Garrett and Massie Publishers, 1934), pp. 15-16.

23. Excerpts from the Petersburg *Republican* and *Fredericksburg Recorder* quoted in Richmond *Enquirer*, March 3, 1847; *Lynchburg Republican*, quoted ibid., March 12, 1847. Ibid., March 5, March 26, and April 30, 1847. GFH to Eliza Floyd Holmes, February 24, 1847, Holmes Papers, Duke. NBT to JHH, March 13 and April 24, 1847, Hammond Papers, LC.

24. NBT, "Judge Tucker's Address." *SLM* 13 (September 1847):569-70. See also JHH to WGS, July 23, 1847, and WGS to JHH, August 21, [1847,] *Letters of William Gilmore Simms*, 2:343-45; NBT to JHH, March 13 and October 13, 1847, Hammond Papers, LC.

25. Holmes came to William and Mary with the recommendations of William Campbell Preston, Tucker's old friend, and of the states' rights Democrat R. M. T. Hunter. Hunter to Robert McCandlish, January 20, 1847, Holmes Papers, Duke; R. M. McCandlish to GFH, February 24, 1847, Holmes Letterbook, Holmes Papers, Duke. WCP to NBT, October 3, 1846; William Berkley to Cynthia Tucker, March 8, 1847; Berkeley to NBT, March 26, 1847; all in T-C. William Meade and John Johns to McCandlish, May 27, 1847, College Papers, WM. NBT to JHH, October 13, 1847, Hammond Papers, LC. See also Neal C. Gillespie, *The Collapse of Orthodoxy; The Intellectual Ordeal of George Frederick Holmes* (Charlottesville: The University Press of Virginia, 1972), pp. 24-27.

26. NBT to CBT, November 1, November 15, November 28, and December 7, 1847, T-C; Richmond *Enquirer*, November 23 and December 10, 1847.

27. NBT to CBT, January 12, 1848; GFH to McCandlish, January 23, 1848, Holmes Papers, Duke; ECB to NBT, January 1, 1849, T-C. See also William Crump to NBT, February 1, 1848; Robert Ould to NBT, February 1, 1848; William M. Burnwell to NBT, February 8, 1848; Henry A. Wise to NBT, February 22, 1848; Beverley Tucker to NBT, March 28, 1848; Charles Minnegerode to [Dr. L. C.] G[arland], August 31, 1848; NBT to LST, October 1, 1848; John Murdaugh to NBT, October 6, 1849; all in T-C. GFH to McCandlish, August 16, 1848, and Millington to GFH, July 29, 1848, Holmes Papers, Duke. NBT to JHH, August 20, 1849, Hammond Papers, LC. Richmond *Enquirer*, March 10 and 28, and July 18, 1848, cited in Gillespie, *Collapse of Orthodoxy*, p. 27; also see *Enquirer*, January 21, 1851. *History of the College of William and Mary*, pp. 141-43.

28. NBT to JHH, [April 20, 1848,] Hammond Papers, LC.

29. JHH to NBT, June 1, 1848, T-C; NBT to JHH, October 11, 1848, Hammond Papers, LC.

30. See "Essay on Sources" for the secondary literature on antebellum Virginia constitutional reform.

31. A Slaveholder of West Virginia [Henry Ruffner], *Address to the People of West Virginia; Shewing That Slavery Is Injurious To the Public Welfare, And That It May Be Gradually Abolished, Without Detriment To The Rights and Interests of Slaveholders* (Lexington, Va.: R. C. Noel, 1847), pp. 9, 14; JHH to NBT, May 12, 1848, and Bayly to NBT, September 6, 1848, T-C. See also William Gleason Bean, "The Ruffner Pamphlet of 1847: An Antislavery Aspect of Virginia Sectionalism," *VMHB* 61 (July 1953):260-82.

32. JHH to NBT, May 12 and November 28, 1848, T-C; NBT to JHH, October 13, 1847, Hammond Papers, LC; Beverley Tucker to NBT, December 14, 1848, T-C. See also NBT to JHH, June 12, November 20, and December 6, 1848, Hammond Papers, LC; JHH to NBT, July 11 and December 26, 1848, T-C; Jefferson Davis to NBT, April 12, 1848, T-C.

33. NBT to JHH, May 29 and July 12, 1849, Hammond Papers, LC.

34. NBT to ECB, March 31, 1849, T-C; NBT to JHH, March 28 and August 20, 1849, Hammond Papers, LC. NBT to CBT, February 24, 1849, T-C. For an account of the Taylor inauguration, see Thomas Ritchie to George [Ritchie], March 12, 1849, acc. #5867, pt. 1, 1835-54, Ritchie Papers, LC.

35. Eby, " 'Porte Crayon' in the Tidewater," pp. 444-45.

36. Ibid.; WGS to GFH, August 13, 1851, *Letters of William Gilmore Simms,* 3:139-40; [NBT,] [Review of] *"The History of England, from the accession of James II;* by Thomas Badington Macaulay," *SQR* 15 (July 1849):376, 394 ff., 406 ff.; NBT to JHH, July 27, 1851, Hammond Papers, LC. See also NBT to JHH, August 20, 1849, Hammond Papers, LC. For a contemporary complaint that Virginia suffered from "sluggishness and imbecility," and that—compared with Northern states—she resembled a heavy, horse-drawn coach of the eighteenth century "competing with the flying steam-car of the present," see Robert Reid Howison, *A History of Virginia From Its Discovery and Settlement by Europeans to the Present Time.* 2 vols. (Philadelphia: Carey & Hart, 1846-1848),2:510 ff.

37. NBT to JHH, November 20, 1848, and December 4, 1849, Hammond Papers, LC. [NBT,] "A Son of Virginia," *Richmond Semi-Weekly Examiner,* March 1, 1850.

38. NBT to JHH, December 4, 1849, Hammond Papers, LC.

39. NBT to JHH, December 4, 1849, ibid. Cf. Calhoun to JHH, January 4, 1850, ibid.

40. NBT to JHH, December 4 and December 27, 1849, ibid.

41. WGS to NBT, January 30, 1850, *Letters of William Gilmore Simms,* 3:9. Tucker placed his hope in a friend's proposed resolution asking the governor, after the elections, to add to the delegation a few "such men as . . . Virginia ought to listen to on such an occasion." NBT to JHH, February 8, 1850, Hammond Papers, LC. See also NBT to JHH, January 27 and February 2, 1850, ibid. Hammond himself cared to attend the convention only if "there was a handsome & spontaneous call" on him; miffed at the support he received in the legislature, he prepared for Nashville with little enthusiasm. JHH to WGS, December 20, 1849, ibid. See also Hammond's Diary, December 15, 1849, March 17, 1850, and April-May (dates uncertain), 1850, ibid. Tucker's piece for Simms was "The Present State of Europe," *SQR* 15 (January 1850):277-323.

42. NBT to JHH, February 21-22 [addendum to letter dated February 8], Hammond Papers, LC.

43. "A Son of Virginia," *Richmond Semi-Weekly Examiner,* especially February 5 and February 15, 1850. Tucker's faithful student William Crump handled the publishing details in Richmond; another former Tucker student was an editorial assistant at the *Examiner.* Crump to NBT, March 14, 1850, T-C. From South Carolina Simms reported that he read Tucker's "bold & eloquent" letters to Floyd and Virginia with "rising pulsation." WGS to NBT, February 11, [1850,] *Letters of William Gilmore Simms,* 3:13-14. Besides the "Son of Virginia" articles, Tucker agitated in favor of the Nashville Convention by writing Virginia Senator James M. Mason and Alabama Senator Jeremiah Clemens—who filled the space the death of Tucker's friend of nullification days, Dixon H. Lewis, had caused. Mason to NBT, March 1, 1850; Clemens to NBT, March 3, 1850, T-C. Tucker and Hammond spoke of republishing *The Partisan Leader* as a tract for the times, and Tucker considered issuing a pamphlet made up of the "Son of Virginia" essays. Neither idea materialized. NBT to JHH, February 21-22 [addendum to the letter of February 8], Hammond Papers, LC; JHH to WGS, March 8, 1850, ibid.; Lucian Minor to NBT, April 6, 1850, T-C.

44. NBT to JHH, March 13 and March 26, 1850, Hammond Papers, LC. On the role Democrats played in the work of compromise, see Holman Hamilton, *Prologue to Conflict: The Crisis and Compromise of 1850* (Lexington: University of Kentucky Press, 1964), pp. 86 ff.

45. NBT to JHH, April 18 and February 21-22 [addendum to letter dated February 8], 1850, Hammond Papers, LC; "A Son of Virginia," *Richmond Semi-Weekly Examiner,* March 19, 1850. See also JHH to NBT, April 28, 1850, T-C.

46. "A Son of Virginia," *Richmond Semi-Weekly Examiner,* February 22, March 8, March 13, and March 19, 1850. NBT to JHH, December 4, 1849, February 2, February 8 [et seq.], March 13, and April 18, 1850, Hammond Papers, LC.

47. NBT to JHH, February 2, March 13, and April 18, 1850, Hammond Papers, LC.

48. Wise to NBT, May 14, 1850, T-C; NBT to JHH, May 7, 1850, Hammond Papers, LC. See also JHH to NBT, May 14, 1850; William Crump to NBT, May 8, 1850; W. H. Ray [chairman of the district convention] to NBT, May 21, 1850; all in T-C; Richmond *Semi-Weekly Examiner,* April

19 and May 10, 1850; Richmond *Enquirer,* May 10, 1850. The General Assembly, instead of making the election of delegates to Nashville part of the regular spring canvass, gave citizens in all congressional districts the option of choosing representatives in semiofficial gatherings. Most Virginia districts made no effort to stage such meetings. Besides the one in Tucker's district between the York and James rivers, caucuses were held in the Southside, along the Rappahanock, and in scattered Shenandoah Valley communities. Of fifteen districts in Virginia, seven held conferences; of the fourteen men selected to attend the Convention in Nashville only six appeared there (see below, note 52). The Virginia legislature refused to reimburse them for travel expenses.

49. NBT to LST, May 28 and 29, 1850, T-C.

50. Ibid.

51. NBT to LST, June 3 and 4, 1850, T-C. Many, perhaps most, Nashville citizens opposed the convention but it seems nonetheless to have been a local festival. St. George Leakin Sioussat, "Tennessee, the Compromise of 1850, and the Nashville Convention," *MVHR* 2 (December 1915): 330.

52. "Miss Kate Conynham" [pseud.], *Nashville Union,* July 24, 1850, quoted in Sioussat, "Tennessee, the Compromise of 1850, and the Nashville Convention," pp. 331–32; JHH to WGS, June 16, 1850, Hammond Papers, LC. NBT to LST, June 3 and 4, 1850, T-C. See also *Letters of William Gilmore Simms,* 3:53n. Joining Tucker in Hammond's quarters were William F. Gordon, a Charlottesville Democrat and former congressman, and William O. Goode, a William and Mary graduate from the Southside who had been speaker of the House of Delegates. Of the other Virginians, Thomas S. Gholson, a pro-Unionist from Goode's district, balanced his colleague's states' rights militancy; Willoughby Newton, a Westmoreland County Whig who had served in Congress before his 1844 defeat, was a moderate in 1850. Tucker's colleague from the first district, R. H. Claybrook, was the Whig party representative from the Tidewater and another moderate. *BDAC,* pp. 1013, 1018, 1470; Shanks, *Secession Movement in Virginia,* pp. 33–34.

53. NBT to JHH, May 7 and January 27, 1850, Hammond Papers, LC. See also NBT to JHH, February 21 and 22 [addendum to letter of February 8], 1850, ibid., and JHH to NBT, February 7, 1850, T-C. Early in the year Tucker had considered a constitutional amendment with even more abrasive propositions. He spoke of a requirement that Congress pass tariff bills only with a two-thirds majority; he mentioned an excise tax on machine-made domestic products that would balance import duties on like articles. Tucker thought about claiming full congressional represenation of Southern slaves, since "the proportion of weight in the *common council* of allied states should be adopted to their capacity to contribute to the common need. . . ." According to another Tucker idea, the federal government in peacetime would distribute a quarter of its revenues among the states. When Southerners could show that Northern states frustrated the return of their fugitive slaves, the Treasury Department would deduct the value of the slaves from the funds due the state where "kidnapping" had occurred and pay the slave owners. NBT to JHH, January 17, 1850, Hammond Papers, LC.

54. NBT to JHH, May 7, 1850, ibid.; NBT to LST, June 3 and 4, June 8 and 13, 1850, T-C. Though surely Hammond and Rhett played important parts in drafting the radical resolutions, one member of the Carolina delegation claimed that he and his colleagues were "determined to take the initiative in no measure—letting it be understood that we were prepared to toe the furthest mark that would be made." Next time, he promised, "we will probably do something, or at least show our hand." David F. Jamison to GFH, September 20, 1850, Holmes Papers, LC.

55. Johnson to Buchanan, June 6, 1850, Buchanan Papers, LC, quoted in Sioussat, "Tennessee, the Compromise of 1850, and the Nashville Convention," pp. 333–34. See also Dallas Tabor Herndon, "The Nashville Convention of 1850," *Transactions of the Alabama Historical Society* 5 (1904):217–18; Cleo Hearon, "Mississippi and the Compromise of 1850," *Publications of the Mississippi Historical Society* 14 (1914):119–20, 123–24.

56. For the membership of the Nashville Convention, see Herndon, "Nashville Convention of 1850," pp. 216–17. The South Carolina delegation, perhaps the most distinguished at Nashville, included Langdon Cheves, Francis W. Pickens, Robert Barnwell Rhett, David Flavel Jamison, and Charleston mayor T. L. Hutchinson.

57. Cave Johnson to James Buchanan, June 6, 1850, Buchanan Papers, LC; "Miss Kate Conynham" [pseud.], *Nashville Union,* July 24, 1850. Both Johnson and Conynham quoted in Sioussat, "Tennessee, the Compromise of 1850, and the Nashville Convention," pp. 331–34. For a brief

reference to "Conynham," see Joseph Holt Ingraham, *The Sunny South; or, The Southerner At Home, Embracing Five Years Experience of a Northern Governess in the Land of the Sugar and the Cotton* (Philadelphia: G. G. Evans, 1860), pp. 3-4. On the confusion of parliamentary maneuvering at Nashville, see the *Richmond Semi-Weekly Examiner*, June 11 and 14, 1850. See also F. Newburg, "The Nashville Convention and Southern Sentiment of 1850," *SAQ* 11 (July 1912):263-65.

58. NBT to LST, June 8 and 13, 1850, T-C.

59. *Resolutions and Address of the Southern Convention: June 8, 1850* (Nashville: Harvey M. Watterson, Printer, 1850); Herndon, "Nashville Convention of 1850," pp. 219-22.

60. *Remarks*, p. 1. For a full citation see chapter 1, note 1. NBT to LST, June 8 and 13, 1850, T-C.

61. *Remarks*, p. 2.

62. Ibid., p. 4.

63. Ibid., pp. 2-3.

64. Ibid., pp. 9-11.

65. Ibid., p. 13.

66. Ibid., p. 12.

67. JHH to WGS, June 27, 1850, *Letters of William Gilmore Simms*, 3:53n.; NBT to LST, June 8 and 13, 1850, T-C.

68. *Richmond Semi-Weekly Examiner*, June 18, 1850.

69. [NBT], "South Carolina: Her Present Attitude and Future Action," a review of the *Proceedings of the meeting of Delegates from the Southern Rights Associations of South-Carolina; held at Charleston, May, 1851, SQR* 20 (October, 1851):274-75; NBT to LST, June 21, 1850, T-C. JHH to WGS, June 16, 1850, Hammond Papers, LC.

70. NBT to LST, July 2, 1850, T-C. See also NBT to LST, June 26, 1850; A. B. O'Bannon, Silverton, to NBT, June 25, 1850; S. W. Trotti, Barnwell C. H., to NBT, June 25, 1850; A. P. Aldrich, Barnwell C. H., to NBT, June 25, 1850; all in T-C; JHH to WGS, July 9 and July 25, 1850, Tucker Papers, Duke; NBT to JHH, March 15, 1851, Hammond Papers, LC.

71. JHH to WGS, July 9 and July 25, 1850 (copies), Tucker Papers, Duke; WGS to JHH, July 15, 1847, *Letters of William Gilmore Simms*, 2:330. JHH to WGS, July 7, 1850, ibid., 3:53n.; WGS to NBT, July 11, 1850, ibid., pp. 52-54.

72. J. M. Daniel to NBT, [c. July 20, 1850]; William W. Crump to NBT, July 24, 1850; Mason to NBT, December 21, 1850; all T-C. *Congressional Globe*, 31st Cong., 1st sess., 1850, vol. 22, Appendix, pt. 2:1389-90. Tucker thought his Nashville speech would leave his sons "a name they shall be proud to uphold. . . ." NBT to LST, September 1, 1850; see also his letter to Lucy, June 8 and 13, 1850, T-C. Friends, relatives, and former students cheered Tucker. W. L. French to NBT, June 21, 1850; J. R. Bryan to NBT, July 13, 1850; JHH to NBT, August 11, 1850; Edmund C. Murdaugh, Union-Town, Ala., to NBT, August 12, 1850; Henry C. Semple, Montgomery, Ala., to NBT, August 26, 1850; R. S. French, Lumberton, N.C., to NBT, September 20, 1850; George M. Dallas, [Philadelphia?], to NBT, October 8, 1850; George F. Harrison to NBT, October 15, 1850; all in T-C. "The Southern Convention," *SQR* 18 (September 1850):217. The belief among Northern vacationers at Newport, Rhode Island, was that Tucker "must be insane." William B. Hodgson to JHH, August 6, 1850 (copy), Tucker Papers, Duke. On Southern "acquiescence," see David F. Jamison to GFH, September 20, December 24, 1850, Holmes Papers, LC.

73. NBT to LST, October 21, 1850, T-C; NBT to JHH, March 15, 1851, Hammond Papers, LC. Tucker discussed the value of county justices of the peace in a lecture draft, Essays, Lectures, and Fragments, box 83, T-C. See also St. George Tucker (nephew of NBT studying law at the University of Virginia) to NBT, July 8, 1850, and JHH to NBT, November 8, 1850, T-C; [NBT,] "Garland's Life of Randolph," *SQR* 20 (July 1851):58n., and "South Carolina: Her Present Attitude and Future Action," pp. 275, 278.

74. For examples of the rising pitch of Tucker's rhetoric, see NBT to JHH, October 9, October 18, November 15, 1850 and March 15, 1851, Hammond Papers, LC, and "South Carolina: Her Present Attitude and Future Action," passim.

75. NBT to JHH, December 18, 1850, Hammond Papers, LC. J. H. Means, Columbia, to NBT, February 18, 1851, T-C.

76. WGS to NBT, March 12 and April 7, 1851, *Letters of William Gilmore Simms*, 3:99, 107; JHH to NBT, February 23, 1851, T-C. See also J. H. Means to NBT, February 18, 1851, T-C.

77. JHH to NBT, February 23, 1851, T-C; NBT to JHH, April 19, 1851, Hammond Papers, LC.

78. NBT to JHH, April 19, 1851, Hammond Papers, LC. "South Carolina: Her Present Attitude and Future Action," pp. 284–88. See also WGS to NBT, March 2, April 7, May 12, and May 13, 1851, T-C; JHH to NBT, May 27 and June 13, 1851, T-C.

79. NBT to JHH, May 25 and March 15, 1851, Hammond Papers, LC; "South Carolina: Her Present Attitude and Future Action," p. 283 and passim. WGS to NBT, March 12 and May 13, 1851, *Letters of William Gilmore Simms,* 3:99, 124.

80. JHH to NBT, May 27, 1851, T-C.

81. NBT to JHH, February 6, 1847; NBT to Thomas Hart Benton, February 6, 1833; Hugh A. Garland, Washington, to NBT, July 13, 1850, all in T-C. "Sawyer's Life of Randolph," *SLM* 10 (April 1844):272. See also J. R. Bryan to NBT, October 8, 1838; G. Lane Corbin to NBT, August 9, 1850, and March 15, 1851; John M. Lea, Nashville, to NBT, October 25, 1850; Elizabeth L. Stuart to NBT, May 5, 1851; all in T-C. WGS to NBT, August 7, [1850,] November 27, [1850,] December 17, [1850,] and February 7, 1851, *Letters of William Gilmore Simms,* 3:57–58, 75–78, 84, 90.

82. "Garland's Life of Randolph," pp. 45–46, 51 ff.

83. Ibid., pp. 41–43 and passim.

84. I have drawn Tucker's final charge to Hammond from his letters dated June 6, June 23, and July 27, 1851, Hammond Papers, LC. See also "South Carolina: Her Present Attitude and Future Action," p. 283.

85. WGS to GFH, August 13, 1851, *Letters of William Gilmore Simms,* 3:140. See also Simms's letter in the Charleston *Evening News,* September 20, 1851, and *Letters of William Gilmore Simms,* 3:140n.

86. [WGS,] "My Ways—Along the Highways and Byways," Charleston *Evening News,* August 18, 1851, CHS.

Afterword

1. Board of Visitors Resolutions, October 14, 1851, T-C. See also *The Virginia Historical Register and Literary Note Book* 4 (October 1851):234–35.

2. Williamsburg *Virginia Gazette,* March 8, 1855, in College Papers, WM. Henry A. Washington, *The Virginia Constitution of 1776: A Discourse Delivered Before the Virginia Historical Society, at Their Annual Meeting, January 17, 1852* (Richmond: MacFarlane and Fergusson, 1852); Williamsburg *Virginia Gazette,* June 22, 1854; WGS to Evert Augustus Duyckinck, July 17 and December 6, 1854, *Letters of William Gilmore Simms,* 3:313–14, 339–46; JHH to WGS, July 24, 1854, ibid., 3:312n. For Simms's note on Tucker, see Evert A. Duyckinck and George L. Duyckinck, eds., *Cyclopaedia of American Literature; Embracing Critical Notices of Authors, and Selections From Their Writings....* 2 vols. (New York: Charles Scribner, 1856), 1:665–66.

3. NBT to JHH, December 27, 1849, Hammond Papers, LC. See also Tucker's references to civil conflict in notebook on law, folder 7, NBT Papers, WM, and his comment on the English civil war in [review of] *"The History of England ... by Thomas Babington Macaulay,"* p. 388. "Your choice is now between submission and secession," Tucker wrote Hammond after the Nashville Convention; "Hereafter between oppression and civil war." (NBT to JHH, September 21, 1850, Hammond Papers, LC.) On the literary weakness of the South, see APU to NBT, February 1, 1841; WT to NBT, March 22, 1841; and Tucker's essay on postrevolutionary changes, North and South, in Essays, Lectures, and Fragments, box 83; all in T-C. The leading study of Northern republican ideology is Eric Foner, *Free Soil, Free Labor, Free Men: The Ideology of the Republican Party Before the Civil War* (New York: Oxford University Press, 1970).

4. NBT to JHH, January 2, 1851, Hammond Papers, LC; Carlyle to NBT, October 31, 1850, T-C. On the Russell and Palmerston ministries and foreign affairs, see Sir Llewellyn Woodward, *The Age of Reform, 1815–1870,* vol. 13 of *The Oxford History of England,* 2d ed., ed. Sir George Clark (Oxford: Oxford University Press, 1967).

5. On the various political settings in which secession occurred, see Michael F. Holt, *The Political Crisis of the 1850s* (forthcoming, John Wiley & Sons).

6. In this discussion of Southern culture, I draw on and somewhat modify Bertram Wyatt-Brown, "The Ideal Typology and Antebellum History: A Testing of a New Approach," *Societas* 5 (winter 1975):1–29. For a recent essay on the patron-client relationship in political life, see J. G. A. Pocock,

"The Classical Theory of Deference," *AHR* 81 (June 1976):516–23; see also John B. Kirby, "Early American Politics—the Search for Ideology: An Historiographical Analysis and Critique of the Concept of 'Deference,' " *JP* 32 (November 1970):808–38. On slavery in the setting of Southern culture, see Morgan, *American Slavery, American Freedom;* Wyatt-Brown, "Ideal Typology and Antebellum History"; and David Bertelson, *The Lazy South* (New York: Oxford University Press, 1967).

7. NBT to JHH, November 15, 1850, Hammond Papers, LC; Wise to NBT, February 22, 1848, T-C; NBT to JHH, March 13, 1847, and May 25, 1851, Hammond Papers, LC. See also NBT to JHH, May 29, 1849, Hammond Papers, LC.

8. WT to NBT, December 20, 1848, T-C; WGS to NBT, July 14, 1851, ibid. See also JHH to WGS, February 13, 1850 and NBT to JHH, October 9, 1850, and January 2, 1851, Hammond Papers, LC; WGS to NBT, July 14, 1851, T-C.

9. NBT to JHH, December 6, 1848, Hammond Papers, LC. NBT to JHH, June 12 and November 20, 1848, ibid.

10. [Review of] *"The History of England . . .* by Thomas Babington Macaulay," p. 399; WGS to NBT, January 30, 1850, T-C; NBT to JHH, May 25, 1851, Hammond Papers, LC.

11. "Gertrude," *SLM* 11:182; NBT, "The Nature and Function of the Commercial Profession," *Waldie's Select Circulating Library* 16 (July 1841):6. See also *The Partisan Leader,* pp. 205, 231; NBT to JHH, March 16, 1848, February 2, 1850, and September 21, 1850, Hammond Papers, LC; Richard E. Crallé to NBT, June 29, 1837, T-C. For a study of antebellum attitudes toward money and banking, see James Rogers Sharp, *The Jacksonians versus the Banks: Politics in the States After the Panic of 1837* (New York: Columbia University Press, 1970).

12. NBT to JHH, April 24, 1847, Hammond Papers, LC. See also NBT to JHH, April 18, 1850, and February 4, 1851, ibid., and Tucker's *Remarks* at the Nashville Convention, pp. 13–14.

13. Davis, *Problem of Slavery in the Age of Revolution;* Catherine Kish Sklar, *Catherine Beecher: A Study in American Domesticity* (New Haven: Yale University Press, 1973); Thomas, "Romantic Reform in America."

14. [NBT,] [Review of] "An Oration, delivered before the two Societies of the South-Carolina College, on the 4th of December, 1849," *SQR* 17 (April 1850):44; Waldie to NBT, November 3, 1840, T-C. See also Waldie to NBT, August 21, 1841, T-C.

15. NBT to JHH, April 24, 1847, Hammond Papers, LC. My thoughts in this paragraph and the next develop from readings in Thomas S. Kuhn, *The Structure of Scientific Revolutions* (Chicago: University of Chicago Press, 1962); Erving Goffman, *Frame Analysis: An Essay on the Organization of Experience* (Cambridge, Mass.: Harvard University Press, 1974); and J. G. A. Pocock, *Politics, Language, and Time: Essays on Political Thought and History,* Studies in Political Theory, Michael Walzer, gen. ed. (New York: Atheneum, 1973). A pathbreaking work exploring the part that available language plays in shaping thought patterns is John B. Carroll, ed., *Language, Thought, and Reality: Selected Writings of Benjamin Lee Whorf* (Cambridge, Mass.: The MIT Press, 1956).

16. "Whoso would be a man," wrote Emerson in a discussion of moral and intellectual independence, "must be a nonconformist." Emerson, "Self-Reliance," *Works,* 2:51–52. The few studies we have of Northern and Southern intellectual settings are mentioned in the Essay on Sources. A suggestive collection of essays, including pieces on Poe's critical theory and his literary ideals as distancing devices, is Lewis P. Simpson, *The Man of Letters in New England and the South: Essays on the History of the Literary Vocation in America* (Baton Rouge: Louisiana State University Press, 1973). See also Tucker's commentary on Tocqueville, 2[d] R[eading, foolscap sheet] 2, folder #324, box 84, T-C.

17. Waldie to NBT, November 3, 1840, T-C; NBT to JHH, April 20–21 [and May 7] and May 25, 1851, Hammond Papers, LC; [review of] *"The History of England . . .* by Thomas Babington Macaulay," pp. 376–77.

18. [Review of] "An Oration, delivered before the two Societies of South-Carolina College," pp. 44–45.

19. NBT to JHH, August 20, 1849, Hammond Papers, LC. See also [review of] *"The History of England . . .* by Thomas Babington Macaulay," pp. 408–9, where Tucker wrote, "We have indeed not yet caught the devil-may-care air of the whiskered Snob . . . nor the tranquil indifference to the comfort and suffering of all but ourselves, which constitute the last refinement of the *polisson poli.*"

20. [Review of] "An Oration, delivered before the two Societies of South-Carolina College," pp. 44–45.

21. For sources helpful in making these observations, see "Note on Psychological References."

22. David Campbell to William Campbell, November 15, 1850, Campbell Papers, Duke. I am indebted to Michael Holt for bringing this reference to my attention.

23. NBT to JHH, March 15, January 2, and May 25, 1851, Hammond Papers, LC. See also above, chapter 8, section VI.

24. J. D. Davidson to William Cabell Rives, February 1, 1861, William Cabell Rives Papers, LC, quoted in Robert G. Gunderson, "William Cabell Rives and the 'Old Gentlemen's Convention,'" *JSH* 22 (November 1956):460.

Essay on Sources

LUCKILY HISTORIANS HAVE escaped subjection to full disclosure rules. No politician could suffer keeping track of campaign contributors as historians would keeping a record of all their bibliographical debts. Thus my accounting, too, is selective rather than comprehensive. Interested persons will find a longer catalog of things used and consulted in my doctoral dissertation, copies of which are available in the Eisenhower Library, Johns Hopkins University, and in the Special Collections department of the Earl Gregg Swem Library, College of William and Mary. I have listed here the bulk of the published primary sources I have used, most of the works Tucker himself wrote, and those secondary references—by subject category—which I either dropped from the notes for reasons of space or include here again as worthy of special mention.

This study is based largely on manuscript collections at several Southern academic libraries and the Library of Congress. My richest source was of course the Tucker-Coleman Collection at the Swem Library, William and Mary, which contains several thousand pieces of Tucker family correspondence, a number of scrapbooks and notebooks, several boxes of lectures and essays, legal papers, and the remains of the family library. Altogether it comprises one of the best single collections we have pertaining to late-eighteenth- and early-nineteenth-century Virginia society and intellectual life. Also at William and Mary are two boxes of Nathaniel Beverley Tucker Papers, deposited earlier than the Tucker-Coleman papers and cataloged separately; in the William and Mary College Papers there is an assortment of items relating to college academic affairs in the antebellum period. The lamentably small number of Thomas R. Dew Papers that survive are also in the Swem Library, as are a few George Frederick Holmes pieces, about a thousand Thomas Ritchie items—covering mostly family, rather than political, matters—and the papers of Tucker's fellow faculty members, John Millington and Adam Empie. The Harris Whitaker bound volume of notes on political science and government at William and Mary is one of the all-too-rare examples of student lesson books that we have from the antebellum period. Finally, the college archivist, whose vaults are also in the Swem Library, is custodian of the Faculty Minutes that were kept in the nineteenth century; permission of the current president is necessary to use these volumes. Elsewhere in Williamsburg, the holdings of Colonial Williamsburg, Inc., include a small number of St. George Tucker letters.

My travels while researching the dissertation included pleasant trips to two other Virginia cities. The Archives Division of the Virginia State Library in Richmond, besides having copies or originals of Bryan and Tazewell family papers, makes available a complete set of General Assembly journals, is the repository for the highly interesting petitions citizens made to the governors and assemblies of the antebellum years, and contains in its vast storage bays a wealth of state records that call for methodical analysis. Of the considerable holdings of the Virginia Historical Society, also in Richmond, most valuable to me were the Bryan family scrapbook, the Elizabeth Coalter Bryan diary with its biographical sketch of John Coalter, and the Grinnan Family Papers. But in addition, the society has a large number of John Randolph of Roanoke letters and Edmund Ruffin papers; a few pieces in the Preston Family Papers relate to the Dardenne community that Tucker tried to establish in Missouri. The Thomas B. Montague notebook contains jottings he took in Dew's world-history classes at William and Mary in 1838. In Charlottesville the manuscripts division, Alderman Library, University of Virginia, includes in its holdings manuscripts that are among the richest available to students of the antebellum South. For my purposes the Bryan Papers (acquisition no. 3400), containing Tucker's intimate letters to Bet Coalter (Bryan) and his manuscript sermons, were the most immediately helpful. Also important were the Grinnan (2118) and the Cabell papers (38-111) for their family correspondence and references to professional and political life. The Rawlings Family Papers (6436) include a notebook James Rawlings kept as a Tucker law student in 1839-40. One should also see the important Alderman holdings of John Randolph letters (3321 and others) and, on legal training in the antebellum south, the John B. Minor Papers (3114 and 5657); on the *Southern Literary Messenger,* one should look at the disappointingly few papers surviving of Thomas Willis White (3435) and John Reuben Thompson (38-705 and others), its editors, and at the Virginia collection of Edgar Allan Poe (6012 and others) letters.

The major North Carolina repositories contain material exceedingly valuable to a researcher of antebellum Southern history. At the Perkins Library, Duke University, there are collected "Lawyers" and "Professors" papers that provide highly interesting mosaics of law practice and academic life in the nineteenth century. I found the George Frederick Holmes Letterbook useful and the fifty items of the Thomas Willis White manuscripts suggestive because so little remains to tell us how White or his successors conducted the *Messenger,* sought subscribers and contributors, or handled controversy. The David Campbell Papers at Duke is a full collection for antebellum Virginia political and social life; though it is perhaps most interesting on the legal profession, it contains several Tucker letters to Hugh Lawson White—twenty-seven of whose own letters Duke holds as well. In addition, the Perkins

Library has typed copies of the Tucker letters in the Hammond Papers, Library of Congress, and also copies of fifty William Gilmore Simms pieces. The Southern Historical Collection at the nearby University of North Carolina, Chapel Hill, includes two boxes of Tucker Family Papers (2605), and while most of that material deals with Henry St. George Tucker's son John Randolph Tucker—law professor at Washington and Lee after the Civil War— it also yielded several pieces of more immediate interest to me. The Duff Green Papers (993), also available on microfilm, contain a wealth of information about antebellum Southern politics—both electoral and literary; the John Overton Papers (571) and the James Henry Hammond Papers (304) include scattered material of value.

Among the Library of Congress holdings helpful to me in writing this book, the Hammond Papers were cited the most often in the notes. Though Tucker's correspondence with Hammond was limited almost entirely to the years 1848–51, the Hammond collection is invaluable for the picture it gives of South Carolina political and literary life—especially since William Gilmore Simms's incoming letters were largely destroyed in the Civil War. The Edmund Ruffin, Duff Green, and George Frederick Holmes papers at the Library of Congress reveal much about the effort to build a Southern consciousness in the 1830s and 40s; the John Randolph and Thomas Ritchie manuscripts contained only a few letters usable in this biography but helped to set the political climate in Tucker's Virginia.

After these major manuscript holdings, my most important primary sources were Tucker's own writings. Below is a chronological listing of the Tucker publications that were material to this study. Omitted are a few minor poems and book reviews of little relevance or doubtful authorship. For what seems to be a full inventory of Tucker's published works, see the late Percy Winfield Turrentine's "The Life and Works of Nathaniel Beverley Tucker" (Ph.D. dissertation in American Literature, 3 vols., Harvard University, 1952).

[Tucker, Nathaniel Beverley.] Letters signed "Hampden." *Missouri Gazette & Public Advertiser* (Saint Louis), April 22, May 5, and June 16, 1819.
[——.] Letters of "A Friend to State Rights." *Western Monitor* (Fayette, Missouri), August 25, September 15, October 13, November 3 and 24, and December 1, 1830.
——. "To the People of Missouri." *Jeffersonian Republican . . . Extra* (Jefferson City, Missouri), March 24, 1832.
——. "To the People of Missouri." Saint Louis *Free Press*, January 10, 1833. Reprinted in *Richmond Whig and Public Advertiser*, February 8, 1833.
——. "Communicated . . . extract from a Speech Delivered on the 24th of April, last, at St. Louis, Missouri, by Beverley Tucker, Esq.," Richmond *Enquirer*, February 7, 1833.
[——.] "The Charlotte Resolutions." Richmond *Enquirer*, February 9, 1833.
[——.] Letter signed "A Friend of State Rights." Richmond *Enquirer*, February 19, 1833.

[———.] Letter signed "A Friend of State Rights." *Richmond Whig and Public Adver-tiser*, February 21, 1833.

[———.] Letter signed "A Friend to Andrew Jackson, Esq." *United States Telegraph* (Washington, D.C.), February 23, 1833.

[———.] Letter signed "A Friend to State Rights, because a Friend of Union." *United States Telegraph* (Washington, D.C.), March 6, 7, 12, 13, and 14, 1833.

[———.] Letter signed "A Friend to State Rights, because a Friend of Union." Rich-mond *Enquirer*, April 5, 1833.

———. *A Lecture on the Study of the Law; Being an Introduction to a Course of Lec-tures on That Subject in the College of William and Mary*. Richmond: Printed by T. W. White, 1834. Reprinted in *SLM* 1 (December 1834):145-54.

[———.] "Western Scenery. Extract of a Letter from a Western Traveller." *SLM* 1 (December 1834):139.

[———.] "Note to Blackstone's Commentaries, Vol. I. Page 423. Being the Substance of Remarks on the Subject of Domestic Slavery, delivered to the Law Class of William and Mary College, December 2d, 1834." *SLM* 1 (January 1835):227-231.

[———.] "Original Literary Notices." [Review of John Quincy Adams, *An Oration on the Life and Character of Gilbert Motier de Lafayette*, . . . and Edward Everett, *Eulogy on La Fayette, delivered in Fanueil Hall, at the request of the Young Men of Boston, September 6, 1834*. . . .] *SLM* 1 (February 1835):307-12.

[———.] [Review of Anna Brownell (Murphy) Jameson,] "The Beauties of the Court of Charles the Second. . . ." *SLM* 1 (February 1835):312-14.

[———.] "The Romance of Real Life." *SLM* 1 (February 1835):271-72.

[———.] "Extract From Reminiscences of a Western Traveller." *SLM* 1 (March 1835): 336-40.

[———.] "From the Author of the 'Note to Blackstone's Commentaries.'" *SLM* 1 (March 1835):336-40.

[———.] "Extract of a Letter from the Reviewer of Messrs. Adams' and Everett's Ora-tions." *SLM* 1 (March 1835):388.

[———.] "Christian Education." *SLM* 1 (April 1835):432-35.

[———.] "Literary Notices." [Review of Alessandro Manzoni, *I Promessi Sposi, or the Betrothed Lovers*. . . .] *SLM* 1 (May 1835):520-22.

[———.] [Review of vol. 1, George Bancroft,] "A History of the United States. . . ." *SLM* 1 (June 1835):587-91.

[———.] [Review of vols. 2-6, Jared Sparks, ed.,] "The Writings of George Washington. . . ." *SLM* 1 (June 1835):591-94.

———. "Professor Beverley Tucker's Valedictory Address to his Class." *SLM* 1 (July 1835): 597-602.

[———.] "Charlot Tayon." *SLM* 2 (January 1836):71-74.

[———.] "Slavery." [Review of James Kirke Paulding, *Slavery in the United States*, and (William Drayton,) *The South Vindicated from the Treason and Fanaticism of the Northern Abolitionists*.] *SLM* 2 (April 1836):336-39.

[———.] *George Balcombe. A Novel*. 2 vols. New York: Harper and Brothers, 1836.

[———.] *The Partisan Leader: A Tale of the Future*. "By Edward William Sidney." 2 vols. "Printed for the Publishers, by James Caxton, 1856." [Washington: Duff Green, 1836.]

[———.] "Bulwer's New Play." [Review of Edward Bulwer, *The Duchess de la Valliere: A Play in Five Acts*. . . .] *SLM* 3 (January 1837):90-95.

———. "A Lecture on Government." *SLM* 3 (April 1837):209-16. Reprinted in *Lectures*, pp. 30-51.

[———.] [Review of Robert Montgomery Bird,] "Nick of the Woods, Or the Jibbenainosay. A Tale of Kentucky. . . ." *SLM* 3 (April 1837):254-57.

[——.] "To Our Readers." [Reply to the] "Review of President Dew's Address." *SLM* 3 (April 1837):268-70.

[——.] "Tulrumble and Oliver Twist." [Review of (Charles Dickens,) *The Public Life of Mr. Tulrumble, once Mayor of Mudfrog . . . and Oliver Twist, or the Parish Boy's Progress. . . .*] *SLM* 3 (May 1837):323-25.

[——.] [Review of Benjamin D'Israeli,] "Henrietta Temple: A Love Story. . . ." *SLM* 3 (May 1837):325-31.

[——.] [Review of Charles Dickens,] "The Pickwick Papers." *SLM* 3 (September 1837): 525-32.

[——.] "Washington's Writings." [Review of vols. 11 and 12, Jared Sparks, ed., *The Writings of George Washington. . . .*] *SLM* 4 (May 1838):328-35.

[——.] Letters to Henry Clay signed "A Friend of State Rights." *Richmond Whig and Public Advertiser*, June 12, 15, 19, 22, 26, and 29, and July 6, 20, 24, 27, and 31, 1838.

——. *A Discourse on the Genius of the Federative System of the United States*. Richmond: Printed by T. W. White, 1839. Earlier published in the *SLM* 4 (December 1838):761-69. Reprinted in *Lectures*, pp. 350-72.

——. "A Lecture, Delivered to the Law Class of William and Mary College, June 19, 1839, being the last of a course of Lectures on the Philosophy of Government and Constitutional Law." Richmond *Enquirer*, July 2, 1839. Reprinted in *SLM* 5 (September 1839): 587-92, and in *Lectures*, pp. 448-64.

——. "Political Science; A Discourse on the Questions, 'What is the seat of sovereignty in the United States, and what the relation of the People of those States to the Federal and State Governments respectively,' read before the Petersburg Lyceum on the 15th of May, 1839." *SLM* 5 (August 1839):559-66. Reprinted in *Lectures*, pp. 372-96.

[——.] Letters to Henry Clay signed "A Friend of State Rights." *Richmond Whig and Public Advertiser*, February 7 and 10, 1840.

——. *A Discourse on the Importance of the Study of Political Science, as a Branch of Academic Education in the United States*. Richmond: Printed by Peter D. Bernard, 1840. Reprinted in *Lectures*, pp. 1-30.

[——.] "Liberal and Strict Construction of the Federal Constitution." *The Southern Magazine and Monthly Review* 1 (February 1841): 129-47. Reprinted in *Lectures*, pp. 415-48.

——. "The Nature and Function of the Commercial Profession." *Waldie's Select Circulating Library* (Printed and Published by A. Waldie and Company, Philadelphia) 16 (July 1841):1-4. Reprinted in *Lectures*, pp. 396-415.

[——.] Letters to John Tyler signed "A States Rights Man." Richmond *Enquirer*, August 10, 13, 17, 24, 27, and 31, and September 3, 7, and 10, 1841.

——. *A Discourse on the Dangers That Threaten the Free Institutions of the United States, Being an Address to the Literary Societies of Hampden Sidney College, Virginia, Read on the 22nd of September, 1841, at the Request of the Philanthropic Society of That College*. Richmond: John B. Martin and Company, Printers, 1841.

——. "Temperance. An Address read before the Temperance Society of William & Mary College. . . ." *SLM* 8 (July 1842):439-44.

——. *An Address Delivered Before the Society of the Alumni of William and Mary College, Upon the 5th of July, 1842*. Richmond: Printed by P. D. Bernard, 1842.

[——.] "Sawyer's Life of Randolph." *SLM* 10 (April 1844):262.

[——.] "An Essay on the Moral and Political Effect of the Relation between the Caucasian Master and the African Slave." *SLM* 10 (June 1844):329-39 and (August 1844):470-80. Reprinted in *Lectures*, pp. 290-350.

[——.] "Gertrude; An Original Novel." *SLM* 10 (September 1844):513-19, (November 1844):641-47, and (December 1844):705-13; 11 (March 1845):178-86, (April 1845):

219–30, (May 1845):257–65, (June 1845):377–82, (July 1845):434–41, (November 1845):690–94, and (December 1845):705–12.

——. *A Series of Lectures on the Science of Government, Intended to Prepare the Student for the Study of the Constitution of the United States.* Philadelphia: Carey and Hart, 1845.

——. *The Principles of Pleading.* Boston: Charles C. Little and James Brown, 1846.

——. "Judge Tucker's Address." *SLM* 13 (September 1847):568–70.

[——.] [Review of] "*The History of England, from the accession of James II;* by Thomas Babington Macaulay." *SQR* 15 (July 1849): 374–410.

[——.] "The Present State of Europe." *SQR* 16 (January 1850): 277–323.

[——.] Letters signed "A Son of Virginia." *Richmond Semi-Weekly Examiner,* January 18, February 1, 5, 15, and 22, March 8, 12, 19, and 26, 1850.

[——.] [Review of James Henry Hammond.] "An Oration, delivered before the two Societies of the South-Carolina College, on the 4th of December, 1849." *SQR* 17 (April 1850):37–48.

——. *Southern Convention. Remarks of the Hon. Beverley Tucker of Virginia.* [Richmond:] Colin, Baptist and Nowlan [1850].

[——.] [Review of] "Garland's Life of Randolph." *SQR* 20 (July 1851):41–61.

[——.] "South Carolina: Her Present Attitude and Future Action." *SQR* 20 (October 1851):273–98.

There is no adequate history of Virginia in the antebellum period, and at one level this book has aimed to suggest how such a study might be written. When it is, it will build on Robert McColley's valuable *Slavery and Jeffersonian Virginia* (Urbana: University of Illinois Press, 1973), and Joseph Clark Robert's sketchy *The Road From Monticello: A Study of the Virginia Slavery Debate of 1832,* Historical Papers of the Trinity College Historical Society, series 24 (Durham, N.C.: Duke University Press, 1941), and on Patricia Hicken's suggestive "'Situation Ethics' and Antislavery Attitudes in Virginia Churches," in *America, The Middle Period: Essays in Honor of Bernard Mayo,* ed. John B. Boles (Charlottesville: University Press of Virginia, 1974), pp. 188–215. In addition, there are several standard works on antebellum Virginia: the outdated but still useful chronicle of intra-state conflict, Charles Henry Ambler, *Sectionalism in Virginia from 1776 to 1861* (Chicago: University of Chicago Press, 1910), and James Clyde MacGregor's account of east-west tension in the state, *The Disruption of Virginia* (New York: The Macmillan Company, 1922). Henry Harrison Simms, *The Rise of the Whigs in Virginia, 1824–1840* (Richmond: The William Byrd Press, 1929), offers an equally unpretentious rendering of party strife. Henry T. Shanks, *The Secession Movement in Virginia, 1847–1861* (Richmond: Garrett and Massie Publishers, 1934), is a revisionist treatment of leadership failure.

Except for the Virginia section in Richard P. McCormick's *The Second American Party System: Party Formation in the Jacksonian Era* (Chapel Hill: University of North Carolina Press, 1966), recent accounts of antebellum Virginia public life have in common the attempt to tie together growing social hetereogenity and political change. Norman K. Risjord, "The Virginia Federalists" (*JSH* 33 [November 1967]:486-517), puts to rest notions of political consensus in the state during the "Jeffersonian" years; Joseph H. Harrison, Jr., "Oligarchs and Democrats: The Richmond Junto" (*VMHB* 78 [January 1970]:148-98), offers a lively account of that pseudoorganization and the limits of its power; James Roger Sharp, *The Jacksonians versus the Banks: Politics in the States After the Panic of 1837* (New York: Columbia University Press, 1970), has a solid section on the Virginia Democracy; J. R. Pole's "Representation and Authority in Virginia in the Early Nineteenth Century" (*JSH* 24 [February 1958]:16-50) and the sections on Virginia in his *Political Representation in England and the Origins of the American Republic* (London: St. Martins Press, 1966) remain authoritative on the politics of suffrage reform and legislature reapportionment. Craig Simpson, "Political Compromise and the Protection of Slavery: Henry A. Wise and the Virginia Constitutional Convention of 1850-1851" (*VMHB* 83 [October 1975]:387-405), argues that Wise was no liberal and the new constitution no defeat for the pro-slavery east. Two dissertations supplement our knowledge of the pre–Civil War Virginia constitutional conventions: Robert P. Sutton, "The Virginia Constitutional Convention of 1829-30: A Profile Analysis of Late Jeffersonian Virginia" (Ph.D. dissertation, University of Virginia, 1967), and Francis Pendleton Gaines, Jr., "The Virginia Constitutional Convention of 1850-51: A Study in Sectionalism" (Ph.D. dissertation, University of Virginia, 1950). One should also see Sutton's "Sectionalism and Social Structure: A Case Study of Jeffersonian Democracy" (*VMHB* 80 [January 1972]:70-84); J. Stephen Knight, Jr., "Discontent, Disunity, and Dissent in the Antebellum South: Virginia as a Test Case, 1844-1846" (*VMHB* 81 [October 1973]:437-56); and Daniel Porter Jordan, Jr., "Virginia Congressmen, 1801-1825" (Ph.D. dissertation, University of Virginia, 1970), a survey of sectionalism, ideology, and leadership change containing evidence that law practice was widely frustrating in these years as increasing numbers of men tried to make it a career. On that same point, Anthony F. Upton, "The Road to Power in Virginia in the early Nineteenth Century" (*VMHB* 62 [July 1954]:259-80), uses the Campbell Family Papers at Duke to argue the decline of planting and the rise of the law as the antebellum "highroad" to distinction. All these conventional studies suggest that any comprehensive study of antebellum Virginia will have to devise a scheme for the scaling of measurable things, and perhaps to measure more than we have tried until now. Standing alone in the literature on early republican Virginia, and tantalizing, is Van Beck Hall's interim report on demographic, denominational, economic, and voting correlations, "A Quantitative Approach to the Social, Economic, and Political Structure of Virginia, 1790-1810," a paper read at the 1969 meeting of the Southern Historical Association.

    Studies in antebellum Virginia economic history likewise continue traditional and incomplete. Several interesting essays explore the concepts of political economy that underwrote antebellum development. Carter Goodrich, "The Virginia System of Mixed Enterprise: A Study of State Planning of Internal Improvements" (*PSQ* 64 [September 1949]:355-87), examines the effort—largely successful—to raise private monies for public works; Wiley E. Hodges, in "The Theoretical Basis for Anti-Governmentalism in Virginia, 1789-1836" (*JP* 9 [August 1947]:325-54) and "Pro-Governmentalism in Virginia, 1789-1836: A Pragmatic Pattern in the Political Heritage" (*JP* 25 [May 1963]:333-60), sets out to do for Virginia what Louis Hartz has done for Pennsylvania and Oscar and Mary Handlin for Massachusetts. The sad narrative of agricultural decline in late-eighteenth- and early-nineteenth-century Virginia was the subject of Avery's Craven's now classic monograph, *Soil Exhaustion as a Factor in the Agricultural History of Virginia and Maryland, 1606-1860* (University of Illinois Studies in the Social Sciences, vol. 12, no. 1 [Urbana: University of Illinois Press, 1926]—a study that should be compared to Lewis C. Gray's *History of Agriculture in the Southern States to 1860* (2 vols. [Washington: Carnegie Institution, 1933]) and Kathleen Bruce's "Virginia Agricultural Decline to 1860: A Fallacy" (*AgHist* 6 [January 1932]:3-13). See also W. A. Low, "The Farmer in Post-Revolutionary Virginia, 1783-1789" (*AgHist* 25 [July 1951]:122-27); Charles W. Turner, "Virginia Agricultural Reform, 1815-1860" (*AgHist* 26 [July 1952]:80-89); and Charles D. Lowrey, "James Barbour: Progressive Farmer in Antebellum Virginia" (in *America, The Middle Period: Essays in Honor of Bernard Mayo,* ed. John B. Boles), pp. 168-87.

Though the troubles that beset antebellum Virginia planters have provided a central theme to studies of the state economy, historians have not overlooked the important transportation and manufacturing developments of those years. Kathleen Bruce, *Virginia Iron Manufacturers in the Slave Era* (New York: The Century Company, 1930), is an early study of slave labor in an industrial setting and of economic growth in the Richmond-Petersburg area; Thomas S. Berry, "The Rise of Flour Milling in Richmond" (*VMHB* 78 [October 1970]:387-408), discusses another highly important enterprise on the falls on the James River. Charles W. Turner, "The Early Railroad Movement in Virginia" (*VMHB* 55 [October 1947]:350-71), and Philip Morison Rice, "Internal Improvements in Virginia, 1775-1860" (Ph.D. dissertation, University of North Carolina, 1949), are among the early studies of transportation improvements. George T. Starnes, *Sixty Years of Branch Banking in Virginia* (New York: The Macmillan Company, 1931), and Peter C. Stewart, "Railroads and Urban Rivalries in Antebellum Eastern Virginia" (*VMHB* 81 [January 1973]:3-22), emphasize the internal tensions that legislative and corporate decisions produced. Charles B. Dew, "Disciplining Iron Workers in the Antebellum South: Coercion, Conciliation, Accommodation" (*AHR* 79 [April 1974]:393-418), examines a Rockbridge County attempt to reconcile slave labor with industrial growth.

Chapter five treats two subjects worthy of bibliographical comment. Legal training in antebellum America, for one, has not received the attention it deserves and was one of the threads that led me to Tucker in the first place. It is an interesting question—still unsettled—whether differing approaches to legal training North and South, academic schooling and apprenticeship method, affected one's theoretical perspective on the Constitution or one's attitude toward constitutional theory. In an age when political leaders necessarily approached so many questions in terms of theory, the question deserves asking. Most studies of legal training take the broad sweep through time, make little attempt to compare sectional differences, or look at only one institution. Charles F. Warren's *History of the Harvard Law School and of Legal Conditions in America* (3 vols. [New York: Lewis Publishing Company, 1908]) pays most attention to the late nineteenth century. The most ambitious survey of American legal education, and still the most nearly complete, is Alfred Zantzinger Reed, *Training for the Public Profession of the Law: Historical Development and Principal Contemporary Problems of Legal Education in the United States with Some Account of Conditions in England and Canada* (Bulletin No. 15 of the Carnegie Foundation for the Advancement of Teaching [Boston: D. P. Updike and the Merrymount Press, 1921]). Anton-Hermann Chroust, *The Rise of the Legal Profession in America* (2 vols. [Norman: University of Oklahoma Press, 1965]) adds some color but few changes to the framework Reed provides; Robert Steven, "Two Cheers for 1870: The American Law School" (in *Perspectives in American History,* ed. Donald Fleming and Bernard Bailyn [Harvard University: The Charles Warren Center for Studies in American History, 1967-], vol. 5, *Law in American History* [1971]), depends heavily on Reed and moves quickly over the pre–Civil War period. A superb examination of legal training in the context of late-eighteenth- and early-nineteenth-century social change is Gerald W. Gawalt, "Massachusetts Legal Education in Transition, 1766–1840" (*AmJLH* 17 [January 1973]:27–50). Skirting this subject, and useful as references, are Anna Haddow, *Political Science in American Colleges and Universities, 1636–1900* (ed. with an introduction and concluding chapter by William Anderson [New York: D. Appleton-Century Company, (1939)]), and Elizabeth Kelley Bauer, *Commentaries on the Constitution, 1790–1860* (New York: Columbia University Press, 1952).

Second, historians long have puzzled over the relationship between the legal profession and antebellum society. Space is too short here for a full discussion of the controversy, but most students agree at least that the English common law was the subject of considerable hostility in post-revolutionary America, and that the bar and judiciary were subject to the same pressures. Julius S. Waterman, "Thomas Jefferson and Blackstone's Commentaries" (27 *Illinois Law Review* 629 [1933]), discusses suspicion of residual English influence after independence; W. Raymond Blackard,

"The Demoralization of the Legal Profession in Nineteenth Century America" (16 *Tennessee Law Review* 314 [1940]), brings the standard argument through the Jacksonian period. Chroust's *Rise of the Legal Profession in America* documents this hostility further, describing state by state how legislators sought to make the judiciary elective and to widen access to the practice of law. A more sophisticated study in ideas and society, though unfinished and published posthumously, is Perry Miller, *The Life of the Mind in America: From the Revolution to the Civil War* (New York: Harcourt, Brace & World, 1965). Miller portrays a legal profession on the defensive trying—both by means of frank obfuscation and serious intellectual labor—to preserve its social position while making the law demonstrably "American" and responsive as necessary. In the decade and more since Miller's book appeared, the drift of scholarship has been to modify and clarify this prevailing view. Lawrence M. Friedman, first in "Heart Against Head: Perry Miller and the Legal Mind" (77 *Yale Law Journal* 1244 [1968]) and more recently in *A History of American Law* (New York: Simon and Schuster, 1973), argues that the bar was itself divided on issues of "openness" and concerned itself with theoretical questions that Miller misunderstood; David C. Calhoun, *Professional Lives in America: Structure and Aspiration, 1750–1850* (Cambridge, Mass.: Harvard University Press, 1965), takes the case-study approach, looking at the professional impact of circuit riding on the Tennessee frontier. Richard E. Ellis, *The Jeffersonian Crisis: Courts and Politics in the Young Republic* (New York: Oxford University Press, 1971), fits antibar and antijudiciary sentiment into the left wing of the Jeffersonian coalition and sees attitudes towards the courts as the key to political differences in Congress during these years and in Kentucky, Pennsylvania, and Massachusetts. The most comprehensive treatment of the profession and its setting, however, is Maxwell Bloomfield's collection of essays, previewed in several published articles, *American Lawyers in a Changing Society, 1776–1876* (Cambridge, Mass.: Harvard University Press, 1976). Among other things, Bloomfield shows how lawyers tried to redress their public image in an egalitarian society and even, in some parts of the profession, began specializing to the degree that politics came to be viewed as a separate and distinct career pattern.

Tucker's story provides a detailed picture of how republican political concepts, so critical to an understanding of the revolutionary debate in America, fared in the nineteenth century. The pathbreaking monographical treatment of those principles in the Revolution is Bernard Bailyn, *The Ideological Origins of the American Revolution* (Cambridge, Mass.: Harvard University Press, 1967), though perhaps the most succinct introduction is part one of Gordon Wood's *The Creation of the American Republic, 1776–1787* (Chapel Hill: University of North Carolina Press, 1969), in which Wood also analyzes changes revolutionary and postrevolutionary Americans made in that body of thought. Also valuable to my study were G. H. Guttridge, *English Whiggism and the American Revolution* (Berkeley and Los Angeles: University of California Press, 1966); James T. Boulton, *Arbitrary Power: An Eighteenth Century Obsession* (Nottingham, England: University of Nottingham, 1967); and Caroline Robbins, *The Eighteenth Century Commonwealthman: Studies in the Transmission, Development, and Circumstances of English Liberal Thought from the Restoration of Charles II until the War with the Thirteen Colonies* (Cambridge, Mass.: Harvard University Press, 1959). See also Robbins, comp., *Two English Republican Tracts* (London: Cambridge University Press, 1969). But the student of classical republican thought whose work is most exciting in its effort to explore the relationship between society and ideas is J. G. A. Pocock; see especially his "Virtue and Commerce in the Eighteenth Century," *Journal of Interdisciplinary History* 3 (Summer 1972):119-34; *Politics, Language, and Time: Essays in Political Thought and History,* in Studies in Political Theory, Michael Walzer, gen. ed. (New York: Atheneum, 1973); and *The Machiavellian Moment: Florentine Political Thought and the Atlantic Republican Tradition* (Princeton: Princeton University Press, 1975). On early-nineteenth-century changes that many republican Americans could easily have viewed as dangerous, see Michael Wallace, "Changing Concepts of Party in the United States: New York, 1815-1828" (*AHR* 74 [December 1968]:453-91); Ronald Formisano, "Political Character, Antipartyism and the Second American Party System" (*AmQ* 21 [winter 1969]: 683-709); and Formisano, "Deferential-Participant Politics: The Early Republic's Political Culture, 1789-1840" (*American Political Science Review* 68 [June 1974]:473-87). For the relationship that developed in some quarters between republicanism and the scriptural tradition, see William Gribbin, "Republicanism, Reform, and the Sense of Sin in Ante Bellum America" (*Cithara* 14 [December 1974]:25-41). A useful historiographical survey of republicanism in the writing of American history since the work of Robbins and Bailyn is Robert E. Shalhope, "Toward a Republican Synthesis: The Emergence of an Understanding of Republicanism in American Historiography" (*WMQ* 29 [January 1972]:49-80).

Republicanism shaped Tucker's perceptions of political events; his ways of thinking developed from broader intellectual themes of common sense and romanticism. Peter Gay, *The Enlightenment: An Interpretation* (2 vols. [New York: Alfred A. Knopf, 1967-69]), examines the tradition out of which Tucker's father grew. A recent survey, arguing for the peculiar form that movement took in this country, is Henry F. May, *The Enlightenment in America* (New York: Oxford University Press, 1976); Donald H. Meyer, *The Democratic Enlightenment* (New York: Capricorn Books, 1976) likewise describes the distinctive pattern of the Enlightenment in America, where theory could be put into practice and where the active public role of its adherents dissuaded them from pursuing the radical possibilities of that theory. Richard Gummere, *The American Colonial Mind and the Classical Tradition: Essays in Comparative Culture* (Cambridge, Mass.: Harvard University Press, 1963), offers a suggestive view of the different impressions classicism made, North and South, as does Harvey Wish, "Aristotle, Plato, and the Mason-Dixon Line," (*JHI* 10 [April 1949]:254-66). Little scholarship focuses on the shift from enlightened to romantic modes of thought in America, but one might refer to H.V.S. Ogden, "The State of Nature and the Decline of Lockean Political Theory in England" (*AHR* 46 [October 1940]:31-44); Osborn Earle, "The Reputation and Influence of William Godwin in America" (Ph.D. dissertation, Harvard University, 1938); Howard Mumford Jones, "The Influence of European Ideas in Nineteenth-Century America" (*American Literature* 7 [November 1935]:241-73); and Herbert W. Schneider, "A Century of Romantic Imagination in America" (*Philosophical Review* 56 [July 1947]:351-56). For a monumental study of nineteenth-century ideas quite apart from their social setting, see Maurice Mandelbaum, *History, Man, and Reason: A Study in Nineteenth-Century Thought* (Baltimore: The Johns Hopkins University Press, 1971); on the aesthetic differences between the ages of St. George Tucker and Beverley Tucker, and a comparison with contemporary sensibility, see Jacques Barzun, *Classic, Romantic, and Modern* (Boston: Little, Brown and Company, 1961). Demonstrating the persistence of Scottish common-sense philosophy in American moral studies and aesthetics, are Daniel Walker Howe, *The Unitarian Conscience: Harvard Moral Philosophy, 1805-1861* (Cambridge, Mass.: Harvard University Press, 1970) and William Charvat, *The Origins of American Critical Thought, 1810-1835* (Philadelphia: University of Pennsylvania Press, 1936).

What we might call the intellectual culture of antebellum America—the setting and tone of scholarly and literary life—has been the subject of only a few studies. F. O. Matthiessen, *American Renaissance: Art and Expression in the Age of Emerson and Whitman* (New York: Oxford University Press, 1941) provides an enduring analysis of literary purpose in the pre-Civil War years and of the debts leading writers owed one another; Perry Miller, *The Raven and the Whale: The War of Words and Wits in the Era of Poe and Melville* (New York: Harcourt, Brace and Company, 1956), treats the quality of intellectual-literary life in antebellum New York City. Though the literati in New England and especially New York did offer one another sustenance, both social and intellectual, Matthiessen and Miller demonstrate clearly a vitality among Northerners that few Southerners could experience or take to their work. The reasons for this qualitative difference have not been fully examined. The chapter outlines of Perry Miller's *Life of the Mind in America* suggests how critical to his book the move from rational to romantic modes of thought would have been, but give little hint of an intention to look closely at sectional differences. The most recent general history of American intellectual life in this period, Rush Welter, *The Mind of America, 1820–1860* (New York: Columbia University Press, 1975), for the most part neglects North-South variations; instead Welter surveys popular expression in terms of "Democratic" and "Whig" categories. An important brief commentary on antinomianism among antebellum Americans, with the observation that there was "little humility or reflection on either side of the Potomac" (p. 176), is Bertram Wyatt-Brown, "Stanley Elkins' *Slavery*: The Antislavery Interpretation Reexamined" (*AmQ* 25 [May 1973]: 154–76).

Studies of Southern intellectual life in this period suffer their own limitations. At first glance the ground is admittedly barren. Thus historians frequently recount the suppression of dissent in that society, the "foreignness" of its ideas, and the simplicity of motive underlying the thinking and writing that antebellum Southerners did. Long ago Arthur M. Schlesinger, Sr., passed off the states' rights argument as a "fetish," and little work historians have done since his *New Viewpoints in American History* (New York: The Macmillan Company, 1929) has challenged his assumption that Southern states' rights theory was a stratagem, a ruse that grew out of sectional conflict. Jesse Carpenter, *The South as a Sectional Minority, 1789–1861: A Study in Political Thought* (New York: New York University Press, 1930) largely shared that assumption. Understandably it is easiest to look at constitutional development in light of what has triumphed. For example Bernard Schwartz, *The Reins of Power: A Constitutional History of the United States,* American Century Series (New York: Hill & Wang, 1963), sees the "Marshall conception of the Constitution" (Schwartz gives short shrift to the controversies of the antebellum period) as "a necessary prerequisite to the achievement of the nation's manifest destiny"; for Schwartz and many other constitutional historians, "the notion of state sovereignty has never had any valid *legal* basis" (pp. 63, 22). As in political thought, so in social theory. Students of the antebellum South have generally discounted the proslavery argument as the product of sectional defense. The standard treatment is William Sumner Jenkins, *Proslavery Thought in the Old South* (Chapel Hill: University of North Carolina Press, 1935). The logical extension of this approach is to see that society, as does Clement Eaton, *The Freedom-of-Thought Struggle in the Old South* (New York: Harper and Row, 1964), as a kind of iron-curtain country. Finally, studies of antebellum Southern literature often have made the most of the connection between Southern fiction and secession, implying that it may be enough merely to draw that connection. See, for example, Ulrich Bonnell Phillips, "The Literary Movement for Secession" (in *Studies in Southern History and Politics, Inscribed to William Archibald Dunning* [New York: Columbia University Press, 1914]); John Pendleton Gaines, *The Southern Plantation: A Study in the Development and Accuracy of a*

Tradition (New York: Columbia University Press, 1925); and Jay Hubbell, "Literary Nationalism in the Old South" (in *American Studies in Honor of William Kenneth Boyd by Members of the Americana Club of Duke University*, ed. David Kelley Jackson [(Durham): Duke University Press, 1952]).

Seeing Southern expression as so much propaganda is one traditional weakness in this literature; others are a willingness to be satisfied without examining the whole, to ignore change, and to try to explain too much. Each commentator on the proslavery argument since Jenkins has had his own impression of it, based on the part of the elephant he has been in touch with. William B. Hesseltine, "Some New Aspects of the Pro-Slavery Argument" (*Journal of Negro History* 21 [January 1936]:1–15), and Kenneth M. Stampp, "An Analysis of T. R. Dew's *Review of the Debates in the Virginia Legislature*" (*Journal of Negro History* 26 [October 1942]:380–87), agree that defense of slavery was a means by which planters could smooth over economic differences with poor whites, appealing to their race pride and raising the spectre of black revolt if slavery were abolished. Wilfred Carsel, "Slaveholders' Indictment of Northern Wage Slavery" (*JSH* 6 [November 1940]:504–20), argues that the proslavery appeal was part of an attempt to build a united front of wealthy Americans, North and South, against lower-class demands for economic democracy. Ralph E. Morrow, "The Proslavery Argument Revisited" (*MVHR* 48 [June 1961]:79–94), offers the suggestion that proslavery writers were really talking to themselves and to other slaveholders—trying to convince themselves of the justice of the slave regime. Two additional general works, Rollin Osterweis, *Romanticism and Nationalism in the Old South* (New Haven: Yale University Press, 1949), and Richard Beale Davis, *Intellectual Life in Jefferson's Virginia, 1790–1830* (Chapel Hill: University of North Carolina Press, 1964), though useful, illustrate the limits of an approach that minimizes intellectual and social change.

Eugene Genovese's studies of slavery and slaveholders are valuable for reminding us of U. B. Phillips's cultural insights and for making provocative conceptual contributions. In several respects his books and essays (see especially his piece on George Fitzhugh in *The World the Slaveholders Made: Two Essays in Interpretation* [New York: Pantheon Books, 1969] and *Roll, Jordan, Roll: The World the Slaves Made* [New York: Pantheon Books, 1974]) have transfixed his readers. Few of us any longer doubt, if we ever did, that society in the Old South was hierarchical, that slaveholders exercised considerable power, and that the slave system embalmed traditional patterns of social interaction. My own work seems to fall into line. One might say that if I have explored anything in this book it is the ideology of Southern slaveholders, the world–view of a distinctive elite, and a way of life threatened by nineteenth-century changes that perhaps we should describe as encroaching "modernity." Professor Genovese will find much here to support his view of antebellum Southern society as pre-capitalist and to buttress his argument that slaveholders exercised hegemony over it.

Yet he and I begin with quite different theoretical assumptions, and I would call attention to the ways in which the Tucker story as I have told it revises Genovese or, more to my liking, stands on its own. For one thing, the experience of Tucker and his friends suggests that only with important qualifications may we speak of a slaveholding ideology dominating or suffusing life in the Old South. Slaveholders were divided among themselves; in Virginia nonslaveholders chafed under disproportionate eastern power in the Assembly and doubted the viability of the slave system just as they rendered slaveholders the deference they expected begrudgingly if at all. Proslavery spokesmen, rather than exemplars of a hegemonic class, were often men neglected or trying to win back influence within it. For most of the antebellum period, party membership among Southerners produced deep and abiding allegiances which, in turn, divided loyalties among both slaveholders and nonslaveholders and led to political divisions that Genovese's theory would have us slight. To the importance of evangelical faith Genovese would probably devote much space were he to revise his essay on "the world the slaveholders made," for not many Southerners escaped the influence of those churches; the beliefs of evangelicals about the world and time and God's part in both had much more to do with their behavior than historians have realized until recently. The theory of paternalism, rightly focusing attention on the reciprocity in master-slave relationships, minimizes differences in the treatment of slaves in different localities at different times.

My principal quarrel with Genovese is with his model of history, which strives for a fundamental causality that tends to reduction. His interpretive framework throttles us because it leaves no room for an over-arching aesthetic mode, for a consideration of generational themes, or for intellectual volition—the awareness of the need to try to transcend one's class or culture or time. Perhaps we delude ourselves when we think about such intellectual autonomy; in any case, my choice is to believe such choice possible and necessary, and it seems to me that Tucker's intellectual limits were not simply the limits of a slaveholder. An approach more interesting than Genovese's, I think, is to examine the arrangements of politics, society, and economic life (the order outside oneself), intellectual paradigms, and unconscious needs and processes as three interacting but independent variables. My effort in this book has been to create in analytical narrative the vibrations, the sounds these elements make together—the harmony they usually produce, the noise noticeable when changes alter that harmonic "fit." I have tried in my writing and in the structure I have given the book to whirl these things together, the "white" of the spinning disc (one searches for acoustic or visual rather than mechanical images) disguising what in my own experience at least are really several separate "colors." For a further word on this point, see below p. 283.

My argument is that we are closest to the complexity of the past, and write the most exciting history, when we work on several levels at once. Especially helpful to me have been studies in the Old South that involve two of them—structure and ideas—in exploring antebellum social change and the writing of commentary on it or fiction reflecting it. William R. Taylor's *Cavalier & Yankee: The Old South and American National Character* (New York: Harper & Row, 1969) remains an important study of the way Northern and Southern writers defined Southern life because it places that process in the setting of growing social complexity. David Herbert Donald, in "The Proslavery Argument Reconsidered" (*JSH* 37 [February 1971]:3–18), suggests that the loudest pro-Southern publicists were social aspirants hoping to win entry into the elite inner circle of Southerners. While I would go further to include variations on the "social origins" theme, generational cleavage, and an appreciation for the integrity of the ideas many of those publicists drew upon, nonetheless, this article is valuable because it begins to lay back layers of motivation and points out the need to examine the social setting of pro- and antislavery writing alike. Two more recent essays, interesting in their effort to interweave political-social realities with prevailing political ideas, are Robert M. Weir, "The South Carolinian as Extremist" (*SAQ* 74 [Winter 1975]:86–103), and Kenneth S. Greenberg, "Revolutionary Ideology and the Proslavery Argument: The Abolition of Slavery in Antebellum South Carolina" (*JSH* 42 [August 1976]:365–84). An important analysis of denominational values in changing circumstances is Donald G. Mathews, *Slavery and Methodism: A Chapter in American Morality, 1780–1845* (Princeton: Princeton University Press, 1965). In *Religion in the Old South,* in the Chicago History of American Religion series, Martin E. Marty, ed. (Chicago: The University of Chicago Press, 1977), Professor Mathews elaborates on his view, highly persuasive, that we must place evangelical faith on a "religious-social continuum," seeing it as an "organizing experience" or means by which its adherents could order the world they moved in; evangelical religion, shaped by social realities, helped give shape to the realities its believers saw about them. Three additional works, though limited in scope, will prove useful in any future studies of intellectual parameters in the Old South. For a brief discussion of the writer's difficulty in obtaining an appreciative readership, see Willard Thorp, "The Writer as Pariah in the Old South" (in *Southern Writers,* ed. J. C. Simonini, Jr. [Charlottesville: The University Press of Virginia, 1964]); Edd Winfield Parks, *Ante-Bellum Southern Literary Critics* (Athens, Ga.: University of Georgia Press, 1962), provides interesting but one-dimensional essays on the influence of critical standards; highly suggestive of what inferences one can draw from literary sources about the role intellectuals played in the Old South, and about the limits they worked within, is Lewis P. Simpson, *The Man of Letters in New England*

and the South: Essays on the History of the Literary Vocation in America (Baton Rouge: Louisiana State University Press, 1973). Along with Drew Gilpin Faust, *A Sacred Circle: The Dilemma of the Intellectual in the Old South, 1840–1860* (Baltimore: The Johns Hopkins University Press, 1977), I hope to deepen our self-understanding by examining thought and stress in that society. With tangled roots in reason, unreason, energy, and apprehension, it is more familiar than at first appears.

Note on Pyschological References

FROM THE BEGINNING of my research in this topic, Tucker was irresistibly a problem in personality. Several features of that problem—motives, quirks, social adjustment—were, I realized, of traditional concern to historians; one can rightly say that all historians are to some degree psycho-historians. Yet the longer I studied Tucker, the more reasons I found to go beyond my intuitive interest in character, my native sense of people. First I wanted to learn whether, given theories of personality structure, the recognizable features of Tucker's character formed patterns that might profit me in interpreting him or that might suggest new questions. Too, I thought it best to know how personality development usually takes place, what psychological issues life histories generally raise, and what connections one might find between personality and society. Third, in my study Tucker was an intellectual subject, and therefore the quality of his perception and his capacities for judging and comparing were of critical importance to me; answering the questions whether these skills declined during his late years and how sharp they were from his early life, required reading in theoretical and clinical literature. Finally, it seemed clear to me from my own self-examination that an important part of one's mind lies beneath the usual level of consciousness. Thus the urges that drive us from beneath the surface of awareness and the processes that take place there both seemed critical to any analysis of Tucker and his writing.

This last point led to my first readings. Most everyone becomes acquainted with Freud's writings in their undergraduate years and therefore knows something of psychoanalysis; analytic theory has in fact altered or at least contributed greatly to the language we commonly use to describe ourselves and one another. To refresh such passing familiarity, one might read either Freud's Clark University lectures of 1909, "The Origin and Development of Psychoanalysis" (*The American Journal of Psychology* 21 [April 1910]:181–218), or his "Introductory Lectures on Psycho-Analysis" [written in 1915–17] (in vols. 16 and 17 of *The Complete Works of Sigmund Freud*, 24 vols. [London: The Hogarth Press, 1953–74]). Also useful, as a later discussion of Freud's theory, is James' Strachey, ed. and trans., *An Outline of Psycho-Analysis* [first published in 1938] (New York: W. W. Norton & Company, 1969); a standard selection of Freud's work is A. A. Brill, ed. and trans., *The Basic*

Writings of Sigmund Freud (New York: The Modern Library, 1938). Among the commentaries on Freud that I have discovered to be of value are Franz Alexander, *Fundamentals of Psychoanalysis* (New York: W. W. Norton & Company, 1963); Raymond E. Fancher, *Psychoanalytic Psychology: The Development of Freud's Thought* (New York: W. W. Norton & Company, 1973); part one of Daniel Yankelovich and William Barrett, *Ego and Instinct: The Psychoanalytic View of Human Nature,* (rev. ed. [New York: Vintage Books, 1970]); S. G. M. Lee and Martin Herbert, eds., *Freud and Psychology: Selected Readings* (Baltimore: Penguin Books, 1970); and most useful of all —a study that one simply must read along with Freud's original essays— Philip Rieff, *Freud: The Mind of the Moralist* (Garden City, N.Y.: Anchor Books, 1961). Insofar as this study of Tucker involves an unresolved oedipal dilemma and unconscious processes of repression, regression, projection, and the like, it obviously bears the imprint of Freudian theory.

Nonetheless I have made no effort to write a purely or classically psycho- analytic interpretation of Tucker. As a system of ideas psychoanalysis suf- fers from logical weaknesses; as a clinical method it has its detractors. See, for example, Rieff, *Freud;* William Gass, "The Scientific Psychology of Sig- mund Freud," (*New York Review of Books,* May 15, 1975); Andrew Salter, *The Case Against Psychoanalysis* (New York: Harper & Row, 1952); and— leveling general charges against psychiatric therapy that include criticisms of psychoanalytic jargon—Thomas S. Szasz, *Ideology and Insanity: Essays on the Psychiatric Dehumanization of Man* (Garden City, N.Y.: Anchor Books, 1970). Besides, for the historian rigorous use of psychoanalysis presents special problems of logic and method. Calling for evidence that is often un- available to us, it tends to reduce human behavior to causes that lie in early experiences and to minimize social and cultural influences on personality. Psychoanalysis entails doctrinal niceties and private language; piously ad- hered to, it can as much clutter the historian's path as clear it. Freud's theory, like Charles A. Beard's economic interpretation of the Constitution, is neces- sary to know, not because definitive, but because it does contain truths, raises important questions, and calls for clarification of one's own thinking.

An educated eclecticism is the best rule in writing what I would call psychologically-informed history. Several surveys of personality theory sug- gest the rich deposits that are available to historians who are willing to mine them. Hendrik M. Ruitenbeek, ed., *Varieties of Personality Theory* (New York: E. P. Dutton & Co., 1964), provides, in addition to Freud's Clark University lectures, brief excerpts from the writings of leading authorities since Freud, among them Carl Jung, Alfred Adler, Erich Fromm, Karen Horney, Harry Stack Sullivan, Gordon Allport, Carl Rogers, and Henry Murray. Ruitenbeek offers headnotes to each selection. An even more am- bitious anthology, containing essays exploring everything from medical to existential models of personality and including critical exchanges on each one, is Theodore Millon, ed., *Theories of Psychopathology and Personality: Essays and Critiques* (Philadelphia: W. B. Saunders Company, 1967). An especially clear and readable introduction is Robert T. Hogan, *Personality Theory: The Personological Tradition* (in The Prentice-Hall Series in Personality, ed. Richard S. Lazarus [Englewood Cliffs, N.J.: Prentice-Hall, 1976]).

While searching theories of personality, I also examined writings on psychological issues that increasingly seemed of importance in Tucker's case. Extensive clinical work, for example, has been done on the effect of parental death on child development. *Separation: Anxiety and Anger,* vol. 2 in John Bowlby's *Attachment and Loss,* (2 vols., in The International Psycho-Analytical Library, M. Masud R. Khan, ed. [London: The Hogarth Press, 1969]), speaks of the intense protest, despair, and detachment that the conjunction of loss of mother, strange people, and puzzling events causes in early childhood; the classic psychoanalytic study of object loss in death is Freud's "Mourning and Melancholia" (in *Complete Works,* 14:243–58). Definitions of mourning vary, and discussion among clinicians continues on the question whether young children are capable of mourning as postadolescents experience it. R. Furman, "A Child's Capacity for Mourning" (in *The Child in His Family,* ed. E. J. Anthony and C. Koupernik [New York: John Wiley & Sons, 1973]), argues that a child of four (Tucker's age when he lost his mother) can undergo that trial in most of its complexity.

Clinicians agree, however, on the lasting impact a child's loss of parent can have. John E. Schowalter, "Parent Death and Child Bereavement" (in *Bereavement: Its Psychosocial Aspects,* ed. Bernard Schoenberg, Irwin Gerber, Alfred Wiener, Austin H. Kutscher, David Peretz, and Arthur C. Carr [New York: Columbia University Press, 1975]), explains that the death of a parent "is so painful for preadolescent children that in addition to their cognitive limitations in accepting the finality of the loss, they must idealize, identify with, and cling to the image of the dead caretaker rather than face the intrapsychic separations inherent in the work of mourning" (p. 174). The clinical evidence also strongly suggests that the length and circumstances of illness before death may cause phobic reactions in young children, and by the reports available Tucker's mother suffered considerably in her last weeks of life; her husband's delay in returning to her side may easily have left an indelible impression on Beverley. We know too that young children, in idealizing the deceased parent, often turn the negative feelings felt at this loss outward—perhaps in Tucker's case against his father. But one can also direct that aggression or anger against oneself, and the resulting loss of self-esteem, Schowalter points out (p. 176), can remain a problem throughout life: depressive illness and suicide, for example, are statistically higher among persons who lose a parent in early life. Tucker's anxiety over being left alone while his family traveled, his depressive moods and glorification of the past, and his constant dwelling on his self-esteem all conform to the pattern one finds in the clinical literature on child bereavement. I have tried to show how important this psychological theme was in Tucker's life without placing on it more weight than it will bear.

Both Beverley and Henry, so different in their personalities, suffered that loss of mother; obviously something besides bereavement influenced their individual development. Studies in sibling relationships and the psychodynamics of the family helped to arrange the material I had on the quite dissimilar boyhoods the two brothers experienced. The pioneering student of these relationships is Alfred Adler; see, for example, his *Understanding Human Nature* [first published in 1927] (New York: Fawcett Premier Books, 1959), pp. 125–28. A more recent effort to deal with sibling rivalry is the excellent study of Brian Sutton-Smith and B. G. Rosenberg, *The Sibling* (New York: Holt, Rinehart and Winston, 1970). The patterns Sutton-Smith and Rosenberg find in their work bore out my impressions of the Henry-Beverley relationship and the jealousy it aroused in the younger brother, particularly since St. George Tucker's judicial duties took him away from home for weeks at a time, with Henry "in charge" in his absence. Firstborn children, according to Sutton-Smith and Rosenberg, commonly "perceived themselves and were perceived by the second born as exercising higher power—that is, they commanded, reprimanded, scolded and bossed. Reciprocally, the second born pleaded, whined, sulked, and appealed for help and sympathy from the firstborn and others" (p. 57). Henry's comparative success as a student likewise confirmed findings of an "academic primogeniture" that benefits the firstborn (pp. 69–79, 94–96). For the ways in which one's perception of the family as a set of relationships can make it either "a web, a flower, a tomb, a prison, a castle," see R. D. Laing, *The Politics of the Family* (New York: Pantheon Books, 1969); see also Anthony and Koupernik, eds., *The Child in His Family,* and Donald W. Winnicott, *The Child, The Family, and the Outside World* (Baltimore: Penguin Books, 1969). Reading about sibling rivalry and the ambiguity of family ties did not so much point out what I would have missed otherwise as it confirmed my suspicions and emphasized how intense and longstanding, in Tucker's instance, brotherly rivalry could be. These special studies made clear the pattern of recurrent trauma and conflict in Tucker's life.

They did little to form links between his character and society or to suggest what issues the life cycle past childhood might raise. Psychological role theory offers one means of making ties between personality and society. By this approach, a primary goal in interpersonal relations is to maximize friendly attention and to minimize hostility; recurrent social interactions tend to become ritualized, and one soon develops ways of presenting himself so as to ease interaction and to present the "image" he wishes. See Erving Goffman, *The Presentation of Self in Everyday Life* (Garden City, N.Y.: Doubleday Anchor Books, 1959) and *Interaction Ritual: Essays on Face-to-Face*

Behavior (Garden City, N.Y.: Doubleday Anchor Books, 1967), and Hogan, *Personality Theory,* pp. 187-205. Since these ways of presenting oneself depend in great measure on the setting in which the "interaction ritual" takes place, examining personality in terms of the roles one plays can be instructive. In Tucker's day, and in certain respects the pattern continues, Southern life required highly specific manners of behavior according to one's place on the social scale; antebellum Northern life—socially more fluid and more demanding in its commercial character—required a multiplicity of roles from nearly everyone. Such "splitting" of oneself between the "public" and "private" spheres and the need, so to speak, to "be different things to different people," was what bothered Tucker about that social system. He, on the other hand, can be understood as a personality made up of strategies designed to maximize a social situation that was changing too rapidly for him to adjust. Studied as such, Tucker's case lends support to David Brion Davis's role-theoretical analysis of antebellum society in *The Slave Power Conspiracy and the Paranoid Style* (Baton Rouge: Louisiana State University Press, 1969). Valuable as role theory is, it nonetheless seems overly confined to the superficial, the conscious, the normative to provide a satisfactory account of Tucker's personality.

The closest thing to a scheme in which I could fit all the pieces of Tucker's psychological puzzle was the framework of psychoanalytic ego psychology. This highly serviceable view of personality has developed since Freud's death and has both built on his theories and, in crucial respects, modified them. See, for example, Anna Freud, *The Ego and the Mechanisms of Defense* (London: The Hogarth Press, 1937); David Rapaport, "Historical Survey of Psychoanalytical Ego Psychology" (*Psychological Issues,* monograph I [1959], pp. 5-17); Heinz Hartmann, *Essays in Ego Psychology* (New York: International Universities Press, 1964); and Erik Erikson, *Childhood and Society* (2d rev. ed. [New York: W. W. Norton & Company, 1963]). Erikson proved particularly useful because of the stress he places on the cultural setting of psychological growth, the social possibilities open to the developing person. One may question whether the stages man moves through in life number eight, as Erikson says, or whether there are eight in every society, time notwithstanding; for critical reviews of Erikson's theory, see Frederick Crews, "American Prophet" (*New York Review of Books,* October 16, 1975 and, a special issue on Erikson, *The Psychohistory Review* 5 [December 1976]).

Still, there is abundant evidence of Tucker's passing through several psychological zones that left their mark on him. Erikson in *Childhood and Society* first of all provides a pertinent discussion of the challenge young persons face when, at the same age Beverley was in Williamsburg, they begin to extend their ego boundaries and to gain a sense of competence or confidence outside the home. In going off to school, Beverley had the psycho-

social task of proving himself "workable," of showing his power to be useful in a situation involving other people. His failure to establish that
"industry" made the school experience unfortunate and apparently left him,
as Erikson suggests often occurs in such cases, with a feeling of "inadequacy
and inferiority" (p. 260); given Tucker's later memories of being, as a schoolboy, hitched like a colt to a heavy wagon, he seems indeed to have suffered
the pressures of what Erikson refers to as *"outer and inner hindrances"* (p.
260). Then, in Tucker's late adolescence, his effort to imitate and to please
John Randolph leaves little room to doubt that the young man found his
older half brother a figure after whom he could shape his own sense of self-
hood, or, as Erikson describes it, his identity. Tucker in fact took every
opportunity at the time and thereafter to liken himself to Randolph, after
Randolph's death describing himself as his intellectual heir. That their relationship was stormy only testifies to the investment of feeling Tucker made
in this man who, as another "self," could so easily be the subject of projected hopes and fears. Finally, in Tucker's last months as a dejected
widower and shortly afterwards as the husband of a much younger woman,
he himself questioned the value and lasting importance of his work, his
production, and his generative powers. He seems to have reached the impasse
that Erikson describes as the crisis of generativity. In Tucker's talk of somehow achieving immortality, in his realization that he was a man of mean
accomplishment who, soon "dead and gone," was facing his last chance,
there are striking parallels to the same turning point in Ghandi's life, which
Erikson treats in *Ghandi's Truth: On the Origins of Militant Nonviolence*
([New York: W. W. Norton & Company, 1969], pp. 153-57, 180, 395-96).
Tucker's confidence in divinely appointed mission resembled Ghandi's sense
of special mandate, as did the techniques the two men used to attract young
disciples and to provide them a means of organizing a view of the world:
making the most of the search for identity among young men, both Tucker
and Ghandi offered a lifting camaraderie that demanded sacrifice and promised purpose larger than each individual. See *Ghandi's Truth,* pp. 406-9.

   Ego psychology offers several advantages to the historian. It directs attention beyond the psychosexual development of early life and avoids reducing
the causes of behavior and beliefs to the dynamics of the unconscious alone.
Focusing instead on the process of ego defense, on the capacity for choice,
on the need to deal with ongoing difficulties of life, and on the need to find
useful work and esteem in society, ego psychology allows us to see society
and subject continuously acting on one another. The capacity to cope is
revealing both of the social circumstances of the distress and of the culturally
approved ways of coping; life crises, if not psychologically inevitable, are
socially imposed. Thus Tucker, rather than being the victim of childhood
misfortune, was subject to unfolding problems of life, each of them aggra-
vated by social shifts; instead of being doomed by the psychological fates,

Tucker dueled with them, and his struggle suggests what measures he believed were necessary and proper to his setting. Ego psychology enabled me to treat Tucker as I thought I had to in order to make his life fully illuminating. Neither slave society nor unconscious drives nor ideas by themselves made him what he was. He was instead a study in the twisting together of these shaping elements, in the resonance between ideas and psychological processes, between society and ideas, and between social change and psychological pressures.

The most interesting yet difficult of these connections is that between intellectual growth (or decline) and psychological development (or decay). I know of nothing written that offers a helpful theoretical outline of these processes; clinicians apparently find them as puzzling as the rest of us. Psychoanalytic theory contains references to "reality testing," by which a person because of ego functioning is either well or poorly able to measure wishes against their likely fulfillment; several introductory essays on this subject are chapters six through eight of Leopold Bellak, Marvin Hurvich, and Helen K. Gediman, *Ego Functions In Schizophrenics, Neurotics, And Normals: A Systematic Study of Conceptual, Diagnostic, and Therapeutic Aspects* (in the Wiley-Interscience Series, Irving B. Weiner, ed. [New York: John Wiley & Sons, 1973]). Tucker's capacity for such judgment so ill served him by his later life that he developed what seem to have been paranoid personality traits—though he was never psychotic by any current definition. For a discussion of this pattern, which includes blame transfer, harboring injustices done to one, suspicion, a belief in one's central importance, delusions of grandeur, and intense fear of losing control over one's life, see David Swanson, Philip J. Bohnert, and Jackson A. Smith, *The Paranoid* (Boston: Little, Brown and Company, 1970). Considering Tucker a paranoid personality does not mean that I see his beliefs as altogether illogical (paranoids are frequently bright and, given their assumptions, coherent) or that he was completely wrong in his view of the Northern threat. Taken as a psychological subject, however, he was by the late 1830s a poor judge of his ability to deal with that phenomenon.

Other studies in this vein are of less value. Tucker may have been an authoritarian personality, but the classic treatment of that topic, T. W. Adorno, Else Frenkel-Brunswik, D. J. Levinson, and R. N. Sanford, *The Authoritarian Personality* (New York: Harper & Row, 1950), is riddled with logical and methodological holes. I have avoided referring to Tucker as a "closed mind" because that term—relative, failing to distinguish among the subjects or kinds of thought—had little utility in this case. On the "closed" posture of prejudiced and dogmatic thinking, see Milton Rokeach, *The Open and Closed Mind: Investigations Into the Nature of Belief Systems and Personality Systems* (New York: Basic Books, 1960); another group of essays, also concerned with cognitive styles, is Peter B. Warr, ed., *Thought and Personality: Selected Readings* (Baltimore: Penguin Books, 1970). Such writings tend to be taxonomic and experimental—concerned with definitions, techniques of measurement, and the contradictions or dissonance discovered within the belief structure. A monumental effort to bring together this research is David Rapaport, ed. and trans., *Organization and Pathology of Thought: Selected Sources* (New York: Columbia University Press, 1951). The title is beguiling; the contents dense and discouraging. Perhaps what they demonstrate is that the job of learning why people believe what they do is too important to be left to the psychologists. Or that only in biography can we tackle such problems with any satisfaction.

A final word is in order here, because a good question is what the historian should expect from psychological sources. Not everything, I would answer, but I think we should look at them all the same. My own readings in psychology and in psychohistory lead me to believe that there probably is here no new science, no need for an elaborate new method, and that psychohistorians often ask too much of their theory. But the worse error is to avoid the thinking that such theory prompts us to do. Surely we must be as fully informed as possible when we deal with human motives and experience, and we should keep in mind ways of measuring historical findings against the work of personality theorists and clinicians. If Tucker demonstrates anything, it is that even common sense can be sharpened. Readings in classical and current psychological sources can help to frame questions of the evidence, to give the most meaning to our treatment of psychological themes, and—as unobtrusively as possible—to inform our conclusions. While this pragmatic approach does sidestep for the moment certain theoretical issues, my object has been at once simpler and more difficult than "merging" history and psychology, each with its own methods and purposes. Instead of "explaining" Tucker, I have tried to understand him. Rather than depending on psychological theory, I have used it to shape and strengthen what is primarily an historical argument.

Index

A guide to the abbreviations used in this volume is found on p. 211.

Adams, John, NBT on death of, 69
Adams, John Quincy, 71, 140, 148, 151
Adams-Onis agreement, 149
Aldrich, Alfred Proctor, 188
Alien and Sedition Acts: StGT's response to the, 9; and William and Mary students, 15; Virginia Assembly condemns the, 22–23, 79
American Jurist, 98, 99, 153
Andover, seminary at, 68–69
Annapolis Convention, 5
Antislavery: poses threat to Virginia slaveholders, 93–95; and perfectionism, 110, 144; latent in the movement for Virginia constitutional reform, 174; NBT's fears of, realized, 197; proponents of, view slaves as commodities, 202
Archer, William S., 151
Ardmore (NBT's estate), 74, 80
Aristotle, NBT's reliance on, 109
Articles of Confederation, 6
Ashley, William H., 80–81
Authority, locus of, shifting in antebellum America, 207

Bancroft, George, 128, 164, 237–38 n.26; *History of the United States*, reviewed by NBT, 103
Banking: NBT proposes plan on, 140–42; NBT's attitude toward, and money, 201–2
Bar. *See* Lawyers
Barraud, Phillip, 20
Barton, David, 75–76
Bates, Edward, 53, 59, 96
Bates, Frederick, 51
Bates, Julia Coalter, 59
Bayly, Thomas H., 150, 154, 175
Beecher, Catherine, 203
Belsham, William, NBT reads *Memoirs of the Reign of George III*, by, 25
Bench. *See* Judiciary, federal; Judiciary, Missouri; Judiciary, Virginia
Bentham, Jeremy, 17
Benton, Thomas Hart, 75–76, 80–81, 89–90, 234 n.57
Berkeley, George, 17

Bermuda: Nathaniel Tucker's poetic description of, as the family home, 1–2; NBT's pride in, 40
Bibb, George M., 176, 230 n.11, 246 n.26
Bizarre (Randolph family estate), 4, 11, 29; loneliness of, 25; NBT tries to remain close to, 32
Blackstone, Sir William, 29, 38, 53, 83, 98, 99, 104, 158, 204; *Commentaries on the Laws of England*, edited by StGT, 21–22; conservative tone of, 23–24; NBT complains of reading, 25; NBT uses, in teaching law, 102–4, NBT refutes, on subject of slavery, 108–9; logical problems inherent in, 111
Blackwood's Magazine, 123
Blair, Hugh: text on rhetoric by, used at William and Mary, 17; on the sublime, 66; as influence in NBT's fiction, 123
Botts, John M., 142, 171
Bouldin, James Wood, 39
Bracken, Reverend John, 11
Browne, Dabney, 98
Bruce, William, 39
Bryan, Elizabeth Coalter (niece of NBT), 175; relationship of, with NBT, 70, 72, 229 n.11; on *The Partisan Leader*, 133; tries to boost NBT's spirits, 162; and William and Mary disturbances of 1847–48, 173
Buchanan, James, 184
Buckner, Alexander, 78
Bulwer-Lytton, Edward, 121
Burke, Edmund, 104, 130, 158, 204, 219 n.24; and American regard for liberty, 21; JR finds, appealing, 28–29; distinguishes between beautiful and sublime, 66; NBT invokes, in connecting love of liberty and slaveholding, 109; NBT's grounding in principles of, 111, 166
Burnley, Albert T., 148
Burns, Robert, 86
Bushnell, Horace, 157
Byron, Lord, 29, 162, 219 n.25

Cabell, Joseph C., 15, 24
Calhoun, John C., 87, 89, 116, 139, 170, 181, 184; breaks with Jackson, 78; theory of, on

Calhoun, John C. *(continued)* state veto criticized by NBT, 83–85; and controversy over abolitionist petitions, 118–19; involved in Texas annexation policy, 149–50; group of NBT students support, 171; involved in calling Nashville Convention, 178; plea of, for sectional conciliation in Senate, 179–80

Campbell, David, 208

Carlyle, Thomas: intellectual affinity of, with NBT, 145–46, 246–47 n.29; NBT tries to engage in correspondence, 168; NBT believes ready to support Southern secession, 190; rebuffs NBT on morality of slavery, 197

Carrington, Joseph, 170

Carter, George, 11

Caruthers, Alexander, 123

Cass, Lewis, 186

Cavaignac, General Louis, 173

Chamberlin, Reverend Hiram, 69, 72, 229 n.8

Charless, Joseph, 60–61

Charlotte Court House (Maryville), 101; NBT's disappointments in the, as novice lawyer, 32–34, 39, 66, 72; as site of 1833 anti-Force Bill meeting, 87–88

Cheves, Langdon, 184–85

Christian Spectator, 69, 229 n.8

Clarkson, Thomas, 169

Clay, Henry, 139, 150, 180, 182, 186, 189; JR embarrasses, 71; supporters of, in Missouri politics, 75–76, 78, 80; and tariff compromise, 87, 89; opposes Tyler and NBT on banking policy, 140–42, 245 nn.11, 14; criticizes NBT's expediency on Texas issue, 151; NBT comments on notoriety of, 190

Coalter, David, 58

Coalter, John, 51, 70; tutors NBT, 11; on lawyer's duty, 21; NBT studies law with, 24–25; advises NBT, 44; underwrites Missouri venture, 46, 49; disgust of, at Virginia politics, 117

Cocke, Richard, 132

Codification, NBT opposes, 152–53

Coke, Sir Edward: NBT reads *Institutes* and Coke on Littleton by, 24–25; NBT seeks escape from, 29; NBT's reliance on, 111

Commerce, NBT's attitude toward, 201–2

Common law: logic and wisdom of, according to Blackstone, 23; as instrument of social order in NBT's view, 64; and purview of federal and state courts, 84; NBT celebrates, while opposing codification, 152–54, 158. *See also* Judiciary, federal; Judiciary, Missouri; Judiciary, Virginia; Law; Lawyers

Common sense, Scottish philosophy of, 29, 143, 146, 217 n.45; among subjects taught at William and Mary in 1790s, 17–18; NBT attracted to, 18–19; as influence in NBT's moderate evangelism, 68–69; evidenced in NBT's fiction, 123; and NBT's consciousness of, as compared to the transcendentalists', 166; as intellectual framework, 204, 205–6, 209

Compromise of 1850: introduced, 180; details of, 182–83; passes, 189; limits of, 196

Constitution, federal: StGT opposes ratification of, 6; and Missouri statehood controversy, 53–55; and impairment of contracts, 62; Calhoun's interpretation of, 83; NBT's treatment of, as law professor, 102–3; NBT's confidence in, falters, 138, 153; and NBT's view of a national bank, 141–42; and fugitive slaves, 152. *See also* Judiciary, federal; Sovereignty, concept of; States' rights, constitutional theory of

Constitution, Virginia: of 1776, 35, 220–21 n.39; calls for reform of, during 1820s, 71; of 1829–30, 93, 111–12; revised in 1850–51 convention, 189

Cooper, James Fenimore, 121

Cornwallis, Lord, 4

Courts. *See* Judiciary, federal; Judiciary, Missouri; Judiciary, Virginia

Cowper, William, 162

Coynynham, Kate, 184

Crallé, Richard, 128

Crittenden, John J., 91

Crump, William W., 171, 189

Curriculum, NBT's legal, 101–3, 237 n.22. *See also* Education; Teaching, NBT's approach to; William and Mary, College of

Dallas, George M., 164, 168

Dane, Nathan, 99

Daniel, John Moncure, 189

Dardenne Creek, Missouri, slaveholder community at, 147, 207; development and meaning of, 57–60, 226 nn.33, 34, 36; resistance to, 60–61; breakup of, 70–71; relation of, to NBT's social ideal as expressed in fiction, 124

Davis, David Brion, 202

Democracy. *See* Egalitarianism

Dew, Thomas R., xiv, 93, 96, 98, 114; appearance and background of, 107–8; arguments on slavery and NBT, 108–10; assumes presidency of William and Mary and receives criticism, 133–34; as informal advisor during the Tyler presidency, 139–40; effect on William and Mary of death of, 172

Douglas, Stephen A., 164, 180

Duncan, William, NBT reads, at William and Mary, 17

Duyckinck, Evert A. and George L., 196

Edinburgh Review, 123

Education: StGT on republican need for, 20–21; NBT on need for moral lessons in, 115–16

Egalitarianism: and quality of early-nineteenth-century Virginia bar in NBT's perception, 38–41; in Missouri in 1820s, 60–65 passim, 199; in NBT's fiction, 123–25; Tocqueville on, 136–37; NBT comments on, in 1840s, 143, 145–46, 160–61, 173–74; and NBT's proslavery argument, 147, 202. *See also* Majoritarianism, NBT warns of, in Missouri statehood debates; Politics, character of; Universal suffrage

Emerson, Ralph Waldo, 165–66, 205
Empie, Reverend Adam, 98
England (and Scotland): influence of, on
NBT's view of the country gentleman and
Virginia, 24, 29, 159–61, 176–77, 201;
dependency of, upon cotton in NBT's view,
and likelihood of, supporting a separate
South, 186–87, 190, 197; as cultural
influence in antebellum South, 199, 201
Enlightenment: StGT as exemplary of the,
7–8, 10; William Godwin parodies, in
NBT's view, 16–17. See also Rationalism
Evangelism. See Theology
Everett, Edward, 142
Ewell, Benjamin S., 196

Federalist Papers: StGT refers to, in edition
of Blackstone, 22; NBT uses, in his law
course, 103
Federalist Party, and William and Mary stu-
dents in 1790s, 15
Finney, Reverend Charles Grandison, 110
Fitzhugh, George, 147
Flaubert, Gustave, NBT reads Madame Bovary
by, 168
Flint, Timothy, 57, 58
Floyd, John, 178–79
Foote, Henry S., xiii, 180, 189
Force Bill, 87–89
Foster, Sir John, 37
Free Soil Party, 175
Free trade, doctrine of: in Thomas R. Dew's
lectures, 108; in NBT's fiction, 124
French Revolution, 9, 144; reaction to, among
William and Mary students in 1790s, 15–17;
NBT's memories of, reawakened in 1848,
173–74

"Gag rule" controversy, NBT's involvement in,
118–19
Garland, Hugh, 193
Garrison, William Lloyd, 151
Genêt, Citizen, 16
George Balcombe, xiii, 164, 167; plot summary
of, 121–22; and literary convention, 123;
principal character of, in an exemplar of virtue, 124; western Virginians in, 124–25; and
NBT's love of Virginia, 129; as discussion of
womanhood, 156; Simms praises, 169; reception of, 241 n.19
"Gertrude," 167; NBT serializes, 155; political
lessons in, 155–56; as essay on womanhood,
156–58; and value of land, 159–60
Gibbon, Edward, NBT reads Decline and Fall of
the Roman Empire by, 25
Glasscock v. Steen, NBT's decision in, 63–64
Godwin, William: NBT acquainted with the
Enquiry Concerning Political Justice by, 16–
17; NBT's response to, 18–19; NBT detects,
as an influence in Northern reform movements, 144
Goode, William O., 183

Goodrich, Reverend Chauncey Allen, 69
Gordon, William F., 183, 185
Government, theory of, taught by NBT, 104–6
Green, Duff, xiv, 200; edits United States Tele-
graph, 88; supports Tucker in law professor-
ship, 96; aids in anti-Van Buren effort, 117; con-
sults NBT on Southern schoolbooks project,
120; and publication of The Partisan Leader,
122, 127, 133; proposes publishing schemes to
NBT, 154
Greene, Nathaniel, 184
Greenhow, Washington, 171
Greenleaf, Simon, 158, 165
Grotius, Hugo, 108

Hamilton, Alexander, 22
Hamilton, James, Jr., 234 n.56; NBT writes, 78–
79; distaste of, for Jackson and Van Buren, 117
Hammond, James Henry, xiv, 127, 177, 185, 189,
197, 199, 201, 203, 204, 205, 206; attracts
NBT by his political daring, 117–19; leaves Congress, 119; NBT re-opens friendship with,
168–70; fears European revolutions of 1848,
174; and NBT's preparation for Nashville Convention, 178–81, 183; first meeting of, with
NBT and mutual descriptions, 182; and
maneuverings at Nashville Convention, 183–
84; invites NBT to Silver Bluff, 188; and NBT's
plans for South Carolina secession in 1850–51,
190–92; quarrels with Rhett and doubts expediency of secession, 190–91; admits defeat on
secession issue in South Carolina, 192; expectations of secession, 200
Hampden, John: mentioned in StGT's poem
Liberty, 8; as NBT's pseudonym during Mis-
souri statehood debate, 55–56
Hampden-Sidney College, NBT addresses
Philanthropic Society of, 131
Hancock, John, 177
Harper, Catherine Coalter, 58
Harper, William, xiv, 59, 71, 172, 200, 235 n.61;
and proslavery argument, 146–47
Harrison, William Henry, 116, 138–39
Hartz, Louis, xv
Harvard University, early legal training at, 98,
99–100, 237 n.17
Hay, George, 25
Henry, Patrick, 130, 184
History, NBT's conception and use of, 128–29,
243 n.40; weight of, in NBT's character and
manners, 176–77
Hoffman, David, 98–99
Holmes, George Frederick, 172–73
Homine replegiando, writ de, 153, 249 n.54
Hopedale, utopian settlement of, 143
Hopkins, Reverend Samuel, 68–69
Horace, StGT cites Odes of, 6
Hume, David, 17, 24

Ingersoll, Charles J., 148

Jackson, Andrew: supporters of, in Missouri

Jackson, Andrew *(continued)* politics, 75–76, 78–81; NBT sees, as dangerously charismatic, 81; condemns South Carolina during nullification crisis, 82–83, 86–87; NBT visits and talks with, 88–89, 234 n.58

Jacobinism. *See* Egalitarianism; French Revolution

Jay, John, 22

Jefferson, Thomas, xv, 100, 108, 193; acquaintance of StGT with, 7; and William and Mary curriculum reform, 14; on appearance of Wren Building, 14; break with JR, 28; invoked during Missouri statehood controversy, 54; NBT contradicts western vision of, 59; NBT on death of, 69

Johns, Bishop John, 172

Johnson, Cave, 14

Johnson, Chapman, 15–16, 24

Jones, James B., 171

Jordan, Winthrop, xv

Judiciary, federal, as treated in NBT's fiction, 124. *See also* Common law; Constitution, federal

Judiciary, Missouri: 51–52, 225 n.17; problems of, 51–52, 225 n.17; NBT upholds independence of, 64

Judiciary, Virginia: early-nineteenth-century structure of, 32, 35, 219–20 n.28; attempted reforms of, 36–37; independence of, 37–38; NBT criticizes, 38, 44; changes in, affect Virginia bar, 38–39, 199; NBT champions justices of the peace in, 189. *See also* Common law; Law; Lawyers

Kant, Immanuel, 17

"Kate Coynynham," 184

Kennedy, John Pendleton, 123, 156

Kent, Chancellor James, 98, 99, 103, 142, 237–38 n.26, 244–45 n.5

Lacy, Reverend William, 58

Lafayette, Marquis de, 4

Lamartine, Alphonse de, 113, 173

Lamb, William, 196

Land, as part of NBT's view of stable society, 159–61

Law: and liberty, 21, 23; study of, by means of StGT's edition of Blackstone, 21–22, 98, 99, 103, 218 n.13; practice of, in early-nineteenth-century Virginia, 38–39, 44, 222 n.46; practice of, in frontier Missouri, 51; training in, as NBT assumes professorship at William and Mary, 98–100, 236 n.13; NBT's curriculum and approach to schooling in, 100–103, 237 n.22; procedural reform of, in Virginia, NBT cautions against, 152–53; NBT plans text on Virginian, 162. *See also* Common law; Judiciary, federal; Judiciary, Missouri; Judiciary, Virginia; Lawyers

Law of Nature. *See* Natural law and natural rights

Law Reporter, 165

Lawyers: hostility toward, in early-nineteenth-century Virginia, 37–38; NBT sees distinctions among, and criticizes, 38, 44, 50, 222 n.46; gentlemanly ethic among, difficult to pass on, 39, 222 n.48; NBT tries to shape professional character of, in Missouri, 51; NBT lectures, on value of common law pleading, 152–53, 158. *See also* Judiciary, federal; Judiciary, Missouri; Judiciary, Virginia; Law

Leake, Walter D., 171

Lectures on the Science of Government: NBT publishes, 154–55; lessons from English history in, 159; value of war in, 161; copy of, sent Carlyle, 168; Simms applauds, 169

Leigh, Benjamin Watkins, 15, 86, 88, 101

Leigh, William, 39

Lewis, Dixon H., 89

Liberty: StGT's concept of, 2; as goddess in StGT's patriotic poetry, 8; as an issue in Missouri statehood controversy, 55–56; Burke on slaveholders' love of, 109; fleeting quality of, 114; and slavery in common law, 153; sense of, NBT believes inherent in common law, 154. *See also* Republicanism; States' rights, constitutional theory of

Liberty, A Poem on the Independence of America, 8

Lieber, Francis: and NBT's reception of *Political Ethics,* 144–45, 152–53; breaks off relationship with NBT, 164–65

Littleton, Sir Thomas, 24, 29

Livingston, Edward, 83–84

Locke, John, 15, 17. *See also* Government, theory of, taught by; Social theory

Louis-Phillipe (French emperor), 173

Lowell, James Russell, 165–66

Lynchburg Young Men's Society, 129, 132

Macaulay, Thomas, NBT's reviews *History of England* by, 177

McCulloch v. Maryland, 55

McNair, Alexander, 62

Macon, Nathaniel, 43, 101

McPheeter family, 58

Madison, Bishop James, 15–16

Madison, James, 22, 84, 103

Majoritarianism: NBT warns of, in Missouri statehood debate, 56; judiciary as a bulwark against, 64; and minority rights in democratic reform, 143; and growing political power of the North, 199. *See also* Egalitarianism; Universal suffrage

Marx, Karl, comments on 1848 revolutions, 173

Mason, Senator James, 189

Mason, Senator John Y., 164

Matoax: as boyhood home of NBT, 4–5; NBT's mother buried at, 6; in NBT's later imagination, 7; reflected in NBT's Missouri community, 59; NBT's lingering hurt over loss of, 70

Maysville Road veto, 75

Means, Doctor David H., 58, 71

Means, Frances Coalter, 58

Means, James, 190
Melville, Herman, 205
Mexican War, as political-moral issue, 165–66
Miller, John, 76, 78–79, 81, 231 n.26
Millington, John, 98, 173
Minnegerode, Charles, 172–73
Minor, Benjamin Blake, 155
Missouri Compromise, 183, 185, 227 n.46
Missouri statehood controversy: NBT involvement in, 52–57; and conditions of Texas annexation, 150
Missouri v. *Lane,* NBT's decision in, 63–64
Monroe, James, 83; NBT addresses, on Missouri statehood issue, 53, 57
Montague, Robert L., xiv, 171
Montesquieu, Baron de: quoted in foreword to StGT's antislavery tract, 10; NBT reads *Spirit of the Laws* by, 15; and republican virtue, 18; NBT's grounding in, 111
Morgan, Edmund S., 200
Mormons, and polygamy, NBT's view of, 144
Morse, Jedidiah, comments on Williamsburg in *American Geography,* 7

Nashville Convention: calling of the, 177–78; NBT sets out for the, 181–82; deliberations of and delegates to the, 182–85; NBT addresses the, 185–87; reaction to the, 189
National Institute for the Promotion of Science, 148–49, 165
Nationalism, Southern: NBT's effort to build sense of, 116–19; and schoolbooks, 120; in NBT's reviews of Northern and British literature, 121; eventual failure of, 197–98
Natural law and natural rights: in StGT's teaching and writing, 9–10; and NBT's lectures, 106–7, 238 nn.32, 33
Naylor, John, 46, 58
North American Review, 131, 142, 243 n.47
Nott, Abraham, 58
Nullification, theory of: NBT's criticism of, 83–85, 233 n.46; condemned in Charlotte County resolutions, 88
Nullification crisis: NBT's behavior during, 82–90; reaction in Virginia to Jackson's handling of, 96

Oratory: importance of, in nineteenth-century Virginia and NBT's lack of skill in, 34; NBT anxious about his talents in, 50, 180, 185
Ould, Robert, 151, 170–71
Owen, Robert, 143–44

Page, John, 6, 8
Paine, Thomas, 15, 28
Paley, William: NBT reads *Principles of Moral and Political Philosophy* by, at William and Mary, 17; NBT's attraction to, 18–19; and NBT's revolt against rationality, 29
Palmerston, Lord, 197
Parrington, Vernon Louis, xiii
Partisan Leader, The, xiii, 135, 138, 152, 197;

plot summary of, 122–23; and contemporary literary forms, 123; political commentary in, 123–24; western Virginians in, 124–25; and NBT's view of himself and brother, 125–27; and NBT's love of Virginia, 129; ruin of Virginia in, 131; reception of, 132–33, 241 n.20, 244 nn.51, 52; and womanhood, 156
Paulding, James Kirke, 109
Peachy, Archibald, 172–73
Peachy, Thomas G., 96
Peachy, William S., 171
Pedagogy. *See* Education; Teaching, NBT's approach to
Peel, Sir Robert: 197, 247 n.29; NBT relies on reports of, 145; receives letter from NBT, 168
Perfectionism, NBT on, 110, 112–13, 239 n.49
Pettis, Spencer, 76
Pickering, Henry L., 119
Pillow, General Gideon, 184
Pleading: practice of irregular, in Virginia, 152–53; NBT publishes text on, 158, 250 n.66
Pleasants, John Hampden, 97
Poe, Edgar Allan: NBT writes, on critical theory, 123, 205, 242 n.23; comments on NBT's portrayal of Balcombe, 125
Politics, character of: in early-nineteenth-century Virginia, 35, 198–99; and changing governmental responsibilities, 36; and growth of party changes, 81, 199, 233 n.39; NBT's fictional comments on the, 124; and 1840 presidential election, 135; and the early Tyler administration, 142–43; lessons on the, learned by NBT students in Virginia, 171; angers NBT for encouraging compromise, 180; and secession of Southern states in 1860-61, 197–98
Polk, James K., 150, 164, 171
Polk, William H., 184
Pragmatism, as one of StGT's intellectual principles, 10, 19
Presbyterian Church: NBT a member of, in early 1820s, 67; and NBT's dancing, 74, 77, 231 n.28; NBT's later standing in, 239 n.49
Preston, Maria Coalter, 59
Preston, William Campbell, 59, 71, 96, 117, 139, 200
Prigg v. *Pennsylvania,* 151–52
"Probatory Odes of Jonathan Pindar," 9
Property rights: in Blackstone, 23; at issue in Missouri statehood debate, 53; NBT defends, in debtor relief controversy, 64; NBT's teachings on, 105–6, 238 n.32; socialism and communism threaten, 144
Proslavery argument: NBT's contribution to, 146–47, 158, 202; as "reform" effort, 202–3. *See also* Slavery; Social theory

Quarterly Christian Spectator, 69, 229 n.8
Quids: JR and the, 28; NBT feels himself one of the, 29, 40; meaning of the, for NBT, 42

Randolph, Colonel Beverley, 2–4, 6

Randolph, Jane Bolling, 4

Randolph, John (first husband of Frances Bland), 4

Randolph, John, of Roanoke, xiii, 11, 71, 75, 76, 126, 135, 185, 207, 219 n.22; early character of, 4; refers to StGT's fatherly discipline, 12; at William and Mary, 20; relationship of, with NBT, 26–28, 43–44; breaks with StGT, 28; falls out with Jefferson administration, 28; sensibility of, as model for NBT, 41; beckons NBT back to Virginia, 82; NBT works with, during nullification crisis, 86–90; death of, 90; NBT plans but fails to write biography of, 112, 192–94; NBT wishes for oratorical powers of, 180

Randolph, Judith (sister-in-law of JR), 26, 44

Randolph, Nancy (sister of Judith Randolph), 25

Randolph, Richard (older half-brother of NBT), 4, 11

Randolph, Richard, of Curles, 4

Randolph, Theodorick (older half-brother of NBT), 4, 11

Randolph-Macon College, NBT addresses Franklin Literary Society of, 131, 135

Rationalism: as waning intellectual framework in 1790s, 16–19; coldness of, attacked in NBT's religious writings, 68; NBT sees, in Northern reform movements, 144. See also Enlightenment, StGT as exemplary of the; Tucker, St. George, secular and practical cast of mind of

Realism. See Common sense

Reid, Thomas, NBT studies, at William and Mary, 17

Religion. See Theology

Republicanism: reflected in StGT's poetry and law lectures, 8–9; as an element in StGT's child-rearing practice, 12; at William and Mary in 1790s, 15–16; tensions within, for Southerners, 18; and need for education in StGT's view, 20–21; in Missouri statehood controversy, 52, 54–57; and the requirement for austerity, 63–64; intermeshes with religious impulse in NBT's mind, 69; reflected in NBT's 1830 newspaper essays, 76–77; and opposition to the Force Bill, 87; and slavery, 109; invoked in NBT's teaching, 114–16; and society in the antebellum South, 200–201; as a frame of reference for NBT and other Southerners, 204

Rhett, Robert Barnwell, 205, 208; at Nashville Convention, 183–86; quarrels with Hammond and Simms, 190–91

Rice, Reverend John Holt, 69

Ritchie, Thomas, 50, 65, 87–88, 141, 171, 180

Roanoke, Randolph family estate at, 4, 43, 86

Robinson, Powhatan, 170

Robinson, Reverend Charles S., 58

Rogers, William Barton, 98, 236 n.11

Romanticism: NBT's inclination toward, 41–43; and NBT's expectation of political crisis, 66, 70; in NBT's fictional self-images, 125–26;

134–35; and the tournament season at the Virginia springs, 163; comparative quality of, in NBT and Concord circle, 166; as mode of thought in NBT's society and lifetime, 204, 205–6, 209

Rousseau, Jean-Jacques, 24, 143–44; NBT reads, at William and Mary in 1790s, 15

Ruffin, Edmund, xiv, 91, 96, 139, 200, 208; and Southern publishing efforts, 120; collects the Westover Manuscripts, 128; publishes the Southern Magazine, 138, 245 n.5

Ruffner, Henry, 174

Saunders, Robert, 98, 172–73

Sawyer, Lemuel, 193

Scott, Judge John, 164

Scott, Sir Walter, as influence in NBT's fiction, 123

Secession: NBT calls for, in 1832, 85–86; called for in Charlotte County resolutions, 88; as NBT's means to immortality, 125–27, 199–200, 208–9; and plans for Nashville Convention, 178–81, 183, 254 n.53; NBT calls for, at Nashville, 185–87; object of post-Nashville NBT letters to Hammond, 189–92, 194; immediate political causes of, in 1860–61, 197; anticipated socio-political effect of, in minds of NBT, Hammond, and Simms, 200; as "reform," 202–3. See also Constitution, federal; Sovereignty, concept of; States' rights, constitutional theory of

Shakers, celibacy among, 144

Shakespeare, William, writings of, as a lawyer's balm, 25

Sharkey, William, 184

Sidney, Algernon: mentioned in StGT's Liberty, 8; referred to during Missouri statehood controversy, 56

Simms, William Gilmore, xiv, 156, 176–77, 197, 201, 203, 205; edits Southern Quarterly Review, 162; develops correspondence with NBT, 169–70; publishes NBT essay on revolutions of 1848, 178; misses NBT on his South Carolina trip, 188; and NBT's hope that Carolinians would secede in 1850–51, 191–92; visits NBT in summer of 1851, 194–95; and expectations of secession, 200

Slavery: StGT proposes gradual abolition of, 10, 22, 107, 112; and Missouri statehood controversy, 52–56; NBT discusses Blackstone on, 107–9, 239 n.47; and love of liberty, 109; NBT tries to square, with StGT's antislavery argument, 112–13; overlooked in Lieber's Political Ethics, 145; NBT fashions argument in favor of, 146–47; as a moral challenge, 158; and social change, 159; and white male prestige in slave culture, 199; holding out the promise of "control" in NBT's life, 207. See also Proslavery argument; Social theory

Slaves, NBT's relations with and attitude toward, 46, 55, 93

Smith, Adam, NBT reads Wealth of Nations by, 15

Smith, General Thomas A., 72, 74, 80
Social theory: NBT's teachings on, 104-6, 143-45, 238nn.28, 33; as reflected in NBT's therapeutic proposals, 157-61, 202-3; and frames of reference available to NBT, 204. *See also* Common law; Slavery; Womanhood, NBT discusses
South Carolina: NBT's conception of, 44, 187-88; as the probable leading state in secession movement, 118-19, 189-91, 197, 200, 208
South Carolina, College of, 58, 144, 206, 226n.36
Southern Literary Messenger, 101, 107, 110, 115, 129, 132, 133, 155, 193; NBT as key contributor to, 120
Southern Magazine and Monthly Review, 138, 245n.5
Southern Quarterly Review, 162, 169, 177, 178, 191, 193, 206
Sovereignty, concept of: in Calhoun's theory of nullification, 83; NBT's view of, 84, 105; and NBT's view of the common law, 153-54. *See also* Constitution, federal; States' rights, constitutional theory of
Sparks, Jared, 129
States' rights, constitutional theory of: outlined in StGT's edition of Blackstone, 22-23; and Missouri statehood controversy, 53-55; love of soil builds appreciation for, in NBT's view, 70; Andrew Jackson and, 75-76; South Carolina invokes, 76; in NBT's 1830 essays, 76; in Virginia Resolution of 1798, 84, 233n.46; denounced by Jackson, 83; Calhoun's version of, criticized by NBT, 83-85, 233n.46; supported in NBT's writings during the nullification crisis, 87-88, 233n.42, 235n.62; Jackson's transgression of, attacked in Virginia, 96; NBT's teachings on, as law professor, 102-3, 243n.44; in Upshur's *Brief Enquiry,* 138; influences NBT's banking proposal, 140-42. *See also* Constitution, federal; Sovereignty, concept of
Stewart, Dugald, writings in William and Mary curriculum in 1790s, 17
Story, Joseph, 128, 138, 142, 144, 154, 237-38 n.26, 244-45n.5; law professor at Harvard, 99-100; writes *Commentaries on the Constitution,* 103
Stowe, Harriet Beecher, 196
Stringfellow, Thornton, 147
Strother, David Hunter, 176-77

Taliaferro, John, 117
Tallmadge, John, 52
Tappan, Arthur and Lewis, 118
Taylor, John, of Caroline, 91
Taylor, Reverend Nathaniel William, 69
Taylor, Zachary, 175; NBT visits, at inaugural reception, 176; failure of NBT to influence, 177
Tazewell, Littleton Waller, 96, 117

Teaching, NBT's approach to, 115-16, 128-29, 134-35, 240nn.3, 7, 243-44n.50. *See also* Education
Texas: NBT's interest in, 148; NBT's involvement in Tyler's policy of annexing, 149-51, 154; as challenge restoring social binding, 160-61
Theology: NBT's reflections on, 67-70, 72, 81-82; and issue of slavery in NBT's mind, 111, 146; influences NBT's approach to teaching law, 114-16
Thompson, Waddy, 200; NBT recommends appointment of, as minister to Mexico, 149, 247n.37
Thoreau, Henry David, 165-66, 205
Thruston, John Buckner, 164
Tocqueville, Alexis de, 138, 143, 160; and *Democracy in America,* 136-37; NBT plans to critique commentaries of, 144, 154; view of atomistic individualism of, jibes with NBT's, 145, 246n.28
Transcendentalists, views of, compared to NBT's, 165-66
Trotti, Samuel Wilds, 188
Tucker, Ann Frances Bland (older sister of NBT), 4, 11, 24
Tucker, Berkeley Montague Beverley (son of NBT), 167
Tucker, Beverley (nephew of NBT), 175-76
Tucker, Cynthia (daughter of NBT), 176, 196; described, 167; NBT's relationship with, 168
Tucker, Eliza Naylor (second wife of NBT), 46, 72
Tucker, "Fanny" (daughter of NBT), 45, 47
Tucker, Frances (daughter of NBT), 167
Tucker, Frances Bland Randolph (mother of NBT), 4-6
Tucker, Henrietta (daughter of NBT), 167
Tucker, Henry (father of StGT), 1
Tucker, Henry St. George (older brother of NBT), 4, 11; and the public service ideal, 13; place of, in family, 13; performance of, at William and Mary, 13-14; begins law course, 15; early professional successes of, 25, 32, 34; service of, in War of 1812, 45; and federal internal improvements, 55; as moderate in nullification crisis, 85; and Winchester law school, 98; writes on Virginia law, 101; moderation of, as law professor, 116; unflatteringly referred to in *The Partisan Leader,* 126-27; honored by William and Mary, 127; reacts to *The Partisan Leader,* 133; and constitutional safeguards, 151-52; NBT jealous of, 154; death of, 175; family of, cares for NBT in his last hours, 194
Tucker, "Jack" (son of NBT), 43, 45, 47
Tucker, Lelia Skipworth Carter (stepmother of NBT), 11
Tucker, Lucy Ann Smith (third wife of NBT), 86, 101, 114, 119, 148, 181, 184; weds NBT, 74; NBT's need to please, 74, 80; as niece of Hugh Lawson White, 116; and

Tucker, Lucy Ann Smith *(continued)* NBT's ideal Christian mother, 157; relationship of, with NBT, 166

Tucker, Mary ("Polly") Coalter (first wife of NBT), 45, 47, 49, 57, 58, 77–78; NBT hopes to marry, 33–34; as wife of young lawyer, 43; during NBT's illness of 1825–26, 66; piety of, 67; death of, 71

Tucker, Nathaniel (uncle of NBT), 4

Tucker, Nathaniel Beverley: sense of Virginia ancestry felt by, 1; birth of, 4; boyhood of, at Matoax, 5; loses mother, moves to Williamsburg, 6; experiences family deaths, 11; early schooling and discipline of, 11–12; childhood frustrations of, 12; boyhood relationship of, with HStGT, 13; as student at William and Mary, 14–18; intellectual growth of, 18–20; begins study of law, 20–24; tires of legal readings, 25; early attachment of, to JR, 26–29; attracted to ideas of Burke, 29; opens law practice, 31–39; criticizes social and professional changes, 38–41, 45; romantic self-concept of, 41–43, 223 n.54; early appearance of, 43; marries, 43; complications in relationship of, with JR, 43–44, 223 n.58; service of, in War of 1812, 45; moves to Missouri, 45–47; new self-definition of, in west, 49–50; appointed territorial judge, 51; hopes to influence Missouri bar, 51; and Missouri statehood controversy, 52–57; establishes the Dardenne community, 57–60; fears social fluidity of west, 60–61; and Missouri debtor relief debate, 62–65; illness of, motivates writing, 66–67; theological speculations and evangelical impulse of, 67–70; hopes of, to return to Virginia from the west, 70–72; death stalks, 71–72; middle-aged appearance of, 74; remarries, 74; reevaluates life, 74–75; abortive political career of, 75–82; growing peevishness of, 77; during nullification crisis, 82–90; advocates secession in 1832, 85–86; named law professor at William and Mary, 90, 96–97; attitude of, toward own slaves, 93; view of legal training, 100–102; curriculum and constitutional teachings of, 102–3, 237 n.22; on social and governmental theory, 103–6; early writing and teaching of, on slavery, 107–10; tries to square slavery with StGT's antislavery argument, 110–13; pedagogical style of, 115–16, 240 nn.3, 7, 243–44 n.50; supports Hugh Lawson White's presidential candidacy, 116–17; and "gag rule" controversy, 117–19; engaged with friends in developing Southern consciousness, 119–21, 200; publishes *George Balcombe* and *The Partisan Leader,* 121–23; uses fiction to issue political and social commentary, 123–25; describes himself as a man of heart, 125–27; uses history to build cultural awareness, 128–29; appeals to youth of Virginia, 129–32, 243–44 n.50; defends William and Mary and his own teaching approach, 134; inflated self-

image of, 134–35; and Tocqueville's *Democracy,* 136–37; and Upshur's *Brief Enquiry,* 138; advises President Tyler on banking issue, 140–42; disappointed in Tyler, 142–43; and Lieber's *Political Ethics,* 144–45; comments on social trends in 1840s, 143, 145–56; and Carlyle, 145–56; and proslavery argument, 146–47; involved in Texas policy of Tyler administration, 148–51; constitutional attitude of, compared to HStGT's, 151–52; doubts wisdom of codification, 152–53; reveres common law, 153–54; publishes *Lectures on the Science of Government,* 154–55; and story "Gertrude," 155–56; homilies of, on womanhood, 156–58; on peculiar value of Southern institutions, 158–60; therapeutic message of, 160–61; state of mind of, in later life, 162–63; 178, 180–81, 190, 191–92; relaxing at the Virginia springs, 163–64; loss of relationships with challenging minds, 164–65; views and consciousness of, compared to Concord circle, 165–66; as husband and father, 166–68; re-opens friendship with Hammond, 168–69; begins correspondence with Simms, 169–70; and former students, 170–71; role of, in 1847–48 William and Mary disorders, 172–73; reacts to European events of 1848, 173–74; anxious about stirrings in western Virginia, 174–75; tries to befriend Zachary Taylor, 175–77; finds surcease in the past, 176–77; writes public letters in support of the Nashville Convention, 179; with Hammond plans radical strategy, 178–81, 183, 254 n.53; travels to and participates in Nashville Convention, 181–85; delivers address in favor of secession, 185–87; visits Hammond and addresses Barnwell audience, 188; misses Simms in South Carolina, 188; receives comments on Nashville address, 189; angered over changes in Virginia constitution, 189; prompts South Carolinians to secede, 189–92, 194; plans of, to write biography of Randolph fall through, 192–94; Simms visits, 194–95; death of, 194; burial of, remembered in 1850s, 196; forecasts of, proved correct, 196–97; failure of other prophesies of, 197–98; early life of, illustrative of stable socio-cultural order, 198–99; suggests impact of change on the socio-cultural order, 199–202; compared to Northern reformers, 202–3; friends of, share his moral delicacy, 203; as thoughtful, productive figure, 203–4; intellectual limitations and failure of, 204–6; an example of intellectual constraints on the socially anxious, 206–7; evidences connection between slavery and control, 207; as psychological subject outlines larger intellectual issues and social tensions of antebellum period, 207–8, 278–79

Tucker, St. George (father of NBT), 75, 83, 91, 103, 106, 132, 175; birth and early life of, 1–2; legal training of, 2; as officer in the Revolution, 2–3; marries, 4; attends Annapolis Convention, 5; opposes ratification of

federal Constitution, 6; loses wife, 6; accepts general court judgeship, moves to Williamsburg, 6; offers a description of Williamsburg, 7; secular and practical cast of mind of, 7–8 10, 19, 20–21, 206; as poet of liberty, 8; writes "Probationary Odes," 9; named law professor at William and Mary, 9; proposes end to slavery, 9–10; as demanding father, 12–13; sets intellectual and professional goals for sons, 19–21; on republican value of educated gentlemen, 20–21; elected to Supreme Court of Appeals, 25; breaks with JR, 28; opposes early marriage of NBT, 33–34; on lawyer's demeanor and ethic of the bar, 39; invoked during the Missouri statehood controversy, 53, 55; religious attitudes of, commented on in NBT's religious writings, 68; death of, 71; argues against the existence of a United States Common Law, 84
Tucker, St. George (son of NBT), 167
Tucker, Theodorick Thomas Tudor (oldest brother of NBT), 4, 11
Tucker, Thomas Smith (son of NBT), 167
Tucker, Thomas Tudor (uncle of NBT), 4, 8
Turner, Nat, 93
Tyler, John, 96; early relationship of, and NBT, 138–39; NBT advises, as president, 140–43, 245 n.16; and Texas annexation policy, NBT involvement in, 149–50

Universal suffrage: NBT fears, in Missouri, 64; as dangerous to republican government, 109; and Dorr Rebellion, 143; movement for, in Virginia, 174; and 1850–51 Virginia constitutional convention, 189. See also Egalitarianism; Majoritarianism, NBT warns of, in Missouri statehood debate
Upshur, Abel, P., xiv, 96, 136, 148, 151, 154, 157, 171, 196, 200, 205; as part of NBT's circle of friends, 120; and The Partisan Leader, 132–33; publishes Brief Enquiry, 138; as advisor to President Tyler, 139–42; on Dorr Rebellion, 143; and Texas annexation question, 148–49

Van Buren, Martin, 119, 138; as foil in NBT's efforts to build Southern self-consciousness, 116–17; portrayed in The Partisan Leader, 122–23
"Viola," NBT's lost play entitled, 249 n.62
Virginia: agricultural decline in, 35–36, 199; early-nineteenth-century political and judicial changes in, 36–39, 44, 199; NBT in west hopes to return to, 70–72, 82; calls for constitutional reform in, during 1820s, 71; economy and society of, in mid-1830s, 91–92; movement for constitutional change in, 92–93; policy debates in, during 1830s, 93, 111–12; decline of, worries fathers of NBT's students, 114–15; NBT tries to make the love of, the cause of youth, 129–32; ruin of in The Partisan Leader, and persistent sectionalism in, 131, 199; referred to in Ruffner's

Address, 174; in NBT's later imagination, 176–77, 253 n.36; delegates from, at Nashville Convention, 254 n.52; viewed as a system of subjective relationships in NBT's early years, 198–99; and NBT's hope that secession would restore, 208
Virginia, University of, 101, 121, 152, 154
Virginia Historical Society, 196
Virginia Resolutions of 1798: passed condemning the Alien and Sedition Acts, 22–23; as rallying point for Missouri Democrats, 79; and Calhoun's theory of nullification, 83–84; NBT uses, in law course, 103
Virtue. See Republicanism

Waldie, Adam, 164, 203–5
Walker, Robert J., 164; and Texas annexation, 148–50
Washington, George, 4, 54, 129, 132, 177, 184
Washington, Henry A., 196
Washington College (Lexington, Virginia), 174
Watchman of the South, The, 157
Watson, Joseph, 14
Webster, Daniel, 76, 88, 148, 180, 186
Wells, Robert William, 79, 81
Wetmore, Alphonso, 79
White, Hugh Lawson, 89; NBT works on behalf of, 116–17
White, Thomas W., 101, 129; asks NBT for contributions to Southern Literary Messenger, 120; on reaction to The Partisan Leader, 133
White Sulpher Springs, summer resort at, 163–64
William and Mary, College of, 115, 138–39, 204–5; StGT appointed law professor at, 9; NBT attends, 11; HStGT's record at, 13–14; reputation and appearance of, in 1790s, 14; NBT's experiences at, 14–19, 204; and 1802 student disorders, 20; condition of, in 1834, 91; NBT named professor at, 90, 96–97; as home of states' rights theory, 102–3; students of law at, 114–15, 240 n.3; honors HStGT, 127; historical appreciation of, an object of NBT's teaching, 129; political posture of, as a subject of criticism, 133–34, 142, 244 n.55, 245–46 n.17; NBT delivers 1847 commencement address at, 172; 1847–48 disruptions at, 172–73
Williamsburg, 96, 110, 139; Tucker family moves to, and its impression on NBT as a boy, 7; travelers' accounts of, in 1790s, 7; NBT's boyhood memories of, 11; NBT visits, 25; gives rise to melancholy, 42; appearance of, in 1834, 91; 1848 College disruption effects, 173; as reminiscent of an English village, 201
Wilmot, David, 163; Proviso of, denounced in Virginia General Assembly, 171; as an issue in 1848–50, 175, 180
Wirt, William, comments on civic virtue and bar in Virginia, 37–38
Wise, Henry A., 199; and NBT's banking proposal of 1841, 141; defers to NBT as delegate to Nashville Convention, 181; at Virginia

Wise, Henry A. *(continued)* constitutional convention of 1850–51, 189
Womanhood, NBT discusses, 156–59; in free society, 182. *See also* Social theory
Wright, Frances, 143–44, 156, 158
Wythe, George: StGT's legal training with, 2; vacates law professorship, 9; NBT invokes, 103

Yale Divinity School, 68
"Yankeys": as symbolic of values alien to NBT, 78, 110, 232 n.30; as negative reference group in NBT's talks to young men, 130; interrupt NBT's interview with President Taylor, 176; NBT's first-hand view of, in Cincinnati, 182
Youth, NBT's appeal to, 129–32

Library of Congress Cataloging in Publication Data

Brugger, Robert J.
  Beverley Tucker: Heart over head in the Old South.

  (The Johns Hopkins University studies in historical and political science; 96th ser., no. 2)
  Includes bibliographical references and index.
  1. Tucker, Nathaniel Beverley, 1784–1851.
2. Lawyers—Virginia—Biography. 3. Virginia—Biography. 4. Secession. 5. Slavery in the United States. I. Series: Johns Hopkins University Studies in historical and political science; 96th ser., no. 2.
P230.T92B78   975'.03'0924 [B]   77-16294
ISBN 0-8018-1982-2